STUDIES IN IMPERIALISM

General editor: Andrew S. Thompson

Founding editor: John M. MacKenzie

When the 'Studies in Imperialism' series was founded by Professor John M. MacKenzie more than thirty years ago, emphasis was laid upon the conviction that 'imperialism as a cultural phenomenon had as significant an effect on the dominant as on the subordinate societies'. With well over a hundred titles now published, this remains the prime concern of the series. Cross-disciplinary work has indeed appeared covering the full spectrum of cultural phenomena, as well as examining aspects of gender and sex, frontiers and law, science and the environment, language and literature, migration and patriotic societies, and much else. Moreover, the series has always wished to present comparative work on European and American imperialism, and particularly welcomes the submission of books in these areas. The fascination with imperialism, in all its aspects, shows no sign of abating, and this series will continue to lead the way in encouraging the widest possible range of studies in the field. 'Studies in Imperialism' is fully organic in its development, always seeking to be at the cutting edge, responding to the latest interests of scholars and the needs of this ever-expanding area of scholarship.

Banished potentates

Manchester University Press

SELECTED TITLES AVAILABLE IN THE SERIES

WRITING IMPERIAL HISTORIES
ed. Andrew S. Thompson

EMPIRE OF SCHOLARS
Tamson Pietsch

HISTORY, HERITAGE AND COLONIALISM
Kynan Gentry

COUNTRY HOUSES AND THE BRITISH EMPIRE
Stephanie Barczewski

THE RELIC STATE
Pamila Gupta

WE ARE NO LONGER IN FRANCE
Allison Drew

THE SUPPRESSION OF THE ATLANTIC SLAVE TRADE
ed. Robert Burroughs and Richard Huzzey

HEROIC IMPERIALISTS IN AFRICA
Berny Sèbe

Banished potentates

DETHRONING AND EXILING
INDIGENOUS MONARCHS UNDER
BRITISH AND FRENCH COLONIAL
RULE, 1815–1955

Robert Aldrich

MANCHESTER UNIVERSITY PRESS

Copyright © Robert Aldrich 2018

The right of Robert Aldrich to be identified as the author of this work has been asserted by him in accordance with the Copyright, Designs and Patents Act 1988.

Published by Manchester University Press
Altrincham Street, Manchester M1 7JA
www.manchesteruniversitypress.co.uk

British Library Cataloguing-in-Publication Data
A catalogue record for this book is available from the British Library

ISBN 978 0 7190 9973 1 hardback
ISBN 978 1 5261 5166 7 paperback

First published 2018

The publisher has no responsibility for the persistence or accuracy of URLs for any external or third-party internet websites referred to in this book, and does not guarantee that any content on such websites is, or will remain, accurate or appropriate.

Typeset by Out of House Publishing

CONTENTS

List of figures—vii
Preface—ix

1	Thrones and dominion: European colonisers and indigenous monarchs	1
2	The last king in Ceylon: the British and Sri Vikrama Rajasinha, 1815	32
3	Kings of Orient were: royal exile in British Asia	75
4	'Dragons of Annam': the French and three emperors in Vietnam	117
5	Out of Africa: the British, the French and African monarchs	178
6	The French and the queen of Madagascar: Ranavalona III, 1897	215
7	From conquest to decolonisation: exile from French North Africa	255
	Conclusion	274

Bibliography—283
Index—307

FIGURES

All images are from the author's collection

1	'Les rois en exil', postcard printed by L. Chagny, Algiers, c. 1907.	19
2	'Wickrama Raja Sinha, Last King of Kandy, 1793–1815', postcard printed by British Empire Exhibition, c. 1924.	33
3	'Capture of Sri Wickrama Rajasinghe, Last King of Kandy', unattributed postcard illustration.	44
4	'Bahadurshah & his Queen', unattributed postcard, date unknown.	85
5	Maharaja Tukojirao Holkar III of Indore, international newsreel photograph, c. 1920s.	92
6	'Royal Palace – Mandalay', unattributed and undated postcard printed by D. A. Auja, Rangoon.	98
7	Emperor Ham Nghi and his bride, Marcelle Laloë, unattributed postcard, 1904.	131
8	'Empereur [Thanh Thai] en costume de ville', unattributed postcard, c. 1916.	134
9	'Empereur [Duy Tan] en costume de cour', unattributed postcard, c. 1912.	147
10	'Béhanzin, Ex-Roi du Dahmoney et toute sa famille', unattributed postcard, c. 1900.	179
11	'Le Prince Said Ali. – Ex-Sultan de la Grand Comore', unattributed postcard, c. 1890s.	191
12	'Dinuzulu', unattributed photograph published in *Black & White*, 14 December 1907.	194
13	'S. M. Ranavalona, Ex-Reine de Madagascar', unattributed postcard, after 1897.	218
14	'Moulai-Hafid et son interprète Ben Ghabrit', unattributed postcard, c. 1905.	258
15	'S. A. le Bey de Tunis', postcard published by E. C.	261

PREFACE

Research for this book was greatly facilitated by a Discovery Grant from the Australian Research Council, for which I am extremely grateful. In particular, it made possible work in archives and libraries in Britain and France, and visits to some of the countries from which the rulers were deported and countries to which they were sent. Work for the project began during a visiting fellowship at the Centre for Research in the Arts, Humanities and Social Sciences and Wolfson College at Cambridge University, for which I also express my warm appreciation, and encompassed another sabbatical from the University of Sydney, where the Department of History has provided a continuing source of collegiality and stimulation.

I would like to give particular thanks to Briony Neilson for her research assistance, and acknowledge with appreciation Linh Do for reading and summarising material from Vietnamese sources, and W. Matthew Kennedy for research assistance in the British National Archives. Nicholas Keyzer did great service in digitising and enhancing the illustrations. Trevor Matthews prepared the index. The staff of the British Library, the Bibliothèque Nationale de France, the Archives Nationales d'Outre-Mer, and the Archives Départementales de La Réunion provided invaluable access and assistance to their resources. I owe much merited thanks, too, to the staff of my home library at the University of Sydney. Emma Brennan, the commissioning editor at Manchester University Press, and Andrew Thompson, the general editor of the 'Studies in Imperialism' series, have shown much appreciated enthusiasm for this project. I have had valuable and enjoyable conversations with many scholars who are far more knowledgeable about particular colonial situations than I will ever be. I will forbear naming names, in the hopes of personally thanking them and in an effort to avoid neglecting any by inadvertent omission. However, for reading and commenting on various chapters, I would especially like to thank Eric Jennings, Harshan Kumarasingham, Brad Manera, Jim Masselos, Cindy McCreery, Kirsten McKenzie and Mark Seymour.

Earlier versions of some of these chapters have been presented at seminars and have benefited from the comments from other participants. A conference on 'Exile in Colonial Asia' organised by Ronit Riccit was especially enriching, and I contributed a chapter on Sri Lanka to the resulting collection published under the same title. Another chapter on Sri Lanka appeared in a volume I co-edited with Cindy McCreery,

PREFACE

Crowns and Colonies: European Monarchies and Overseas Empires, and an article on the Vietnamese emperor Duy Tan was published on H-France in a collection of papers from the George Rudé Seminar.

The names of non-European people and places discussed in this book have been transliterated in many different forms, and are still rendered in varying ways. I use forms for individuals' names that have wide currency, and have generally referred to places as they were known during colonial times. The sovereigns who are my subjects held a variety of titles; I often use 'king' or 'monarch' in a generic sense. Titles, in general, are not put in upper-case, except for 'Resident' – the colonial official at a feudatory court – solely to differentiate that figure from 'residents' referring to inhabitants in general. For convenience, I frequently refer to a deposed ruler by his or her reign title without the prefix 'ex-' or 'former'. Since almost all of the deposed rulers were male, 'he' rather than 'he or she' sometimes suffices.

The first chapter explores confrontations and accommodations between European colonisers and indigenous monarchs in a general sense. Three chapters examine particular cases of the deposition and exile of rulers: King Sri Vikrama Rajasinha in Ceylon in 1815, Queen Ranavalona of Madagascar in 1897, and Emperors Ham Nghi, Thanh Thai and Duy Tan in Vietnam over the period 1885 to 1916. Two other chapters provide more composite accounts of Asia and Africa: the British ouster of Indian princes, the last Burmese king and a sultan in Malaya, and then British and French removal of a host of 'chieftains' in sub-Saharan Africa. The final chapter looks at the French colonial removal of rulers in Algeria, Morocco and Tunisia – and the restoration of a Moroccan sultan on the eve of decolonisation.

CHAPTER ONE

Thrones and dominion: European colonisers and indigenous monarchs

'Deposed and pensioned off kings' ran the headline over a two-page article in France's popular *Le Monde illustré* in 1912. Celebrating the colonial exploits of the mother-country, which had just completed the conquest of Morocco, the journalist remarked that on occasion 'political necessity' had required the dethroning and banishment of indigenous rulers, some of whom, he claimed, now lived a life of leisure thanks to the pensions graciously provided by the French. Photographs showed the former Vietnamese emperor Ham Nghi, dressed in a silk tunic, and the ex-sultan of Morocco, wearing a woollen burnous. The melancholy-looking deposed sultan of Grande Comore, sitting in a grand rattan chair, appeared still regal in robes and turban. Two Africans, Dinah Salifou from Guinea and the son of Béhanzin, exiled ruler of Dahomey, were dressed in European style, the first in a dapper three-piece suit, the latter in the bemedalled uniform of a French soldier. Ago-Li-Agbo, Béhanzin's successor, who had also been ousted, wore a distinctive dust-guard strapped over his nose. Ex-Queen Ranavalona of Madagascar, demure in a matronly dress, posed with her cute little great-niece.[1]

The gallery illustrated the breadth of a French empire extending over large parts of Africa, the Indian Ocean and Southeast Asia, but also pointed to a strategy of imperialist rule not reserved to the French: the overthrow and exile of indigenous rulers who resisted foreign takeover, rebelled against the new masters of their countries, or were regarded by colonisers as unfit to remain on their thrones. That phenomenon provides the subject for the present volume, which examines, with varying degrees of detail, the displacement of three dozen 'potentates' by British and French authorities from 1815 until the 1950s.

Royal exile

Throughout history, removal from the body politic – banishment, exile, deportation, transportation – has offered a way to punish criminal offenders and political opponents. The ancient Greek city-states practised ostracism of rebels, generally sent away for ten years. Roman law included provisions for *relegatio in insulam*, the sending of a prisoner to a different city or province for a limited time, though without deprivation of citizenship or property, as well as permanent deportation, with consequent loss of assets and citizen rights. Early modern law perpetuated such types of punishment; Spanish legislation enacted from 1525, for instance, provided for *destierro*, internal exile on the Iberian peninsula, *relegación* or banishment to an overseas colony, and *extranamiento*, permanent exile from the mainland as well as the Spanish empire.[2] Peripheral or overseas territories – Latin America, for early modern Spanish malefactors – provided depositories for those ejected, sufficiently distant to keep undesirables from causing trouble, and with hopes of their rehabilitation and contribution to colonising endeavours.

Colonies gained notoriety as places of banishment for both common criminals and political prisoners. The British sent Irish nationalists to New South Wales in the 1790s and 'patriot exiles' from Canada to Tasmania in the 1830s, taking advantage of the Australian outposts that had been established in large part as penal colonies for those committed of ordinary crimes. From the early 1800s to the mid-1900s, they despatched political prisoners from South Asia to the Andaman Islands, Mauritius and the Seychelles, the 'carceral archipelagos' of the Indian Ocean.[3] In 1871, the French deported several thousand survivors of the Paris Commune to New Caledonia, as well as over two hundred largely Berber participants in an uprising in Algeria. Motley political troublemakers from the metropole and the empire as well as common-law convicts continued to be sent by the French to the 'green hell' of Guiana, in South America, until the mid-twentieth century. Other countries practised similar policies and also found remote destinations for their convicts; the Russians sent political prisoners to Siberia and Sakhalin Island.[4] Some rebels, of course, fled into voluntary exile before they were arrested, fearing for their lives and hoping to rebuild radical or nationalist movements outside their homelands; many nineteenth-century nationalists – Giuseppe Garibaldi from Italy, Adam Mickiewicz from Poland, Lajos Kossuth from Hungary – spent long years abroad because of their political views.

A particular cohort of willing or forced exiles is composed of monarchs, though statistically they accounted for only a very small number of political deportees or refugees, and a minuscule drop in the vast sea of migrants moving around the world in modern times. Monarchs who lost their crowns, accompanied by princely relatives, regularly washed up on foreign shores, seeking shelter when vanquished in battle or ousted by revolutionaries. Jacobites left Britain after the Glorious Revolution; Bourbons who escaped the guillotine fled France in the decade after 1789 and others followed with revolutions in the early nineteenth century.[5] Romanovs who survived the Bolsheviks took flight from Russia after 1917, and Habsburgs, Hohenzollerns and Ottomans sped across borders after the First World War.[6] King Zog of Albania, the only ruler of a short-lived modern dynasty, fled his country after Italy invaded in 1939.[7] Communist takeovers in eastern Europe after the Second World War saw the departure of the kings of Romania, Bulgaria and Yugoslavia, and the Italian king went into exile after his subjects voted for a republic. There would be more royal exiles around the world in subsequent years. Trying to maintain a semblance of the life to which they had been accustomed, they continued to claim thrones, agitate for restoration, observe punctilious court protocol, bestow orders and decorations, and search for marriage partners of appropriate status to assure their lineage.

Royal exile occurred around the world.[8] For instance, the last emperor of China, Puyi, lost his throne in the revolution of 1911–12 and was sent away from the 'forbidden city' in Beijing. Puyi gained a new crown when made ruler of the Japanese puppet state of Manchukuo in 1932, but lost his second throne, too, with Japanese defeat, and spent the rest of his life discreetly in Communist China.[9] One newspaper article on 'kicked-out' rulers, published in 1936 while Puyi was still emperor of occupied Manchuria, spoke of the recently restored King George of Greece (who also later suffered a second deposition) and King Alfonso XIII of Spain, who lost his throne in 1931. It referred to the still living figures profiled in the French account a quarter-century earlier, now joined by such men as Abd el-Krim, the 'Napoleon of the Rif', who led a rebellion in Morocco, and the Maharajah of Indore, removed from his Indian throne because of an *affaire des moeurs*.[10] The year that article was published saw the fall of yet another 'exotic' monarch, as Mussolini's Italian troops chased Emperor Haile Selassie off the throne of Ethiopia. (He, too, would be restored, and deposed once again – proof that crowns were never secure.)[11]

Heirs to thrones and crowned monarchs have always faced dangers from rebellious compatriots, ambitious pretenders and disaffected courtiers. Rivals eliminated competitors by sword, poison or gun. Reigning or aspirant rulers often perished, gloriously or ignominiously, in warfare. Palace intrigues and *coups d'état* replaced one monarch with another. Revolutions abolished monarchies, and victims did not always outrun regicidal opponents. Indeed, many rulers lost their thrones at the hands of fellow countrymen, from Mary Queen of Scots and King Charles I in Britain to Kings Louis XVI, Charles X and Louis-Philippe of France, as well as Emperor Napoleon III.[12]

In other cases, foreign conquerors played a key role in the exile of defeated enemies. Napoleon Bonaparte remains the most legendary of all the royal exiles. Vanquished and forced to abdicate by a coalition of foreign powers, Napoleon was sent to Elba, a relatively comfortable little realm near to home, but he escaped and regained his throne, only to be defeated and banished once again, this time to a far more distant domain.[13] The image of the French emperor in 1815, boarded onto a British ship bound for St Helena, there to spend the remaining years of his life, is well known, the memory, myths and relics of his exile developed into a cult.[14] Less familiar is the fact that only a few months later, the British deposed and exiled the last king of Kandy, from the island of Ceylon (today's Sri Lanka); Sri Vikrama Rajasinha is the subject of the first case study in this volume.

This book concerns such rulers, those who lost their thrones through the actions of colonial overlords, and except for the handful who were restored, lived out their lives in near or distant exile. They were forced to abdicate formally, or arbitrarily removed from office, by invaders from far away, sent into exile as a result of conquest of their countries during the great surge of expansion that saw most of Asia and Africa, and Australasia and Oceania, divided among the great powers. These men, and a couple of women, differed from the dethroned European royals not just because of ouster by colonisers rather than compatriots (though their compatriots often aided the colonisers in their deeds). The royal refugees in Europe generally remained free men and women in the place they found abode, able to move about as they wished, keep contacts with their old countries, even work for their restoration with support from host governments. The deposed colonial rulers, by contrast, were prisoners; though not incarcerated in gaols, they were effectively kept under house arrest, restricted in movement, and forbidden to engage in political activity. European royal exiles might easily travel between London and Paris, or from the Côte d'Azur to the Algarve; if the former 'native' rulers moved about, it was when colonial authorities shifted them from one place to another, or only when they were given leave by their colonial masters.[15]

The Europeans looked for grace and favour to kinsmen in the great royal family tree that had spread over the continent. Connections of birth and marriage as well as political sentiments assured hospitality, and exiles evoked sympathy from monarchs who felt threatening shock waves when thrones tumbled elsewhere. Several Bourbon kings and Napoleon III thus found refuge from French revolutionaries and republicans in staunchly monarchist Britain, and Napoleon III's son, the Prince Imperial, died alongside British troops in the Zulu War in 1879.[16] Several rulers who lost thrones after the unification of Germany in 1871 ended up in Hapsburg Austria. Such congeniality was lacking for non-European rulers, who almost always married into their own societies and could not throw themselves onto the mercies of kin ruling elsewhere. They could, at best, count on the pity of European monarchs for *ci-devant* native emperors, kings, sultans and princes, even if viewed as brutal and licentious Oriental potentates or savage African chiefains. And indeed Queen Victoria, in particular, manifested remarkable sympathy for former native rulers, including those dethroned in her name.

Further differences separated the Europeans and the non-Europeans. Dethroned European rulers had often lived in cosmopolitan courts and moved about their kingdoms, and outside their lands, in great royal progresses. Non-Europeans lived in more restricted courts, in some cases seldom emerging from 'forbidden cities' until bustled into the palanquins, trains and ships that took them into exile. Banished European royals drifted around a continent where they nevertheless benefited from such commonalities of culture as Christian religion (though in varying denominations), the French language that long served as the elite lingua franca, and relatively familiar protocol, customs and daily life. Europeans found burgeoning communities of fellow expatriates, such as the French in London or Russians in Paris. By contrast, normally only a small band of family members and faithful courtiers and servants accompanied royals from the colonies into exile. Those banished from one colony to another encountered far different situations than their displaced European peers. They included Muslim rulers, for instance, deported to places without a mosque, ex-sovereigns who had little if any knowledge of a European language or vernacular ones spoken in their new homes, men deposed from continental kingdoms confined on small and remote islands.

Generations after the deposition of European royals, their heirs might still frequent surviving royal courts and appear as decorative members of high society. The Europeans occasionally found other career possibilities; the last Stuart pretender became a cardinal, Louis XVIII was mooted as a possible king of Poland, later royal exiles entered the world of business. Such possibilities did not exist for deported African or Asian royals. The families and successors of native ex-monarchs, as subjects of the colonial state, might realistically only hope for subaltern positions in the military or administration; most descendants faded into obscurity, and some descended into penury.

There are, of course, exceptions to those dramatic contrasts. Some deposed Indian maharajahs carried considerable fortunes with them into exile and, like European royals, found comfortable niches overseas. A few of the other exiles also accommodated relatively well to new host societies, as shown by images of a Zulu and Asante king dressed in European clothes and worshipping in Christian churches. The European and non-European royal exiles also shared certain traits. They expressed nostalgia for lost homelands and loss of status, and continuously lamented their fate. Both groups railed against the injustice of their removal, recruited support for their causes and campaigned for restoration, though seldom with success. They all faced concerns about finances, marriages, their children's futures, and rivalries among heirs and other claimants to thrones. They resented slights to their dignity, and clung to residues of their former positions, their titles and medals and heirlooms. Many tried to preserve the languages and cultures of their ancestors, and kept as close contact with home societies as was possible or permitted. Sometimes they were eventually able to celebrate regime change, hoping for reinstatement of their rights, compensation for confiscated property, and a welcome home, if not a return to their thrones.

Deposed royals from the colonies were vastly outnumbered by non-regal political exiles, many of them famous. The circumstances of their removal, often by force, sometimes only after a show trial or no trial at all, and little recourse to appeal, often paralleled that of the monarchs. The French, for instance, sent Toussaint-Louverture from Haiti to a fortress in the Vosges in 1802, and a century and a half later, Tunisian nationalist (and future president) Habib Bourghiba was kept in detention in France, and the Polynesian nationalist (and later senator) Pouvanaa a Oopa was deported from Tahiti to the metropole. The British sent the Egyptian nationalist Ahmad Urabi to Ceylon in 1882,[17] and Archbishop Makarios from Cyprus to the Seychelles in 1956. Many others deported or in voluntary exile were less well known, but for the activists banishment to off-shore prison islands, imperial metropoles or foreign countries provided opportunities to gain experience from different colonies or metropoles, forge contacts with other rebels, develop and articulate ideologies, and devise strategies for gaining power.[18]

Royal exiles from the colonies, though they were limited in number compared to other political prisoners and generally did not gain freedom and successfully lead independence movements, are nevertheless an important and fascinating group. Native monarchs and their families stood at the apex of local societies, they claimed by birth (or, sometimes, conquest or usurpation) an inalienable right to rule, they were often regarded by subjects as sacred or semi-divine figures, and they represented – as friends or enemies – key points of contact between colonisers and indigenous masses. The overthrow of a monarch, and his or her execution, imprisonment or banishment, constituted one of the most serious blows delivered by conquerors to local societies and cultures. The removal of royals, as will be seen, posed particular concerns that did not obtain for 'commoners'. The dynasties that survived or were extinguished bequeathed wide-ranging and long-lasting legacies, visible in later anti-colonial resistance and post-independence state-building, national narratives and popular commemoration.

An examination of these figures tells us something about imperial conquest and governance, the exercise of power by colonial states, and the opportunities of indigenous rulers to exercise a counterweight to that power through negotiation, accommodation or resistance. It shows the endurance and sometimes resilience of the principle of monarchy, even in the face of great efforts to diminish royal power and reputation. It evidences the residual influence that the institution of monarchy held as a symbol of national or ethnic identity, even as republicanism replaced monarchism as the central animating force in anti-colonial nationalism. On the side of the colonisers, we see the instability that Antoinette Burton has argued stood at the heart of empire, the continuing difficulties the colonisers faced in maintaining their rule.[19] We see, too, how the imperial monarchy of Britain and its vicegeral officials, and similarly the representatives of republican France, in trying to assert their dominion, assumed the mantle of displaced pre-colonial monarchies, draping themselves in new ceremonial and taking on rights and duties of justice, military command, patronage and preferment. The material culture of the old monarchies revealingly illustrates the metamorphosis: palaces destroyed or repurposed, and regalia appropriated, taken as booty, enshrined in museums, sold at auction, sometimes eventually returned. Furthermore, the itineraries of deposed figures through years or, for some, decades of exile, and the interminable consultations between colonial offices and governors in different overseas outposts about their princely wards, point up the transnational networks created by empire. Concern in Europe about the treatment meted out to indigenous rulers and disagreement about what to do with them and their dynasties disrupts simple notions about imperial consensus and underlines the tensions existing inside empires. In countries where treaties established protectorates, the fate of 'protected' rulers who were 'kicked out'– sovereigns become captives – shows the paradoxes and contradictions of European expansion.

Finally, there are the simple but often poignant life-stories of men and women whirled about in the maelstrom of colonialism.

Monarchs here and there

With the exception of the French after 1870 (and episodically during earlier revolutionary periods), the European military officers and civil servants who conquered and administered colonies in the 1800s and early 1900s planted flags and governed in the name of monarchs. Under new constitutions and increasingly powerful parliaments in the nineteenth century, European sovereigns increasingly reigned rather than ruled, but monarchy endured. In fact, European overseas expansion in the decades preceding the First World War coincided with the last great efflorescence of the European monarchy – fated soon to disappear in some countries – under Queen Victoria and King Edward VII in Britain and fellow sovereigns on the continent. For the Spanish, Portuguese, British, Dutch, Belgian, German, Danish and Italian monarchs, ruling overseas colonies formed part of their brief, and the Russian tsar, too, had his distant domains in Asia.[20] Behind the glitter and glamour of royal courts lay persistent allegiance to the idea of hereditary monarchs who ruled 'by the grace of God', and whose prerogatives, in principle if not in practice, remained wide-ranging. Radicals demanded republics, but the would-be revolutionaries (except in Portugal, which abolished the monarchy in 1910) until the First World War did not seriously endanger the kings and queens whose rule extended to ever wider dominions outside Europe.

Overseas, those claiming possession of new colonies in the name of their sovereigns (or the republic, for the French) confronted indigenous governments that, in most cases, were also organised along monarchical lines. Native emperors, maharajahs, sultans and chieftains inherited their right to rule, or if they had usurped power, hoped to pass it to sons or kinsmen. The authority of Asian and African rulers, at least in European regard, remained absolute, with stereotypes of cruel potentates who enjoyed rights of life and death over subjects, amassed fantastic wealth from land, labour and taxation of impoverished masses, and revelled in the pleasures of palaces and harems. Beyond the fantasies, certain it was that, before colonial takeover, many non-European rulers retained a degree of personal authority that European monarchs no longer wielded. Such sovereigns were also imbued with great spiritual grace as Confucian 'sons of heaven', Buddhist *devarajas* or Africans held sacred in traditional religions. They lorded over extended royal families, bureaucracies, armies and navies, bevies of courtiers and servants and, in some countries, slaves. Monarchs stood as symbols of historical legitimacy, territorial dominion and the cultural identity of their people. They were surrounded by taboos and elaborate ceremonial, monopolised sumptuary privileges, and were protected by laws against *lèse-majesté*. They brandished treasured regalia and awarded honours to worthy subjects. They appointed and dismissed officials, recast institutions, proclaimed law codes and dispensed justice, promoted or restricted trade, dispatched and received diplomatic delegations, contracted alliances and battled enemies, and commissioned public works. Often they carried out these duties personally, whereas in Europe, many had been delegated in practice to parliaments and officials, even if monarchs continued to assent to legislation and sign documents such as military commissions.

In clashes between European and indigenous regimes, imperialists had various options with regard to sovereigns whose realms they conquered. In one scenario, those who resisted might be killed in battle or executed by triumphant foreigners. Neither Europeans nor those they attacked were strangers to warfare, violence and judicial or extrajudicial capital punishment. Colonialist propaganda celebrated the deaths of native enemies to valorous European soldiers bringing civilisation to savages and law and order to the misgoverned. However, the death of a ruler was not necessarily optimal, for an heir or pretender could emerge, death might transform an adversary into a martyr, and the absence of an indigenous figure empowered with sacred aura robbed colonisers of a useful intermediary and interlocutor.

Ideally from the colonialist perspective, local rulers and dynasties would live on as auxiliaries to the imperialists. In return for treaties giving Europeans rights to land, trade, settlement and effective government, they might retain positions, wealth and privileges, even in reduced circumstances. They could assume the position of loyal and docile vassals to European overlords, left to carry out traditional rites and subcontracted to perform administrative functions. Europeans hoped they would convert to Western ways and pursue approved paths to modernisation of their countries. Rulers displaying fealty would be rewarded with recognition of their legitimacy, manifestations of deference, privy purses and other emoluments, decorations and honours, and perhaps the occasional tour of European capitals. In this arrangement of 'overrule', the Europeans as paramount powers left kings, maharajahs, sultans and chieftains in place as feudatories, though colonial overlords and indigenous vassals seldom cohabited without disputes about rights and duties.[21]

When colonisers chose not to annex a territory outright, thus abolishing local dynasties and ruling directly, the usual practice was establishment of a 'protectorate'. In some cases, this lasted until the end of the colonial era, but in others a protectorate provided a first step towards annexation. Conquerors and colonial officials generally chose protectorates when they feared that the other great powers would object to outright annexation of an occupied country, and hoped that retaining a monarch would facilitate rule, perhaps even reducing the manpower and expenses that direct administration would incur. The indigenous sovereign, they expected, would control the local population through his or her traditional political and moral influence, and would aid the Europeans to achieve their own objectives. With native rulers who enjoyed great sway over their subjects, and who seemed not totally opposed to European hegemony, a protectorate appeared a desirable form of overrule.

The legal instrument for setting up a protectorate was normally an agreement between two nominally sovereign powers – the European and the indigenous one – in which a native ruler conceded rights to foreigners who promised 'protection' of his throne and realm. The protected monarch solemnly agreed by treaty, frequently signed after actual or threatened military action, not only to give land and resources to the invader, but also to accord his policies with those of the 'protector', accept the advice and counsel of European administrators (especially the pro-consular European 'Resident' appointed to his court), and maintain law and order in his dominions; he also promised not to engage in any sort of resistance or subversion against the colonisers. The Europeans, for their part, agreed to respect the monarch's dynastic rights and local culture (especially religion), and to protect the sovereign from attack at home or abroad. Protectorates were always ambiguous political arrangements, even for constitutional experts, though always weighted in favour of the coloniser. In principle, protectorate treaties gave the colonisers only 'half-sovereignty' (as one French jurist characterised the arrangement). In practice, they allowed the foreigners near untrammelled power, including the ability to delimit and constrain the rights of reigning sovereigns, and the possibility of getting rid of a 'protected' ruler whom they decided had failed to honour his obligations, and to replace him with another monarch whose selection they sanctioned, or to abolish a dynasty altogether.[22]

If feudatories proved less than docile, engaged in resistance against the new colonial order, or were judged grossly incompetent or immoral, the Europeans in the first instance could formally chastise and threaten them, reminding them of their treaty obligations. A second step would be to remove prerogatives or powers that monarchs still enjoyed, the loss of symbolic rights or real authority a great blow to rulers intent on safeguarding their status. The gradual or abrupt whittling away of power could reduce protected rulers to mere puppets, retaining only the most nominal authority, even becoming near prisoners of the Europeans in the gilded cages of their palaces. If the cautioning of monarchs or curbing of their rights did not achieve colonisers' objectives, Europeans could proceed to more severe measures, and ultimately oust a recalcitrant monarch. The colonisers deployed various strategies to dispossess an inconvenient ruler. They could convince or coerce a sovereign to abdicate, perhaps promising comfortable retirement with lodgings, pension and retention of title and honours to one who went quietly. A ruler might also be threatened with a commission of inquiry, a humiliating prospect that could make him choose abdication rather than trial; if a commission were held, with a judgement of guilt and recommendation for deposition, the ruler's fate would be sealed. Another option was to oust a ruler by force and fiat, often with a simple administrative decree issued by a governor or military commander. Removal of an individual might or might not lead to the abolition of the native monarchy as an institution, the Europeans either placing a more obliging candidate on the throne or annexing the territory and dispensing with the dynasty altogether.

Endorsement of or participation in warfare or rebellion against colonisers, lack of cooperation, or behaviour that went beyond the bounds of European tolerance (though colonisers willingly turned a blind eye to much private misconduct) precipitated the removal of native rulers. Charges of offences that violated treaties establishing protectorates or laws governing princely states, or accusations of belligerency against the colonisers, provided whatever fig leaf of legality seemed necessary. The most senior officials, such as a governor-general or commander-in-chief, often exercised a great deal of personal initiative and discretion, and were not above overturning the verdicts of commissions of inquiry they had constituted if they disagreed with conclusions reached. Colonial offices in London or Paris might caution against hasty action, but eventually approve or ratify decisions made on the ground.

Commission verdicts and gubernatorial decrees could and did provoke criticism at home about the arbitrary powers of officials, unwarranted interference in local affairs and injustices committed on native subjects. Deposed rulers and their defenders might protest, and on occasion deftly pushed back against colonial decisions, rallying support in press and parliament, organising delegations from colony to metropole, and in one or two instances mounting court cases for restoration of rights or property. Avenues for redress, however, were limited given that subjects lacked the rights of citizens, international jurisdiction over colonial territories was limited, and human rights discourse in the late 1800s and early 1900s had not achieved the currency it later earned. Widespread and gung-ho backing for imperialism, mounting jingoism and entrenched belief in the right of the 'whites' to rule the world and stamp out misgovernment often made depositions faits accomplis. European force of arms generally voided the likelihood of success for any uprising in favour of a deposed leader. Moreover, those who were ousted had often become too compromised by the time of their removal to rally compatriots, and the Europeans had usually managed to secure alliances with disaffected factions of the elites in manoeuvring against sovereigns they evicted. A few notable cases provide exceptions.

Once a ruler was deposed, the colonial government faced the question of what to do with the ex-sovereign, as well as family members, courtiers and hangers-on. Executing a deposed sovereign was a step too far by the nineteenth century. Such action would turn the victim into a martyr, perhaps setting off uncontrollable protest, and it hardly matched up with the humanitarian image the European colonisers sought to project. Incarcerating an emperor, king or sultan in gaol was an awkward prospect, with the possibility of escape and the rather unhappy vision of a former sovereign languishing in a prison cell. Letting the ruler remain in his old realm posed manifest dangers: he might try to regain his throne, serve as a rallying-point for resistance, interfere with his successor, and otherwise menace the colonial order. A preferred solution to the problem of what to do with a dethroned ruler, thus, was to exile him (or, rarely, her) to a place far enough away so that possibilities of escape and return, or of marshalling support for restoration, would be minimal. This was ideally a fully-fledged colony where colonial control was not subject to the 'half-sovereignty' of a protectorate, a place where isolation, surveillance and restrictions on the exile's freedom of movement, contacts with others and any political initiative could be assured. An appropriate site for transportation might be an area only a few hundred kilometres away from an exile's former kingdom, for instance another territory securely under European control in Africa for deposed African rulers, or some part of British India for the dethroned ruler of one of the subcontinent's princely states. Ever better, however, was a sleepy island colony, one relatively small and easy to police, a site where an exile could moulder away in safe tropical torpor.

The legal basis for exiling sovereigns from one colonial possession to another was vague, though Britain and France had long histories of transporting criminals and rebels to overseas penal colonies. In Britain, 'The Colonial Prisoners Removal Act', adopted by Parliament in 1869, authorised 'the Removal of Prisoners from one Colony to another for the purposes of Punishment'. It stated that 'Any two colonies may, with the sanction of an order of Her Majesty in Council, agree for the removal of any prisoners under sentence or order of transportation, imprisonment, or penal servitude from one of such colonies to the other for the purpose of their undergoing in such other colony the whole or any part of their punishment'. The careful wording allowed considerable scope for individual situations; a prisoner could be sent away by 'order', which did not require a formal court sentence; a prison was conveniently defined as 'any place of confinement or any place where the prisoners undergo punishment'.[23] The necessary agreement of a host colony to receive a prisoner was not difficult to obtain, though it required discussions about the choice of exact destination, the timing of the exile's arrival, the number of family members or servants who accompanied the ruler, the conditions in which he was kept and the restrictions placed upon him. Those decisions involved substantial negotiation among officials from the exile's country of origin and the host colony, as well as authorities in the metropole. Their correspondence encompassed pensions, accommodation and other benefits, the education of children, the petitions exiles regularly submitted, and the possibilities of repatriation. Two matters held particular concern. One was worry that exiles might escape, undertake anti-colonial agitation, or behave inappropriately. The other was bickering as to which budget – that of the ministry, or of one or other colony – would cover the not inconsiderable costs of an exile's maintenance. As prices rose and families multiplied, financial issues often became consummate; they did not end with the death of the dethroned monarch, as colonial authorities still bore some responsibility for widows, descendants and relatives of banished rulers.

Deposition and exile addressed immediate problems for the colonial power, but created others, including financial burdens that could last for decades and even generations. One priority was the question of whether to abolish a dynasty or enthrone a new ruler. With heirs and kinsmen numbering in the dozens among rulers with multiples wives and concubines, no rule of primogeniture in most non-European dynasties, and the crucial hope that whoever was placed on the throne would be more agreeable to European domination than the one dethroned, that issue represented a great challenge. How could the colonisers assure the legitimacy of a new ruler in the eyes of his subjects while avoiding contamination by the ideas and influences that had undone his predecessor, or misdeeds because of familial character flaws? How could they navigate around court and family factions and intrigues? Should colonisers opt for a mature, experienced and trusted heir, or (as usually proved the case) should they select a child, even an infant, in the hopes that a youngster might be suitably groomed? Might a previously deposed ruler even be brought back from exile? Should the powers of the new nominal sovereign be further curtailed, or would colonial rule benefit by buttressing the throne under its new occupant? Would a new ruler succeed in entrenching his authority and fending off possible rivals, and would he bend to the colonisers' demands?

Abolishing a native dynasty might seem a preferable option, but that also posed risks. There might no longer be a recalcitrant king on the throne, but the aura of an old dynasty could linger, with nationalists invoking glorious ancestors and their achievements, and damning colonisers for getting rid of a hallowed institution. Indeed, monarchism – loyalty to a particular dynasty or the general principle of indigenous monarchy, demands for restitution of pre-colonial native authority, hopes of recruiting a reigning or deposed monarch to an uprising – inspired many early nationalist movements. Extinguishing a dynasty also deprived the Europeans of a potential strength in their overrule: the international image of respecting local customs and the monarch who embodied them, the backing of a sovereign for colonising policies, the use of the pomp and pageantry of kingship as an adjunct to colonial overlordship, and the opportunity to position the monarch and the ideology of monarchism as a bulwark against more radical creeds. Particular circumstances dictated whether a new ruler replaced a deposed old one, with patterns difficult to discern; lack of a credible candidate, however, often inflected officials' decisions to dispense with the throne and rule by direct administration.

Europeans, in short, had an ambiguous relationship with local monarchs, whom they viewed as both enemies and potential friends. Rulers who resisted conquest or rebelled had to be vanquished, but more acquiescent ones could be co-opted into the colonial order (as in Indian princely states, Malay sultanates and French protectorates in North Africa), left in power in their ancestral realms, with greater or lesser remaining powers and rights. European views of native rulers were similarly ambivalent. Europeans damned many as brutal and immoral, yet even denunciations revealed fascination for 'oriental' power and luxuriance. Deposed rulers did not lose their claims to entitlement or celebrity status. The British and the French – the former because of commitment to monarchy at home, the latter because of republican suspicion about kings – retained a wary respect for those who had sat on thrones. Dethroned royals continued to command attention, especially for the British, accustomed to the special place in society occupied by princes and nobles. Salutations of 'Your Highness' were still employed, marks of lingering consideration for those 'born to the purple', even if the colonisers mocked native rulers, their regalia and culture. Queen Victoria was especially sympathetic to deposed feudatories, and senior administrators (many hailing from aristocratic milieus or themselves rewarded with peerages and knighthoods) were sensitive to gradations of privilege. Royals and elites recognised each other across borders, including colonial frontiers.[24] Even France, to judge by popular periodicals, experienced residual royalism. Members of the *ci-devant* nobility often pursued vocations in the military and diplomatic corps. The empire likewise provided a terrain for those who felt that modern France had lost the virtues – *grandeur*, a sense of mission, military prowess, Christian faith – associated with the monarchy. Colonial officials acknowledged a moral obligation, if a reluctant and occasionally onerous one, to see to the needs of the deposed in an appropriate manner, and looking after them well was championed as befitting the superior values of Europeans and magnanimity towards old foes. In a world where hierarchy and deference were enshrined, though highly coloured in the colonies by racialism, royal status meant that the deposed could never be ordinary prisoners.

Colonialism and dethroned monarchs

This study demonstrates how the deposition and exile of indigenous monarchs provided a strategy for colonial authorities to establish, consolidate and maintain their domination. It argues that the displacement of those at the pinnacle of native power, often in arbitrary fashion and by duplicitous means, blatantly manifested the strength of colonisers. Colonial propagandists might laud the banishment of native rulers as removal of cruel potentates, but colonial *raison d'état* rather than the *mission civilisatrice* was the principle. The dethroning of indigenous sovereigns, however, the study suggests, also evidenced the fragility of colonial overlordship. It revealed colonisers' inability to reconcile defeated rulers to the colonial order and successfully to groom new ones as loyal agents. It testified to never-ending worries about rebellion, betrayal and undermining of colonial dominion. It pointed to the instability and mutation of theories and practices of colonial government. In exile, the former monarchs stubbornly represented pre-colonial independence, genealogies of rulership and indigenous cultures, collective identities that could not be effaced by colonialism. Monarchism provided a potent platform for anti-colonialism, even if other ideologies later proved more potent. The diminution of the real powers of rulers that remained on the throne showed the limitations and hypocrisy, even vacuity, of 'protection' as a means of indirect rule. Metropolitan debates about the fate of ousted rulers underlined the lack of consensus about imperialism, and the remonstrations of the banished offered reminders about the colonisers' unhonoured humanitarian claims. After independence, the pulling down of statues of

European monarchs and viceroys in the former colonies, and renewed commemoration of pre-colonial heroes – Kandyan and Burmese kings, Vietnamese 'patriotic' emperors and African resisters to colonialism, among others – provided a retort to colonialism and its mythologies.

It would be simple in this history if colonisers were all villainous and ousted rulers all saintly, but that is not the case. There were indeed displays of great cruelty by several of those the Europeans removed, bloody actions against rivals, abuse of subjects, offensive warfare, backroom plots, maintenance of 'feudal' privileges; some allegations of corruption, maladministration and improper personal behaviour were well substantiated. From the colonialist European viewpoint, warfare and the self-appointed mandate to govern provided justification enough to get rid of opponents. The point is not so much whether an individual was culpable of the accusations made, but the issue of whether colonial authorities who had invaded and occupied foreign countries had the right to depose indigenous rulers, and if so whether the processes used were defensible. Which states have a right to intervene in the domestic affairs of another, and under what circumstances, remains an unresolved questions in present-day international relations.

Such issues will be more fully elucidated in the remainder of this book. To anticipate and summarise key arguments: The first aspect of my topic is the circumstances and steps involved in deposition and banishment of indigenous hereditary rulers by British and French authorities. Other interesting cases – in the Dutch, Belgian, German and Portuguese empires – lie outside my area of study, although those examples confirm the contentions advanced here.[25] The following chapters are also largely limited to consideration of reigning rulers. Other native royals were also subjected to banishment, or went into voluntary exile; some have provided subjects for different authors. Their experiences, too, second my view about the importance of royal figures in colonial situations, and the idea of monarchy as a crucial element in the dynamics of colonialism and anti-colonialism.[26]

Three different but overlapping contexts precipitated removal of indigenous sovereigns, men (and the rare woman) later referred to as 'prisoners of war', 'prisoners of the state' and 'captives'. The first involved incidents in which the British or French, sometimes at the time of a *prise de possession*, but more often in consolidating takeover, defeated by force of arms or otherwise mastered a ruler who resisted invasion and occupation, and then removed him. The Ceylonese king Sri Vikrama Rajasinha, the Asante king Prempeh, the Vietnamese emperor Ham Nghi and the Burmese king Thibaw count among their number. A second cohort suffered deposition when, subsequent to European conquest, they became implicated in rebellions, as occurred with the

Vietnamese emperor Duy Tan, the Malagasy queen Ranavalona, and the maharajah of Manipur; this might occur during the early years of colonial control or, as the cases of Sultan Mohammed V in Morocco and King Mutesa II in Uganda show, near the end of the age of empire. Third, rulers were deposed when they lost the confidence of imperialists and sometimes their countrymen for real or alleged personal failings or plots. Such diverse rulers as one maharajah of Indore and the Vietnamese emperor Thanh Thai were ousted on this basis.

Justifications for displacing a monarch nevertheless melded: when colonisers charged a ruler with resistance, they also blackened his political and moral reputation, and cited familial, regional or court opposition to justify the *coup*. Indeed aspirational rivals for indigenous thrones profited from European clashes with a ruler to improve their own lots, sometimes posing as replacements for evicted or soon to be ousted sovereigns. In many cases, the personal antipathy of an individual colonial administrator or military officer, senior or subaltern, played a decisive role in determining a ruler's fate, and a particular incident or suite of incidents precipitated action that had been premeditated for some time.

Most of the depositions occurred prior to the First World War, over a century when European powers jousted for territory in South and Southeast Asia and in Africa. During these years, colonial conquerors operated with relatively few constraints on their actions other than opposition from big-power rivals and reservations from their compatriots about the merits of imperial expansion. Colonialism raised great protest, except from diehard opponents, largely when abuses were egregious (as in the Congo Free State) or when especially bloody confrontations or scandals erupted. Extension of overseas empires, for most at home and in the concert of nations, especially by the last decades of the 1800s, constituted acceptable international policy, legitimised by racial and civilisational ideas, and promoted as a commercial and geopolitical imperative. Such perspectives excused, and sometimes endorsed, the ouster of those who placed obstacles in the path of European colonisation and who could be depicted as intractable enemies or brutal tyrants. By the 1920s and 1930s, these views had moderated; there were fewer depositions, and they more frequently concerned rulers charged with unredeemable faults of private behaviour. Yet, as cases in Tunisia, Morocco and Uganda in the 1940s and 1950s illustrate, political concerns – now situated in the context of decolonisation – still provided imperatives for toppling rulers who undermined empire.

A second general aspect of this study concerns the life of deposed monarchs and their families, courtiers and servants in exile, with the argument that if the deposed might be out of sight, they seldom were out of the mind of colonisers or compatriots. The life of former rulers was regulated by colonial authorities, who provided pensions and lodgings, but also engaged in constant surveillance and determined the degree of captives' freedom. The paradoxes of former sovereigns becoming prisoners will become apparent from the case studies: whether they accepted their fates, manoeuvred to regain thrones or negotiated for repatriation without restoration, whether they became Westernised or obdurately resisted Europeanisation, whether they lived out their days in celebrity, infamy or obscurity. During their banishment, one also sees the endless concern of colonial officials with the captives-*cum*-wards, the fretting about their activities and sympathies, and preoccupation with expenditures, privileges and demands that deportees submitted. One glimpses how the banished were viewed by those among whom they lived, indigenous people of the host countries, descendants of slaves, European settlers, passing visitors.

Even when only a few hundred kilometres from their homelands, exiles ended up in places with different languages, cultures and landscapes, with many sent to far more distant places of banishment. St Helena in the South Atlantic and the Seychelles islands in the Indian Ocean served as favoured options for British exile of former potentates, though at least one African was sent to the Caribbean, and several Indians ended up in Britain. In the Seychelles, as Uma Kothari has shown, a community of exiled colonial rulers collected in the creole colony, living alongside each other with parallel fates though limited interactions.[27] The French sent one of their African exiles to Martinique in the West Indies, and a Moroccan sultan to Madagascar. As the postcard of 'kings in exile' in this chapter shows, briefly a West African chieftain, a Vietnamese emperor and the last queen of Madagascar metaphorically crossed paths as exiles in Algeria (see Figure 1). Réunion Island in the Indian Ocean, not that distant from the Seychelles, in particular, served the French for deportation of royals and other political exiles from Madagascar, the Comoros Islands, Vietnam and Morocco.[28]

Varying fates awaited the banished. Some remained permanently in exile, though occasionally shifted from one site to another. Many died during their terms of banishment, in several instances, decades after deposition, far away from a homeland where they had never again set foot. A few were allowed to return home, and were even reinstated to some lesser official position if considered sufficiently reconciled to the colonial order or so aged as to be harmless. (Death at home rather than in detention avoided the inconvenient question of local burial or repatriation of remains, and the possibly dangerous sympathies that might provoke.) Only a few exceptional figures re-entered the political arena

Figure 1 'Les rois en exil': This satirical drawing, reproduced as a postcard, shows the exiled Vietnamese emperor Ham Nghi, ex-queen Ranavalona III of Madagascar and Béhanzin, the former sovereign of Dahomey (and his entourage) in Algiers. Although Ham Nghi and Ranavalona were banished to the French North African outpost for long years, Béhanzin spent only a short time there before his death. The caption reads: 'Royal introductions: Friends, all friends!'

of their home countries. Sultan Mohammed of Morocco led his country to independence, while the possibility of a former emperor of Vietnam regaining the throne after the Second World War was foreclosed in tragic circumstances. A return, however, as a couple of instances witness, did not preclude a second deposition and exile, either by colonisers or, after independence, by the rulers' compatriots.

The third general area on which this study focuses is the posthumous life of royal exiles, suggesting that though deposed, dead and buried, they lived on in national memory and commemoration. Some, after death, returned to the countries over which they once reigned. This occasionally occurred under colonial rule when French or British authorities hoped to capitalise on enduring royalist sentiment in the face of more radical nationalist movements. In different cases, repatriation of rulers' remains came only after colonies gained independence, yet with new regimes also hoping to appropriate the aura of pre-colonial dynasties and monarchs. During often lengthy years of exile and after death, the reputation of the banished altered, and their commemoration – in reburials, statuary, national iconography and historical narrative – shows how those considered evil or treasonous by one group and generation might be considered heroic by another, with deposition adding a halo of sacrifice: the deposed and demonised monarchs were now consecrated as state-builders, 'patriotic kings', 'fathers of the country' and exemplars of resistance. In metropoles, as well, anti-colonial and post-independence revisions suggested new views about those the Europeans had removed, now able to be seen as victims of colonialism, defenders of their homelands, and figures bound by the exigencies and mores of their times and cultures rather than violators of universalist European precepts of behaviour. Some are hailed as brave warriors, notable scholars, nation-builders and cultural intermediaries.

Relationships between European colonisers and native rulers remained contingent and opportunistic. Colonisers, it should be noted, both made and unmade monarchies outside Europe. While foreigners overturned kings throughout Africa and Asia, they also helped to establish or entrench dynasties. The British, for instance, in recognising a regional ruler selected as king of Bhutan in 1907, provided an imprimatur for the dynasty that remains on the throne today and confirmed the territorial integrity of a country that had earlier been forced to cede land to Britain. In Uganda, British support for the king of Buganda buttressed his position among the multiple hereditary rulers of that country. The retention of the sultanates in the Malay states led to a unique post-independence arrangement by which one of the hereditary rulers serves a term, as Yang di-Pertuan Agong, effectively the king, of Malaysia. The British played a vital role in creating the monarchies of Jordan and Saudi Arabia, and the ill-fated kingdom of Iraq, after the First World War, and they provided valuable recognition to rulers of the Gulf states. In southern Africa, Britain left intact the monarchies of Lesotho and Swaziland, and in the South Pacific, they did much to secure the monarchies in Tonga and Samoa. In their sphere, the French built up administrative and religious foundations under the king of Cambodia, and they promoted the ruler of Luang Prabang to the position of king of Laos – though the last king of Cambodia under the French, the long-lived Sihanouk, would be on and off the throne for decades afterwards, and the monarchy of Laos disappeared with a Communist coup in 1975. The Moroccan monarchy survived deposition of several sultans, French withdrawal in 1956 and the vagaries of recent history. These cases of the role of colonisers in the creation of monarchies around the world, as well as their destruction, point to the complex intersections of colonial and indigenous rule, and of metropolitan and native monarchies.[29]

Rediscovering the royals in history

A study of exiled colonial rulers fits within several historiographical settings. The 'new imperial history' – now more orthodox than novel – places emphasis on the lived experiences of those affected by colonialism, the life stories of both the famous and the unknown.[30] Each of the royal exiles has a personal history of upbringing, accession, reign and a falling-out with colonial overlords. There are alliances and betrayals, battles and intrigues, high politics and skulduggery. The downfall of monarchs drew in spouses and concubines, extended families, courtiers and servants. Exile raised quotidian concerns about lodgings and pensions, food and clothing, the fate of children and relatives, emotions of nostalgia, resentment and resignation, and dreams of reinstatement. The exiles gained notoriety in the places they were sent but also in Britain and France, in person, when allowed to visit, or through newspapers and images reproduced in periodicals and on postcards (some of which appear as illustrations in this volume). Images are major resources and subjects for both royal and colonial history, and here are native rulers portrayed in word portraits by friends and foes, and photographed arrayed in traditional finery or European dress. They are exotic potentates, defeated enemies or would-be European bourgeois, the depictions mirrors of European visions as much as the realities of their lives.

Also influenced by the new imperial history, this study underlines the ways in which such categories as class and gender, and ethnicity and religion, structured colonial encounters. Traits of what Europeans perceived as manly rule in indigenous societies – strength and a warrior spirit – appear in many of the exile stories, and triumphant Europeans proved capable of paying tribute to brave adversaries even when they impugned the morals of the defeated. Women appear on several occasions as regnant queens, but more often as powerful queen mothers, wives who followed husbands into exile, mothers of potential heirs, and concubines brought into royal courts by means fair and foul. In a couple of cases, they also fight for kings as 'amazon' soldiers. Colonial officials were troubled by male heirs, but also concerned with marriage partners for the daughters of exiles. The banishment of the queen of Madagascar shows distinct gendering of that monarch on the throne and in exile. Race, not surprisingly, looms large: the notion of 'savage' or 'degenerate' potentates in Africa or Asia, intimations of in-born flaws of inconstancy, duplicity, dishonesty and depravity, questions about the capacity of 'natives' to become civilised to European standards. Omnipresent in officials' correspondence, journalists' reports and participants' recollections are assumptions about race, assertion of Western and 'white' superiority over 'yellow' or 'black' peoples.

Recent colonial history has placed much emphasis on webs of empire. Dispossession and exile created and reinforced links across the map. Deportation created or added to connections between Vietnam and Réunion, Madagascar and Algeria, Uganda and the Seychelles, Zululand and St Helena, West Africa and the West Indies. Such webs illustrate the 'spatial turn' in colonial studies, a new focus on space and place.[31] They show how St Helena and the Seychelles, Algeria, Madagascar and Réunion became places of confinement of political prisoners from diverse backgrounds, royals and commoners. In a neat switch, the British exiled the last Mughal emperor from India to Burma in 1857, and the last king of Burma to India in 1885. Pathways crisscrossed the map. The last ruler of the Punjab went into exile in Britain, later visited India again, travelled around Europe and died in France. A Zulu king from southeastern Africa was sent to the Cape Colony, then back to Zululand, to be deported once again, this time to St Helena; he subsequently visited Britain, and finally returned to southern Africa. Others travelled along equally complex itineraries. Exile involved a geometry of imperial connections: the country from which a ruler came, the one to which he was sent, and the metropole, where ultimate decisions were made and where ex-rulers were occasionally allowed to sojourn. Place was crucial, for royal exiles lost homelands where they claimed ancestral rights, and were forced to settle temporarily or permanently in very different countries.

The 'spectacle of empire', a phrase popularised by Jan Morris, contributes an integral part of the story.[32] The pomp and ceremony of courts were not just window-dressing, but central to the exercise of royal power. Symbols of authority, royal prerogatives and protocol were vital to rule, and failure to observe conventions, whether by the colonising or the colonised, could lead to troubles. Enthronements of monarchs followed traditional rites but the presence of colonial authorities provided public endorsement of their mandate while affirming the paramountcy of the foreigners. Performance of duties such as Confucian rites counted among the major duties of monarchs, both before and after the arrival of Europeans. Funerals and interments confirmed monarchs' status in national memory, explaining why burial or reburial of exiled leaders in their homelands, even decades after death, assumed such symbolic importance. In establishing overrule, colonial governments, the monarchs and viceregal representatives, alongside the republican administrators of France, assumed the powers of old dynasts, building new government palaces, introducing new flags and anthems, parading with the pageantry of authority, taking on guardianship of sacred sites and dispensing honours; in an expression of Sujit Sivasundaram, the British 'recycled' old forms and expressions of majesty inherited from rulers they displaced, and so did the French.[33]

Essential in the story, as well, is the administrative and political history of deposition and exile, including the question of law and its execution: an area of growing interest in colonial studies. Law was much more than a façade of colonial rule, for it erected the architecture inside which colonial authorities acted. Protectorate treaties, though often honoured in the breach, determined the rights of the colonisers and those whom they vowed to 'protect'; gubernatorial decrees recognised or deposed local rulers. Protectorates, often too easily conflated with colonies, had a dynamics induced by negotiations – leveraged towards Europeans, to be sure – between colonial overlords and indigenous sovereigns. Native rulers, though severely constricted in their actions, were never incapable of manoeuvre, and indeed, they suffered punishment because they dared to exercise authority and behave in ways that did not suit the colonisers. Colonial authority was not absolute, nor was pacification total. Factions jostled each other in royal palaces and colonial government houses as well. Imperial authority was uneasily shared among metropolitan officials, governors and subaltern appointees, military commanders and civilians, men with different views and policies, some acting at the limit of their briefs. The history of royal exiles illustrates the latitudes of law and its enforcement, and the constant legislative and administrative experimentation involved in governing a colony.

Another historiographical context here, beyond the field of colonial and imperial history, is the study of royalty. For long a scent of political conservatism, nostalgia, antiquarianism or obsession with tittle-tattle about royal celebrities clung to writing about modern monarchy. However, a revived serious interest has recently emerged, typified by a *Royal Studies Journal* (complementing a more veteran journal, *Court Studies*) and an innovative series of 'studies of modern monarchy'.[34] European monarchs, scholars increasingly argue, were far from bystanders in modern history, and many engaged actively with colonial endeavours. Colonial possessions were integral 'realms and territories' of the British Crown and other monarchies, and the presence of the monarch overseas – in person during tours, by proxy through viceregal officials, in the symbolism of monuments, fêtes and proclamations – was part and parcel of imperial governance.

The late 1800s and early 1900s saw what Jürgen Osterhammel calls the 'reinvention' of monarchies.[35] Monarchies in Europe underwent major transformations in the face of revolutions, national unification, rising republicanism, exertion of greater political control by parliaments, and the extension of the suffrage. Colonialism, too, instigated change – the assumption of the title of 'Empress of India' by Queen Victoria, the acquisition of a vast personal colony by King Leopold II of the Belgians, the evolution of German and Italian kingship into imperial monarchies after unification. Indigenous monarchies were much influenced by European ones: resisting European domination or accommodating overrule, remodelling themselves along European lines, adopting European-style uniforms, orders of chivalry and ceremonial, developing personal ties between counterparts through royal tours.[36] In the 'high colonial age', monarchies in Europe and abroad remained forces to be reckoned with, to a degree perhaps less than fully appreciated, and historians are now exploring anew the dimensions and dynamics of royalty in the modern world.

The complicated relationship between the crown of a colonising country and colonial monarchies has often lain in the background of historical research, but relatively seldom appeared in the forefront except in the case of the Indian princely states.[37] David Cannadine's *Ornamentalism* famously suggested a community of interests between British and colonised elites, and argued that societies with hereditary privileges for royals and nobles, as existed in Britain and India, for instance, found shared bases for interaction.[38] Coronations, decorations, durbars and royal prerogatives provided ways of tethering the maharajas and other rulers to the British colonial state. The 'paramountcy' of the imperial government nevertheless was non-negotiable. Nicholas Dirks suggests, in the Indian case, that British rule 'hollowed out' indigenous crowns, eviscerating rulers of any real power.[39] A more nuanced view comes from Colin Newbury, who argues that 'overrule', whether in Africa, Asia or other colonial theatres, allowed for significant variations in power-sharing, and D. A. Low traces the way this worked in practice in what he sees as the most 'successful' example of British indirect rule, in the kingdoms of Uganda.[40] Whatever the particular valences of links between metropolitan monarchies and the colonies, the relationships open avenues of research on such issues as royal prerogatives, the involvement of individual royals in colonial undertakings, royal tours (including visits by European royals to colonies and indigenous royals to Europe), regalia and its despoliation, colonial ceremonies and the rituals of monarchical regimes, and expressions of royalist sentiment by elites and ordinary people.[41]

Several rulers deposed by the British have attracted attention from recent historians, including full-scale biographies that provide more detail than can be given here. Indeed, a landmark study of the Punjab maharajah Duleep Singh by Tony Ballantyne – his exile and life in Europe, and his legacy to Sikh communities around the world – provided much inspiration for the present volume.[42] There have been other works on the Punjab ruler, too, as well as an excellent biography of his daughter Sophia.[43] William Dalrymple on the last Mughal emperor of India, Rosie Llewelyn-Jones on the last king of Awadh, and Sudha Shah on the last king of Burma offer comprehensive inquiries.[44] (Shah acknowledges the influence of Amitav Ghosh's splendid novel about the Burmese king, *The Glass Palace* – another of my own inspirations.[45]) Caroline Keene has examined the case of the deposition of the ruler of Manipur.[46] Jeff Guy's studies of the Zulu kings Cetshwayo and Dinuzulu cover their epic lives and also the remarkable support they enjoyed from an Anglican bishop and his daughters.[47] Uma Kothari's article on exiles in the Seychelles, already mentioned, is a pioneering work on an entire group of the banished in one location.[48] The present work builds on these studies, which have presented new insights into the lives and fates of important figures in world history and have broadened understanding of the workings of colonialism.

Royal exile in the colonies: a prelude

The modern exile of royal personnages by colonial overlords has a long history. In 1619, for instance, when the Portuguese conquered the Jaffna region of northern Ceylon, they captured and deposed its ruler, Cankili II. The former king was deported to Goa, put on trial, convicted and sentenced to death. Franciscan friars convinced Cankili that, doomed in this world, he must consider his eternal life; converted and baptised, 'Dom Felipe' was nevertheless decapitated around 1623. His two queens, children and other family members, also sent to Portuguese India and converted, were persuaded to enter religious orders, where the vow of chastity meant they would produce no further claimants to the Jaffna throne.[49] The Dutch, who soon wrested Ceylon from the Portuguese, chose the island as a place to deport rebels from the East Indies, including the king of Kartasura (in central Java), Amangkurat III, in the early years of the seventeenth century, after he had been overthrown in a palace coup but then unsuccessfully battled the Dutch and his usurper.[50] Amangkurat III was the first in a succession of East Indian exiles to Ceylon, and the Dutch also banished prisoners to the Cape Colony in southern Africa.[51] After being ousted by the British from these two possessions, the Dutch used the huge territory of the East Indies for 'internal' exile of rulers from one city or island to another, the most famous, in 1830, Diponegoro, the ruler of Yogyakarta.[52]

The British also had early experience with exile of native royals. One example came after the defeat by the armies of the East India Company of Tipu Sultan, the famous 'tiger of Mysore', at Seringapatam in 1799. Tipu was killed in battle, but the British captured his twelve sons and banished them to Vellore, near Calcutta (though one youngster died on the day of their arrival). Some three thousand compatriots joined Tipu's family in the 'little Mysore' that spread around the fort. In 1806, a mutiny by Indian soldiers serving under British command broke out in the fort, precipitated by orders that they wear a leather-ornamented hat rather than turbans, shave their beards and dispense with jewellery and markers of caste. (The rebellion has been seen as foreshadowing the great uprising of 1857.) The rebels raised the banner of Tipu Sultan, and proclaimed one of his sons their leader, though none of the princes had in fact played an active role in the mutiny. The British quelled the insurrection, with considerable bloodshed, and moved Tipu's sons to Calcutta. Most seemed to accommodate to British rule – one, later living in London, won election to the posh Oriental Club in 1837, and another was received by Queen Victoria and awarded a knighthood for his charitable works.[53]

Fourteen years after the banishment of Tipu Sultan's sons, the British exiled a sultan on the island of Java. When Napoleon occupied and then in 1810 annexed Holland to France, the Dutch colonies became nominal French possessions; in 1811, the British sent in troops to take over Java, appointing Thomas Stamford Raffles as lieutenant-governor over their new territories. The reigning sultan in Yogyakarta, Hamengkubuwono II, had come to the throne as the forty-two-year-old son of the former ruler in 1792. Accused of being anti-Dutch and charged with financial mismanagement, lack of Islamic piety and other offences, he was deposed and replaced with his son, Hamengkubuwono III, considered more receptive to the colonisers' demands; the Dutch nevertheless allowed the dethroned ruler to remain in Yogyakarta. When the British occupied Java – pillaging the sultan's palace and setting up a new sub-kingdom, Pakualam, for one of their allies (who was Hamengkubuwono II's brother) – Raffles restored Hamengkubuwono II to the throne, but he proved no more friendly to the British than he had to the Dutch. Correspondence was discovered pointing to a conspiracy to overthrow British rule with the joint forces of the rulers of Yogyakarta and Surakarta.

The British again marched troops on the palace in Yogyakarta, and captured and deposed Hamengkubuwono II, whom they deported with two of his sons and a retinue of fifty others. Their destination was Penang, an island off the coast of peninsula Malaysia that the British had acquired in the 1780s. They initially told Hamengkubuwono II that he would be banished for three months, but his exile lasted for several years, despite the former sultan's official disavowal of any intentions to regain his throne and repeated petitions asking for repatriation. Finally, he was allowed to return to Batavia (present-day Jakarta) in Java – his grandson was now sultan in Yogyakarta – as the British prepared to transfer the East Indies colonies back to the Dutch in 1816. The Dutch, however, still feared Hamengkubuwono II's anti-European feelings, and when they resumed control of Java, they exiled him and his sons to Ambon, in the Moluccas. In a great about-face, in 1826, the Dutch allowed Hamengkubuwono, frail at more than seventy-five years of age but apparently reconciled to Dutch paramountcy, to return to Yogyakarta, and replaced him on the throne. He died as reigning sultan two years later, bringing to an end a remarkable life that had seen an East Indian ruler twice deposed, by two different colonial powers.[54]

Such episodes as the exile of the rulers of Jaffna and Kartasura, Tipu Sultan's sons and Hamengkubuwono provide a prelude to the chapters that follow. They illustrate the complex situations – war, rebellion, court intrigues, imperial rivalries – that precipitated depositions, as well as the various fates – resistance, accommodation, migration, death in exile, repatriation, restoration – that befell those removed. The next chapter looks closely at the overthrow of the king of Kandy, Sri Vikrama Rajasinha, in 1815; his destiny, like that of Hamengkubuwono II, was bound up with domestic conflicts, British expansion in the Indian Ocean and big-power rivalries for acquisition of colonies.

Notes

1 G. Silber, 'Rois déchus et pensionnés', *Le Monde illustré*, 12 October 1912, 236–7.
2 Robert G. Calwell, 'Exile as an Institution', *Political Science Quarterly*, 58:2 (1943), 239–62.
3 Clare Anderson, *Subaltern Lives: Biographies of Colonialism in the Indian Ocean World, 1790–1920* (Cambridge: Cambridge University Press, 2012).
4 Daniel Beer, *The House of the Dead: Siberian Exile under the Tsars* (London: Allen Lane, 2016).
5 In a variation on the theme, Portuguese royals fled Lisbon just before Napoleon's invasion for Brazil, where they ruled Portugal and the empire from a colonial base for thirteen years. See Kirsten Schultz, *Tropical Versailles: Empire, Monarchy and the Portugal Royal Court in Rio de Janeiro, 1808–1821* (London: Routledge, 2001).
6 See Jean des Cars, *Le Sceptre et le sang: Rois et reines en guerre, 1914–1945* (Paris: Perrin, 2014); and Garth Russell, *The Emperors: How Europe's Rulers Were Destroyed by the First World War* (Stroud: Amberley, 2004). Among biographies of the last Habsburgs are Jean Sévilla, *Le Dernier Empereur* (Paris: Perrin, 2009), and *Zita, impératrice courage, 1892–1989* (Paris: Perrin, 2003). On the German royals, see Sally Marks, '"My Name is Ozymandias": The Kaiser in Exile', *Central European History*, 16:2 (1983), 122–70; and on Romanovs who survived the Bolsheviks, Frances Welch, *The Russian Court at Sea: The Voyage of HMS Marlborough, April 1919* (London: Short Books, 2011).

7 Neil Rees, *A Royal Exile: King Zog and Queen Geraldine of Albania* (London: Court of King Zog Research Society, 2010).
8 The website www.royalark.net provides an invaluable reference guide to reigning and deposed royal houses, and to the complex genealogies of these dynasties.
9 Danielle Eliséef, *Puyi* (Paris: Perrin, 2014).
10 'Kicked-Out Rulers Beg to Be Sent Home Again', *The Milwaukee Sentinel*, 12 January 1936.
11 Asfa-Wossen Asserate, *King of Kings: The Triumph and Tragedy of Emperor Haile Selassie I of Ethiopia* (London: Haus Publishing, 2015).
12 Philip Mansel and Torsten Riotte (eds), *Monarchy and Exile: The Politics of Legitimacy from Marie de Médicis to Wilhelm II* (London: Palgrave Macmillan, 2011); Bruno Dumons, *Rois et princes en exil: Une Histoire transnationale du politique dans l'Europe du XIXe siècle* (Paris: Riveneuve, 2015). Alphonse Daudet, *Les Rois en exil* (Paris: Dentu, 1879), provides a comic portrayal of a fictional King of Illyria living a life of louche pleasure in Paris, while the stalwart Queen Frédérique stuggles to maintain royal dignity, and courtiers hatch a plot to reconquer the throne.
13 Paul Ganière, 'L'Embarquement de Napoléon pour Sainte-Hélène', *Le Souvenir napoléonien*, 51 (1988), 8–20. Other members of the Bonaparte family also went into exile; see, e.g., Patricia Tyson Stroud, *The Man Who Had Been King: The American Exile of Napoleon's Brother Joseph* (Philadelphia: University of Pennsylvania Press, 2015).
14 Emilie Robbe (ed.), *La Conquête de la mémoire: Napoléon à Sainte-Hélène* (Paris: Gallimard/Musée de l'Armée, 2016); Sudhir Hazareesingh, *The Legend of Napoleon* (London: Granta Books, 2004).
15 Charles-Philippe d'Orléans, *Rois en Exil: Quand les Cours d'Europe trouvaient refuge au Portugal* (Paris: Express Roularta, 2012).
16 Theo Aronson, *Queen Victoria and the Bonapartes* (London: Thistle, 2014); Ian Knight, *With His Face to the Foe: The Life and Death of Louis Napoleon, the Prince Imperial, Zululand 1879* (Stroud: Spellmount, 2007).
17 The action taken against Urabi, his exile to Ceylon and his return to Egypt has manifest parallels with the fates of the deposed monarchs. See John S. Galbraith, 'The Trial of Arabi Pasha', *Journal of Imperial and Commonwealth History*, 7:3 (1979), 274–92 and Vijaya Samaraweera, 'Arabi Pasha in Ceylon, 1883–1901', *Islamic Culture*, 50:3 (1976), 219–27.
18 See, e.g., Peter Zinoman, *The Colonial Bastille: A History of Imprisonment in Vietnam, 1862–1940* (Berkeley: University of California Press, 2001).
19 See Antoinette Burton, *The Trouble with Empire: Challenges to Modern British Imperialism* (New York: Oxford University Press, 2015).
20 Though the nineteenth-century Habsburgs claimed no overseas colonies, there were colonial aspects to the regime. See Walter Sauer, 'Austria-Hungary: The Making of Central Europe', in Robert Aldrich (ed.), *The Age of Empires* (London: Thames & Hudson, 2007), pp. 196–219.
21 Colin Newbury, *Patrons, Clients, and Empire: Chieftaincy and Over-rule in Asia, Africa, and the Pacific* (Oxford: Oxford University Press, 2003).
22 Frantz Despagnet, *Essai sur les protectorats: Étude de droit international* (Paris: Larose et Forcel, 1896), p. 361. See also Étienne Jacobé de Naurois, *Le Protectorat: Théorie générale et application aux Protectorats français* (Toulouse: Rousseau, 1910); and Louis Rolland and Pierre Lampué, *Précis de législation coloniale* (Paris: Dalloz, 1936).
23 The Colonial Prisoners Removal Act, 1869–32 & 33 Vic. c. 10. (Imperial) Amended by Statute Law Revision Acts, 1883, 46 & 47 Vic. c. 39 and 1893 (No. 2) 56 & 57 Vic. c. 54. (www.legislation.gov.uk/ukpga/Vict/32-33/10).
24 David Cannadine, *Ornamentalism: How the British Saw Their Empire* (London: Allen Lane/The Penguin Press, 2001).
25 On the Dutch, see the chapters by Ronit Ricci and Sri Margana in Ronit Ricci (ed.), *Exile in Colonial Asia: Kings, Convicts, Commemoration* (Honolulu: University of Hawai'i Press, 2016); Peter Carey, *Destiny: The Life of Prince Diponegoro of*

THRONES AND DOMINION

Yogyakarta, 1785–1855 (Bern: Peter Lang, 2014); and A. A. A. Dewi Girindrawardani, Adrian Vickers and Rodney Holt, *The Last Rajah of Karangasem: The Life and Times of Anak Agung Agung Anglurah Karangasem (1887–1966)* (Denpasar: Saritaksu, 2014). A notable Portuguese exile was the African Gungunhana; see Maria de Conceiçao Vilhena, *Gungunhana no seu reino* (Lisbon: Colibri, 1996), and *Gungunhana: Grandeza e decadência de um império africano* (Lisbon: Colibri, 1999). On the Belgian exile of the Rwandan king Yuhi V, see Alison Des Forges, *Defeat is the Only Bad News: Rwanda under Musinga* (Madison: University of Wisconsin Press, 2011). For a case in the German Pacific, Patricia O'Brien, *Tautai: Samoa, World History, and the Life of Ta'isi O. F. Nelson* (Honolulu: University of Hawai'i Press, 2017). The colonising Japanese abolished the dynasty of Korea when it was their colony: Hoo Nam Seelmann, *Lautloses Weinen: Der Untergang des Koreanischen Köninghauses* (Würzburg: Königshauses & Neumann, 2011). I have also not discussed the ouster by the Ottoman sultan of the khedive (viceroy) of Egypt, Ismail Pasha, in 1879, under pressure from the British and French, on the basis of the large debts run up by his government and the khedive's tacit support for Ahmed Urabi's rebellion. Abbas II was removed as khedive by the British in 1914 after they declared war on the Ottoman empire. For Abbas' own account, see Amira Sonbol (ed.), *The Last Khedive of Egypt: The Memoirs of Abbas Hilmi II* (Cairo: American University in Cairo Press, 2006).

26 See Pierre L. Lamant, *L'Affaire Yukanthor: Autopsie d'un scandale colonial* (Paris: Société française d'histoire d'Outre-Mer, 1989); Tran My-Van, *A Vietnamese Royal Exile in Japan: Prince Cuong De (1882–1951)* (London: Routledge, 2005); Søren Ivarsson and Christopher E. Goscha, 'Prince Petsarath (1890–1959): Nationalism and Royalty in the Making of Modern Laos', *Journal of Southeast Asian Studies*, 38:1 (February 2007), 55–81. On the Myingun prince, see Penny Edwards, 'Watching the Detectives: The Elusive Exile of Prince Myngoon of Burma', in Ricci, *Exile in Asia*, pp. 248–278. Natasha Pairaudeau is also doing research on the Myingun prince.

27 Uma Kothari, 'Contesting Colonial Rule: Politics of Exile in the Indian Ocean', *Geoforum*, 43 (2012), 697–706; see also Athol Thomas, *Forgotten Eden: A View of the Seychelles Islands in the Indian Ocean* (London: Longmans, 1968), Ch. 12; Christopher Lee, *Seychelles: Political Castaways* (London: Elm Tree Books, 1976), Ch. 3; William McAteer, *To Be a Nation, being the third part of The History of the Seychelles, 1920–1976* (Mahé, Seychelles: Pristine Books, 2008), Ch. 2.

28 'La Réunion, terre d'exil', in Daniel Vaxelaire (ed.), *Le Mémorial de la Réunion* (Saint-Denis: Australe Éditions, 1979), pp. 284–91; Julian Mockford, *Pursuit of an Island* (London: Staples Press, 1950), Chs 8, 10, 11, 23.

29 Michael Arris, *The Raven Crown: The Origins of Buddhist Monarchy in Bhutan* (Chicago: Serindia Publications, 1994) and Karma Phuntsho, *The History of Bhutan* (London: Random House, 2013); D.A. Low, *Fabrication of Empire: The British and the Uganda Kingdoms, 1890–1902* (Cambridge: Cambridge University Press, 2009); Kobkua Suwannathat-Pian, *Palace, Political Party and Power: A Story of the Socio-Political Development of Malay Kingship* (Singapore: NUS Press, 2011); Matthieu Rey, 'The British, the Hashemites and Monarchies in the Middle East', in Robert Aldrich and Cindy McCreery (eds), *Crowns and Colonies: European Monarchies and Overseas Empires* (Manchester: Manchester University Press, 2016), pp. 227–44; Milton E. Osborne, *Sihanouk: Prince of Light, Prince of Darkness* (Sydney: Allen & Unwin, 1994); Grant Evans, *The Last Century of Lao Royalty: A Documentary History* (Chiang Mai: Silkworm Books, 2004); Mangkra Souvannaphouma, *Laos: Autopsie d'une monarchie assassinée* (Paris: L'Harmattan, 2010); and William Dalrymple, *Return of a King: The Battle for Afghanistan* (London: Bloomsbury, 2013). There is also the phenomenon of Europeans trying to make themselves monarchs of overseas places, successfully in the case of the Brookes of Sarawak, unsuccessfully so for the French 'king of the Sedangs': Nigel Barley, *White Rajah* (London: Little, Brown, 2002); Antoine Michelland, *Marie Ier, le dernier roi français: la conquête d'un aventurier en Indochine* (Paris: Perrin, 2012).

30 See Stephen Howe (ed.), *The New Imperial Histories Reader* (London: Routledge, 2009).

31 Alan Lester, 'Place and Space in British Imperial History Writing', in Robert Aldrich and Kirsten McKenzie (eds), *The Routledge History of Western Empires* (Abingdon: Routledge, 2014), pp. 300–14.
32 Jan Morris, *The Spectacle of Empire: Style, Effect and Pax Britannica* (London: Faber & Faber, 1982).
33 Sujit Sivasundaram, *Islanded: Britain, Sri Lanka and the Bounds of an Indian Ocean Colony* (Chicago: University of Chicago Press, 2013).
34 Frank Lorenz Müller and Heidi Mehrkens (eds), *Sons and Heirs: Succession and Political Culture in Nineteenth-Century Europe* (London: Palgrave Macmillan, 2016); Matthew Glencross, *The State Visits of Edward VII: Reinventing Royal Diplomacy for the Twentieth Century* (London: Palgrave Macmillan, 2016).
35 Jürgen Osterhammel, *The Transformation of the World: A Global History of the Nineteenth Century* (Princeton: Princeton University Press, 2014 [2009]), pp. 579–93.
36 Japan and Thailand are notable examples. See T. Fujitani, *Splendid Monarchy: Power and Pageantry in Modern Japan* (Berkeley: University of California Press, 1998); Maurizio Peleggi, *Lords of Things: The Fashioning of the Siamese Monarchy's Modern Image* (Honolulu: University of Hawai'i Press, 2002) and *Thailand: The Worldly Kingdom* (London: Reaktion Books, 2007); Irene Stengs, *Worshipping the Great Moderniser: King Chulalongkorn, Patron Saint of the Thai Middle Class* (Singapore: NUS Press, 2009). On the diverse fates of monarchies in this region, see Roger Kershaw, *Monarchy in South-East Asia: The Faces of Tradition in Transition* (London: Routledge, 2001).
37 See the references in Chapter 3.
38 Cannadine, *Ornamentalism*.
39 Nicholas Dirks, *The Hollow Crown: Ethnohistory of an Indian Kingdom* (Cambridge: Cambridge University Press, 1988).
40 Newbury, *Patrons, Clients, and Empire*; Low, *Fabrication of Empire*.
41 Robert Aldrich and Cindy McCreery (eds), *Crowns and Colonies: European Monarchies and Overseas Empires* (Manchester: Manchester University Press, 2016) and *Royals on Tour: Politics, Pageantry and Colonialism* (Manchester: Manchester University Press, 2018).
42 Tony Ballantyne, 'Maharajah Dalip Singh, Memory, and the Negotiation of Sikh Identity', in *Between Colonialism and Diaspora: Sikh Cultural Formations in an Imperial World* (Durham, NC: Duke University Press, 2006), pp. 86–120.
43 Michael Alexander and Sushina Anand, *Queen Victoria's Maharajah: Duleep Singh, 1838–93* (London: Weidenfeld & Nicolson, 1980); Anita Anand, *Sophia: Princess, Suffragette, Revolutionary* (London: Bloomsbury, 2015).
44 William Dalrymple, *The Last Mughal: The Fall of a Dynasty, Delhi, 1857* (London: Bloomsbury, 2006); Rosie Llewellyn-Jones, *The Last King in India: Wajid 'Ali Shah* (London: Hurst, 2014); Sudha Shah, *The King in Exile: The Fall of the Royal Family of Burma* (London: HarperCollins, 2012).
45 Amitav Ghosh, *The Glass Palace* (London: HarperCollins, 2000).
46 Caroline Keen, *An Imperial Crisis in British India: The Manipur Uprising of 1891* (London: I.B. Tauris, 2015).
47 Jeff Guy, *The View Across the River: Harriette Colenso and the Zulu Struggle against Imperialism* (Oxford: James Currey, 2002).
48 Kothari, 'Contesting Colonial Rule'.
49 K. M. de Silva, *A History of Sri Lanka* (Colombo: Vijitha Yapa, 2008 [2005]), pp. 166–8.
50 Ronit Ricci, 'From Java to Jaffna: Exile and Return in Dutch Asia in the Eighteenth Century', in Ricci, *Exile in Colonial Asia*, pp. 94–116. See also Timo Kaartinen, 'Exile, Colonial Space, and Deterritorialized People in Eastern Indonesian History', in Ricci, *Exile in Colonial Asia*, pp. 139–64.
51 Kerry Ward, *Networks of Empire: Forced Migration in the Dutch East India Company* (Cambridge: Cambridge University Press, 2009); Jean Gelman Taylor, 'Belongings and Belonging: Indonesian Histories in Inventories from the Cape of Good Hope', in Ricci, *Exile in Colonial Asia*, pp. 164–92.

52 Carey, *Destiny*, and *The Power of Prophecy: Prince Depanagara and the End of an Old Order in Java, 1785–1885* (Leiden: KITLV Press, 2007).
53 Denys Forrest, *Tiger of Mysore: The Life and Death of Tipu Sultan* (London: Chatto & Windus, 1970); Bunny Gupta and Jaya Chaliha, 'Exiles in Calcutta: The Descendants of Tipu Sultan', *India International Centre Quarterly*, 18:1 (1991), 181–8; Siddharth Raja, 'Tipu Sultan: The Forgotten Connection with India's First Sepoy Mutiny', *The Wire*, 30 July 2016, http://thewire.in/54776/tipu-sultan-forgotten-connection-indias-first-sepoy-mutiny, accessed 25 November 2016.
54 Sri Margana, 'Caught between Empires: *Babad Mangkudiningratan* and the Exile of Sultan Hemengkubuwana II of Yogyakarta, 1813–1826', in Ricci, *Exile in Colonial Asia*, pp. 117–38. See also Peter Carey, *The British in Java, 1811–1816: A Javanese Account* (Oxford: Oxford University Press, 1992).

CHAPTER TWO

The last king in Ceylon: the British and Sri Vikrama Rajasinha, 1815

Five months after the British placed Napoleon on a ship in Portsmouth, bound for exile in St Helena, another ship carrying a deposed monarch set sail.[1] On 24 January 1816, HMS *Cornwallis*, armed with seventy-eight guns and conveying six hundred crew and passengers, departed from Colombo in Ceylon, headed for Madras in India. Among those on board was Sri Vikrama Rajasinha, king of Kandy, last reigning monarch on the island and now a 'prisoner of war'[2] (see Figure 2). The thirty-five-year-old former king was accompanied by four wives among a retinue of eleven, including a woman described as court jester. Supervising his banishment was the twenty-seven-year-old William Granville, whose diary recounts the voyage.[3]

The king, noted Granville, had been taken to the ship in the carriage of Sir Robert Brownrigg, the governor of Ceylon, watched by a 'crowd of natives, all eager to witness the embarkation'. The king demanded the procession momentarily halt for spectators on an archway to descend, since subjects ought not to stand higher than the royal personage – even deprived of a throne, Vikrama expected that certain customs be observed. He was 'attired in a red silk cloth wrought with gold thread, and his purple silk trousers, which were baggy, were secured to his ankle with ribbons. He wore an embroidered jacket, and over the jacket a very fine white upper dress with innumerable frills or pleats, and over it he had a green silk mantle edged with gold lace; and a magnificent turban completed the toilette of Rajasingha'. Vikrama's physique as well as his attire impressed Granville. At nearly six feet tall, 'his limbs were of herculean size, but beautifully formed; his head small, his features regular and handsome; his eyes large, and intensely black and piercing; his hands and feet small and elegantly turned'. As the king and his consorts – who had never been on a ship – were hoisted onto *Cornwallis'* deck from a barge, 'an excellent band' played, and the captain 'welcomed the fallen monarch with every mark of proper

THE LAST KING IN CEYLON

Figure 2 A portrait, reproduced on a postcard printed for the 1924 British Empire Exhibition, of the last king of Kandy, Sri Vikrama Rajasinha (1780–1832, r. 1798–1815), deposed by the British and exiled to India.

decorum' (though the governor had forbidden any military salute[4]). The royal party repaired to the dozen cabins set aside for them and cordoned off from fellow travellers.

Granville proved an attentive guardian, seeing to the comfort of the royals, but keeping a close eye on his charges, and daily recording their activities and interactions with the British. The queens suffered seasickness, and the king sometimes turned moody, prone to fits of anger. Once Granville soundly chastised him for beating a wife, conduct he insisted the British would not tolerate; Granville cleverly told His Majesty – the way he addressed the ex-monarch – that 'his dignity and character would suffer in the opinion of everyone on board if he gave way to his passion in that manner'. In another incident, Granville rushed to the king's cabin when he heard disconcerting noises, to discover Vikrama attacking a day bed with a hatchet, outraged that a courtier had the effrontery to sit on the royal couch. Granville acceded to his request that the bed be thrown overboard, and commented: 'I then, for the first time, thought how dreadful his anger must have been when he had occasion to display it on the throne of Kandy, over his defenceless subjects.'

Vikrama at first remained cold towards his captors. He complained repeatedly that Brownrigg had refused to receive him, confiding that he had wanted to reveal the location of secreted treasure (but refusing to tell Granville where it was). He also expressed doubt that the ship was heading to Madras, fearing deportation to London. Gradually, relations became warmer, especially with Granville's solicitousness. (For instance, he fetched smelling salts when the king came down with a headache; the king thought he had to swallow the salts, and an amused Granville marvelled that he finally 'snuffed them with violence' but remarked that they had no scent.) The king and his wives – two sets of two sisters, the oldest 'past her prime', the youngest, around eighteen years old, 'decidedly handsome, and beautifully formed' – timidly began to come onto the deck. Granville encouraged Vikrama's curiosity, and officers showed him navigation charts and equipment; he 'looked with an enquiring eye at everything around him'. He examined a cameo of the captain's wife and children with interest, and asked questions about England. Granville and the king conversed amiably, even laughing together in banter, despite limitations of language; Granville understood neither Sinhala nor Tamil, and often had difficulty with the embroidered rhetorical forms interpreters used when referring to the king. He confessed that with easier communication perhaps he would have learned more. Granville did become bold enough to ask about the king's reputed brutality, but Vikrama brushed off the question.

The king on occasion had an ottoman moved just outside the officers' mess, where he could watch the captain and officers dining, though his own food was prepared by Ceylonese cooks. The officers courteously rose when the king arrived, and the captain toasted his health. Several weeks into the voyage the king invited Captain O'Brien, Granville, a Mrs Sewell and others to dinner, personally and with care and excitement supervising preparation of a spread of Ceylonese specialities. Granville, ungraciously, recorded that 'the greasy slops, and other nausea spread before us, almost overcame me, and produced divers sensations of a tendency which I need not expatiate upon'. The king, however, was 'looking more cheerful and contented than I think I had ever before seen him'. The next morning the king said he was proud of giving pleasure to his guests, but Granville noted dyspeptically that 'the bowels of some of the party spoke pretty plainly an opposite feeling'.

Granville offered a positive characterisation of the ruler the British had damned: 'He appeared to me to possess a very acute intellect, and could penetrate with wonderful precision into the characters of others. His mind, in some respects, was lofty, and he could sometimes hold uncommon control over his feelings. The high notions he had formed from his infancy of his own importance could not in him be impaired or be dismissed by adversity.' Although the king abandoned his ceremonial apparel for an ordinary Ceylonese sarong, 'his person and manner possessed something peculiarly striking and distinguished; and no one, let him be of any civilized country whatsoever, could be five minutes in his presence without discovering a grandeur and superiority about him which is almost impossible to define'. Granville's fascination was shared by the crew, who competed to maintain the king's quarters (which they generally found untidy). Such housework, Granville added, also provided a chance for the tars to eye off the Ceylonese ladies 'though I must say they took no other liberty'.

The voyage to India was long but as time passed, royals and colonisers relaxed, Granville good-humouredly remarking on the jester's jokes at his expense. On some days, the British and Ceylonese settled down in cosy camaraderie, the king staring meditatively out to sea seeming 'to think on the mutability of power, and his own irreparable misfortunes', Granville immersed in a book, Mrs Sewall attending to her needlework and her young son. The king stopped complaining about Brownrigg and showed no resentment at the British taking away his kingdom, though he spoke bitterly of Ehelepola, the former chief minister who had conspired in his overthrow, and he warned the British – presciently, it turned out – to be wary of their new ally. Granville 'expressed to His Majesty my surprise that during the time he was in possession of his throne he had not encouraged more intercourse between his subjects and those of our Gracious Sovereign'. The king replied that he had indeed protected 'Christians' as much as his laws would allow. Granville retorted that 'it would have advanced the Kandyan people in civilization if a free intercourse had existed between the two Governments'. Again daring to raise the question of brutality, Granville asked if the king had approved the mutilation of Ceylonese who had strayed from British territory into the king's realm, a *casus belli* for the British attack on Kandy. Vikrama argued that they were spies and had been justly punished, then 'declined any further discussion on the subject'. The king, determined to counter the blackening of his reputation, told Granville that he bore no responsibility for the incarceration for ten years of a Englishman taken prisoner in 1803, and that he had provided him with land, food and drink, and women.

The *Cornwallis* finally docked in Madras on 21 February with a tired Granville and 'royal captives' (as he called them), though the king refused to disembark until fresh clothing was procured for his women folk. Vikrama donned his ceremonial outfit, including a head covering ornamented with rubies, emeralds, sapphires and gold, and with the ladies in new golden muslins processed off the ship. 'The beach was covered as far as the eye could reach with a dense mass of the native population of Madras, and of the adjacent districts, who were assembled to see the deposed sovereign and witness his landing', Granville observed. As a sloop carried the royal party to land, 'His Majesty stood erect at the stern ... and when the boat reached the shore he received the general homage of the assembled thousands with a slight inclination of his head'. The royals were taken away in palanquins to a tent, the king – still intent on protocol – gently trying to dissuade Granville from entering since 'he thought it degrading to himself to stand upon the same carpet with me'. Granville persisted, and the king relented. Granville said he hoped that his and the crew's attentions had been satisfactory. 'The king replied at great length, in a manner both eloquent and dignified, and ended by saying that he had every reason to approve the conduct of those to whom the care of himself and his people had been entrusted hitherto, and hoped that the gentlemen to whose care he was about to be consigned would treat him as courteously and kindly as we had done.'[5]

Granville's account of the king's journey into exile aboard a Royal Navy ship provides an interesting spectacle of imperial power and human drama. Vikrama had reigned for seventeen years before his removal by foreigners bent on annexing the kingdom, in league with chiefs and ministers who rebelled against their sovereign. He never abdicated, and was never arraigned, brought to trial or convicted. Neither imperial imperatives nor international law offered him an opportunity to appeal his banishment or to confront those who accused him of misrule.

Vikrama was a prisoner, but Granville and the officers treated the king with respect; coming from Regency England, they were sensitive to questions of hierarchy, and somewhat awed by a king in their midst, even an ousted Asian one. There were reciprocal gestures of consideration, the captain's toasts and the king's banquet well-intentioned sharing of food and culture, even if spicy curries did not suit English taste. Granville, though betraying no deep-seated interest in Ceylonese society, seems wistful that language made more expansive conversation impossible. It is noteworthy that, apart from disobliging comments on Ceylonese food and the chaos in the king's quarters, his account remains remarkably spare of orientalist stereotypes, European condescension towards natives, outrage over horrors visited by the king on his subjects, or triumphalism at his defeat. His portrait depicts an attractive, masculine and regal Vikrama, intelligent and inquisitive, dignified and confident, if sometimes fitful. Englishmen such as Granville, of course, might well afford magnanimity: they now controlled the fabled and precious island of Ceylon, and were escorting a dethroned king into permanent exile. It is difficult to discern the king's sentiments except in the interstices of Granville's diary, but his behaviour evidences attachment to royal prerogatives, an effort to defend himself against allegations about his arbitrariness, and melancholy as he stared out to sea. Betrayed by counsellors and captured by the British, he could have harboured few hopes of regaining his crown, and he had little idea of what awaited him.

The voyage out from Colombo, as rendered in Granville's diary, takes on the style of a theatre-piece, the dramatis personae of Britons and Ceylonese moving about on the stage-set of a creaking sailing ship, speaking their scripts in the precise accents of Regency England and the awkward translations of orotund Tamil and Sinhala court language, withdrawing for relief or ructions off stage, coming together under the limelight for dialogues about their countries, habits and fates. Moments of tension, such as evocation of brutalities, were punctuated with the comic monologue of a court-jester and scenes – the king hacking at a desecrated couch, the British trying to stomach fiery morsels – that might have been devised by a comic playwright. Here was human interest, but also the business of empire: colonial conquest, fratricidal conflicts within indigenous societies, the defeat and definitive banishment of a ruler and the abolition of a dynasty, designs for a country newly subjected to colonial dominion.

The monarchy in Ceylon

The events of January 1816 marked a turning point in a confrontation between the British and the Sinhalese, both subjects of divinely ordained kings. The origins of monarchical government on Ceylon stretch back at least to the fifth century BCE; over the centuries, dynasties changed, rulers fought over territory and capitals moved, with the whole island rarely unified under a single sovereign before the British era.[6] Different dynasties and polities continued to exist on the island, for instance, the realms of Kotte and Jaffna, and there were varying ethnic groups and allegiances as well as competing centres of power. The king in Kandy controlled one of the largest territories, and after the incursions of the Portuguese and Dutch, was the last ruler left in control of his dominion.

The duties of the Kandyan king were symbolised by two features on the landscape. In the words of the Sri Lankan historian Vernon L. B. Mendis, 'Temple building and tank building were two sides of the same medal which was the impulsive urge for construction of Sri Lankan rulers'.[7] The *wewas* (or *vevas*) were water reservoirs, or tanks sometimes the size of lakes, that conserved the monsoonal rainwater and provided irrigation during the long dry season; their building exemplified the secular role of the monarchy. Temples, such as the complexes of monasteries and *dagobas* (reliquary stupas) in the ancient capitals of Anuradhapura and Polonnaruwa, symbolised the religious role of the monarch as guardian of Buddhism and protector of the *sangha* (the Buddhist community). A primordial obligation of the king was custodianship of the Sacred Tooth, said to be a relic of the Buddha, housed in golden casks in the inner sanctum of the Dalada Maligawa, the Tooth Temple, in Kandy. The relic was the palladium of the kingdom, its procession around Kandy at the Esala *perahera* festival – accompanied by monks, musicians, dancers, and caparisoned elephants – the culmination of the royal and religious year. The king, viewed as semi-divine, a *boddhisatva*, came from the solar caste of Kshatriya, and generally sought spouses from the appropriate caste in southern India. A bureaucracy grew up around the monarch; particularly important were the chief minister and second minister (the *adigars*) and the provincial governors (*dissaves*). The chief minister executed royal policy but could also be kingmaker, choosing among candidates for the throne when it fell vacant. *Adigars* and *dissaves* belonged to the aristocratic *radala* stratum of the Goyigama caste closely tied to the senior echelons of Buddhist clergy. The Sinhalese kingdom, and the court of its ruler, however, included several ethnic groups, and Tamils in particular held positions of importance as military and administrative officers and as princesses married into the extended royal families.

The king of Kandy historically faced many challenges in securing his throne. Given lack of primogeniture and large numbers of sons born to rulers from multiple wives, contests for succession were intense. Palace coups regularly threatened, with kings sometimes victims of assassination. They also contended with foreign invaders, beginning with the Cholas from southern India, who tried on various occasions to conquer the island. From the early 1500s, rulers met incursions by the

Portuguese, who extinguished the kingdoms of Kotte and Jaffna.[8] That left Kandy the remaining indigenous state to confront the Dutch, who rivalled the Portuguese from the early 1600s. The king hoped that the Dutch would eliminate the Portuguese, and so they did, but with no intention of relinquishing the Portuguese territories they conquered.[9] Taking advantage of a revolt against the king, who appealed unsuccessfully to the British and the French for assistance, the Dutch extended their holdings in the 1660s and an uneasy cohabitation between the Dutch on the coast and the Kandyans in the hinterland endured for a century. In 1761, the Dutch invaded the Kandyan state, and the monarch again asked for European help; the British sent a delegation, but negotiations came to nought. Five years later, the Dutch forced a harsh new treaty on Kandy; the territory they took deprived the kingdom of access to the sea.[10] A brief French occupation of the eastern port of Trincomalee in 1782 and another British mission to Kandy, in 1783, served as reminders of the interests of other powers and the geopolitical importance of Ceylon. With a key position on Indian Ocean trade routes, proximity to British outposts in India, rich resources and fine harbours, Ceylon presented a splendid prize.

In the late 1700s and during the revolutionary and Napoleonic wars, Britain and France were embroiled in commercial rivalries and military conflicts that constituted a world war fought in Europe, the Americas and Asia. In the struggle in South Asia, Britain and France formed alliances with local rulers, all hoping to gain advantage; in India, the British bested the French, and with the battle of Seringapatam and the defeat of France's ally Tipu Sultan, put paid to any realistic French hopes for a large share of India. Britain had meanwhile acquired other territories, the takeover of New South Wales in 1788 giving it a beachhead in Australia, and the capture of Penang, in the Straits of Malacca, in 1786, establishing a foothold in Southeast Asia. The 'French wars' that began in 1793, and lasted intermittently for more than twenty years, provided further opportunities to enrich the imperial portfolio. When French armies took over the United Provinces in the Netherlands, Dutch colonies were potentially placed at their disposal, a situation the British found intolerable. The Dutch ruler, the Prince of Orange, taking refuge in Britain, agreed to British occupation of Dutch colonies with the proviso of their return when peace with France was established. In 1795, the British occupied the Cape Colony at the southern tip of Africa, and set their sights on Ceylon.[11] British ships took Trincomalee in September 1795, moved on to Jaffa in the north, and by February 1796 occupied Colombo. A proud William Pitt boasted to Parliament that this presented 'to us the most valuable colonial possession on the globe, as giving to our Indian empire a security which it has not enjoyed from its first establishment'.[12] The Kandyans cautiously welcomed the British, hoping for greater concessions than from the Dutch, though an initial treaty of friendship delivered little.

The British and the Nayakkars

By this time a new dynasty reigned in Kandy; it may have been ill-fated, though Sujit Sivasundaram refutes an idea current at the time, and among many later historians, that the kingdom was in inevitable and terminal decline during the late eighteenth century. Social structures remained strong, trade thrived, and the king still intended to treat European interlopers on the coast as his vassals – though the foreigners hoped to make the Kandy sovereign their own liegeman.[13] King Narendra, who died in 1739, fathered no sons and named as heir his brother-in-law, Sri Vijaya Rajasinha, an Indian-born prince of the Nayakkar family. He was a Hindu, as were later Nayakkar rulers, but paid tribute to the Buddhist *sangha* and remained guardian of the Buddhist faith. His successor, Kirti Sri Rajasinha, indeed gained renown for building the inner sanctum of the Dalada Maligawa.[14] Under the reign of the next king, Rajadhi Rajasinha, the British seized the Dutch territories that encircled the kingdom of Kandy. At his death in 1798 Rajadhi left no son by the senior queen, but various contenders queued up for the throne. The man who would decide was the chief minister, Pilima Talauve, a strong-minded nobleman who, historians agree, aimed to keep power in his own hands.[15] He opted for Rajadhi's young and, he hoped, pliable nephew, who took the reign name of Sri Vikrama Rajasinha. Pilima nevertheless harboured long-standing resentment against the Nayakkar dynasty, which some Sinhalese nobles regarded as foreign, and whose interests threatened to undermine the Kandyan elite.[16] Pilima cherished hopes that, in due course, the Nayakkar dynasty could be displaced and he himself acclaimed king in a restoration of Sinhalese rule.

The political conjuncture was less than auspicious for the Kandyan kingdom. Soon after the mightiest imperialist country on the globe had taken over the entire coastal area of his island, a youthful monarch was placed on the throne by a minister who intended to use him, or eventually dispense with him, for his own objectives.[17] Relations did not immediately change between the Kandyans and the British, as the incumbent governor, Frederick North, wanted to avoid confrontation; he dutifully sent a delegation to congratulate Vikrama on his enthronement. Pilima, however, saw potential allies in the British and in 1800 even suggested that they depose Vikrama, with himself as replacement. North refused to intervene, but ventured that Vikrama might agree to reign nominally from Colombo, in British territory, much like one of Britain's Indian feudatories. His overtures to Vikrama were not surprisingly rebuffed.

The British, Vikrama and Pilima circled around each other until hostilities finally broke out between the Kandyans and the British in 1802. North was now seriously considering Prince Muttusamy, a strong contender for the throne at the time of Rajadhi's death, as a possible new king, essentially abandoning both Vikrama and Pilima. In February 1803, when British troops marched on Kandy, they found Vikrama had fled. After a bout of pillaging, they brought the potential king, Muttusamy, into the city, but he refused to swear allegiance to the British or agree to cede one of the kingdom's richest provinces, as they demanded. Kandyan soldiers loyal to Vikrama meanwhile went on the offensive against a British military force severely wasted by disease. North withdrew his army from Kandy and, ingloriously, handed over Muttusamy to Vikrama, who ordered his execution. The British subsequently cast their fortunes with Pilima.

The next years saw occasional skirmishes between the British and Kandyans, but also renewed trade, under North's successor, Thomas Maitland. Pilima continued machinations against the king, but in 1811 when a plot to assassinate Vikrama was discovered, Pilima was executed. However, his son (and namesake) was spared, and his nephew, Ehelepola, was appointed chief minister.[18] If Vikrama hoped that Ehelepola would prove loyal, he was mistaken, as Ehelepola soon began manoeuvring as well. For support he approached Robert Brownrigg, who arrived in Colombo as governor in 1812. A veteran of the wars against Napoleon, Brownrigg was more gung-ho about expansion than his predecessors.[19] Caught in the middle – and destined to play a role in Vikrama's removal – was the fascinating John D'Oyly, an archdeacon's son and Cambridge graduate, who had come to Ceylon in 1801 as a writer for the East India Company. He had learned Sinhala (a nearly unique achievement for Britons) and was appointed Government Translator.[20]

The backstory to the mounting tensions of 1813 and 1814 was, thus, growing opposition from Kandyan chiefs against the king, Ehelepola's ambitious ouvertures to the British, Brownrigg's hope to establish full control over Sri Lanka, and the continuing war between Britain and France. The king by this time was faring badly with his subjects. Between 1810 and 1812, he undertook enormous public works in Kandy, building an octagonal tower at the Dalada Maligawa, and constructing new roads and a large lake. The use of corvée labour (*rajakariya*), though hardly new, provoked opposition from commoners. His development efforts also created suspicion among the elite, who feared an attempt to turn Kandy into a copy of the Indian city of Madura from which the Nayakkars originated. The king settled increased numbers of his South Indian relations in Kandy, in what became known as Malabar Street, their presence further menacing Sinhalese nobles. Monks found cause for offence when, contrary to Buddhist doctrines prohibiting killing, goats were slaughtered in the immediate vicinity of the Dalada Maligawa, and Vikrama was rumoured to be practising Indian Saivite rituals of which they disapproved. Furthermore, the king was said to have developed an immoderate taste for alcohol, and was wont to outbursts of temper.

By 1814 Ehelepola was writing regularly to the British governor about the hardships of the Sinhalese; the British replied with concern and expressions of amity for the chief minister, but no commitment. Brownrigg, however, wrote to the colonial secretary in London, in March, that the time was not far off when the Kandyan chiefs would rise up against Vikrama and demand British protection. When rebellion against the king erupted in the southern Kandyan realm in May, D'Oyly suggested that the British strike while the iron was hot. He recommended that the British arm the rebels and encourage support for Ehelepola's forces from Muslims in Ceylon. Brownrigg cautioned that despite his hopes for the rebellion's success, 'it is necessary that we should not appear to have been fomenters of it, but that the work has been the genuine act of the oppressed people, who in their struggle to rid themselves from the Rule of a Tyrant call for our aid'.[21]

When Vikrama learned of the insurrection spearheaded by the chief minister, he exacted dreadful punishment on Ehelepola's family. His four young children, including an infant, were publicly beheaded and their mother forced to pound their heads in a mortar before she was drowned; forty-seven other prisoners died by impalement. Ehelepola managed to escape over the border to British territory, and was given refuge. His rebellion seemed to fizzle, and the British expressed doubt that Kandyans would unite against the king. However, continuing Kandyan actions – including the burning of a Muslim village, and mutilation and torture of the king's opponents – provided Brownrigg with arguments for intervention on what might now be called 'humanitarian grounds', and in a letter to the colonial office in October, the governor pled that for the British to turn a blind eye would 'encourage further barbarities'.[22]

There was also a strategic imperative. Napoleon had been defeated and exiled to Elba, but the British still worried about his possible return (as came to pass in the Hundred Days of rule in 1815). The British wished to consolidate their position in the Indian Ocean: India, the Cape Colony, Mauritius and the Seychelles (islands taken from the

French) and Ceylon. In British eyes, the case for action was strong: a moral crusade to combat barbarity and overthrow a tyrant, an opportunity to gain further geopolitical and commercial advantage, the need to assure defence of British territories in India, the prospect of developing the latent resources of a fertile island. Conveniently, local dissidents – though perhaps not confidence-inspiring allies – provided accomplices, and the British could lend support to their efforts to restore justice and overthrow an alien monarch in Kandy. Brownrigg soon found the precipitants he had awaited: the mutilation of British Ceylonese subjects who had strayed over the border, and an incursion by Kandyan soldiers into British territory. In January 1815 began an invasion of the Kandyan state, with a key goal getting rid of the 'Malabar' king.

The capture of a king, 18 February 1815

The dramatic circumstances of Vikrama's capture were recounted in a memoir by a British-employed interpreter, William Adrian Dias Bandaranayaka.[23] The operations involved D'Oyly as effective manager of the campaign, several British officers, eight hundred troops including reinforcement from India, two leading rebels, Ekneligoda and Molligoda, and other Sinhalese. An advance party, with Ekneligoda and Dias Bandaranayaka, pushed towards Medamahanuvara, where the king was known to have taken refuge after fleeing Kandy. 'A lad of about ten or twelve years of age' whom they took into custody led them to the hideout in return for his life. After a sentry was overpowered, Ekneligoda ordered the king to open the door of the hut in which he was sheltering and give up any weapons. Three rifles and two daggers were passed through a window, but the king would not relinquish his golden sword or open the door. Soldiers broke down the door, 'after which the Sinhalese men entered the house and created a disturbance for a while, meantime snatching all the garments and ornaments from the persons of the queens, only sparing for each of them a piece of cloth of about four cubits in length (just enough to cover their nakedness)'. The distressed queens fell to the floor, 'just as fowls whose necks are just severed do'. The interpreter called out to the women not to be afraid, but noticed his clothing was stained with the queens' blood, as their ears had been torn when their earrings were ripped off in the mêlée; in the chaos Dias Bandaranayaka managed to obtain medicinal leaves for the wounds.

Dias Bandaranayaka continues that 'shortly after the king was forcibly dragged out' – it was *lèse-majesté* to touch the king's person – Ekneligoda shouted harshly: 'Bring me kirindi creepers to have this fellow tied like a pig and taken' (see Figure 3). The interpreter, perhaps

Figure 3 This drawing shows the king of Kandy, his hands bound with vines, taken into custody by British soldiers at his hideout at Medamahanuwara. Of note are his two wives in the background and several Sinhalese dignitaries who had collaborated in his capture.

valorising himself but clearly affronted by the rebels' behaviour, states that 'I stepped forward and said: "Nilame [an honorific for a chief] you Sinhalese were up to this very day and hour subject to and honouring this king ... He is your King, your God, your Master and your Parent. Now what is only necessary is to take him; and it is not right for you to bind, insult or injure him"'. The remark enraged Ekneligoda, but Dias Bandaranayaka offered his shawl as a somewhat more respectful way than vines to bind the king.

> Being grieved at the insults and injury to which the King was being subjected and being able no longer to contain myself, I tried to take pencil and paper from my pocket for the purpose of informing General [sic] D'Oyly about the affair, but I could not make my hands reach my pockets, for the reason that the two queens had clung very close to me and were holding my arms fast.

Finally seizing writing materials, he scribbled a note: 'To General D'Oyly – The Sinhalese King has fallen into our hands, and Ekneligoda Mohottale is fetching him on and has bound him and is subjecting him to much ill-treatment and ignominy. Therefore it is of paramount importance that you should come to meet us with three palanquins. Some wearing apparel is also necessary, as the queens are almost naked.'

Half an hour later, two colonels and 150 British and local soldiers arrived: 'When the two colonels and the officers reached the spot where the king was lying and beheld the ignominy and torture to which they were subjecting him, they whipped and drove the Sinhalese people in all directions.' The British unbound the king, asked if he was hungry or thirsty, and offered brandy, wine, madeira, port, claret or beer – a rather remarkable selection in the situation. The king 'asked for madeira and drank nearly a pint of it with water', but would not take food, while the queens drank claret and water. The royals were then dressed in the fresh apparel that had been brought and led to palanquins. The king beseeched the interpreter: 'Come here, son, these English will take and kill me, but I know they will not kill these ladies, and I ask you to take charge of them and protect them.'[24] The litters were borne off, one British officer riding on either side of the king, backed by others with unsheathed swords and loaded muskets: an honour guard and a police guard. When the party reached the British camp, D'Oyly 'received them very courteously and gave orders to find quarters for them in tents furnished with beds, and to place sentries around them ... and in two days they were carefully transferred to Kandy'. The British had meanwhile occupied the capital. When Brownrigg received D'Oyly's letter reporting the capture, the governor reputedly burst into tears.

The scene in Medamahanuwara was inevitably disorderly and presented risks of serious harm to the king and queens, though at least according to the interpreter and D'Oyly, the British ultimately treated the captives with dignity. The king surrendered without further resistance, though he had little choice; his remarks reveal his fears, and the queens were clearly and understandably distressed. The king had meagre belongings in his redoubt, though assailants took what they could; the British confiscated Vikrama's sword. The end of his reign occurred with neither the glory of victory nor heroic defeat and death in battle, but a rather pitiable last stand against foreigners and rebellious subjects.

Over the next eight days, under D'Oyly's care, the king was moved from one resthouse to another, as lack of supplies, problems with palanquins and bearers, and heavy rains postponed his transfer to Colombo. D'Oyly continued to insist that the royals should be treated with all the respect due to persons of high rank, and he had white cloths draped over chairs where they sat, as royal protocol demanded. D'Oyly met with Vikrama regularly; the king complained of ill treatment at the hands of the Sinhalese who had taken him, and rejected as unsuitable clothing sent at D'Oyly's request (which D'Oyly admitted was of poor quality). Vikrama intimated that treasures had been hidden away, 'intending, as I understand, to offer them as a douceur'; D'Oyly dismissed the talk, and manifestly did not intend to bargain. The monarch asked to meet with Brownrigg, who had come up-country, but D'Oyly refused. D'Oyly did arrange for the king's mother and his two other wives, who had been in hiding at another location, to join him, and Vikrama formally introduced them to the British agent and 'committed them to my charge and protection'. D'Oyly commented that the relatives 'have no participation in his crimes, [and] are certainly deserving of our commiseration and particularly the aged mother, who appears inconsolable'.

More urgent issues compelled D'Oyly's attention. The rebel leader Ehelepola was beseeching the British for preferment, though declining appointment as chief minister: 'He begs to retire from Office, unless he obtains the honours of the Regal Office', an enthronement that the British did not consider. D'Oyly had been relieved when Ehelepola turned over items of the royal regalia he had contrived to obtain, no doubt as a sign of his thwarted hopes to be made king. The ally deserved some compensation, however, and D'Oyly arranged for a sum of money, a testimonial of gratitude as a 'friend of Britain' and a cameo of the Prince Regent – a gift pointedly emphasising the British Crown not a local monarch now ruled in Ceylon. Nevertheless, Ehelepola appeared still to nourish ambitions; when, on 7 April, he insisted on assuming the position at the end of a procession usually reserved for the monarch, D'Oyly noted in his diary that 'many Kandyans say that Ehelepola has to-day been acting the part of the king'. D'Oyly meanwhile received a stream of visitors expressing 'complaints' (as he put it), some about the Sinhalese chiefs, and speculated that they would rather be ruled by the British than the Sinhalese nobles. He also received reports about pillaging by British soldiers, which he tried with some success to stop. The Buddhist hierarchy presented another cause for concern, and D'Oyly learned 'that the priests still express their fears and doubts ... and some of [sic] have spoken that a Singalese king is necessary for protection and increase of their religion'.[25]

On 2 March 1815, an act of settlement, the Kandyan Convention (composed by D'Oyly), was signed in the royal audience hall by Governor Brownrigg and the Kandyan chiefs, Ehelepola first among them. It recorded the 'cruelties and oppressions of the Malabar Ruler', and the king's 'habitual violation of the chief and most sacred duties of a Sovereign' through which he 'has forfeited all claims to that title'. He is thus 'declared fallen and deposed from the Office of King – His family and relatives whether in the ascending, descending or collateral line, and whether by affinity or blood, are also for ever excluded from the Throne – and all claim and title of the Malabar race to the dominion of the Kandyan Provinces is abolished and extinguished'. Moreover, 'all male persons being or pretending to be relations of the late Rajah Sri Wikreme Rajah Sinha ... are hereby declared enemies to the Government of the Kandyan Provinces and excluded and prohibited from entering those Provinces' without British permission. The convention, explicitly characterising the Nayakkars as 'Malabars' and thus foreign, thereby denied legitimacy to the dynasty that had ruled for over seventy-five years, and any claim on the throne by the former king's relations. Sovereignty was ascribed solely to the British Crown, extinguishing a kingdom that traced its history back for over 2,500 years, though the 'rights, privileges and powers' of the *adigars*, *dissaves* and other 'Headmen', 'lawfully appointed by authority of the British Government', were recognised. Crucially, the fifth article read: 'The Religion of Boodoo [sic] professed by the Chiefs and inhabitants of these Provinces is declared inviolable, and its Rites, Ministers and Places of worship are to be maintained and protected.' Further articles prohibited torture, mutilation and execution without warrant of the British authorities, but stated that administration should be carried out 'according to established Forms'.[26]

The British could not convincingly claim authority until the sacred Tooth Relic, taken away by priests when the king fled Kandy, had been brought back to the Dalada Maligawa. A mile-long procession of monks, Kandyan chiefs, drummers, dancers and British soldiers – and Ehelepola in the senior position – returned the relic to the temple.[27] D'Oyly went out to meet the procession, earning respect from Kandyans, and accompanied it to the temple, then excused himself to fetch a gold clock to offer to the clergy. Though all was not settled, D'Oyly could be proud of his first days as British Resident in Kandy, a post he held until his death from illness in 1824. He had seen to the deposition and first steps into exile of the king, arranged a convention that gave Britain sovereignty over Kandy, and gained pledges of allegiance from the Kandyan elite in return for guarantees of the inviolability of Buddhism and recognition of ancestral privileges. Perhaps most importantly, he had seen to the return of the Tooth Relic, showing due reverence for the palladium but, in effect, establishing British guardianship over Ceylonese Buddhism and proprietorship of the Kandyan kingdom.

BANISHED POTENTATES

The Kandyan king in perspective

Casting Sri Vikrama Rajasinha in heroic mode is probably not justified, given his documented excesses (to put it no more strongly). Even Sri Lankan historians generally do not do so,[28] though seeing his deposition as an arbitrary act in British conquest. The *Mahavamsa*, updated in the *Culavamsa*, is an age-old royal chronicle back to the origins of the country. In the 1870s, two Buddhist monks, Hikkaduwe Sumangala and Pandit Batuwantudawa, were commissioned by British authories in Ceylon to write Chapter CI, recounting the last years of the Nayakkar dynasty. It states that Vikrama's reign began well with merit-making sacrifices to the Tooth Relic and gifts to the monks:

> But as he indulged in intercourse with impious people he changed (for the worse). He had the chief councillors, the great dignitaries and many other officials gathered together and destroyed his subjects like a devil. He had the people, many hundreds in number, brought to different spots and had them impaled, merciless as death. Much wealth that had come to the people by inheritance, the King had confiscated like a thief that robs villages. And because the Ruler committed in this way many evil deeds the Sihalas [*sic*] and the inhabitants of the town of Colombo rebelled. They all came hither, captured the criminal king alive when the eighteenth year after his consecration had passed, and brought him to the opposite coast [to India]. After they had brought the King, the torturer of his people, to the opposite coast the Ingirisi [English] seized the kingdom.

Thus ended the *Culavamsa*, with a succinct catalogue of the king's misdeeds.[29] The judgement invites no appeal, though composed under the aegis of the British by monks who perhaps had little innate sympathy for the Nayakkar monarch. The accusation that he was corrupted by 'impious people' is a reference to Tamil kinsmen, but it might be intended as a subtle comment on relations with the British.

Vernon L. B. Mendis declares that Vikrama 'has become in the eyes of posterity a kind of enigma as to whether he was a monster or a victim of circumstances which made him a paranoid'. His interpretation focuses on the king's state of mind. 'Paranoid' suggests a psychohistorical approach, and Mendis reaffirms that the king became a 'maniac driven by paranoid fears of the chiefs and the surroundings which his youthful disposition and immaturity could not cope with'. His later years, and the exactions he carried out, represented 'painful examples of the corrosive effects of fear'. Mendis sets this diagnosis in the context of nobles' conspiracies and British designs.[30] Another Sri Lankan historian, Michael Roberts, contributes a further piece to the psychological puzzle. In 1805, the king suffered an attack of smallpox that 'could provide one part of the explanation for Sri Vikrama Rajainha's subsequent lines of action: that is, his frenetic building projects in later years may have been an attempt to compensate for this ultimate stigma'. His subjects may have seen his illness as a sign of divine displeasure.[31]

Contemporary accounts, including Granville's diary, point to the king's mood swings and depression (hardly surprising on board the ship bearing him into exile), though venturing psychological imbalance as the cause of his behaviour has risks. In any case, the threats to the independence of Kandy, and Vikrama's less than incontrovertible right to the throne, had been apparent since his accession, and both Kandyan chiefs and the British were plotting against the king by 1811. The British demonised Vikrama as foreign, corrupt, alcoholic and sadistic, though these charges, too, need to be placed into context. As Henry Marshall, Inspector-General of the British army hospital, wrote in the mid-1800s (not avoiding a stereotype about Asian rulers), 'He should be tried by the standard of his own country, by the spirit of the Kandyan government, and the usages of Oriental despotisms, together with the circumstances in which he was placed'.[32] The British claimed the Nayakkars were a foreign dynasty, but Britain was ruled by an imported German royal house. Though the king may have enjoyed alcohol, immoderate drinking was far from uncommon among the British; the Prince Regent was said to consume several bottles of wine daily. A king with four wives seemed to confirm prejudices about the licentiousness of Oriental potentates, but a contemporary of Vikrama, Sir David Ochterlony, acclaimed British Resident of Delhi, had no fewer than thirteen concubines; sexual high jinks were hardly uncommon in Regency Britain. Vikrama was particularly blackened for cruelty: execution of opponents by decapitation or impalement, the massacre of Ehelepola's family, and mutilation of captives. Historians such as P. E. Pieris have questioned the reliability of some accounts of Vikrama's brutality, though not denying his authoritarian power or the punishments he ordered. Summary 'barbarities' nevertheless fell within the parameters of Kandyan law. Moreover, hanging, flogging and other types of state violence were regularly practised by the British at home and in the colonies. Vikrama and earlier Kandyan kings indeed used coerced labour, but only during his reign did the British ban the slave trade, and only after his death was slavery abolished throughout the empire. Later British depredations, such as repression of the 1857 Indian 'Mutiny' and the Amritsar massacre, are proof that innocence is a difficult virtue to claim.

Vikrama was manifestly manipulated by those around him, owing his coming to power to Pilima Talauve. Both Pilima and his successor

Ehelepola held hopes for the end of the Nayakkar dynasty. Henry Marshal wrote with perspicacity at the time: 'Having been placed on the throne by a professed friend, but in reality an inveterate intriguing enemy, for the intriguer's own aggrandizement, his situation as king was attended with insuperable difficulties.' Marshall compared Vikrama to 'a man blindfolded and in fetters', unable to act other than according to Pilima's wishes and 'doubtful if any one of the chiefs deserved his confidence'.[33]

Faced with manoeuvres by powerful ministers and their clans, Vikrama also confronted the British, whose territory and garrisons literally encircled his kingdom. British takeover of the maritime provinces was a fait accompli when he ascended the throne. Though initial contacts proved cordial enough, the British early on hoped for his removal, possibly with Muttusamy as replacement. The First Kandyan War in 1803 ended with British retreat but seriously undermined the king's power, and opened the way for further overtures from disaffected Kandyan nobles to the British after the 1811 plot to assassinate Vikrama failed to bring about regime change. Over the next years, the king was unable either to work out a supportive relationship with the nobles or an alliance with the British, who possibly might have been willing to protect his throne. It seemed only a matter of time before he, or a successor, would be overthrown by the Sinhalese elite, the British or, as it happened, the two together. The ouster of a monarch, ostensibly justified by claims to combat barbarism and misgovernment, represented a straightforward strategy of colonial aggrandisement.

The captured king: from Colombo to Vellore

Vikrama was left with few friends or defenders after his capture; no rescue attempts eventuated, though any such plans probably would have failed. The objectives of both the chiefs and the colonisers – different aims, to be sure – could only be accomplished with the king out of the way. For Buddhist priests the overriding concern was protection of the faith, and its venerated Tooth Relic. Commoners in Kandy remained largely in the background, perhaps baffled by the goings-on of their masters in Kandy, but hoping for relief from corvées and taxation. The low-country Ceylonese, far from the ructions up-country, had not been subjects of the kingdom of Kandy for decades or, in some regions, for more than two centuries, and they had accommodated the British for almost twenty years. British writers compared Vikrama to Henry VIII, Richard III and Macbeth, but such references lay outside the purview of Ceylonese in 1815.

Little less than a month after the captured king had been brought to Colombo, Brownrigg sent out feelers to colleagues in India about appropriate sites of exile. British India rather than another colonial outpost was presumably considered a fit place of exile as the Tamils would be 'going home' (at least as his detractors and opponents, including the British, would see it); transporting the king to a near-by destination was cost-effective, and the East India Company there could take charge of the prisoner and his entourage. The exact place of confinement was a matter of considerable discussion, with several rejected because of lack of suitable accommodation or because of too close proximity to Ceylon.[34] Only a short time before the *Cornwallis* set sail was Vellore chosen, with the precedent of the fort there as the place of detention for the sons of Tipu Sultan in 1799. The governor in Madras later affirmed that 'the reputation of our government is concerned in seeing that his [Vikrama's] captivity be accompanied with no more severity than is absolutely requisite for securing his person, and for preventing him, his family, and attendants from carrying on political intrigue'.[35] The twin guidelines – preserving both Britain's reputation in handling a captured king and safeguarding against subversion – are noteworthy. Vikrama was to be maintained in comfort, though 'it is the interest of the Ceylon Government now they have got rid of an Enemy to make the expense of keeping him as small as possible'. No 'marks of distinction' were to be shown, though he and his family should be treated with respect, and publicity was to be avoided.[36]

Five houses were set aside in the Vellore Fort ('Kandi Mahal', now used as a district land registry), for the king and his family, courtiers and servants. It is uncertain how many of those who sailed with Vikrama ended up in Vellore.[37] The Ceylon colonial government paid Vikrama an annual pension and provided provisions (butter, dried fish, coconuts, vegetables, 'currystuffs', spices, citrus fruits, sugar, betel and tobacco figure on a list of daily expenses that ran to seven pages). The authorities engaged eighteen servants for the king's household, later adding eight more, and kept a doctor and barber on retainer. When the king requested a palanquin so that he could move about the Vellore citadel, twelve bearers joined the domestic staff. No armed guards were stationed around the prisoners' quarters, though the fort was already heavily guarded and surrounded by a deep moat, making escape impossible.

On his arrival in India, the king asserted his status, expressing his 'expectation of being honourably received and entertained at Madras'. According to one official, 'altho' [sic] his country has been taken from him he does not thereby lose his dignity as a king, and the implicit obedience he has been in the habit of receiving for the last 19 years ...

makes it a very painful exertion for him now to submit to restrictions which are absolutely necessary for the security of the person'.[38] Initially, 'he talks and acts as if he was yet a rajah', said a paymaster, and 'even forgot himself so far as to threaten to have me discharged from the superintendence of him'.[39] Vikrama's notorious temper and 'sulkiness' occasionally flared, which authorities conceded reflected 'the unpleasant feelings necessarily connected with his degradation and captivity'.[40] He quarrelled intensely with a brother-in-law, but was solicitous about his wives and children.[41]

Though he quietened down as time passed, Vikrama continued to insist on certain considerations, submitting lists of requisites; the British found him 'exorbitant in his demand for money' and of an 'avaricious disposition'.[42] He exchanged some 'valuable cloths' for jewels and ornaments for his queens, presumably in an effort to retain vestiges of courtly luxury. He importuned the British for a larger palanquin after he grew obese, which he got, and a horse, which he did not get. He successfully asked them to build a veranda around his house. He sometimes requested more food, though at other times rejected goods supplied. Petitions for an increased pension regularly occurred; the government comptroller reported that the captives were costing a thousand rix-dollars a month, but that if he agreed to all the king's requests, the outlay would be three times that amount. The government nonetheless appropriated supplementary funds on special occasions, such as the birth of children, coming-of-age ceremony of the king's daughters and cremations of deceased members of his household.[43]

Family life continued as well as it could in confinement, but time took its toll: one of the king's wives (who lived in Tanjore) died in 1818 and a father-in-law four years later. The king's mother passed away in 1831; the government provided an escort of fifty Hindu soldiers, a drummer and a fifer for her cremation. Happier occasions were the birth of two daughters to the king, in 1822 and 1829, and a son in 1831. When the elder daughter was nine, the king asked the British to bring relations from Trichinopoly and Tanjore so that a suitable marriage could be arranged.

The British retained concerns, though not major fears, about political claims by the king or his descendants. When Vikrama requested that gold in his possession be fashioned into some sort of headdress, authorities refused. Brownrigg wrote from Colombo in 1816 that a crown could be seen as 'encouraging troublesome pretensions or generating reflexions which had better be allowed to subside', and added that 'a style of dress and living which may partake more of personal comfort than any tendency to appearances of splendour or royal state will be found most safe and eligible, most consonant with his situation as a prisoner of war and most conductive to his happiness'.[44] The paymaster in Vellore, who held immediate responsibility for Vikrama's finances and provisions, responded perceptively that the British should 'allow him all *reasonable* indulgences without losing sight of his former rank, but not to admit of any thing merely relating to purposes of Pomp and State. The difference betwixt the comforts of a king by state, and those of a private person are too obvious to require pointing out'. He thought the king's reconciliation with his new situation would not be immediate: 'To eradicate the kingly notions of a person (and that person by no means a wise one) who has by his own account been seated on a Throne about nineteen years, must be the work of time and infinite patience ... the utmost that can be done ... must be to give as little room as possible for retrospective views, and to remove all temptations of pomp and state as far out of his way as possible.' This meant, furthermore, that the number of courtiers around the king should be reduced since 'he assembles them in durbar at stated times, and in short uses the utmost effort of his limited power to treat them as the nobles of his court'.[45] The British, in sum, were determined that Vikrama would not establish a court in exile.

Officials in Colombo and Madras had exchanged much correspondence about treatment of the exiles, with the general view that the king could be allowed some liberty, but kept under watch and never fully trusted. Contacts with outsiders should be severely restricted, but his privacy respected. The presence of his family, it was thought, would dissuade him from any effort to escape. In September 1817, with unfortunate timing since Ceylon stood on the verge of rebellion, Madras administrators suggested the prisoners might be freed or placed in less restrictive confinement. Brownrigg vetoed the idea, on the grounds that the king might attempt to return to Ceylon. During the rebellion (on which more presently), the British sought to determine if Vikrama was aware of the disturbances, though apparently he was not; to what extent he was kept apprised of affairs in Ceylon at all remains unclear.

As the years passed, Britain entrenched itself in Ceylon and India, the world largely ignorant about the captive in Vellore.[46] In 1831, more than fifteen years after Vikrama's banishment, officials in Madras noted his declining health – difficulty in breathing, fever, insomnia and swollen limbs – and began discussing funding for his cremation and acquisition of land for burial of his ashes. The ex-king, aged fifty-two, died on 31 January 1832. The government authorised payment for his cremation and interment (though with advice to 'adhere to the strictest economy') in Vellore, with provisions for a military escort and musket fire salute; the paymaster of the fort, writing to colleagues, called attention to the responsibility to see that death rituals were carried out correctly. The government declared that with the king's death, those who had been taken to India in 1815 were free to return to Ceylon. Some remained in the fort long enough for the government to accede to funding a memorial ceremony after Vikrama's death. The king had asked the British to keep his son there. Officials did not fully understand the request, which may have related to brooding rivalry among the surviving queens. Officials engaged in lengthy discussions about whether to send the young prince to Madras or Calcutta for education, or possibly install him on an estate (even in Ceylon), but took no action.[47] The prince's death in 1842 resolved the issue, no doubt to British relief. The queens and king's daughters, who moved to Tanjore, and their descendants continued to receive pensions from the government of Ceylon.

After the exile of Vikrama, the British had also sent relatives, dependents and followers of the king to India; some had requested their return. Five lists enumerated Vikrama's immediate family, near and distant relations, those who had been long-term residents of Kandy and more recent arrivals in 1815. The total of those who left Ceylon in the immediate wake of Vikrama's ouster was put at 250 people, though with confusion about the actual number of men, women and children, and their exact status (relatives, servants or 'slaves').[48] There was concern about possible trouble from those variously referred to as 'prisoners', 'refugees' and even 'these unfortunate persons', and also the obligation to provide allowances, with hopes that those returning would not be reduced to poverty. After negotiations, the East India Company agreed to appropriate money for allowances for the king's relations and others who had lived in Kandy for at least five years. The Resident in Tanjore judged payments 'arranged for the Kandyan prisoners of war ... to be formed with the most humane and liberal consideration for their actual and relative situations and to be fully adequate to the decent subsistence of all in their appropriate classes'.[49] (Some, he noted, had money left over to hire servants.) A few of the deported or repatriated remained in Vellore, but others moved to Tanjore (Thanjavur), Madura (Madurai), Trichinopoly (Tiruchirappalli) and elsewhere, with British hopes they would find a chance to earn their own living.[50] They were not kept under restraint other than their word not to leave places they settled without British permission, and were not allowed to return to Ceylon; the government desired 'that they be treated with respect and kindness'.[51] Occasionally authorities were drawn in to complex family issues – particularly concerning marriage and inheritance – of these people, but they otherwise caused no serious problems.[52]

Many of the other exiles outlived the king, their families now including children born in India: one list from 1830 had counted 98 in Vellore,

159 in Tanjore, 389 in Trichinopoly, 135 in Madura and 80-odd in other locations.[53] Agents reported that most had no means of support other than government pensions. One letter in 1834 pitifully stated: 'As the British government is our benefactor after our own maharajah demised we doubt not that your unbounded generosity will induce your lordship's earliest compliance with the request solicited by the helpless widows. What more is to be written?'[54] The government, fretting about never-ending payments after Vikrama's death, was determined to eliminate as many as possible from the list of pensioners, and not to extend payments to any heirs of those currently given allowances.[55]

Vikrama's direct heirs, through his daughters' lines, made occasional appearances in petitions or in writings about South Asia. In 1889, for instance, Ponnambalam Arunachalam, a Cambridge-educated Ceylonese public servant (and later nationalist), wrote to his close friend Edward Carpenter, the English radical, about his visit to Tanjore. The city was a centre of Tamil civilisation and former capital of several dispossessed dynasties: 'Unjustly deprived of their throne by the English, the representatives of the last dynasty [Mahrattas] are now here in various stages of poverty and distress. Here also, but in far greater and pitiable destitution, are the descendants of the last native dynasty of *Ceylon*. A good deal of the time of the royal folks is spent in building castles in the air and scheming for increased allowances and restoration of the throne.'[56] Five years later, *The Times* published a short news item noting in dry language that M. D. Kavanagh, a barrister, 'who has been during the past seven years advocating the case of the exiled Kandy Prince and followers of the late King of Kandy', had received word that the colonial secretary had given his approval for some supplementary funding.[57] The 'prince' was not further identified, but in 1897, a writer claiming to be a Ceylonese prince sent a letter to Queen Victoria on her jubilee,[58] and a great-nephew of Vikrama, Coomarasamy Rajah, reputedly visited Ceylon in the late 1890s. Afterwards the heirs largely fade away in the records.

A Sri Lankan journalist visiting Vellore in 2007 reported that descendants of the royal family still lived in the city, though in straitened circumstances. He met one fifth-generation descendent, a sixty-seven-year-old ticket-taker at a cinema, the father of a medical college attendant and an electrician. The man, identified only as Prithviraj, lived in a 'shabby one room' and told the visitor that 'only after Independence [of Ceylon in 1948] could the family members reveal that we belonged to the royal family as we were afraid of the British'. He declared that the pension provided by the government had long been discontinued. Notwithstanding Prithviraj's situation, the journalist noticed that 'his pride in his lineage is unmistakable. He goes regularly to the tombs to pay his respects to his royal ancestors and hopes that Time's wheel will take a turn to improve his position'.[59]

Revolts, wars and pretenders, 1817–48

No evidence suggests the British seriously considered coronation of a new king after deposing Vikrama. The existence of a princely state, even landlocked in the interior of Ceylon, had been a thorn in their side since the 1790s and might cause further pain in the future. A promise to protect Buddhism, the British hoped, would defuse opposition, and the nobles and commoners would come round to the colonial regime.

Brownrigg nevertheless wrote to the colonial secretary in mid-1815 that Buddhists feared for the Tooth Relic and 'even ventured to suggest that a Singhalese king would be necessary for the protection of the Temple and of the Buddha [sic] faith, an idea which though natural enough to occur to them was supposed to receive encouragement from Ahelapola [sic] and his adherents'. Another official commented:

> Accustomed to the presence of a king in their capital, to the splendour of his court, and to the complicated arrangements connected with it, they could ill relish the sudden and total abolition of the whole system. The king of Great Britain was to them merely a name; they had no notion of a king ruling over them at the distance of thousands of miles; they had no notion of delegated authority; they wanted a king whom they could see, and before whom they could prostrate and obtain summary justice.[60]

Such comments underlined the stakes and potential impediments to winning Ceylonese hearts and minds.

Brownrigg had stated that one of the aims in deposing Vikrama was 'the subversion of that Malabar dominion which during the three generations has tyrannised over the country',[61] so it appeared unlikely any move for restoration of the Nayakkar dynasty would come from Sinhalese chiefs. It would have been possible for the British to select a new king, and Ehelepola was an aspirant, even behaving as a future monarch by signing his name as *primus inter pares* on the Kandyan Convention, occupying the king's traditional place in a procession, taking possession of the Kandyan regalia, and declining appointment as chief minister in hopes of a better position. The British regarded him as loyal in 1815, and he had certainly proved valuable in galvanising support against Vikrama and facilitating conquest of Kandy. He enjoyed high status and experience in government, though without being universally popular. He nurtured an intense rivalry with Molligoda, whom the British appointed chief minister when Ehelepola declined the post. Ehelepola's undisguised ambitions and past behaviour – after all he conspired against his sovereign – might have given the British pause. Ehelepola as king, indeed any new king, would be more trouble than worth.

Writing 'what if' history is dangerous, but one knowledgeable observer speculated on how Ceylon might have been different if the British had set another king on the throne. Sir A. C. Lawrie, a Scottish jurist who collected several volumes of documents on Kandyan law and history, speculated:

> If Ehelepola had been raised to the throne as a king dependent on England, with a resident English garrison at once to support and to control him, the Kandyans might possibly have been spared the horrors of the insurrection of 1817 and the cruelty of its suppression by the English. The country might have flourished under a native ruler of no mean capacity, whose worst tendencies might have been corrected and his best fostered by English aid.

He concluded with criticism:

> The story of English rule in the Kandyan country during 1817 and 1818 cannot be related without shame. In 1819 hardly a member of the leading families, the heads of the people, remained alive; those whom the sword and the gun had spared, cholera and smallpox and privations had slain by hundreds. The subsequent efforts of Government to rule and assist its Kandyan subjects were, for very many years, only attempts begun and abandoned ... If Ehelepola had reigned, much that must now be regretted might have been avoided, but fate decided otherwise.[62]

Destiny indeed decided that Ehelepola did not become king. Ceylon, however, was not easily pacified. Old frustrations persisted or resurfaced, with new ones induced by colonial rule, taxation and modernisation. The idea of the monarchy provided, for a time, a powerful platform for resistance. In 1816, one of the monks who would take part in a uprising that erupted the following year, Ihagama Ratnapala Unnanse, announced a plan to go to Burma, 'to beg the King of the Country to send a prince to govern Ceylon'.[63] That came to nought, and Britain would not have accepted a foreign prince as king of Kandy, but it underscores sentiments that a Buddhist king would be the best 'defender of the faith'.

Revolts, insurrections and conspiracies occurred with regularity in Ceylon from 1817 to 1848. Hopes for political emancipation, demands for amelioration of social conditions, and millenarianism joined with remnants of monarchism in provoking and sustaining resistance. Kumari Jayarwardena, who has investigated early nineteenth-century anti-colonial uprisings, suggests that such movements brought together four groups in 'attempts to restore the lost monarchy and institutions of the pre-colonial regimes'.[64] First, the Kandy aristocracy, the *radala* that included *adigars*, *dissaves* and other chiefs and headmen, discontented with loss of privilege, influence and income, gave a strong impulse to insurrection. Second, Buddhist monks, worried about the *sangha* under British rule, joined forces. Peasants, angered at new taxes, the establishment of an export-oriented economy and other demands of the colonial authority, provided recruits for rebellion. Finally, the Veddas, often considered Ceylon's aboriginal population, played an active role, their bows and arrows making them the key military force in uprisings. A pretender to the throne, usually self-proclaimed and of dubious merit, provided a rallying-point, continuity with the pre-colonial order, and claims to incarnate Sinhalese tradition. In the movements of 1817–18 and the 1820s, a pretender also generally claimed kinship with the Nayakkar lineage still fresh in collective memory, though later claimants from obscure backgrounds and no genealogical legitimacy abandoned this pretence. The recognition and, in some cases, enthronement of a pretender eventually became what Jayawardena calls nothing more than a 'charade'.[65] She quotes Viscount Torrington, governor in the late 1840s: 'The Pretended King of every successive Rebellion from 1817 to the present time has been merely the fictitious idol of the occasion; the hoped for stepping stone of the chiefs to power and the symbol of the religious ascendancy of the Priests.'[66] A royal claim nonetheless had (just) enough potency to galvanise support, revealing for Jayawardena 'the ideological hold that the concept of monarchy still had over the people'.[67] Demands for a restoration of the *ancien régime*, however, tellingly never called for the return of Vikrama or his son.

A major uprising – the one to which Lawrie referred – took place in 1817–18, touched off in the Uva province. It did not begin as a royalist movement, but a candidate for the throne more or less spontaneously emerged. Named Vibave, the former monk claimed descent from the Nayakkar dynasty, and also declared that the much revered god Skanda had designated him for the throne. A militia mustered, initially composed largely of Veddas, and gradually Kandyan chiefs threw their weight behind the pretender despite his dubious credentials.

The real leaders were several noblemen, the most prominent among them Keppetipola. Coming from a distinguished line of royal officials and a brother-in-law of Ehelepola, he counted among signatories of the Kandyan Convention. Among others who joined were Pilima Talauve – son and namesake of the minister executed by Vikrama – and the chiefs Madugalle and Ellepola. In May 1818, Keppetipola organised a ceremony of enthronement for Vibave before three thousand people and was named his chief minister. Governor Brownrigg commented that the ceremony was intended to 'dazzle the minds of the People who certainly do not think highly of the unostentatious and little ceremonious manner in which the British Government is conducted'.[68] The remark alluded both to the enduring power of the idea of monarchy and to British failure, at that point, to project itself in a way commensurate with local expectations of rulership. Vibave's 'reign' proved short-lived, while the rebels engaged in guerrilla warfare against the British for a year. The colonisers battled dense jungles, rains and disease, with a quarter of their troops victim to illness. British tactics included the burning of villages, destruction of rice paddies and irrigation works, and felling of the fruit trees of rebel supporters; the Ceylonese death toll may have totalled ten thousand.

The Sinhalese leaders never managed a united front. Notables sometimes changed sides, or wavered in loyalty, and intense rivalry divided the chiefs, with the pretender at one point imprisoned by dissidents. The premier chief, Ehelepola, having supported the British in 1815, never fully commited to the uprising, though Vibave spread the word that he was friendly to the cause. In March 1818, the British placed Ehelepola under detention in Colombo, without laying charges against him.

Disunity among rebels and superior British military power spelled the outcome. The uprising's leaders were captured in late 1818, and twenty-three executed, including Pilima Talauve, who had succeeded Keppetipola as chief minister under Vibave. Under court-martial proceedings, Keppetipola and Madugalle were sentenced to death, but allowed a final visit to the Dalada Maligawa for prayers; Keppetipola left his prayer book to a British guard who had treated him kindly. After his execution, Keppetipola's head was shipped to a phrenological society in Edinburgh.[69] Twenty-five of the rebels were exiled to Mauritius, soon joined by Ehelepola, the former minister to Vikrama, though he had taken little part in the 1817-18 uprising; he died in Mauritius in 1829.[70] The pretender Vibave went to hiding and eluded capture until 1830. He was then sentenced to prison or banishment, but a Commission of Eastern Enquiry sent from London to audit colonial governance declared the conviction invalid because of a statute of limitations, and expressed criticism about banishment. Vibave died in obscurity.

Other pretenders to the throne came forward. In 1820, Kumaraswami (Coomarasamy) claimed kinship with the royal family and announced that Vibave had ceded rights to him; a clutch of Kandyan chiefs half-heartedly invested Kumaraswami with symbols of kingship, but he soon fell into British hands and was also banished to Mauritius. Three years later came rumours of another pretender, who was arrested. In

1824, yet another man was proclaimed king by a small band of supporters, but captured and sentenced to two years' hard labour, confiscation of property and one hundred lashes. Other would-be kings followed with increasingly less believable claims to the throne and lessening purchase among the population. A final effort to restore or re-establish a throne took place during a more significant rebellion in 1848, though monarchism did not provide the main thrust of the insurrection in that fateful year of revolutions. Rebellion broke out in Kandy at the beginning of July, and within three weeks a 'king' was proclaimed: Gongalegoda Banda, a forty-year-old bullock-cart driver and ayurvedic medical practitioner. Captured in fairly short order and flogged a hundred times, he was deported to Malacca in the Straits Settlements.[71] Subsequently, new creeds replaced monarchism in animating anti-colonialism in Ceylon, though many nationalists harked back to an idealised Kandyan monarchy as a fount of Sinhalese culture, identity and independence.

The British Crown as successor to the Kandyan throne

Sri Vikrama Rajasinha and his dynasty out of the way, the British monarchy and its viceregal representatives assumed the place of the Kandy monarchy, while extending royal power over the whole island in a way the Nayakkars never managed. Governor Brownrigg commented of the ordinary Kandyans that 'apparently they regarded the transfer of government from the Oriental to an European dynasty with perfect indifference'.[72] Events soon nuanced that degree of 'indifference', but he made a significant point. According to Brandon and Yasmine Gooneratne, 'the meaning of the Act of Settlement as understood by the Kandyans was that Sri Vikrama Rajasinha was being replaced by the King of England. No innovations needed to be introduced since the British governor, acting on behalf of the English king, was expected to govern the country according to its time-honoured institutions and customs'.[73] One monarch, though a British and Christian one in London, assumed the place of a local one, with hopes by some Ceylonese that otherwise the social and cultural universe of the former Kandyan kingdom would change little. The British, too, as Sujit Sivasundaram has shown, hoped to 'recycle' old practices and beliefs to their advantage, though not with the same objectives as the Kandyans.[74]

Initially, expectations on both sides may have been comforted. D'Oyly, British Resident of Kandy, had fluent command of Sinhala and enjoyed respect from Kandyan chiefs. The Kandyan Convention he had written agreed to safeguard Buddhist and Sinhalese rights. Regulations D'Oyly issued acknowledged subtle gradations in chiefly ranks. Sentries were instructed to present arms to the first and second *adigars* and others had to doff their hats. All were to rise for the *adigars* when they entered a room; at audiences *adigars* were seated on chairs, lesser officials on benches, and subalterns on the floor. Such protocol remained important to those accustomed to privilege, and rankling at the former king's transgressions on prerogatives. These niceties were also hardly foreign to British etiquette.

The deferential fashion in which D'Oyly received the procession returning the Tooth Relic, and his presentation of a gift to the temple, augured well. He clearly understood that its return meant the British could step into the royal role of guardian of the relic, the *sangha* and Buddhism itself. Brownrigg, a perceptive if patronising commentator, was exactly right when he wrote to London about the return of the relic: 'Its recovery had a manifest effect on all classes and its having fallen into our hands again ... was considered by this superstitious people as a demonstration of its being the destiny of the British Nation to govern the Kandyans.'[75]

D'Oyly was also aware of the importance of the Kandyan regalia to the Sinhalese. When they were recovered, he wrote to Brownrigg that he wanted to inform the chiefs 'and assure them that the Government is well aware of the high honour and estimation in which they are held by the Nation, and that having become the property of the king of Great Britain, they will be preserved with the same respect as the Regalia of the British Crown'.[76] The fine words, however, remained that, as the precious symbols of Kandyan rule, including the king's throne, were taken to Britain. Some entered the Royal Collection – the throne was placed in Windsor Castle – but other items were auctioned off; the crown and throne would not be returned to Ceylon until the 1930s.[77]

As the governor generally remained in Colombo, D'Oyly exercised pro-consular powers in Kandy, and he attempted to situate the British Crown as honourable successor to the old monarchy. Though he lived modestly, dressing informally, eating only vegetarian food, and seemingly forswearing wife or concubines, D'Oyly's 'subjects' sometimes performed ritual marks of obeisance to him, including prostrations. In his office in the old royal palace, he enjoyed a 'virtual kingship' for which he was fit by temperament and sense of duty.[78] He also played the part of the traditional royal patron, particularly in his (possibly intimate) relationship with the poet Gajaman Nona, or Perumal, who reciprocated with verses addressed to D'Oyly much as if he were a monarch.[79] D'Oyly nevertheless suffered great disappointment with the uprising of 1817–18, for which superiors and colleagues held him to a degree responsible. For the remainder of his tenure, D'Oyly did not benefit from his earlier esteem at Government House and the Colonial Office; the delay in awarding him an honour, a baronetcy, signalled his partial eclipse. The British, however, continued to fill the role as true successors to the Sinhalese and Nayakkar dynasties.

The governor issued a proclamation on 21 November 1818 to mark the end of the 'rebellion'.[80] It drew back on promises in the Kandyan Convention, most significantly, in toning down protection for Buddhism. 'The priests as all the ceremonies and processions of the Budhoo religion shall receive the respect which in former times was shewn them', the document stated, but immediately it added that 'at the same time it is in no wise to be understood that the protection of government is to be denied to the peaceable exercise by all other persons of the religion which they respectively profess'. (The building of an Anglican church in the shadow of the Dalada Maligawa in 1846 underscored the point.) The proclamation constituted a magnificently self-serving document, beginning with a sweeping statement about Britain's conquest of Kandy: 'The chiefs and people of the Kandyan nation no longer able to endure the cruelties and oppressions which the late King Sri Wikreme Raja Singha tyrannically practiced towards them prayed the assistance of the British Government for their relief and by a solemn act declared the late king deposed.' Further paragraphs detailed the evils of the *ancien régime*, counterposed to the benefits of British rule. The proclamation castigated the rebels as 'plotters' bent on subverting the government and appropriating power. Though Vibave went unnamed, it alluded to the pretender in saying that 'the people had been deluded to prostrate before the phantom', and for good measure, referring to his enthronement, ridiculed 'the pageant [where the one] whom the people were called to recognize as the descendant of the gods [was] exposed as the offspring of a poor Cingalese empyric'.

One of the proclamation's main objectives was to reaffirm British control, leaving no question as to who was master: 'His Excellency the Governor therefore now calls to the mind of every person and of every class within these settlements, that the Sovereign Majesty of the King of Great Britain and Ireland exercised by His Representative the Governor of Ceylon and his Agents in the Kandyan Provinces is the source alone from which all Power emanates, to which obedience is due.' It directed 'that on entering the Hall of Audience, every person shall make obeisance to the portrait of His Majesty there suspended; and as well there as in any other Court of Justice to the presiding Authority'. On the governor's tours, 'he shall be attended by all the persons in office belonging to each province in manner as they attended the former Kings of Kandy'. All must show signs of deference: 'all chiefs and other persons coming before, meeting or passing any British officer, civil or military, of rank and authority in the Island of Ceylon shall give up the middle of the road, and if sitting rise and make a suitable obeisance, which will be always duly acknowledged and returned'. Only the *adigars* enjoyed similar rights. Appointment of officers, including *adigars* and *dissaves*, came only through a warrant from the governor. The proclamation also laid down rules of precedence and honours for native chieftains, and exempted from taxation lands held by chiefs who had remained loyal to the British. In matters of protocol, as well as entitlements, the document thus shifted the weight from the Kandyans to the British, conceding rights to their loyal allies. It demanded obedience from all, especially the chiefs, 'as they shall answer the contrary at their peril'.[81]

The document could not be clearer: the British both reigned and ruled. Not only had transfer of sovereignty from the Kandyan monarch to the British monarch been confirmed, but the governor assumed absolute powers not dissimilar to those of the deposed 'tyrant', including the meting out of rewards and punishments to both noble vassals and commoners. Over the next decades, the British imprinted the signs and symbols of their monarchy on the new crown colony. Decrees were issued in the name of the British sovereign, royal monograms ornamented public buildings, portraits of the monarch were hung, the governor decorated eminent local men with British orders and medals, and by the late 1800s a few received knighthoods. Ceylon boasted viceregal splendour: a show of majesty that Brownrigg, it might be remembered, had once remarked was singularly lacking, to the detriment of the British. Thus, during the 1817–18 rebellion, Brownrigg had instructed British officers to appropriate Nayakkar ceremony and dress.[82] The governor moved about his newly conquered territory with great pomp, met with prostrations by local people until the practice was outlawed in 1818.[83] Flags and gun salutes, processions and assemblies, soldiers in uniform and judges in wigs dramatically and ceremoniously heralded the British as successors to the Kandyan monarchy.

The respect shown to the Tooth Relic and the Buddhist hierarchy, especially during the first decades of British rule, perpetuated the position of the colonial state as guardians of local religion. In 1828, the governor served as patron for an exhibition of the Tooth Relic in the sort of festival not held since the late 1700s. The interest the British displayed for sacred sites such as Sri Pada mountain, ancient temples in Anuradhapura and Pollonaruwa, and antique palm-leaf manuscripts similarly recalled old royal patronage of religion and the arts. They established the Royal Asiatic Society of Ceylon in 1845, and later an 'Oriental library' and Museum of Natural History and Antiquities. In Sivasundaram's words, 'the performance of orientalism by the British was an act of good governance that made it possible for the British to be seen as inheritors of Kandyan kingship and the rightful governors of the island'.[84] For good measure, they constructed a grand new botanical garden at Peredeniya on the site of an old royal garden. The restoration of temples, building programmes, support for pilgrimages and viceregal travels, Sivasundaram adds, strategically connected the British colonial state to the kingdom that it had conquered.[85]

The first British royal tour of Ceylon occurred only fifty-five years after Vikrama's deposition. Such tours provided opportunities to show off the British monarchy in person and with considerable spectacular, political and propagandistic value.[86] In 1870 Prince Alfred, Duke of Edinburgh, second son of Queen Victoria, was the first member of the royal family to visit Ceylon, arriving aboard the Royal Navy ship he commanded. Thousands had laboured on the decorations and amenities. (Did local people see a parallel with the old corvées?) As guns fired in salute, the *Galatea* steamed into the port, escorted by hundreds of fishing canoes. 'Chiefs and headmen who had not left their jungle homes for half a lifetime', according to a commemorative volume, were invited to a reception at Queen's House, where 'the blending of the Native and European costumes – official and unofficial – has at all times a striking effect'. After these formalities, the prince and governor headed up-country, heavy rains making the journey a misery, but brandy and champagne at a resthouse providing cheer. An archway erected by British planters, but unaccountably made out of old bottles, offered a sight at another stop. Ten thousand people joined the prince at a kraal to witness the gunning down of an elephant judged dangerous to the local population, but His Royal Highness appeared to more taken with the daughter of the Sinhalese official organising the festivities. The prince continued his five-week stay with a visit to Kandy, where the official memoirist noted the picturesque costumes but also the sorry state (in the Englishman's view) of a party of Veddas. Alfred viewed the Tooth Relic, then took in some shooting in the countryside. More receptions and entertainments followed, including a show for children put on by 'a famous Hungarian wizard', and performances by 'nautch-girls' and 'a band of boy dancers'. A visit to the south coast city of Galle concluded the royal progress, which did not stretch to the sites of Anaradhapura and Polonnaruwa, rather slighting the island's cultural patrimony.[87] The published account shows that some Ceylonese, including those hosting private receptions, had been well integrated into the colonial order. The Kandyan aristocrats scored meetings with the duke, mingling with officials and planters. One can only wonder what 'common' people thought of the spectacle; at the least, it would have been an impressive display of majesty.

Other royal visitors arrived in 1901, the Duke of Corwall and York, son of King Edward VII, and his wife. An Australian newspaper reported that for four days the future King George V and Queen Mary 'saw many interesting and amusing sights'. The 'ancient Kings and Queens of Kandy' (presumably, the Kandyan nobles) were mustered to meet them, and 'the Duke and Duchess were taken by train to the old castle [sic] of the Kandyan Kings'. The visitors toured the Dalada Maligawa, and also 'At Kandy, the Duke received the chiefs (who were barefooted, if not bareheaded), and saw a procession of elephants, each of which made obeisance to Royalty'. The duke accepted an ivory and gem-studded casket ('which had been in the last Paris Exhibition') offered by planters, presented new colours to the infantry, awarded medals to twenty veterans of the South African war, and planted a sacred bodhi tree. The article, though betraying imprecision and stereotypes, underlined the pageant of royalty without remarking on the irony of the heir to the British throne rubbing shoulders with the 'ancient Kings and Queens of Kandy' whose own sovereign had been ousted. The feelings of the Kandyans and other Ceylonese are hard to discern.

Later British royal visitors included the Prince of Wales (the future Edward VIII) in 1921, the Duke of Gloucester in 1934 – returning Vikrama's throne during his stay – and Queen Elizabeth II in 1954, taking the place of her father, who died before a planned tour could take place. Ceylon had gained independence as a dominion in the Commonwealth in 1948, the throne and crown of the Kandyan king meaningfully placed on the dais behind the representative of the queen, the Duke of Gloucester (on another visit), and the Ceylonese dignitaries. The visit of Queen Elizabeth was the first by a British monarch to a realm over which she would reign until Ceylon became a republic in 1972.[88] Her tour continued the deployment of the British monarchy – in person, by proxy and through law and symbols – that had been the practice for a century and a half since the deposition of Vikrama from the throne.

The legacy of a deposition

The extinction of a monarchy, or its replacement by another (in this case, a colonial one), produced many collateral effects in addition to obvious changes in government. Ananda Coomaraswamy, the preeminent historian of traditional Sinhalese art, bemoaned the decline of art and architecture on the island, which he attributed generally to British conquest and disestablishment of the monarchy, the end of the patronage it provided, and disruption of the social structures of the pre-colonial order. Though unsparing in his criticism of Vikrama, whom he labelled a deranged tyrant, Coomaraswamy, writing in 1907, condemned the British for exactions after the 1817–18 uprising: 'The results of foreign rule and of the insurrection and its suppression were disastrous. It was many years before the country began to recover its prosperity, while the breach in the continuity of national traditions and culture has never been spanned.' Colonialism had introduced a foreign materialist order unsympathetic to Buddhist values, and the end of the Kandyan monarchy led to loss of royal and aristocratic interest and commissions, as well as artisan skills. The integral links between monarchy, people and culture were sundered: 'The people were very dependent on the royal patronage, looking to the king for support in all religious and social undertakings. During the succeeding century this sympathetic patronage was lacking, and a secular and alien government, whose main business was that of the policeman, ignored indigenous culture and social life.' Cultural decadence was not surprising: 'How impossible it was that the arts should continue to flourish under foreign rulers, ignorant of, and in the main opposed, to the perpetuation of that culture and religion', Coomaraswamy wrote:

> What befell the royal craftsmen when the Buddhist king was replaced by the Christian Governor? How could there continue that identification of sentiment between ruler and craftsmen which made possible the building of Gangarama [a temple in Colombo], the Dalada Maligawa, or the last festival at Asgiriya [another temple in Kandy]? Imagine the effect on English art if English independence had ceased in the reign of Henry III, and the Government had passed into the hands of a nation of materialists – Westminster Abbey left unfinished, Gothic art no more the vehicle of the national religious sentiment.[89]

Cooomaraswamy was overly pessimistic. Buddhism experienced a revival as philosophy and practice in the last decades of the nineteenth century, owning much to Hikkaduve Sumangala and Angarika Dharmapala, but also the interest of local and foreign Theosophists.[90] Traditional crafts, such as wood- and metal-working, sculpting and temple decoration, have continued to be practised to this day. New sorts of art emerged, and in the 1930s and 1940s, Ceylon played host to an innovative cohort of modern artists, who drew on indigenous and European avant-garde influences. There was also eventually a revival of Kandyan and low-country ('devil') dance.[91] In some ways, these movements were revivifications of artistic practices fallen into abeyance after the British takeover and the Westernisation it engendered.

The end of the Kandyan kingship did not annul a sense of Kandyan identity. Kandyans, argues Nira Wickramasinghe, regarded themselves as the repository of true Sinhalese and Buddhist culture, and the British likewise considered Kandy the most 'authentic' region of the island. Low-country Sinhalese showed themselves more open to Westernisation (and, in British views, modernisation), leading to competition between the two Sinhalese populations. Fearing domination by the coastal Sinhalese, a Kandyan Association was set up in 1917; delegates at the inaugural meeting claimed a privileged relationship between Kandyans and the British Crown. There followed efforts to secure greater representation in the Ceylon Legislative Council, alongside proposals in 1924 for establishment of a Kandyan National Assembly. The Kandyans manifested vigilance against the growing influence of the Ceylon National Congress, dominated by low-country Sinhalese, unsuccessfully championing a federal political structure for the dominion in which Ceylon would be divided into autonomous Kandyan, low-country and Tamil regions. Meanwhile, nationalists, including those in the Congress organisation, adopted specifically Kandyan cultural symbols of Sinhalese identity, leading eventually to a considerable but incomplete fusion of ideologies and nationalist groups.[92] The patrimony of the Kandyan kingdom, *sans* king, became the symbolic core of Ceylonese culture, in the eyes of the British, local residents and tourists. Among the signifiers are the Kandyan royal symbol of a golden sword-bearing lion *passant* on a maroon background, which figures on the Sri Lankan flag, and the iconic status of the Dalada Maligawa, closely linked to the pre-colonial monarchy.

British colonisation produced profound long-term effects on the ecology, economics, government, society and culture of Ceylon – the introduction and spread of plantations of tea, the product with which the island became most identified, one of the greatest sources of the transformation.[93] Although monarchism lost its attraction as a rallying point for resistance and emerging nationalism, the abolition of the dynasty did not reconcile all Ceylonese with untrammelled British dominion. The move towards independence was remarkably peaceful and gradualist compared to some other colonies, and separation from Britain amicable and gradual. For the most part, the first generation of political leaders in independent Ceylon, many British educated, expressed pride in the political, judicial and educational systems they inherited from Britain and continued to pledge loyalty to the distant queen who still reigned over them.[94] The pre-colonial dynasties, however, did provide a referent for those who hailed kings of the often distant past as nation-builders and builders of temples, tanks and cities, and as heroes who for centuries fought off foreign invasions.[95] According to some commentators, elements of an ideology and political practice connected with monarchism, as portrayed in the *Mahavamsa* and *Culavamsa*,[96] persisted after independence and even after the declaration of a republic in 1972: hope for strong leaders who resembled the ancient kings, the imperative to attend to the needs of common people, a mandate to promote unity and combat enemies from home or abroad. New political dynasties were often related to old elite families, and some recent political rulers have seemed to enjoy near royal privileges and immunities. The ethno-nationalistic positioning of prime ministers and presidents as defenders of Sinhalese people and the Buddhist faith links them to the pre-colonial regime, sometimes to the detriment of other communities.

Ehelepola, as much or more than Vikrama, has kept a position in Sri Lankan memory and culture, most recently through a novel by Romesh Gunesekera about the prisoners transported to Mauritius.[97] Keppetipola, executed leader of the 1817 uprising, is honoured with a stele on the esplanade of the Kandy lake and a statue in his ancestral village. Unveiled by William Gopallawa, the last governor-general before Ceylon became a republic, it shows a commanding figure, dressed in the apparel of a Kandyan chief, ready to draw his sword. The inscription includes the words: 'I would rather lay down my life as a Sinhalese in the struggle for the liberation of the Sinhala country than live in servility under foreigners.' The Kandy lake itself, and the octagonal tower of the Dalada Maligawa, testify to Vikrama's building programmes in his capital. An hour's drive from Kandy, near Medamahanuwara, an austere monument, looking like an Ionic cross without the crossbeam, recalls the site of Vikrama's capture; it was erected in 1908 at the behest of John Penry Lewis, an 'antiquarian government agent'.[98] It attracts few visitors – a monument to the defeat and capture of a country's sovereign that outlives colonialism is hardly likely to be a celebrated memorial. Nor is a small structure resembling a guard post in central Colombo that claims to be the king's gaol cell; the view through the window shows pictures of Vikrama, Queen Venkata, Adigar Pilima Talauve and Governor Brownrigg, as well as a ship, presumably the one that carried the king into exile.[99]

Artefacts in the National Museum more dramatically recall the last king of Kandy. A portrait shows Vikrama wearing a golden crown, red brocaded coat and white ruff collar. As Granville said, he is a handsome figure, his face encircled by a thick neatly trimmed beard, a Hindu *bindi* marking his forehead. One hand, bracelets on the wrist, delicately holds a handkerchief. Nearby is a painting of Queen Venkata Rengammal, the king's beautiful youngest spouse, posed on a terrace against misty hillsides and palm trees.[100] Also on display is a stained cloth, said to be marked with the blood of a queen whose earring was torn off. The exhibition includes several of the king's garments as well, and a gold watch 'Presented by the king of Holland to king Sri Vikrama

Rajasimha'.[101] The regalia of the dynasty are some of the most important treasures of the museum: the golden throne, decorated with gemstones, and ornamented with lions and images of the sun representing the monarchy, and the jewel-encrusted crown. Their repatriation to Ceylon in the 1930s was meant by the British as a generous gesture to loyal subjects, though for many they represented booty stolen in 1815 and remain symbols of Ceylon's independence – before foreign invasion, and after 1948 – and of Sinhalese culture.[102]

Sri Vikrama Rajasinha, his queens, a grandson and his wife are interred in small whitewashed *mandapas*, pillared Hindu-style pavilions, in Vellore. A descendant of the king renovated the graves on the centenary of his death, and in 1990, the Tamil Nadu state government built a lotus-shaped outer structure to enclose the tombs. At the State Museum in the Vellore fort, a small exhibition displays Vikrama's ivory chessboard, coins and hunting gear.[103]

Vikrama was one of first monarchs in the nineteenth-century British colonies to be deposed and exiled, and his case provides a template for ones that followed. Indigenous sovereigns stood as obstacles to expansion of colonial dominion; sometimes Europeans could treat with them, obtaining concessions of territory, trading privileges and acknowledgement of the colonisers' paramountcy, or at least they could work out a modus vivendi for uneasy neighbourliness (as indeed occurred in Ceylon between 1796 and 1815), though generally after exacting painful concessions. When international circumstances – such as the Napoleonic Wars, and new geostrategic and commercial aspirations – warranted further incursions in European eyes, monarchs could be deposed, dynasties abolished and territories annexed; that was the fate of Vikrama and his kingdom in 1815. To do so, the reputations of native rulers had to be blackened, foreigners brought into league with disaffected subjects, and military might deployed. Vikrama's banishment to a foreign country – not coincidentally, another colonial outpost under his captors' sovereignty – removed the man, though it did not necessarily efface memories of old regimes, or in the long term thwart nationalism. The British experience with Vikrama nevertheless inaugurated a strategy they would essay elsewhere.

Notes

1 I have also written about the exile of the Kandyan king in 'Out of Ceylon: The Exile of the Last King of Kandy', in Ronit Ricci (ed.), *Exile in Colonial Asia: Kings, Convicts, Commemoration* (Honolulu: University of Hawai'i Press, 2016), pp. 48–70.
2 Governor Robert Brownrigg to captain of the *Cornwallis*, 24 January 1816, IOR/F/4/515 Volume 2 12365, India Office Records, British Library; the phrase reappears in other correspondence as well.

3 This account and all quotations are taken from William Granville's 'Journal of Reminiscences relating to the late king of Kandy when on his voyage from Colombo to Madras in 1816, a prisoner-of-war on board His Majesty's Ship "Cornwallis"'. It was published as 'Deportation of Sri Vikrama Rajasinha', in two parts, in *The Ceylon Literary Register*, 3:11 (1936), 487–504, and 3:12 (1936), 543–50. The most recent study of Ceylon under the British is Sujit Sivasundaram, *Islanded: Britain, Sri Lanka and the Bounds of an Indian Ocean Colony* (Chicago: University of Chicago Press, 2013). Longer-range perspectives come from K. M. de Silva, *A History of Sri Lanka* (Colombo: Vijitha Yapa Publications, 2008 [2005]); and Nira Wickramasinghe, *Sri Lanka in the Modern Age: A History of Contested Identities* (London: Hurst, 2006). Alicia Frederika Schrikker, 'Dutch and British Colonial Intervention in Sri Lanka, c. 1780–1815: Expansion and Reform' (PhD dissertation, University of Leiden, 1976), gives details of the transition from Dutch to British rule. John Clifford Holt (ed.), *The Sri Lanka Reader: History, Culture, Politics* (Durham, NC: Duke University Press, 2011) contains many valuable original documents and academic studies. C. A. Gunawardena, *Encyclopedia of Sri Lanka* (New Delhi: New Dawn Press, 2006), is a useful reference work.

4 Brownrigg to the captain of the *Cornwallis*.

5 Granville subsequently held various positions in the colonial government in Ceylon, returned with his wife to Britain in 1834, and died in 1864.

6 Vernon L. B. Mendis, *The Rulers of Sri Lanka* (Colombo: S. Godage & Bros, 2000); and J. B. Disanayaka, *Lanka: The Land of Kings* (Maharagama: Sumitha Publishers, 2007). Michael Roberts, *Sinhala Consciousness in the Kandyan Period, 1590s–1815* (Colombo: Vijitha Yapa, 2003), provides the fullest account of the ideology of rule at this period. On early modern kingship, see Alan Strathern, *Kingship and Conversion in Sixteenth-Century Sri Lanka: Portuguese Imperialism in a Buddhist Land* (New Delhi: Cambridge University Press, 2010).

7 Mendis, *The Rulers of Sri Lanka*, p. 194.

8 P. E. Pieris, *Ceylon and the Portuguese, 1505–1658* (Delhi: Sri Satguru Pub., 1986 [1920]).

9 Tikiri Abeyasinghe, 'Princes and Merchants: Relations between the Kings of Kandy and the Dutch East India Company in Sri Lanka, 1688–1740', *Sri Lanka Archives*, 4 (1984), 35–59.

10 S. Arasaratnam, *Ceylon and the Dutch, 1600–1800* (Aldershot: Ashgate, 1996); for a travelling artist's images of a still grand court, see Max de Bruijn and Remco Raben, *The World of Jan Brandes, 1743–1808* (Amsterdam: Waanders and Rijksmuseum, 2004).

11 P. E. Pieris, *Tri Sinhala: The Last Phase, 1796–1815* (New Delhi: Asia Educational Services, 2001 [1939]); Colvin R. De Silva, *Ceylon under the British Occupation, 1795–1833* (New Delhi: Navrang, 1995 [1941]); Channa Wickremesekera, *Kandy at War: Indigenous Military Resistance to the European Expansion in Sri Lanka, 1594–1818* (New Delhi: Manohar, 2004); and Upali C. Wickremeratne, *Hearsay and Versions in British Relations with the Kingdom of Kandy, 1796–1818* (Colombo: Vijitha Yapa, 2012).

12 Quoted in De Silva, *Ceylon under the British Occupation*, p. 20.

13 Sivasundaram, *Islanded*, p. 71.

14 John Clifford Holt, *The Religious World of Kirti Sri: Buddhism, Art, and Politics in Late Medieval Sri Lanka* (New York: Oxford University Press, 1996).

15 Ananda S. Pilimatalavuva, *The Pilimatalavuvas in the Last Phase of the Kandyan Kingdom* (Pannipitiya: Stamford Lake, 2008), and *The Chieftains in the Last Phase of the Kandyan Kingdom (Sinhalé)* (Pannipitiya: Stamford Lake, 2008).

16 Opinion differs on the degree of the Nayakkars' acceptance and assimilation. L. S. Dewaraja argues that there were seen as aliens and unpopular, whereas H. L. Seneviratne suggests they were accepted. (H. L. Seneviratne, 'The Alien King: Nayakkars on the Throne of Kandy', *Ceylon Journal of Historical and Social Studies*, 6:1 (1976), 55–61.) K. N. O. Dharmadasa credits the Nayakkars as patrons of Buddhism and Sinhalese culture, but also points to rebellions in 1749 and 1760, and proposals that a Siamese prince be recruited to head a new dynasty. (Dharmadasa, 'The

THE LAST KING IN CEYLON

Sinhala Buddhist Identity and the Nayakkar Dynasty in the Politics of the Kandyan Kingdom, 1739–1815', in Michael Roberts (ed.), *Sri Lanka: Collective Identities Revisited* (Colombo: Marga Institute, 1997), pp. 79–104.) Sivasundaram points to the Nayakkar dynasty as a 'transregional kingship' (pp. 31ff.) and suggests that the British arbitrarily but unsuccessfully attempted to separate Sinhalese and 'Malabar' identity (p. 50). Michael Roberts suggests that the question of the '"homogeneity" of the Sinahalese' is a 'non-issue'; though there was a 'Sinhalaness', or Sinhala consciousness, in opposition to the intrusion of foreign armies, it encompassed others, including migrants. (Roberts, *Sinhala Consciousness*, pp. 14–16.) R. A. L. H. Gunawardana shows how the Nayakkars were fashioned as Sinhalese after their rule began, then later as 'Malabars', but also were transformed from 'Aryans' into 'Dravidians'. (R. A. L. H. Gunawardena, 'Colonialism, Ethnicity and the Construction of the Past: The Changing "Ethnic Identity" of the Last Four Kings of the Kandyan Kingdom', in Martin van Bakel, Renée Hagesteijn and Pieter van de Velde (eds), *Pivot Politics: Changing Cultural Identities in Early State Formation Processes* (Amsterdam: Het Spinhuis, 1994), pp. 197–221.) See also S. Gopalakrishnan, *The Nayaks of Sri Lanka, 1739–1815: Political Relations with the British in South India* (Madras: New Era, 1988).

17 On his reign, see Punchibandara Dolapihilla, *In the Days of Sri Wickramarajasingha, Last King of Kandy* (Ratmalana: Vishva Lekha, 2006 [1959]).
18 See T. B. Pohath-Kehelpannala, *The Life of Ehelapola, Prime Minister to the Last King of Kandy* (Colombo: The Observer, 1896).
19 Geoffrey S. Powell, 'Brownrigg, Sir Robert', *Oxford Dictionary of National Biography*, www.oxforddnb.com/index/3/101003718/, accessed 25 November 2016.
20 Brendon Gooneratne and Yasmine Gooneratne, *This Inscrutable Englishman: Sir John D'Oyly (1774–1824)* (London: Cassell, 1999); see also H. W. Codrington (ed.), *Diary of Mr. John D'Oyly* (New Delhi: Navrang, 1995 [1917]), which finishes in April 1815.
21 Quoted in Tannakoon Vimalananda, *Sir Wickrema, Brownrigg and Ehelepola* (Colombo: Gunasena, 1984), p. 269.
22 Vimalananda, *Sir Wickrema*, p. 323.
23 William Dias Bandaranayaka, 'How the Last King of Kandy was Captured by the British: An Eye-Witness's Account, Rendered from the Sinhalese', *Journal of the Royal Asiatic Society (Ceylon)*, 14:47 (1896), 107–11, from which quotations are taken. The journal raised questions about its reliability, since it had been first published only in 1860 and contained several factual errors (e.g. the number of soldiers taking part), but does not discount the document. D'Oyly's account of the capture largely accords with Dias Bandaranayaka, though he mentions a skirmish in which shots were fired and several men injured.
24 Dias Bandaranayaka, 'How the Last King of Kandy was Captured by the British'.
25 Codrington, *Diary of Mr John D'Oyly*, quotations from pp. 223, 254 and 250.
26 The convention is reproduced in De Silva, *Ceylon under the British Occupation*, pp. 227–30.
27 Reprinted in Codrington, *Diary of Mr John D'Oyly*, pp. 267–9.
28 Sivasundarm, *Islanded*, p. 44, does point to positive views in some chronicles.
29 *Culavamsa, being the more Recent Part of the Mahavamsa, Part I*, trans. Wilhem Geiger and C. Mabel Rickmers (London, 1973), p. 302.
30 Mendis, *The Rulers of Sri Lanka*, pp. 191 and 28.
31 Roberts, *Sinhala Consciousness*, p. 50.
32 Henry Marshall, *Ceylon: A General Description of the Island and Its Inhabitants* (London: William H. Allen, 1846), p. 168.
33 Marshall, *Ceylon*, p. 167.
34 Letter of Brownrigg, 24 January 1816, in the India Office Records, IOR/F/4/545, Vol. 2 12365, British Library, London; the following details come from documents in this bound manuscript volume.
35 Governor, Fort St George, political letter, 28 January 1818, IOR/E/4/920.
36 Extract from consultations with Fort St. George (Madras), 17 April 1816, IOR/F/4/515/12364.

37 P. E. E. Fernando, 'The Deportation of King Sri Vikrama Rajaimha and His Exile in India (Based on Archival Documents in Madras)', *University of Ceylon Review*, 20:3–4 (1962), 163–87.
38 Paymaster, Mysore stipends, to Chief Secretary, Fort St George, 12 March 1816, IOR/F/4/515, Vol. 2 12365.
39 Extract, Fort St George consultations, 10 May 1816, IOR/F/4/515/12364.
40 Governor, Fort St George, political letter, 28 January 1818, IOR/E/4/920.
41 Various correspondence in IOR/F/947/26578; see also IOR/E/4/935.
42 Report by Lieutenant-Colonel Stewart, 31 October 1827, IOR/F/f/1418/56111.
43 IOR/E/4/944 and IOR/F/4/1418/56111.
44 Letter of Brownrigg, 5 October 1816, and other correspondence, IOR/F/4/527/12639.
45 Report of paymaster, 16 October 1816, IOR/F/527/12639.
46 The following details come from IOR/F/4/1461/57493, India Office Records, British Library.
47 In particular, Paymaster of Vellore to Chief Secretary, 9 March 1832, and Deputy Secretary, Colombo, to Chief Secretary, 27 March 1833, IOR/F/4/1461/57493; see also IOR/F/4/1432/56581.
48 Chief Secretary, Colombo, to Chief Secretary, Fort St George (Madras), 20 January 1816, IOR/F/4/515, Vol. 2 12365, British Library.
49 Resident, Tanjore, to Chief Secretary, Fort St George, 4 March 1816, IOR/F/4/515, Vol. 2 12365, British Library.
50 Correspondence in early 1815, IOR/F/4/515, Vol. 1 12364.
51 Resident, Tanjore, 31 January 1816, IOR/F/4/515, Vol. 2 12365.
52 See, e.g. letters from October 1827 about the family of 'Gumpal Naick', IOR/F/4/1418/56111, and voluminous correspondence from 1832 to 1833 about others in F/4/1461/57493.
53 IOR/F/4/1518/56110.
54 Peddaswamooloo and Chiniaswamooloo to Governor-in-Council, 23 March 1832, IOR/F/4/146/57493; see also petitions in IOR/F/4/1418/56110.
55 Governor, Fort St George, 23 Febuary 1835, IOR/E/4/945.
56 Ponnambalam Arunachalam, *Light from the East, being Letters on Gnanam, the Divine Knowledge*, ed. Edward Carpenter (London: Allen & Unwin, 1927), pp. 33–4.
57 *The Times*, 26 November 1894, p. 6.
58 PP 1/648/2515, National Archives, Kew.
59 Kausalya Santhanam, 'Lankan Legacy', *The Hindu*, 6 May 2007, www.thehindu.com/todays-paper/tp-features/tp-sundaymagazine/lankan-legacy/article2275191.ece, accessed 25 November 2016. See also Satharathilaka Banda Atugoda, 'Tomb of King Wickrama Rajasinhe in Vellore – India', http://amazinglanka.com/wp/tomb-of-sri-wickrama-rajasinhe-2/, accessed 25 November 2016.
60 Quoted in A. D. Appuhamy, *The Rebels, Outlaws and Enemies to the British* (Colombo: M. D. Gunasena, 1990), p. 23.
61 Quoted in Appuhamy, *The Rebels*, p. 2.
62 Quoted in Ananda K. Coomaraswamy, *Mediaeval Sinhalese Art* (New York: Pantheon Books, revised edition, 1956 [1907]), p. 15.
63 Kumari Jayawardena, *Perpetual Ferment: Popular Revolts in Sri Lanka in the 18th and 19th Centuries* (Colombo: Social Scientists' Association, 2010), p. 74.
64 Jayawardena, *Perpetual Ferment*, p. 1.
65 Jayawardena, *Perpetual Ferment*, p. 4.
66 Jayawardena, *Perpetual Ferment*, p. 121.
67 Jayawardena, *Perpetual Ferment*, p. 16.
68 Quoted in Jayawardena, *Perpetual Ferment*, p. 77.
69 Returned to Sri Lanka, it was interred in a memorial in 1954.
70 Appuhamy, *The Rebels*, pp. 150–4; Raja C. Bandaranayake, *Betwixt Isles: The Story of the Kandyan Prisoneers in Mauritius* (Colombo: Vijitha Yapa, 2006). On Ehelepola, see also Sheila Ward, *Prisoners in Paradise* (Rose Hill, Mauritius: Éditions de l'Océan Indien, 1986), pp. 21–33.

71 Anoma Pieris, 'The "Other" Side of Labor Reform: Accounts of Incarceration and Resistance in the Straits Settlements Penal System, 1825–1873', *Journal of Social History*, 45:2 (2011), 453–79.
72 Quoted in Appuhamy, *The Rebels*, p. 6.
73 Gooneratne and Gooneratne, *This Inscrutable Englishman*, p. 150.
74 Sivasundaram, *Islanded*, p. 11.
75 Quoted in Appuhamy, *The Rebels*, p. 64.
76 Quoted in Gooneratne and Gooneratne, *This Inscrutable Englishman*, p. 243.
77 Robert Aldrich, 'The Return of the Throne: The Repatriation of the Kandyan Regalia to Ceylon', in Robert Aldrich and Cindy McCreery (eds), *Crowns and Colonies: European Monarchies and Overseas Empires* (Manchester: Manchester University Press, 2016), pp. 139–62.
78 Gooneratne and Gooneratne, *This Inscrutable Englishman*, p. 165.
79 Sivasundaram, *Islanded*, p. 99.
80 The proclamation is printed in John Davy, *An Account of the Interior of Ceylon* (London: Longman, 1821), pp. 505–17, from which quotations are taken, and in G. C. Mendis (ed.), *The Colebrooke-Cameron Papers* (Oxford: Oxford University Press, 1956), pp. 231–43.
81 Davy, *An Account of the Interior of Ceylon*.
82 Sivasundaram, *Islanded*, p. 148.
83 Sivasundaram, *Islanded*, p. 170.
84 Sivasundaram, *Islanded*, p. 134.
85 Sivasundarm, *Islanded*, p. 322.
86 Richard Boyle, 'British Royal Encounters with Sri Lanka', *Explore Sri Lanka*, November 2013, http://exploresrilanka.lk/2013/11/british-royal-encounters-with-sri-lanka/, accessed 25 November 2016.
87 Richard Boyle, 'A Right Royal Tour', *Himal Magazine*, June 2009, http://old.himalmag.com/component/content/article/539-a-right-royal-tour.html, accessed 25 November 2016. Based on the commemorative volume by John Capper, *The Duke of Edinburgh in Ceylon: A Book of Elephant and Elk Sport* (London: Provost & Co., 1871), from which the quotations are taken.
88 Harshan Kumarasingham, *A Political Legacy of the British Empire: Power and the Parliamentary System in Post-Colonial India and Sri Lanka* (London: I. B. Tauris, 2013), Chs 5–7.
89 Coomaraswamy, *Mediaeval Sinhalese Art*, p. 17.
90 Anne M. Blackburn, *Locations of Buddhism: Colonialism and Modernity in Sri Lanka* (Chicago: University of Chicago Press, 2010); Steven Kemper, *Rescued from the Nation: Angarika Dharmapala and the Buddhist World* (Chicago: University of Chicago Press, 2015).
91 See Senake Bandaranayake and Albert Dharmasiri, *Sri Lankan Painting in the Twentieth Century* (Colombo: The National Trust Sri Lanka, 2009); Rajiva Wijesinha, *Breaking Bounds: Essays on Sri Lankan Writing in English* (Colombo: Sabaragamuwa University Press, 1998); Susan A. Reed, *Dance and the Nation: Performance, Ritual, and Politics in Sri Lanka* (Madison: University of Wisconsin Press, 2010).
92 Nira Wickramasinghe, 'The Return of Keppetipola's Cranium: Authenticity in a New Nation', *Economic and Political Weekly*, 26 July 1997, pp. 85–92.
93 See Kumari Jayawardena, *Nobodies to Somebodies: The Rise of the Colonial Bourgeoisie in Sri Lanka* (Colombo: Social Scientists' Association and Sanjiva Books, 2000); John D. Rogers, 'Early British Rule and Social Classification in Lanka', *Modern Asian Studies*, 38:3 (2004), 625–47; Newton Gunasinghe, *Changing Socio-Economic Relations in the Kandyan Countryside* (Colombo: Social Scientists' Association, 2007); James L. A. Webb, *Tropical Pioneers: Human Agency and Ecological Change in the Highlands of Sri Lanka, 1800–1900* (Athens, Ohio: Ohio University Press, 2002); Nira Wickramasinghe, *Metallic Modern: Everyday Machines in Colonial Sri Lanka* (New York: Berghahn, 2014).
94 Kumarasingham, *A Political Legacy of the British Empire*.

95 James S. Duncan, 'The Power of Place in Kandy, Sri Lanka: 1780–1980', in John A. Agnew and James S. Duncan (eds), *The Power of Place: Bringing Together Geographical and Sociological Imaginations* (Boston: Unwin Hyman, 1989), pp. 185–201.
96 Kemper, *Rescued from the Nation*, pp. 95–104.
97 Romesh Gunesekera, *The Prisoner of Paradise* (London: Bloomsbury, 2012).
98 Christopher Ondaatje, *Woolf in Ceylon: An Imperial Journey in the Shadow of Leonard Woolf, 1904–1911* (London: HarperCollins, 2005), pp. 180–1.
99 'The Last King's Jail Cell', www.yamu.lk/place/the-last-kings-jail-cell/review-41889, accessed 25 November 2016.
100 Gooneratne and Gooneratne, *This Inscrutable Englishman*, pp. 139–42 on the portrait of the queen.
101 Leelananda Prematilleke and Ranjith Hewage, *A Guide to the National Museum, Colombo* (Colombo: Department of National Museums, 2012).
102 Aldrich, 'The Return of the Throne', based largely on materials in CO 54/921/3, National Archives, Kew, and materials in the Royal Archives used by permission of Her Majesty Queen Elizabeth II.
103 Ajith Amarasinghe, 'Rediscovering the Tomb of the Our Last King', *Sunday Times* (Colombo), 11 March 2012, www.sundaytimes.lk/120311/Plus/plus_01.html#top, accessed 25 November 2016.

CHAPTER THREE

Kings of Orient were: royal exile in British Asia

The nineteenth century saw unparalleled British empire-building in Asia after the consolidation of its position in Ceylon in 1815. Through conquest and treaty, the East India Company increased its holdings, and after the Great Indian Uprising of 1857, the British government assumed administration of the Indian colonies, and overrule in the princely states of the subcontinent. In Southeast Asia, wars in the 1820s, 1850s and 1880s brought Burma (Myanmar) under British control. The British had taken possession of the Straits Settlements – including Penang, Malacca and Singapore – in the late 1700s and early 1800s, and under Queen Victoria, they expanded throughout the Malay peninsula and on Borneo. The 'Opium Wars' led to acquisition of Hong Kong and later concessions in China. In the march eastwards, the British faced off indigenous emperors, kings, maharajas and sultans, defeating them in battle, annexing territory or establishing protectorates, and extending imperium in the Orient.[1] Victoria's assumption of the title Empress of India in 1876 attested to her sovereignty over vast Asian domains and paramountcy over surviving dynasties.

The years of British expansion in Asia coincided with significant changes in metropolitan politics, typified by voting reform and granting of the suffrage to virtually all adult men (though not women). Walter Bagehot's *The English Constitution*, published in the 1860s, articulated the theory of British governance as a partnership between Crown and Parliament. The pomp and pageantry of the monarchy were carefully choreographed into spectacular displays of royal power and prerogative. The jubilees of 1887 and 1897 underlined the central position of the monarchy in the United Kingdom and the empire. Victoria, her beloved husband and many children became the model of bourgeois family values lauded throughout her realms, and she occasionally dispatched a son to fly the flag in the colonies. Victoria herself, though never travelling to her possessions, manifested ardent interest in the empire, especially India. Her sympathies reached even to those rulers whom her representatives dethroned: 'I always feel so much for these poor deposed Indian Princes', she wrote in her journal in 1854.[2]

This chapter begins with an overview of the ouster of Indian 'princes' – a generic term for the native sovereigns – who were taken as prisoners of war, or deposed on grounds of resistance, maladministration and character defects, from the early 1800s until the 1940s. It then examines the overthrow of the last king of Burma following the conquest of Mandalay in 1885. Finally, it looks at the removal of a Southeast Asian monarch, the Sultan of Perak in Malaya.

Indian princes and British overlords

Deposition under the Company Raj

The charter issued by the Crown to the East India Company gave the enterprise capacious rights to sign treaties with Asian rulers, govern territories conceded to the company, raise armies and levy taxes. The Company arrogated even greater powers to itself, often to the consternation of critics who accused it of rapacity and corruption in the quest for territory and resources. Many of the Indian princes with whom the company treated came under the nominal suzerainty of the Mughal dynasty, much diminished from its glory of the sixteenth century. With the death of Emperor Aurangzeb in 1704, three large states – Bengal, Mysore (Mysuru) and Oudh (Awadh) – gained virtual independence, and others flung out of the orbit of the emperor, including the Maratha ad Sikh states. Wars mounted by the Company by the early 1800s left the 'King of Delhi', as the British called him, master of little territory beyond his capital, though the East India Company remained, in strict terms, one of his vassals.

The Company directly ruled many of the territories it occupied. In others, where princes were vanquished or forced to accommodate the foreigners but remained on thrones, treaties imposed trade concessions, exterritorial legal rights for Europeans, land grants, pledges of good government and the acceptance of powerful British Residents at royal courts. In return, princes received British recognition for their rule, the cessation of military hostilities, and promises of commercial and other benefits of British overrule. Under a 'doctrine of lapse', articulated in the early 1800s, the Company claimed the right to annex any territory with which it had an agreement if the incumbent ruler died without a legitimate heir or one the Company judged competent; on this basis, the Company took over several dozen states, of varying sizes, from the 1830s until the mid-1850s. The appointed Residents interfered to varying degree in local affairs, but any perceived failure on the princes' part to honour treaty obligations allowed the Company to take action against sovereigns.

The Residents, or technically their superior the governor-general of India, deployed various strategies towards rulers accused of resistance to the supreme British power, misgovernment, corruption or personal failings. They might first admonish a prince to mend his ways or risk severer sanction. The threat of a formal commission of inquiry or trial, with public humiliation and possible conviction, provided a particularly strong weapon that could secure either better behaviour or abdication. As the next step, the British could punish a prince in symbolic ways by withholding much valued honours or gun salutes to which sovereigns felt entitled. Residents could also temporarily or permanently remove from monarchs some of their powers of administering justice, collecting taxes, appointing officials or otherwise exercising sovereign rights. More dramatically, the British overlords could suspend a ruler or, in the worst scenario, depose and banish a sovereign.

With or without a trial – or after 1858, a commission of inquiry – a decree by the governor-general, with the imprimatur of the central government in London, sufficed to oust a sovereign despite occasional political challenges to such actions. Rather than incarcerate a dethroned sovereign, the preferred alternative was to send him off to an appropriately distant part of 'British India'.[3] On occasion, the toppled ruler might be allowed to live overseas, even in Britain, so long as the colonial authorities felt confident that, nearby or far away, he had no chance of escaping, avoiding surveillance, rallying supporters or undermining the British imperium.

The first major nineteenth-century conflict in India nicely illustrates the twists and turns in relationships between colonisers and princes, but is also a rare case of a dethroned ruler evading the British. In the small central state of Nagpur, Maharaja Mudhoji II Bhonsle ('Appa Sahib') came to power, with British approbation, in 1816, having wrested the *gadi* (throne) from a kinsman. Foreshadowing continued palace intrigues, he took up residence near the security of the British cantonment. Soon he turned against the British and leagued with other Maratha chiefs in a short war, won by the British, in 1817. Appa Sahib clung to his throne, though forced to cede territory, but the British feared another conspiracy, and arrested him in 1818 on charges of involvement in the murder of a rival. They deposed the sovereign, placed on the *gadi* a minor too young to be a menace, and banished Appa Sahib to Allahabad. However, he escaped with the connivance of sentries and headed for the Mahadeo Hills. (The British captain responsible for the captive was put on trial for neglect in letting a 'state prisoner' escape.) With contradictory reports that the fugitive was either rallying several thousand men, or suffering from lack of provisions, the British offered him safe passage and 'a competent provision for his future maintenance with his family at a station within the British territories'. Appa Sahib replied that 'he preferred to live and die a beggar, rather than enter on any conditions which might appear a relinquishment of what he considered his right to the Throne'. He continued to elude the British, and died of illness in Jodhpur in 1840.[4]

The Nagpur affair showed how the British could strike to get rid of an opponent, though he might first be given an extra chance. After the episode, colonial officials indeed debated whether deposition and exile provided the best strategies for eliminating inconvenient rulers, but over the next decades they nevertheless repeated the action several times. Four cases stand out in the first half of the century: the removal of the maharaja of Coorg in 1834, the raja of Satara in 1839, the famous Sikh Maharaja Duleep Singh of Punjab in 1849, and the king of Oudh in 1856. Space is lacking for comprehensive examination of each case, and they have been extensively covered in other studies, but some details evidence the circumstances and consequences of the dethroning of these Indian princes. A grab for territory, and the commercial and geopolitical resources it offered, provides the simple explanation for such moves, though the exact conditions differed in each incident.

The British courted Chikka Virarajendra, raja of Coorg (Kodagu, in present-day Karnataka) in the 1790s, during their struggle against Tipu Sultan; a treaty declared him 'the friend and ally of the Honourable Company'. The relationship soured after a rival (who was also Virarajendra's brother-in-law) tried to unseat him from the throne; the plot was discovered, and the conspirator fled with his wife to British territory in Mysore. The raja wrote to the British for assistance, saying that since his ancestors' times, 'we have been blended together, like sugar and milk, or, as you would express it, we have been hand-and-glove together', and requested the British to hand over his enemy. Despite repeated demands over two years, the British refused to extradite the raja's rival. Finally, in 1834, the Company issued a statement saying that 'the conduct of the Raja of Coorg has, for a long time past, been of such a nature as to render him unworthy of the friendship and protection of the British Government'. It accused him of 'the greatest oppression' of his subjects and disrespect for allies; his sister and her husband had sought asylum with the British because of 'his oppression', and the raja's requests for extradition had been 'replete with the most insulting expression' to British authorities. Promising to bring 'the blessings of a just and equitable government to Coorg', the proclamation continued: 'It is accordingly hereby notified, that a British army is about to invade the Coorg frontier; [and] that Virarajendra Wodear is no longer to be considered as rajah of Coorg.' Invasion and fighting took place before Virarajendra gave in to an ultimatum for his surrender; the British also demanded his entire treasury, some of which they distributed as prize money to soldiers. They annexed Coorg, granted the deposed ruler a small pension, and exiled him first to Vellore (where Tipu's sons had been confined), then to Benares (Varanasi); for seventeen years, he remained a state prisoner.[5]

Relations between the Company and the Maratha empire – a large confederation of Hindu states in western India – had been belligerent since the 1700s, and a war between them concluded in 1817 with British takeover of much of the Maratha territory. In hopes of reconciling the vanquished Marathas, the British allowed Pratap Singh (who had ascended the Maratha throne in 1808 at the age of fifteen) to retain sovereignty over the territory of Satara. He was not permitted an army or 'intercourse with foreign powers' and Montstuart Elphinstone, lieutenant-governor of Bombay, straightforwardly remarked that the aim of the settlement was 'keeping the entire control of his Government in the hands of the British'.[6] Elphinstone personally escorted Pratap Singh to Satara, 'in procession with the pomp of a prince and the delight of a schoolboy'. He remarked four years later on 'what a good fellow [is] the little Raja of Satara', and the comment was echoed by the Company's Board of Directors: 'He appears to be remarkable among the princes of India for his mildness, frugality, and attention to business, to be sensible of what he owes to the British.'

A decade further on, however, a dispute erupted over jurisdiction of lands the raja claimed, but which the Company said lay outside his domains. Court politics concerning appointment of the prime minister complicated matters. The British set up a commission of inquiry, which found Pratap Singh guilty of various offenses that violated his settlement with the British, including establishing contacts with the Portuguese in Goa, intrigues with the deposed ruler of Nagpur and attempts to spread subversion among soldiers. The British presented Pratap Singh with three options: a formal trial, hostile operations by which they would take full possession of Satara, or admission of his misdeeds and chastisement. The raja pled his innocence and refused to sign a statement acknowledging breach of the treaty with the British. Recalling Appa Sahib's words, he stated that he would not retain sovereignty at the expense of honour. He was thus deposed, and transported to Benares, his second procession under the British including a retinue of 2,700 family members, servants and followers, and over 1,300 animals.[7]

The next Indian monarch to suffer deposition was undoubtedly the most famous, Duleep Singh, the Sikh ruler of Punjab and 'Queen Victoria's maharaja'.[8] Duleep Singh came to the throne at the age of five in 1843 on the death of his father, Ranjit Singh, 'lion of the Punjab'. Two years later his subjects and the East India Company engaged in a war precipitated by border disputes. The treaty ending the conflict turned Punjab effectively into a British protectorate but did not still Sikh opposition, even in the palace. In 1847, the British placed the regent, Duleep Singh's mother Jindan Kaur, in detention, moving her the following year to the remote North West Provinces; she managed to escape and made her way to Nepal, whose ruler provided refuge. Meanwhile, the death of a British agent ignited a second Anglo-Sikh War, won by the British in 1849. The British ominously told the now eleven-year-old maharaja that he must sign away his rights to Punjab or risk his safety. On 30 March, holding his last durbar, Duleep Singh renounced the throne, and the British annexed Punjab. They removed Duleep to Fategarh in the North West Provinces.

A final deposition occurred in 1856, the year before the 'Mutiny'.[9] The scene was Oudh, another state under Company control. Its last ruler, Wajid Ali Shah, was enthroned in 1847, though the British found him spendthrifty and dissipated. Their antagonism mounted at the ruler's appointment of a chief minister without British consent, and spread to issues surrounding taxation and the question of succession (since Wajid's eldest son was deaf and dumb). With antipathy reaching a climax, the British demanded that Wajid abdicate, or he would be forcibly removed. In a scene memorably dramatised in Satyajit Ray's 1977 film *The Chess Players*, in a meeting with the British commander James Outram, Wajid removed his turban and handed it to the general as a sign of his submission.[10] He agreed to leave Oudh for Calcutta (Kolkata).

Thus were five early nineteenth-century sovereigns arbitrarily deposed under the East India Company. The fates of the deposed varied considerably, though none went quietly. Pratap Singh continued to protest his ouster, and particularly lack of due process in his removal. In a letter published in 1845, he bemoaned:

> My State Territories and my Private Property have been confiscated, and I have been consigned to degradation, ignominy, banishment, and perpetual exile, *without a hearing*, on charges, which have never yet been stated to me – on evidence, collected in secrecy, and never yet submitted to me for examination. I have been condemned to the forfeiture of my throne, my reputation, and my property. In pursuance of this arbitrary sentence, I have been driven from my palace and my country.[11]

Several champions took up his cause in Britain, though more in opposition to the East India Company than sympathy for an Indian raja. The Court of Directors of the Company eventually examined his case in a stormy session. George Thompson, a shipper and shareholder, argued that the government in Bombay, eager to acquire Pratap's realm, had manoeuvred to take him down in contravention of a law requiring an 'express' order from the governor-general against a ruler for commencing hostilities against the British or negotiating with foreign powers; moreover, testimony at the inquiry had been fraudulent. Thompson railed:

> That you condemned the Raja, wholly unheard [in his own defence], is notorious. That you dethroned him, in violation of the express provisions of a Statue Law of this realm, is, to me, a fact equally clear and unquestionable ... I put the question of guilt or innocence aside. The point for which I contend is that, that guilty, or not guilty – heard or unheard – the dethronement of the Raja was a manifestly illegal act, and is therefore null and void.

A Mr Gordon, alluding to earlier business scandals, criticised the directors as 'unworthy to be entrusted with administration of justice, as they were formerly unworthy to be entrusted with the affairs of commerce'. 'Great interruption' and 'confusion' broke out at this point, and 'during these, and the subsequent remarks of Mr. Gordon, a large number of the Proprietors created at intervals great noise, by beating the floor and the benches with their umbrellas and heels'. Gordon continued (to 'laughter and uproar'): 'By your conduct in the case of this unfortunate Raja, you have for ever damned yourself in public estimation.'[12]

Nothing came of the appeal, though the stir further compromised the parlous reputation of the Company. What was at stake in London was not so much the fate of Pratap as that of the Company, which had been on the receiving end of mounting criticism since the late 1700s for corruption, illegal enrichment of its administrators and blatant exploitation of its territories.[13] Back in Benares, however, there was no joy for Pratap, who died in 1847, just three months before the death of his successor, a brother who produced no male heir – the British refused to recognise a youth adopted on his deathbed. Implementing the doctrine of lapse, the British annexed Satara.

The king of Oudh also protested innocence, and dispatched his mother, brother and son to Britain to seek reversal of the takeover of Oudh; they hoped at least to get leave for the family to return to Lucknow, a city famous for its architecture and glittering culture.[14] Several sympathetic newspaper articles greeted their arrival, Queen Victoria received the rani, and a few ministers seemed well disposed to Wajid. The Oudh royals were still in Britain when the 1857 rebellion broke out, which changed both the situation and British perspectives. The British, fearing Wajid might become a focus of resistance in Calcutta, though he condemned the uprising, placed him in detention in Fort William. The focus of the emissaries in London now became his release from incarceration, though the British refused any accommodation, and the Indians left London. (The rani died unexpectedly on the return home, and was buried in Paris.) The British released Wajid in July 1859, and he returned to his Calcutta residence on the banks of the Hughli River. Wajid there recreated a court with between 5,000 and 8,000 people, including sentinels, servants and tradesmen, eunuchs, and reportedly thieves, prostitutes and other hangers-on. There was also a printing press, steam engines, and a collection of peacocks, monkeys, tigers, leopards and bears. Wajid's domain, in Rosie Llewelyn-Jones' words, was 'a small but exotic town, a miniature Lucknow, which provided a home to the king and a steady irritant to the government of India for thirty years'. Wajid continued to enjoy the title of 'king' or at least 'ex-king' in British usage, though he lost his gun salute. He died in 1887, leaving twenty-two surviving sons; the last, Prince Asfar, became a sheriff of Calcutta, member of the Executive Council of Bengal and mainstay of the Bengal Flying Club, and died in 1940.[15]

Both Virarajendra, after years of banishment in Benares, and Duleep Singh of Punjab ended up in Britain.[16] Virarajenda planned to file suit in the London chancery court against the East India Company for recovery of his confiscated wealth, but the ostensible reason he used to gain British permission to travel was so that his daughter Gowramma could have a Christian education. This successfully played on British sentiment, and after their arrival, Gowramma was baptised, Queen Victoria serving as godmother – Gowramma took Victoria as her Christian name – and presenting an inscribed Bible.[17] In 1853, Duleep Singh also converted to Christianity and was allowed to go to Britain, and the handsome Indian prince quickly became a favourite of Queen Victoria and Prince Albert. On one of his visits, the queen showed him the Koh-i-noor diamond – one of the largest in existence and a Sikh treasure – which the British had seized when they took over Punjab and had recut; Duleep Singh left Victoria greatly touched when he handed it back and formally 'presented' it to the queen.[18]

Victoria commissioned portraits and busts of Duleep Singh and Gowramma,[19] and tried to play match-maker between the two Christian converts. The pair did not hit it off, however. Duleep Singh ended up marrying the German-Ethiopian daughter of a merchant he met in Cairo after a trip back to India, while Gowramma chose a much older but dashing British officer. Her father, the Coorg raja, never gained satisfaction from the East India Company, and his status as a celebrity had waned by his death in 1863; Gowramma, whose husband had abandoned her and their daughter, died just a year later.

Duleep Singh had a dramatic life after his deposition. Given a generous pension by the British, the debonair Sikh became a fixture in high society and eventually lived on a 17,000-acre estate, Elveden Hall, in Suffolk, where he enjoyed sports, carousing and womanising, often in the company of British aristocrats. As he ran up high debts, creditors warned of bankruptcy and the British government proved increasingly reluctant to cover his expenses. (The queen chided him gently: 'as an old friend, excuse me for saying that I think, you are considered a little inclined to extravagance'.[20]) By the 1880s his alienation had grown alongside his debts: he abandoned his wife, kept limited contact with his children, and took to drink. Duleep Singh also turned fiercely against the British, now signing himself 'the lawful Sovereign of the Sikhs', co-authoring a book highly critical of annexation of Punjab, and accusing the British government of trying to ruin him by not providing sufficient means. He began calling the British his bitterest enemies, made contact with Irish rebels, and approached the Russian tsar with proposals to rout the British from India. He renounced Christianity and reconverted to the Sikh faith. In 1886, Duleep Singh determined to go to India once again – he had visited twice since his exile – but the British, concerned about his new attitudes, turned him back in Aden. He fled to Europe, and spent most of the rest of his life in Paris, where he died in 1893, though not before a final audience with Queen Victoria, in the south of France, where he wept as he beseeched her to forgive his waywardness. She gave her pardon, and later sent a wreath to his funeral.

The lives of Duleep Singh's children were similarly dramatic. Two sons were educated at Cambridge (and held army officer commissions), two daughters at Oxford. Victor lived as a country squire with a particular passion for shooting; another passion, spending money like his father, led him into bankruptcy. Frederick acquired a Tudor manor house, entertained titled British personages, took a near professional interest in archaeology and architecture, and collected art and antiques. Neither set foot in India. Catherine, a supporter of women's suffrage and Indian nationalism, spent much of her adult life in Berlin, in an intimate relationship with a German woman. Bamba briefly studied medicine in Chicago, and eventually moved to Lahore, where she married a British academic. The remarkable Sophia, whose life story has been deftly told by Sushila Anand, became involved as activist and donor in the campaign for votes for women. Regularly taking part in public protests, she escaped arrest only because the police did not want to charge a woman still officially recognised as a princess. She lived in a grace and favour residence provided by the monarch until her death in 1948. None of Duleep Singh's offspring had children.[21]

Duleep Singh, as Tony Ballantyne has shown, is a legendary figure, portrayed variously as an English gentleman from India, Victoria's indulgently treated protégé, a victim of British aggression, and a man whose anti-British pronouncements pointed towards India's struggle for independence. For a few British conservatives, he seems a pioneer in an unwelcome movement of migration from the subcontinent. For the proud Sikhs, including pilgrims to his tomb near the Suffolk estate, he remains an iconic symbol of culture and traditions, identity and nationhood. In 1999, the Prince of Wales unveiled a grand equestrian statue of the Punjab ruler in Thetford; the inscription in English and Punjabi speaks of 'bringing history and cultures together', and concludes: 'To this day the Sikh nation aspires to regain its sovereignty.'[22]

Princely exiles under the East India Company included rulers of powerful states such as Punjab and Oudh, as well as lesser ones. Duleep Singh, for a time, flourished in his banishment in Britain, and Wajid Ali Shah reigned over a reconstructed if diminished court in exile. The maharaja of Coorg struggled on in Britain, and the raja of Satara lived out his days in straitened circumstances in Benares, while Appa Sahib finished his life as a fugitive from the British. The Company attracted damnation for unbounded aggrandisement of territory and dubious processes of deposition. The queen looked fondly on the deposed princes even while she took pride and pleasure in the expansion of her dominion and added Duleep Singh's diamond to her jewellery-box. Soon India would be convulsed by an uprising and war that would lead to dissolution of the East India Company, bring down a native emperor, and make Victoria Empress of India.

The 1857 uprising and the exile of the Mughal emperor

In 1857, what the British branded the 'Mutiny' erupted, allegedly sparked by orders that Indian soldiers use their teeth to open paper cartridges that contained gunpowder and musket balls, but that was greased in pork and beef fat; the animal fat was highly offensive to Muslims and Hindus. The conflagration, now generally called the Great Uprising or Great Rebellion, and by some judged the first war of independence against the British in India, spread throughout the subcontinent, with much loss of life from attacks on the British and

Bahadurshah & his Queen

Figure 4 A postcard showing portraits of the last Mughal emperor, Bahadur Shah Zafar (1775–1862, r. 1837–57), alongside his consort. The emperor, deposed after the Indian 'Mutiny' of 1857, is shown here wearing his ceremonial robes, headdress and jewels.

bloodthirsty repression of the Indians. The events resulted, as well, in deposition of the Mughal emperor, Bahadur Shah Zafar (see Figure 4).

Zafar had succeeded to the throne two decades earlier, by which time the Mughal empire was in grave decline and the new emperor was already sixty years old.[23] His reign did mark a fine twilight for the dynasty with a blaze of cultural achievements, including the emperor's own Urdu poetry, while the British appropriated more and more territory that nominally came under Mughal suzerainty.[24] When the rebelling sepoys took control of Delhi in 1857, they acclaimed Zafar as emperor and titular leader of their efforts to eject the British from India. Zafar named his eldest son, Mirza, as commander-in-chief of the uprising, though he later claimed he did so under duress. When the British invaded Delhi, Zafar and his sons took refuge at Hamayun's Tomb, the burial-ground of the Mughal emperor. Major William Hodson surrounded the site and forced Zafar's surrender, then shot two of Zafar's sons and his grandson. Meanwhile, the British pillaged the emperor's Red Fort.

A frightened Zafar was held in conditions so miserable that they evoked pity from a visiting former British MP who questioned, 'Is that the way, as Christians, we ought to treat a King?'[25] The British placed Zafar on trial, on the shaky legal grounds that since he received a pension from the Company and was its subject, he was liable to British justice. As William Dalrymple suggests, however, the Company's authority issued from the emperor, and he was, in principle, their master.[26] Zafar, in any case, was charged with aiding the rebels, treason against the British, and being accessory to murder of British subjects. Zafar remained disconnected from the proceedings held by the military tribunal, though he presented one short written defence. Judges unanimously found him guilty on all charges. The British honoured Hodson's unauthorised promise that Zafar's life would be spared, and he was exiled, along with a wife and two surviving sons, to Burma (after the Cape Colony had been rejected as a site of detention).[27]

In Rangoon (Yangon) in 1859, according to Captain H. N. Davies, the eighty-odd-year-old Zafar's 'memory is still good, where time is allowed him to fix his ideas, but his articulation is indistinct consequent on the loss of his teeth. He certainly does not now give the impression of being capable of any extended mental energy or capacity but on the whole he appears to bear his weight of years remarkably well'. His consort, Zenat Mahal, spoke to the official from behind a screen, and unlike the apathetic emperor, continued to voice remonstrations, argued that during the uprising, 'the Royal family were at the mercy of the Rebels and she constantly avers that they were thus helpless'. She also complained about loss of her jewels and other treasures confiscated after the emperor's conviction. The emperor's sons, around ten and fifteen, 'are both healthy and promising youths'. The older, Jawan Bakht, 'exhibits an appearance and deportment of superiority ... induced more from his present recognized position in the family, rather than from any decided superiority in his character and attainments, he having been born a prince, whereas his less fortunate half brother is but the son of a "Hand Maiden"'. Davies found both 'extremely ignorant', but noted that they wished to learn English and hoped to be sent to Britain.[28]

A report by Lieutenant-Colonel Arthur Phayre, filed the following year, concluded: 'Zafar and his family are in every respect, as regards their wants, comforts and occupations, as well cared for as possible.' They lived in a wooden bungalow, and the emperor spent much time on the veranda, watching passers-by through bamboo blinds that shielded him from their gaze. Jawan Bakht now left each morning for instruction in English, and Phayre suggested that he and his half-brother might be allowed greater liberties (although with attendants on their walks 'so as to prevent intercourse with the inhabitants'). Phayre assured London that 'there is nothing in the present status of these prisoners which excites any sympathy in any class of the population. It is known that they are well treated. The Burmese seem scarcely to know of their presence here'.[29]

The emperor died in 1862 and was buried by the British, intentionally, in a nondescript tomb.[30] In 1903, a visiting Indian was so concerned about the dilapidated state of the grave and lack of a monument that he published a book echoing the MP's comment about the treatment of the captive emperor (and quoted Thomas Grey's line, 'in this neglected spot is laid'): 'To the Britons who read this, may I point out that there is more at stake than the mere granting of a favour asked by the Muslims ... more than courtesy to a dead sovereign's remains or statues to a poet's memory – the honour of our nation, the honour of Britain is at stake.'[31] The site nevertheless received little attention, though the Indian nationalist Subhas Chandra Bose was said to issue his Second World War call for the liberation of India from Zafar's tomb in Japanese-occupied Burma. Only in the 1990s were the bodies of the emperor, his wife and a granddaughter disinterred and housed in a befitting mausoleum. Surrounded by a metal rail, covered in richly patterned cloths strewn with flowers by guardians and visitors, the emperor's sarcophagus is surmounted by a large metal crown-like ornament. There are colourful banners, commemorative plaques and photographs of the emperor and his family, as well as of Indian and Pakistani dignitaries who come to pay their respects. In 2009, the Indian vice-president, Hamid Ansari, after reciting a prayer, remarked, 'The people of India cherish the memory of that moment in the First War of Independence whose rallying point was Bahadur Shah Zafar'.[32] Two years later, the Indian External Affairs Minister S. M. Krishna spoke in Rangoon of Zafar as a 'great patriot'.[33] An Indian newspaper reports that each November 'thousands of people' attend an annual prayer service at the tomb.[34] The Burmese also honour the emperor; according to a mausoleum guardian, 'Bahadur Shah was not only an emperor, but also a poet-scholar and he is recognised here as a *pir* or saint. Along with Muslims, Buddhists, Hindus and Christians come here to seek his blessings'.[35] The last emperor thus continues to occupy a place in Indian, Pakistani and Burmese memory, and thanks largely to Dalrymple's best-selling book, perhaps a niche in British memory.[36]

The new order: India after 1857

In a proclamation in 1858, Queen Victoria announced 'to the Native Princes of India that all Treaties and Engagements made with them by or under the authority of the Honourable East India Company are by Us accepted, and will be scrupulously maintained'. The Crown foreswore any territorial aggrandisement of British possessions, and promised that 'We shall respect the Rights, Dignity, and Honour of Native Princes as Our own'; it would also respect the religions practised in India. Lamenting the 'evils and misery' of 1857, it declared an amnesty for all except rebels who took part directly in the 'Murder of British Subjects'. The proclamation concluded with 'Our earnest Desire to stimulate the peaceful Industry of India, to promote Works of Public Utility and Improvement, and to administer its Government for the benefit of all Our Subjects resident therein'.[37] The people of India, including the 'Native Princes', were now British subjects. The princes reigned as feudatories of the British Crown, liege-men of the monarch represented by the governor-general, who took on the further title of viceroy. At an Imperial Assembly of 1877, held after the proclamation of Victoria as empress, and the imperial durbars of 1903 and 1911, the rulers were called upon to make public obeisance to the viceroy or, on the last occasion, to the king-emperor in person. The relationship between the British monarch and the Indian princes was hierarchical, but also considered a partnership in which British governing elites and Indian rulers could collaborate for the betterment of the empire. That collaboration depended on the princes' willingness to prove themselves worthy of the colonisers and submit to the demands of the British.

The British hoped to achieve this result by keeping close watch on the princes and their administrations through Residents and Agents at their courts. Heirs to the throne were carefully groomed, sent to elite schools in India and sometimes on to British universities; a classical education and initiation into sport provided proper preparation for competent rule and loyalty. Princes who did well earned rewards through marks of respect, such as gun salutes, the number carefully calculated (and alterable) to reflect a state's significance and viceregal pleasure. Return visits by the viceroy after a prince paid a visit to the Crown's representative were a coveted entitlement. Queen Victoria also established orders of chivalry for the Raj – the Orders of the Indian Empire, the Star of India and Crown of India – complete with mantles, sashes and medals. Visits to London, subject to viceregal authorisation, offered yet another benefit for loyal vassals.[38] The princes retained control of their families and extensive courts, certain rights in dispensation of justice, taxation, local lawmaking and other areas of administration, the performance of dynastic and religious ceremonies.[39] The grander princes enjoyed wealth – land, palaces, jewellery, artwork – that even to European royals was fantastic.

The sentiments of respect expressed in the 1858 proclamation did not keep the government of India from censuring rulers, following precedents established by the defunct East India Company. Fiona Groenhout, who has explored post-Uprising depositions most fully, emphasises that the outright ouster of a ruler became a relatively rarely used strategy. She suggests that in late Victorian India and afterwards, the primary situation in which it was deployed occurred when the British decided a ruler was morally and politically irredeemable, or when he had directly threatened Britons in India.[40]

Commissions of inquiry and viceregal ouster of a ruler represented very serious actions, generally reserved for princes who repeatedly refused to adhere to British demands or who were implicated in offences that would have been deemed criminal if princes did not have immunity to criminal prosecution. Such extreme measures, Groenhout stresses, ran the risk of alienating other princes by endangering the autonomy they claimed; the colonial order rested on continued acknowledgement of princes' rights and cordial relations. When other attempts to persuade a ruler to mend his ways failed, dethroning, accompanied by banishment from the prince's capital or state, nevertheless remained an option. The major difference after 1858 was that overthrowing a ruler did not result in British annexation of a state, but the replacement of the offending ruler by another, a carefully selected and frequently very youthful one.

The pages that follow, evoking ten cases of deposition, illustrate the cirumstances in which dethroning was precipitated, and also some of the ways in which the practice of kingship by Indians regularly contrasted with proclaimed British principles of governance. The innocence or guilt of individuals might still be debated – few were accorded real opportunities to exonerate themselves – and standards of probity and morality, of course, depended on varying perspectives of the period, culture and country. Maintenance of British rule, when all was said and done, trumped any other consideration in decisions about accused rulers. The targeted figures constituted only a small fraction of the many hundreds of maharajas and other princes who reigned from the Uprising until British withdrawal nine decades later. There were, after all, some six hundred princely states encompassed in the British empire in India, from Hyderabad, roughly the size of Britain, to polities little larger than a British country town. These cases show, however, the dynamics of personal and political interactions among indigenous and foreign governing elites, and the consequences of perceived misrule and challenges to imperialist power.

The details of some episodes could fill the pages of pulp novels. The first major post-Uprising deposition occurred in Baroda (Valdodara), one of the largest and richest states of Gujarat, whose ruler in the 1870s, Gaekwar Mulhar Rao, was entitled to the maximum twenty-one gun salute.⁴¹ The British Resident at his court, Colonel Robert Phayre, accused the gaekwar of ill treatment of his subjects, extortion of payment for appointments, seizure of women for the palace harem and torture of opponents. An initial investigation led to removal of the state's chief minister. The gaekwar kept his throne, but asked the viceroy to remove Phayre. The Resident then alleged that Mulhar Rao had tried to kill him by having arsenic and diamond dust mixed into the pomelo sherbet he drank after his habitual morning walk. A formal commission of inquiry, with three European members and three Indians (including two fellow maharajas), took testimony from courtiers and servants, Indians and British, but the inquiry ended with a 'hung jury'. The Europeans concluded that the charges against the gaekwar were proven, the Indian members that evidence was neither credible nor corroborated. The viceroy adjudicated, deciding in 1875 that Mulhar Rao would be deposed, not for culpability in the alleged poisoning, but for 'his noxious misconduct, his gross misgovernment of the State, and his evident incapacity to carry into effect reforms'.⁴² The British took away the gaekwar to Madras (Chennai), where he died in obscurity seven years later, with a youthful member of a cadet branch of his family placed on the throne in his stead.

Several decades later, in Rewa, a state now in Madhya Pradesh, the process of removing a maharaja reprised the Baroda affair. Maharaja Gulab Singh came to the throne at the age of fifteen, in 1918, but his sexual proclivities incurred British disapproval. The Resident reported that he 'takes about with him quite openly ... about two dozen young boys known as the "Anandi ['pleasure' or 'bliss'] Party". I have even got a photograph of this party all in women's clothes and ornaments, and ... letters in His Highness's own handwriting ... showing the degree and manner of his degradation'. Private conduct was generally not enough to censure a ruler, though British concern mounted with manifestations of the maharaja's sympathies for the Congress Party and because of petitions from subjects discontented with new taxes. Issues of morals again arose, now mixed with bloodshed, in 1937, when one of the maharaja's aides-de-camp, Shankar Prasad, shot another aide-de-camp, Uma Prasad, supposedly on the maharaja's orders. The two were reputed to be competing for the prince's sexual attentions. Shankar was then also killed, the maharaja personally escorting his murderer out of Rewa. Gulab Singh surprisingly still survived on the throne, but the trial for bribery of one of his clerks in 1941 added another point to his charge sheet. The British suspended the maharaja and organised a commission of inquiry, the first convened according to new regulations that had come into force in 1920. The members' verdict, as in Baroda, split along ethnic lines, and the viceroy again found against the maharaja.

Declaring Gulah Singh implicated in bribery, he finessed the added accusations into conviction for 'other delinquencies and defects in your capacity for rulership'. Yet once more, Gulab Singh was nevertheless allowed to remain on the throne, though now stripped of real power. He was finally done in with a speech in 1945 promising responsible government for his state and adult franchise. When his removal was ordered, Groenhout recounts how the Resident, in a late-night chase, pursued the maharaja as he tried to escape by motorcar, took him into custody and spirited him across the state border to exile in Allahabad; he died in 1950. The catalogue of misdeeds against Gulab Singh was long and varied – his sexual behaviour, implication in bribery and murder, anti-British political sympathies – but what is striking, perhaps, is British forbearance to take decisive action against him over so many years.[43]

Allegations of sexual shenanigans and death plots also figured in removal of Maharaja Madho Singh in the small state of Panna (also in Madhya Pradesh). The Hindu prince, after fathering no children with the maharani, expressed his intention to marry his pregnant mistress, a Muslim dancing-girl. The ruler's powerful uncle strongly opposed the union and eventual succession by their child, but he was found poisoned with strychnine and arsenic. A formal inquiry mandated Madho Singh's deposition – which Groenhout says was a foregone conclusion since the British thought him a debauched despot – and he died in Ballary, in Karnataka, in 1931.[44]

An earlier incident occurred in the neighbouring, but much more prominent state of Indore in 1925, and a prince's mistress again was at the centre. Maharaja Tukoji Rao III was known as a handsome lothario; one of his paramours was Mumtaz Begun, who had entered his court as a girl (see Figure 5).

According to her later statements, the maharaja had forced his attentions on her and kept her as a virtual prisoner, though showering her with gifts; she broke with him in her mid-twenties when her newly-born child, she alleged, had been killed by nurses. She fled from Indore to Bombay with her new lover, a man called Abdul Kadir Bawla. Driving on Malabar Hill, their car was attacked by men said to be acting for the maharaja and intending to kidnap Mumtaz Begun; she was injured, and Bawla killed. The 'Bawla case' excited public opinion, and three men convicted for the attack were hanged. The British offered Tukoji Rao a choice between abdication and a commission of inquiry. He chose the former, and spent much of the rest of his life – he died only in 1978 – in considerable luxury and married to an American, in Switzerland.[45]

Irregular sexual activities – irregular at least in British eyes – elsewhere contributed to the overthrow of rulers. Maharaja Shivaji Rao of

Figure 5 An International Newsreel photo of Maharaja Tukojirao Holkar II (1890–1978, r. 1903–26), with a note on the back explaining that it 'shows the wealthy Maharaja of Indore, storm center in international scandal, involving the murder of Abdul Kadir Bawla, rich Bombay merchant, who befriended Mumtaz Begum, formerly one of the maharaja's favorite dancing girls'.

Indore (Tukoji Rao's father) came to the throne in 1886 with the promise that his male lover would not attend events at which British officers were present. He was characterised in officials' correspondence as a lunatic and sodomite, with a propensity to 'gross and unnatural sexual indulgence' – the secretary of state for India lamented to the viceroy that 'so considerable a proportion of the Chiefs of India are addicted to unnatural vices'. The British and the ruler had a rocky relationship and, on and off for years, the maharaja offered to abdicate only to withdraw the offer, though finally he agreed to go once he had attended the 1903 durbar celebrating the coronation of Edward VII. After the durbar and enthronement of his son, Shivaji Rao gave up his position and retired to a country estate eight kilometres from his old capital, the viceroy smugly noting that 'nothing in Maharaja Shivaji Rao's official life became him so well as his leaving it'.[46]

A fourth case of sexual impropriety concerned the Maharaja of Dewas Senior (in a Maratha state in western India). He was Tukoji Rao III Puar, fondly recalled in *The Hill of Devi* by E. M. Forster, who was employed for a time at his court. The maharaja's homosexual inclinations hardly pleased the British in Dewas or elsewhere – homosexual acts had been criminalised in British India – but they were more anxious about the near bankruptcy of the state. When a commission of inquiry was threatened in 1931, Tukoji Rao fled to the French territory of Pondichéry (Puducherry), where he lived the remainder of his life.[47]

The Maharaja of Datia (yet another state in Madhya Pradesh), Govindh Singh, who had come to power in 1907, also earned a reputation for licence, including homosexuality; the British first tried to set him straight by sending him on manly hunting expeditions to rural India and South Africa in the years before the First World War. He returned, resumed his powers, and took up his old ways. The maharaja by the 1920s was said to suffer from syphilis and an ulcerated anus as a consequence, and the British accused him with neglect of duty, profligacy, depletion of the state's reserves and a range of other misdeeds. Once again, the British threatened a commission of inquiry, which inspired Govind Singh to reform (and he apparently recovered from his maladies). When he slid back into his old practices, the British finally had enough and deposed him in 1946.[48]

Maharajas' morals, especially if they had a homosexual bent, regularly raised British eyebrows, but did not suffice to provoke deposition unless accompanied by financial and political failings or murderous plots.[49] Affairs of state held more importance than *affaires des moeurs*, though some connections existed, notably in the way that 'improper' sexual liaisons compromised a prince's reputation in the eyes of the British, suggesting or confirming character defects that undermined a ruler. If admonitions (or a hunting trip) did not 'man up' and moralise a prince, the British could resort to other tactics, notably the threat of a commission of inquiry. If that secured abdication (or flight for the maharaja of Dewas Senior), so much the better, and this avoided the need for removal directly by viceregal decree. The offending prince was thus shifted safely away, with what the British hoped was an appropriate heir installed on the throne.

In a few cases, more explicit worries about a ruler's political behaviour rather than just immorality or incompetence loomed larger. In the Rajput state of Alwar, Maharaja Jay Singh began his reign, as a youth, in 1892 and developed a reputation as a model monarch for his modernisation programmes. Reports circulated, however, about his eccentricity, including a newsworthy incident in which he was slighted by a dealer at a Rolls-Royce showroom in London, and bought six of the automobiles, shipped them home and used them for rubbish collection. He was also accused of cruelty – he allegedly staged combats between wild animals, and once doused with oil and set alight an underperforming polo pony – and for failure to show proper respect to British officials. (He dared, for instance, to wear gloves when shaking viceregal hands.) Central to his deposition, however, were conflicts with the Meo, a Muslim minority in Alwar, who complained that Jay Singh was pursuing a policy of Hinduisation – giving Hindi names to government departments, banning Urdu and Persian in state schools, demolishing mosques. After rioting and the sending in of troops to restore order, the British gave the maharaja forty-eight hours to leave Alwar. Though he did not abdicate, Jay Singh moved to Europe and lived there until he was found dead at the bottom of a stairway in Paris, presumably following an accident, in 1937.[50]

In the small but strategically placed far northeastern state of Manipur, at the confines of India and the recently conquered northern Burma, the end of the reign of Maharaja Surchandra in 1891 followed on dramatic palace intrigues, in which two half-brothers wrested away Surchandra's throne. The rebels attacked the British; the Resident was murdered, and his widow heroically escaped, made her way back to Britain, was comforted by Queen Victoria, and wrote an account of her experiences. The British captured the maharaja's palace, held by the usurpers, in the culmination of the brief 'Anglo-Manipur War', which was nevertheless 'the greatest single military challenge to British rule' in India since 1857, according to Caroline Keen. The British arrested the two rebel leaders, and their trial came to the attention of Queen Victoria. She wired the secretary of state for India to express disapproval of any execution of the two princes, as it 'would create bad feeling in Manipur and in all India. But shut him up in some distant part. Think no prince was ever hung'. When she learned that the death sentence would be carried out on one of the men – the other was deported to the Andaman Islands – she wrote again, doubting that the measure would 'be of use in deterring others', and adding that 'hanging a person (and he a Prince) so long after he has been kept a prisoner [in fact, it was only a few months] has something cruel and cold-blooded about it'. Using the third person, as was her custom, she expressed 'great and strong feeling that the principle of governing India by fear and *crushing* them, instead of by firmness and conciliation, *is one* which will never answer to the end and which the Queen-Empress would wish to see more and more altered'.[51] The rebels were punished despite the queen's objections – reservations that echoed the sentiments confided to her diary about deposed Indian princes almost forty years earlier in the context of her contacts with the Coorg and Punjab maharajas – and the British refused to restore Surchandra, thus effectively confirming his deposition; he died in Calcutta in 1892.[52]

In the Sikh state of Nabha, which has been analysed by Barbara Ramusack, Maharaja Ripudaman Singh lost his position in 1928 after a long-standing dynastic conflict with a neighbouring maharaja. However, his sympathies with nationalists, and particularly his support for an anti-British Sikh organisation, the Akali Dal, so worried the British that they forced him to leave his state – he was driven away in an armoured vehicle to Dehra Dun, 240 kilometres from Nabha. Ripudaman kept his title and gun salute, as well as a yearly pension, and promised formally to abdicate when his son and heir came of age. Several Sikh groups, however, took up his cause and organised protests centred on ritual recitation of the Sikh scriptures. The British proceeded with arrests, and violence threatened. The Congress Party became interested in the affair and sent a committee, including Jawaharlal Nehru, to investigate, and they too were arrested and briefly detained, then expelled from Nabha. Unrest continued for several years. In 1928, the British managed to wring out Ripudaman's formal abdication, and he was sent to live in the Madras region, where he died in 1942.[53]

These summaries of the incidents in Manipur and Nabha do not do justice to the complexity of the political issues or manoeuvres there. They do show that challenges to British overrule could not go unanswered. In the case of Manipur, the British quelled a revolt at the end of the nineteenth century that played out with an armed confrontation that harked back to conquests of territory at the time of the East India Company half a century earlier. In Nabha, the clash revealed the ferment of nationalist sentiment, opposition to British rule and the various anti-colonial strategies of such political organisations as the Congress Party and Akali Dal that would lead to the independence of India less than two decades later.

Both in Manipur and Nabha, and in the cases going back to the early 1800s, determination to extend and maintain British imperial authority prompted removal of native princes who represented obstacles. Before 1857, the Company did not hesitate to strike when it wanted to increase the territory under its control, ready to withstand the criticism that actions sometimes provoked, as shown in the experience of the raja of Satara. Under the new regime after 1858, the British government was more guarded in 'firing' its feudatories, but criticisms still arose, including from the pen of the queen. However, when officials decided that a prince was incorrigible and irredeemable, or if personal conduct, provocation of subjects' discontent, flagrant lack of financial probity or sympathy for nationalists threatened the British, then a ruler had to go – usually pushed to do so by strong-armed persuasion, threats of an inquiry or, when necessary, by viceregal decree even if a 'jury' had not agreed on a guilty verdict.

Deposed maharajas never won satisfaction for their grievances. Some gained celebrity or notoriety in Britain, even if latter-day exiles almost never garnered the attention of Duleep Singh, who for a time was the darling of the court, London society and the country gentry. The Coorg maharajah had his moment of fame in London in the mid-1800s, but the other deposed rulers did not visit Britain, with the exception of the ousted Tukoji Rao of Indore in 1928 – and the British fretted about the influence he might exercise when he called on his son and successor, Yashwant, who was a student at Christ Church, Oxford. Most of the other dethroned rulers were distant from Britain, their removal sideshows in the bigger spectacle of empire. In the case of Zafar, deposition was thought payment for the infamy of the 'Mutiny', and most Britons likely considered the ouster of others – if they kept themselves apprised of Indian news – as the just deserts for immorality, corruption and anti-British agitation. Avenues of appeal for the toppled rulers were effectively limited to the court of public opinion, difficult to stimulate from far away and in the context of imperialist fervour. None of the princes was reinstated, and most of the successors – though the Indore father and son exiles proved an exception – more or less satisfied British expectations. The princely dynasties continued to reign during the twilight years of the empire, the majority considered by Indian nationalists to have a too accommodating relationship with the British overlords. Many princes, though handicapped by the might of Britannia, had played the imperial game against the British with great strategic skill through conflicts and warfare, negotiations and compromises, enthronements, depositions and successions to thrones: the metaphor of a chess match used in Satyajit Ray's film about Oudh is brilliantly pertinent. Just a year before the British quit India, they could still move to dethrone a maharaja who failed to play by their rules, but when checkmate was called in 1947, it was the British king who was toppled.

The road from Mandalay: the exile of the king of Burma

East of India lay Burma, whose king enjoyed a spiritual aura as protector of the Buddhist faith as well as wide powers of administration, justice and taxation, though much administration remained in the hands of the heads of townships, the Shan princes in the eastern parts of the country, and 'tribal' chiefs elsewhere. Though to outsiders it thus sometimes appeared a lawless land over which bandits ('dacoits') swarmed, Burma beguiled travellers with grand golden temples, green rice paddies, the magnificent Irrawaddy river and images of friendly people leading a simple village life. Rudyard Kipling's 'The Road to Mandalay', one of the canonical colonial-era poems, memorialised the allure. Burma's strategic position between India and China, fertile land, good ports and powerful river systems, as well precious gemstones – including one of the world's largest deposits of rubies – and tropical hardwoods meant Burma offered much to excite colonisers.

After a war in 1825, Britain acquired the southern provinces of Arakan and Tenarassim; following a second war, in 1853, their holdings expanded to include Rangoon and the rest of 'Lower Burma'. In 1885, Britain completed the conquest by taking over the royal capital of Mandalay and 'Upper Burma', and as part of that third campaign, the colonisers dethroned and exiled King Thibaw and his consort Queen Supayalat.[54]

Thibaw's predecessor, King Mindon, who ruled from 1853 to 1878, had been considered by foreigners a modernising monarch; he had signed treaties with the British and French conceding rights of trade, though retaining royal monopolies over timber, precious stones and oil. In a dynastic tradition lacking primogeniture, a struggle for power generally followed the death of a king. Among Mindon's surviving twenty-two sons, Thibaw, a junior member of the extended royal family and at the time of his selection a monk, emerged triumphant. Much credit for his success went to Supayalat's deftly manoevuring mother. Foreign commentators found Thibaw a weak, unassuming figure, and pointed to Supayalat and her mother as continuing powers behind the throne. A German newspaper recorded one traveller's portrait of the king, muddling physical description with character assessment:

> somewhat stout for his age, being only twenty-one; but otherwise the best looking Burmese he had seen ... His hair was arranged in a big

top-knot on the top of his head, surrounded by a narrow band of white muslin; his round face, which was almost white, made a very pleasant impression; his eyes are small and slightly almond-shaped; and with his full lips and small moustache he makes the impression of an indolent, blasé, perhaps rather sensual young man. Cruelty is stamped upon his features, but not intemperance.[55]

Almost immediately after Thibaw took the throne, a massacre of between thirty and eighty rival princes and princesses took place in the grounds of the royal palace (see Figure 6). Whether the king or queen ordered the killings remains unknown; Supayalat said not, though many held her responsible.[56] Foreigners condemned the bloodletting – seen as further proof of Oriental despotism – and Britain withdrew its representative from Mandalay. Trading nevertheless continued, though the British faced political and commercial competition from France. Having taken over southern Vietnam in the late 1850s and 1860s and established a protectorate over the centre of the country in the 1870s, the French were expanding further north. For avid expansionists in Paris, Upper Burma also beckoned, especially with Anglo-Burmese

Figure 6 'Royal Palace – Mandalay', the palace of the Konbaung kings of Burma, from which King Thibaw (1859–1916, r. 1878–85) and Queen Supayalat (1859–1925) were deported by the British in 1885. Most of the palace was destroyed in Second World War bombing, but parts have now been reconstructed.

estrangement. The French pursued diplomatic contacts and commercial contracts that eventuated in a beneficial treaty in April 1884, and a formal Franco-Burmese alliance was mooted. Paris's ambassador in London hinted that Thibaw might be replaced by Prince Myingun, a French protégé.[57]

British officials looked with rising consternation on French actions (especially as France moved into Tonkin, northern Vietnam, in 1885). British merchants in Rangoon stepped up pressure for the takeover of Thibaw's kingdom, citing French designs, Burmese brutalities, the maintenance of Burmese royal trade monopolies that disadvantaged British business, and various slights to compatriots. The British found a *casus belli* in a conflict between the Mandalay government and the Bombay Burma Trading Corporation, which held leases for felling timber in return for payments to the royal treasury. The Burmese discovered that the British had not paid the commission on most of the logs delivered to the company, and demanded both payment and a hefty fine. Rejecting the demand, London ordered General Harry Prendergast to occupy Mandalay.

As a flotilla of British vessels set sail on the Irrawaddy, Prendergast issued an ultimatum to Thibaw to grant the British free trade and waive the fine imposed on the teak company. On 14 November 1885, the British then formally declared war and crossed the border between Lower and Upper Burma. Opinion divided in the Burmese court about the reaction. Queen Supayalat headed a faction calling for armed resistance, but the prime minister, the Kinwun Myingyi, arguing for negotiation, won over the king. When a message accepting the British ultimatum was sent, Prendergast announced that it was too late for conciliation – the British, in fact, had never intended negotiation.[58]

On 28 November, the British landed in Mandalay, having resisted a last-minute offer from Thibaw to settle their dispute. Prendergast and the senior British political officer, Colonel (later Sir) Edward Sladen, marched to the royal palace, and summoned Thibaw, Supayalat and the queen's mother.[59] Thibaw surrendered peacefully, and was peremptorily told that he was deposed and that his family would be sent to India, though the king for some time understood this to mean he would be taken to Calcutta for negotiations with the viceroy and might in due course return. Prendergast gave the royals one night to pack their belongings. Scenes of distress and chaos ensued as Burmese commoners forced their way into the palace. Many court treasures not packed away by the royals were stolen by the British or Burmese; the most valuable royal jewel, the ninety-carat Nga Mauk ruby, disappeared – according to Burmese royals, casually pocketed by Sladen – and has never been found.[60]

On 30 November, Thibaw, his wife and daughters, alongside other family members, after a final bow towards King Mindon's tomb, were led out of the palace compound, the senior royals transported in a covered bullock-cart, over which royal white umbrellas were still carried, the procession passing between lines of red-coated British soldiers. In scenes depicted by the court painter, Saya Chone, crowds of Burmese looked on, some prostrating themselves and wailing as the cortège made its way to the river port.[61] The royal family were placed aboard a ship for Rangoon, whence they set sail for India. Their eventual destination was Ratnagiri, on the western coast of the subcontinent, two hundred miles from Bombay. There Thibaw lived the rest of his life.

In London, Lord Randolph Churchill, secretary of state for India, celebrated what he called a New Year's gift for Queen Victoria, while Lord Dufferin, the viceroy, on 1 January 1886, formally proclaimed the deposition of Thibaw and annexation of Burma, but promised respect for Buddhism and its clergy. Reports of British pillage in Mandalay, summary executions, the burning of villages and what would now be regarded as torture nevertheless sparked much adverse reaction in Britain, especially one incident in which an army photographer got an execution delayed while he adjusted his camera to record the scene. Occupying the royal palace, British soldiers used the grand audience hall as a chapel, with an altar placed before the throne; the queen's throne room became the Upper Burma Club, complete with bar and billiard tables.

With Thibaw removed, the British hesitated about whether to find a replacement king. A Rangoon newspaper reported that 'the ministers comprising the Hlutdaw [privy council] have threatened to resign unless a prince be put on the throne'.[62] When the viceroy triumphantly visited Upper Burma in February 1886, he reported 'a great deal of sentimental reverence for Royal Blood', and noted that ministers would 'naturally prefer a king, provided we undertook to restrain him from abusing his authority'. There was no shortage of candidates despite the 1879 massacre, though Dufferin rejected the Myingun Prince because 'he would probably fall into the hands of French adventurers and concessionaires who would be constantly giving us trouble'. Dufferin ruled out another as 'disobedient to orders'. One option would be the 'placing on the throne of some child, but it would be tying ourselves down for the future without curtailing our obligations or reaping any present advantage'. Thus, 'the best course will be to assume at once and without further delay direct administration of the country', the viceroy concluded, sealing the end of the Burmese monarchy.[63]

Royalist resistance movements soon emerged, with Burmese rallying around one or another pretender (some with very dubious claims) – as had occurred seventy years earlier in Ceylon. The most significant was Myinzaing, a sixteen-year-old son of King Mindon. His supporters established a base east of Mandalay and recognised the young prince as king. A British official fretted that 'he was an important potential centre of disaffection' and 'many rebels chiefs ... professed to be fighting on his behalf'. Forced to retreat to a border province, Myinzaing's death of fever in late 1886 brought a premature end to his campaign. Other claimants failed to galvanise support, their movements suppressed by the British with considerable violence.[64]

Royalism, however, was not dead in Burma, even if it was over forty years before British rule was endangered by another man who would be king, Saya San. A fortune-teller (an honoured profession in Burma) and traditional doctor, in the late 1920s, Saya San became active in a nationalist group and called for the setting up of a monarchy with himself as sovereign. He adopted as emblem the Garuda bird ('Galon' in Burmese), the mystical creature that killed snakes: the Galon represented the Burmese, the snake the British.[65] In 1930, his followers proclaimed Saya San king, and the 'Galon King' was crowned at a pagoda. He recruited an army, its members tattooed with talismanic symbols to protect them from the enemy, and began a guerrilla war against the British. The British captured Saya San in 1931, and convicted and hanged the erstwhile king, making him a martyr for Burmese nationalists. Though historical judgements about the revolt differ, it underlined the potency of the monarchical idea, long after the ouster of Thibaw, as a symbol of resistance to colonialism and a rallying-point for national sentiment.

By the time of the Saya San uprising, the older members of the exiled Konbaung royal family had died: King Thibaw in 1916, Queen Supayalat in 1925. Sudha Shah's study has comprehensively traced the fate of the royals in exile,[66] and Amitav Ghosh's novel *The Glass Palace* provides a fascinating fictionalised portrayal.[67] The story is full of family dramas, attempts to maintain some semblance of the Konbaungs' former status, remonstrations to the British for better treatment, and British feelings of annoyance at what they regarded as the difficult behaviour of those who were both state prisoners and state pensioners in Ratnagiri. Thibaw and Supayalat eventually lived in a sixteen-room residence on a twenty-seven-acre estate, with garages for several carriages and motorcar, and quarters for around sixty servants. Though relatively comfortable, the court in exile could hardly compare with Mandalay, where Supyalat had three hundred maids of honour. 'His Highness the ex-King Thibaw', as he was officially addressed by the British (though informally allowed the superior style of 'His Majesty'), had seemed reconciled with his fate, though Supayalat remained resentful. When Thibaw died, the British refused to allow his burial in Burma, fearful that his grave might become a symbol for nationalists, but Supayalat and several of her daughters were allowed to go back to Rangoon. The queen lived the rest of her life there, and her remains are interred near the city's most famous temple, the Shwedagon Pagoda.

Four daughters of Thibaw and Supayalat, two born after the king's deposition, survived to adulthood. The eldest fell in love with an Indian gatekeeper in Ratnagiri; she accompanied her mother to Rangoon, but then renounced her title and moved back to Ratnagiri. The second daughter married a Burmese commoner – for which she was disowned by her mother – and did not return to Burma, but shifted her family to Kalimpong in eastern India. The third daughter, most popular of the children, after falling pregnant to a chauffeur, married a prince, though he was considered a wastrel; she was the last of the princesses to die, in Maymyo, in southern Burma, in 1962. The fourth daughter was the most militant guardian of the family's heritage, and in the early 1930s sent petitions to the British and the League of Nations demanding restitution of assets taken from her father and re-establishment of a Burmese kingdom within the British empire. She spent her later life in Mandalay.[68]

The present senior member of the royal family is Prince Taw Phaya (or Edward), son of the youngest of the princesses. Communists assassinated his eldest brother shortly after Burmese independence in 1948, and the military junta that came to power in 1962 imprisoned another brother – known as 'The Red Prince', because of Communist sympathies – on three occasions. Taw Phaya set up a successful import–export business, but fell on hard times with the socialism and nationalisation policies of the dictatorship after the 1962 military coup in Burma. Taw Phaya has remarked on the meanness of the pension given to his grandfather ('a small pittance for a former sovereign'), and British treatment of his descendants: 'We were always shunted off here and there ... The British had no concern for what today you would call human rights. We were told what to do and what not to do.' Though Taw Phaya has addressed letters to Queen Elizabeth and British officials complaining that the Burmese royals had 'lost their rightful prerogative and dignity of birthright and suffered all sorts of indignities and inconveniences', he acknowledges the good administration Burma enjoyed under British rule and adds, 'it's no use crying over spilt milk'. The prince, now in his nineties, lives modestly in Maymyo, two hours from Mandalay. Journalists regularly call on 'the long-lost heir to the Burmese throne', who says that he has never wanted to be king, but who points out that 'the sympathy for us is still quite strong'. In 2015, Taw Phaya and his family were allowed for the first time to hold a commemorative ceremony in Mandalay.⁶⁹ Four years earlier, the reformist Burmese president Thein Sein had laid a wreath at the tomb of King Thibaw in Ratnagiri, the first Burmese head of state to do so.⁷⁰

The history of the last Burmese king and his queen, their exile and the life of their descendants long after his deposition has continued to intrigue both the Burmese, for whom this is a part of their national heritage, and outsiders, for whom there is a story full of drama and tragedy, poignancy and resilience. Ghosh's novel, Shah's detective-like tracing of Thibaw's fate and of his family over several generations, and the commentaries in the press and various books have now been joined by a documentary film, *Burma's Lost Royals*, made by a team from London's Grammar Productions. Premiered in 2017, it features interviews with several amiable and articulate grandchildren and great-grandchilden of Thibaw. 'After 130 years, Burma's royal family lives on, hidden among the people their ancestors used to rule', states the film-makers' website, and Taw Phaya says, 'It is a surprise to some of them that we are still alive'. Grammar Production's website adds of the documentary that 'in their story [the film-makers] found the story of modern Burma itself'.⁷¹ Those words might well apply to the stories of many deposed rulers and abolished dynasties.

As with other cases of deposition, there is a history not only of the descendants of the former monarch, but also the dynasty's regalia and palace. The Burmese king had nine 'Lion Thrones', each used for different occasions. Eight that remained in the royal palace were destroyed when the British bombed the palace, trying to flush out Japanese garrisoned in the Mandalay citadel, in March 1945.⁷² In 1885 they had taken the other throne to a museum in Calcutta, but it was returned to Burma after independence, and is now a featured attraction at the National Museum in Rangoon. Dating from 1858, the spectacular throne, very different from a Western throne, is effectively a raised platform backed by grand doors from which the king would emerge to sit cross-legged while princes, ministers and supplicants prostrated themselves. The monumental ten-metre-high structure is gilded and highly decorated with figures of the Celestial King, precious stones representing glory, honour, grace and other virtues, and figures of heavenly and mythological beings, as well as a fighting lion and elephant, as impressive in reality as in Saya Chone's painting of a royal audience.⁷³ Near-by in the Rangoon museum are displayed some of the 154 Burmese items returned from the Victoria and Albert Museum in London in 1964 and various other artefacts – clothing, furniture, manuscripts – from the old royal palace and its last occupant.⁷⁴ They stand as items of heritage, memorials to a dynasty, and survivors of the troubled history of modern Burma.

Little but the walls of the royal citadel in Mandalay remained in place after the Second World War, and the site was then used as a Burmese military base.[75] In the 1990s, the military government of Myanmar reconstructed the old royal palace within the fortress. There are concrete replicas of the audience hall and other buildings, complete with an imitation throne and a few mannequins of Thibaw, Supayalat and courtiers, in a largely bare and soulless reconstructed compound, an unconvincing attempt (at least to foreign visitors) by the former authoritarian government to appropriate the aura and patrimony of the pre-colonial monarchy. The new national capital commissioned by the generals, Naypyidaw, with a version of the Shwedagon pagoda and statues of ancient Burmese kings, similarly represents an effort to recreate the glory of old royal capitals, but now serves as the décor for the democratic government of Aung San Suu Kyi.[76]

The British abolished the monarchy in Burma, and symbolically as well as politically replaced it with the British monarchy, under the authority of the viceroy of India (until Burma was given a separate administration in the 1930s). The government houses, viceregal ceremonies, systems of honours and royal tours instituted a new regal panoply, and the British even attended to the conservation of surviving old royal sites, now as part of colonial heritage.[77] However, while setting itself in place of the Konbaung dynasty, the British imperial government set itself over other surviving hereditary monarchs in the country. The British left in place after 1885 the rulers of the Shan states, an area the size of England and Wales combined. Over thirty *sawbwas* – 'lords of the sky', generally referred to as 'princes' – had owed allegiance and tribute to the Burmese king. Many welcomed emancipation from Konbaung hegemony, and some supported an ill-fated claimant to the throne, the Limbin prince, after the deposition of Thibaw in hopes of gaining greater autonomy. When the Limbin prince surrendered (and went into voluntary exile in India), the effort petered out, and the *sawbwas* now became feudatories of the British Crown, paying tribute as well as tax on opium and alcoholic spirits to the colonial state. The British prohibited them from making treaties with any other rulers, required them to accept and act upon the advice of British agents at their courts, and enjoined them to preserve law and order and to govern without oppression. The colonisers treated the Shan rulers deferentially, granting them from one- to nine-gun salutes, and they invited *sawbwas* to Delhi for the 1903 durbar. They opened a school in Taunggyi for the education of young Shan royals, and a few continued their education in England. Travellers often wrote roseate descriptions of the small courts and their colourful sovereigns in the picturesque hill country of Burma. The *sawbwas* generally cooperated with the

British, and some showed their Anglophilia by building new English-style palaces. The *sawbwas* accepted incorporation of their realms into a newly independent state in 1948, just as the Indian princes had done, with moderate enthusiasm, though they retained a formal right to secede; a Shan prince was elected first president of Burma. After the 1962 coup, the military forced the *sawbwas* to renounce their rights; many disappeared in suspicious circumstances, and most of the Shan palaces were ransacked. Many Shan fled into exile in Thailand or further away, though others formed a 'resistance army' that continued to fight the Burmese military for decades. The post-independence extinction of the Shan principalities marked a postscript to the end of the monarchy in Mandalay.[78]

The Sultan of Perak

From the late 1700s, Britain had acquired outposts in the East Indies, Penang in the 1780s, then Malacca, and Singapore in 1819; constituted as the Straits Settlements, these provided valuable points of international trade and access to the resources of the Malay peninsula. The discovery in 1848 of tin in Larut, the northern part of the state of Perak, itself on the northern part of the peninsula, provided another lure, though not until the last quarter of the nineteenth century, as tin dramatically increased in value, did Britain impose its hegemony. The interest of other powers, notably France and, incipiently, Germany also prompted British moves to gain sway over what is today Malaysia.[79] Although they abolished thrones in annexed territories, such as Singapore, elsewhere indigenous rulers were left in place.

Heirs, pretenders and vassals contested positions as Islamic sultans and rajas who wielded near absolute power over largely peasant subjects in the Malay states; succession was decided by consensus or might rather than foreordained. Internecine conflicts offered opportunities for intervention to ambitious Europeans. Indeed, one adventurer, Charles Brooke, had provided such services to the Sultan of Brunei that he was ceded a realm on the island of Borneo, and in 1846 became the ruler of Sarawak; the family of 'white rajas' ruled for a century.[80]

Perak experienced several particularly ferocious contests involving Malay claimants to the sultanate, with occasional intervention by powerful Chinese miners.[81] When the heir apparent, Raja Muda Abdullah, failed to attend the funeral of the deceased sultan in 1871, the chiefs present elected as ruler another senior prince, Ismail (the Raja Bendahara, or vizier), and presented him with the sacred dagger (*kris*) of the state. Abdullah nevertheless then proclaimed himself as sultan. For good measure, a third candidate, Yusuf, came forward. The conflict embodied a joust between kinsmen, but with elements of regionalism as well, since chiefs from northern Perak supported Ismail, while Abdullah won loyalty primarily from southern chiefs. Abdullah let it be known that in return for British recognition, he would accept appointment of a Resident to his court.

British officials in Singapore, the capital of the Straits Settlements, fearing anarchy in Perak, seized a chance to gain leverage. They summoned tribal headmen, subaltern chiefs, Ismail and Abdullah for a meeting in Pangkor in 1874. Ismail refused to attend, but the others agreed to allow the British to place a Resident in Perak. The British thus made Perak a protectorate, and Abdullah won acknowledgement for his right to the throne. Ismail refused to relinquish the *kris* and other regalia, and fled to the southern city of Johore to live out his days in obscurity.

The British chose as Resident James Wheeler Woodford Birch, a fifty-year-old who had served as colonial secretary of the Straits Settlements. He arrived in Perak in November 1874, and immediately began to antagonise Abdullah and his entourage. Birch judged Abdullah extravagant; the Malays considered Birch arrogant and disrespectful of local customs. Birch's attempted reforms of taxation and justice, and his opposition to the bearing of arms by chiefs, endangered the rights of the Malay elite. He also attempted to outlaw slavery, with a deleterious effect on those who made handsome profits from slave-trading. Birch allowed escaped slaves to take refuge in his compound; since many were women, rumours circulated that he was recruiting a harem. He made no secret that his aim was full British control of Perak, with the sultan retaining only a nominal title, and threatened that if Abdullah did not agree, he would be replaced.[82] By March of 1875, even the governor of the Straits Settlements confessed that he was 'very much annoyed with Birch and the head-over-heels way in which he does things'. Abdullah was even more annoyed, and his relations with Birch went from bad to worse. In November, Birch was found murdered, speared in the bathhouse of his boat.

The British sent in troops, and so began the brief 'Perak War' that lasted until mid-1876. The British captured Birch's murderer, a vassal of Abdullah, and he was charged, convicted and executed, along with four others. Suspecting that the sultan and his associates were behind Birch's death, they summoned Abdullah to Singapore. They kept him under house arrest for eight months, followed by four months in gaol. The colonial secretary had accused him of ten offences, though producing no evidence for the allegations. According to the British, Abdullah had attended meetings where Birch's murder was planned, purchased arms and delivered instructions to the assassin. The murder was carried out with Abdullah's knowledge and authority. Despite the written accusations, a prosecutor never officially charged Abdullah, as the British determined that no court in the Straits Settlements was competent to judge a sultan. It was thus the governor's Executive Council that decided on Abdullah's fate, by a single vote deposing and banishing him. The Colonial Office in London confirmed the decision, though as Abdullah and his supporters argued long afterwards, it had dubious legality in British jurisprudence or according to the Pangkor Treaty. With Abdullah nevertheless ousted, the British named Yusuf – the third man from the mid-1870s – as Regent, though not until 1886 (the year before his death) did they grant him full recognition as sultan of Perak.

Abdullah, along with the headman of Larut and two senior officials, was transported to the Seychelles. Thus began Abdullah's fourteen years of exile. Following the practice for other dethroned royals, the British gave him a pension and a house, where he lived with two wives who accompanied him, one of whom died in the Seychelles, and the seven children he fathered in the islands. A son who had remained in Singapore on occasion came to visit, and the ex-sultan was also once allowed to go to Mauritius for a holiday. He learned basic English, began to wear European clothes, and showed a passion for cricket and football, as well as traditional Malay kite-flying. Little else is known about his daily life,[83] but there is information on his appeals to the British.

Over the years Abdullah sent a dozen deferential letters to Queen Victoria and colonial officials, trying various arguments to secure his release. In an 1877 missive pledging loyalty, he conceded that 'youth and inexperience' had combined with the 'hostility of many of the chiefs, partisans of the Ex-Sultan', to unseat him. A letter two years later protested that 'I have never had the chance of being tried at all, nor that of refuting and rebutting my false accusers, and also the different charges which were brought against me'. In 1882, after five years in the Seychelles, Abdullah asked to journey to England to present his case directly, mentioning that the Zulu king Cetshwayo had been permitted to do so; officials remained unmoved. Two years later, Abdullah simply asked to be repatriated, evidencing his impeccable behaviour in the Seychelles with testimonials. Having received no answer for the next fourteen months, Abdullah wrote again, stating that even after eight years, 'I believe that I will receive justice from the British Government' despite the 'illegal' action of the Straits government in exiling him. On the tenth anniversary of his banishment, he threw himself on the goodwill of the British, speaking of 'my now failing health'. In 1887, as Queen Victoria celebrated her jubilee, he called on 'the most beneficent prerogative attached to your Majesty's Crown: the prerogative of mercy'. Two years later, London agreed, for no obvious reason for the change of heart, to let Abdullah and the other Perak exiles return to Southeast Asia, but only to Raja Brooke's Sarawak; one of them took up the offer, but Abdullah refused. Sarawak, he pointed out, was not his native land, and accepting the offer would constitute tacit admission of guilt in Birch's death. He said that 'my habits and likings have been so far altered as to make me prefer my present surroundings in a British colony'. He disavowed political intentions, repeated claims of complete innocence, and stated that his detention had taken place 'in violation of British law'.[84] The following year, he essayed yet another strategy, stating that his sons required a Muslim education and his daughters needed to wed suitable husbands; neither school nor suitors were available in the Seychelles. Finally, a compromise eventuated, and Abdullah accepted a proposal that he move to Singapore.

Abdullah had not campaigned alone. Letters from the Seychelles and Mauritius spoke of his sterling behaviour, and one petition on his behalf gained over two hundred signatures. Supporters variously argued that Abdullah was innocent of the accusations, that he deserved a fair trial, or that his exemplary behaviour in exile justified return home.[85] Key among the advocates was Sir Peter Benson Maxwell, an Irish-born barrister with a long career in the colonial service in Penang and Singapore culminating in a position as chief justice of the Straits Settlements from 1867 to 1871. His son, Sir William Edward Maxwell, followed in his father's footsteps as an administrator in Malaya. In 1875, the younger Maxwell, as deputy commissioner, had taken part in investigations surrounding Birch's murder.[86] Maxwell *père*, who was affiliated with the Aborigines Protection Society in Britain, wrote to the secretary of war that the exile of the Malays was 'repugnant not only to the most elementary principles of justice and fair play, but also to all English political traditions; nor can it be defended by any plea of necessity'.[87] Maxwell's *Our Malayan Conquests*, published in 1878 after his return to London, concluded that on the basis of available evidence, Birch's murder was not the result of a plot and that the testimony on which the Straits government had based Abdullah's deposition was hardly above suspicion.

Several Members of Parliament also raised questions in the House of Commons and official correspondence. Among them was Charles Bradlaugh, a prominent atheist, republican and advocate of women's suffrage and trade unions. The Mauritian-born Liberal MP Francis Seymour Stevenson, known otherwise for efforts on behalf of Armenians, lent his support, as did the Liberal MP Lyulph (later Fourth Baron) Stanley. Another was Sir John Henniker Heaton, who returned to England in 1881, after three decades in Australia, to serve as Conservative member for Canterbury.[88] Best known for his campaign for an imperial penny post, he was a fellow of the Royal Colonial Institute and lectured on Aboriginal affairs. The backgrounds and party affiliations showed the breadth of interest in the exiled Malay. All considered his treatment a miscarriage of justice – or rather a complete lack of justice, given the lack of a trial.

Perak was not the only region where the British faced problems in anchoring their authority in the Malay peninsula, and commentators voiced fears that contagion might spread from Abdullah's state. One official remarked: 'The Malays are much encouraged by the affairs in Perak ... They say they will make white men into white curry.'[89] Concern that Abdullah could become a focus for resistance if allowed to return, as well as the not surprising opposition of Sultan Yusuf to his repatriation, kept the exile in the Seychelles. Even when he went free, the British admitted to no error.

On his departure from the Seychelles in 1893, Abdullah fulfilled a long-expressed wish to visit London, where he continued to wear a brocaded and medal-laden uniform, an indication of refusal to acquiesce to his dethronement. He then went to Singapore, where he lived until he moved in 1903 to Penang. He gained permission from the British and Yusuf's successor to visit Perak, and in 1922, received approval to move to the royal capital of Kuala Kangsar, arriving shortly before his death.

Whether Abdullah was implicated in Birch's murder remains unknown. For D. R. SarDesai, 'there is no doubt that the sultan had acquiesced in the ghastly act and that the chiefs had almost unanimously supported it'. By contrast, a Seychellois historian, Cheah Boon Kheng, refers to the 'innocent' sultan; the nationalist narrative in Malaysia, he says, generally concedes Abdullah's involvement in the killing of Birch, but treats him as an anti-British patriot and freedom fighter (just as those executed for the deed are considered folk heroes). For Abdullah's supporters then and now, refusal to give him a right of defence through a trial represents an indictment of the British if not vindication of the sultan.[90]

Abdullah was accompanied to Britain by his handsome twenty-seven-year-old elder son Raja Mansur, who became an aide-de-camp to the ruling sultan in the 1880s and later a magistrate. Abdullah's other son, Raja Chulan, later took part in the setting up of the Federated Malay States in 1896 and held a position on the Malay law commission, for which he was knighted. One of the sultan's daughters, Raja Hadya Abdullah, born in the Seychelles in 1883, was an accomplished pianist; having heard a band performing 'La Rosalie', she took to playing a version of the old French love song. Raja Mansur added words, and it became the anthem of Perak; after independence, the tune was adapted as the national anthem of Malaysia – a curious postscript to Abdullah's exile. In 1909, however, the British formally forbade Abdullah's direct descendants from taking the throne of Perak. A collateral descendant reigns as the present-day sultan, eligible like other hereditary rulers for election as head of state of Malaysia.[91]

Deposed monarchs in British Asia

In India, Burma and the Malay states, the colonial British during the nineteenth and early twentieth centuries deposed and exiled a considerable number of hereditary rulers, abolishing many traditional dynasties – including those of the Mughal emperor and Konbaung king, among other victims of British conquest – in the process. Annexing some states, they established the British Crown as paramount ruler over surviving lineages, including Indian princes, Shan *sawbwas* and Malay sultans. Overrule was not without its conflicts and dangers, which led to ouster of rulers from Nagpur to Perak, over the period from 1817 to 1946, the native 'potentates' undone by allegations of misgovernment or unacceptable personal behaviour. A feudatory was neither independent nor, in practice, fully autonomous, and overrule meant that colonisers could intervene when they deemed it necessary, and displace a ruler by coerced abdication, trial or decree.

In exile, the banished Indian, Burmese and Malay rulers, like the Kandyan king before them, and notwithstanding real or alleged misdeeds, generally present sad spectacles, having lost their thrones, being deported from their native countries, kept as 'state prisoners', and clinging to vestiges of their royal ways. The procedures in their removal, even by colonial standards, were sometimes dubious, at best, and what would now be called their 'human rights' were violated. The British state after 1857 did not displace rulers for the annexation of territory, as the East India Company had rapaciously done in earlier decades, and deposition might now be a last resort rather than a primary strategy. However, that strategy did not disappear from the colonial toolkit. Old precedents served for new circumstances, as shown by the dethroning and banishment of Sri Vikrama Rajasinha and Thibaw at an interval of seventy years, and in the efforts of the British monarchical state to assume the place of the old regime in both Ceylon and Burma with the pageantry of its power, promises to protect Buddhism, and violent actions against pretenders to the native thrones. Rulers who remained in place, whether Indian maharajas, Shan princes or Malay sultans, needed not only to pledge but to prove their allegiance to the imperial overlords.

KINGS OF ORIENT WERE

Few of the deposed lived to see their rehabilitation, though the memory of kings and thrones did inspire some royalist movements, later nationalists and post-independence governments intent on appropriating the heritage of ancestral dynasties. Only in Malaysia do traditional sovereigns retain positions of official authority. Throughout southern and southeastern Asia, the clashes of monarchies – British and indigenous – formed part of the dynamics of imperial takeover. During the colonial period, Britannic majesty reigned supreme (or at least the British liked to think), though native rulers called upon a range of strategies of resistance, accommodation, cooperation and shifting alliances to position themselves vis-à-vis the foreigners occupying their countries. Those who did not manoeuvre deftly enough lost their thrones, while British overrule leached away the powers of heirs and successors who did survive. This left very few of the old dynasties in a position to serve as rallying-points for the independence movements that finally emancipated the colonies or to regain in the post-colonial period the status and authority that their ancestors had once enjoyed.

Notes

1. Barbara Ramusack, *The Indian Princes and Their States*, Vol. III:6 of *The New Cambridge History of India* (Cambridge: Cambridge University Press, 2004); see also Waltraud Ernst and Biswamoy Pati (eds), *India's Princely States: People, Princes and Colonialism* (London: Routledge, 2007).
2. Quoted in Anita Anand, *Sophia: Princess, Suffragette, Revolutionary* (London: Bloomsbury, 2015), p. 26; see Miles Taylor, 'Queen Victoria and India, 1837–61', *Victorian Studies*, 46:2 (2004), 264–74.
3. 'British India', territories ruled directly, comprised about three-fifths of the subcontinent. In the 'princely states', 600-odd territories of greatly varying size and population, indigenous rulers – bearing titles of maharaja, raja, nizam, and so on – were nominally sovereign under the 'paramount' power of the British government.
4. Government of the Central Provinces and Berar, *Collection of Correspondence relating to the Escape and Subsequent Adventures of Appa Sahib, Ex-Raja of Nagpur 1818–1840* (Nagpur: C. P. & Berar, 1939); quotations from pp. 56 and 132–3.
5. An Officer formerly in the service of His Highness Veer Rajunder Wadeer, Rajah of Coorg, *Coorg and its Rajahs* (London: John Bumpus, 1857); quotations from pp. 25, xx and xxx.
6. This account follows Sumitra Kulkarni, *The Satara Raj (1818–1848): A Study in History, Administration and Culture* (New Delhi: Mittal Publications, 1995); see also Enrico Fasana, 'Pratap Singh a Satara: "Rise and Fall" di un principe indiano (1818–1848)', *Annali della Facoltà di Scienze Politiche, Università di Studi di Trieste* (1980), 759–814. Various relevant documents are contained in R. D. Choksey (ed.), *Raja Pratapsingh of Satara* (Poona: Bharata Itihasa Samshodhaka Mandala, 1970); and *Raja Shahji of Satara, 1839–1848* (Poona: self-published, 1974). For a compilation of documents, see Terence R. Blackburn (ed.), *Justice for the Raja of Sattara?* (New Delhi: APH Publishing Corporation, 2007).
7. Quotations in Kulkarni, *The Satara Raj*, pp. 18–19, 21.
8. Michael Alexander and Sushila Anand, *Queen Victoria's Maharajah: Duleep Singh, 1838–93* (London: Weidenfeld & Nicolson, 1980), one of a number of works on the Punjab prince.

9 Rosie Llewellyn-Jones, *The Last King in India: Wajid 'Ali Shah* (London: Hurst, 2014).
10 'Shatranj Ke Khiladi', directed by Satyajit Ray, based on a short story by Munshi Premchand.
11 Raja of Satara, *A Letter to the Right Hon. Sir Henry Hardinge* (London: Alex Munro, 1845), pp. 1–2.
12 *Debates at the India House: August 22nd, 23rd and September 24th 1845, on the case of the deposed raja of Sattara, and the impeachment of Col. C. Ovans*, www.archive.org/stream/debatesatindiaho00east/debatesatindiaho00east_djvu.txt.
13 See Nicholas B. Dirks, *The Scandal of Empire: India and the Creation of Imperial Britain* (Cambridge, MA: Harvard University Press, 2006).
14 Rosie Llewellyn-Jones (ed.), *Lucknow: City of Illusion* (Munich: Prestel, 2006).
15 Llewellyn-Jones, *The Last King in India*; quotation from p. 202.
16 On other Indian princes in Britain, see Rozina Visram, *Ayahs, Lascars and Princes: Indians in Britain, 1700–1947* (London: Pluto Press, 1986); and Amin Jaffer, 'Indian Princes and the West', in Anna Jackson and Amin Jaffer with Deepika Ahlawat (eds), *Maharaja: The Splendour of India's Royal Courts* (London: V&A Publishing, 2009), pp. 194–227.
17 C. P. Belliappa, *Victoria Gowramma: The Lost Princess of Coorg* (New Delhi: Rupa, 2014).
18 See William Dalrymple and Anita Anand, *Koh-i-Noor: The History of the World's Most Infamous Diamond* (London: Bloomsbury, 2017).
19 Alison Smith, David Blayney Brown and Carol Jacobi (eds), *Artist and Empire: Facing Britain's Imperial Past* (London: Tate Publishing, 2015), pp. 138–9.
20 Anand, *Sophia*, p. 50.
21 Anand, *Sophia*; Peter Bance, *Sovereign, Squire and Rebel: Maharajah Duleep Singh and the Heirs of a Lost Kingdom* (London: Coronet House, 2009), and *The Duleep Singhs: The Photograph Album of Queen Victoria's Maharajah* (Stroud: Sutton, 2004).
22 Image of Statue of Maharajah Duleep Singh by Denise Dutton, 'Statues – Hither and Thither', http://statues.vanderkrogt.net/object.php?record=gbee020, accessed 25 November 2016.
23 The authoritative account, on which the following is based, is William Dalrymple, *The Last Mughal: The Fall of a Dynasty, Delhi, 1857* (London: Bloomsbury, 2006); there is, as well, a huge literature on the Uprising, including Saul David, *The Indian Mutiny: 1857* (London: Viking, 2002), and the multi-volume work of Andrea Major and Crispin Bates (eds), *Mutiny at the Margins: New Perspectives on the Indian Uprising of 1857* (London: Sage, 2013).
24 See Amar Farooqui, *Zafar and the Raj: Anglo-Mughal Delhi, c. 1800–1850* (New Delhi: Primus Books, 2013).
25 Quoted in Dalrymple, *The Last Mughal*, p. 409.
26 Dalrymple, *The Last Mughal*, p. 432.
27 Donovan Williams, 'An Echo of the Indian Mutiny: the Proposed Banishment of Bahadur Shah II to the Cape Colony, 1857', *Historia*, 17:4 (1972), 265–8.
28 IOR/L/PS/6/466, Coll. 69/1, Captain H. N. Davies, 10 July 1859, British Library.
29 IOR/L/PS/6/503, Coll. 28, report by Phayre in message from Viceroy to Secretary of State, 27 November 1860.
30 In 1866 Jawan Bakht petitioned the British for release, pleading he had been too young to take part in the 1857 rebellion. He noted that his half-brother Shah Abbas had been released a year previously and was employed in the Public Works Department in Rangoon. The request was granted, and the government provided a monthly pension as well as a once-off grant for Jawan Bakht to furnish a house. (Provisions were also made for his surveillance in case he tried to return to India.) In the same year, Zafar's widow was released, and also given an allowance; she lived in Rangoon until her death in 1886 (IOR/L/PS/6/545/76). The emperor's descendants continue to live in Burma and India, though in modest conditions (*Daily Mail*, London, 1 February 2016). There have been several calls for Zafar's remains to be repatriated to Delhi. (*Daily Telegraph*, 8 April 2009).

31 A. S. Rafiqi, *Inversion of Times*, ed. Yehya En-Nasr Parkinson (London: Luzac, 1911), first published in 1906, quotations from pp. 6–7, 12–13, 23.
32 *The Hindu*, 8 February 2009.
33 *The Economic Times*, 30 January 2011.
34 *The Hindu*, 16 February 2001.
35 *Mizzima News*, 28 July 2005.
36 Rudyard Kipling's story 'On the City Wall' is a fictionalised portrayal of the exiled Mughal, though in his version the captive emperor manages to escape; finding that his leadership is no longer wanted, he gives himself up. ('On the City Wall', originally published in *Soldiers Three and Other Stories*.)
37 The proclamation is available on the British Library website: www.bl.uk/collection-items/proclamation-by-the-queen-in-council-to-the-princes-chiefs-and-people-of-india, accessed 25 November 2016.
38 Ramusack, *Indian Princes*; Caroline Keen, *Princely India and the British: Political Development and the Operation of Empire* (New Delhi: Viva Books, 2012); Ian Copland, *The Princes of India in the Endgame of Empire, 1917–1947* (Cambridge: Cambridge University Press, 1997), and *The British Raj and the Princes: Paramountcy in Western India, 1857–1930* (Bombay: Orient Longman, 1982).
39 Nicholas Dirks, *The Hollow Crown: Ethnohistory of an Indian Kingdom* (Ann Arbor: University of Michigan, 1988), argues that the princes were little more than puppets, though other authors, such as Ramusack, in *The Indian Princes*, do not fully agree.
40 Fiona Elizabeth Groenhout, 'Debauchery, Disloyalty, and Other Deficiencies: The Impact of Ideas of Princely Character Upon Indirect Rule in Central India, c. 1886–1946' (PhD dissertation, University of Western Australia, 2007). I am much indebted to this thesis for accounts of several cases. See also her 'The History of the Indian Princely States: Bringing the Puppets Back onto Centre Stage', *History Compass*, 4:4 (2006), 629–44.
41 I. F. S. Copland, 'The Baroda Crisis of 1873–77: A Study in Governmental Rivalry', *Modern Asian Studies*, 2:2 (1968), 97–123; Mulhar Rao Gaekwar, *The Trial and Deposition of Mulhar Rae Gaekwar of Baroda* (Bombay: Gazette Steam Press, 1875); Mulhar Rao Gaekwar, Maharaja of Baroda, *The Great Baroda Case: Being a Full Report of the Proceedings of the Trial and Deposition of His Highness Mulhar Rao, Gaekwar of Baroda for Instigating an Attempt to Poison the British Resident at His Court* (Calcutta: R. Cambray & Co., 1905), pp. xxx–xxxi.
42 Mulhar Rao Gaekwar, *The Great Baroda Case*, p. xx.
43 Fiona Groenhout, 'Loyal Feudatories or Depraved Despots? The Deposition of Princes in the Central India Agency, c. 1880–1947', in Waltraud Ernst and Biswamoy Pati (eds), *India's Princely States: People, Princes and Colonialism* (London: Routledge, 2007), pp. 99–117.
44 Groenhout, 'Debauchery, Disloyalty, and Other Deficiencies', Ch. 1.
45 Groenhout, 'Debauchery, Disloyalty, and Other Deficiencies', Ch. 4.
46 Groenhout, 'Debauchery, Disloyalty, and Other Deficiencies', Ch. 2.
47 Groenhout, 'Debauchery, Disloyalty, and Other Deficiencies', Ch. 5.
48 Fiona Groenhout, 'Educating Govind Singh: "Princely Character" and the Failure of Indirect Rule in Colonial India', in Peter Limb (ed.), *Orb and Sceptre: Studies on British Imperialism and its Legacies in Honour of Norman Etherington* (Clayton, Victoria: Monash University Press, 2008), pp. 1–23.
49 Influence, subtle or otherwise, might be placed on maharajas, however, to relinquish power in other circumstances. The marriage of the Raja of Pudukottai to an Australian woman, Molly Fink, in 1915 disconcerted the British and the ruler's subjects; the raja gave up his rights to the throne in favour of his brother, and the couple lived largely overseas. See Edward Duyker and Coralie Younger, *Molly and the Rajah* (Sydney: Australian-Mauritian Press, 1991), and on other *mésalliances*, Coralie Younger, *Wicked Women of the Raj: European Women Who Broke Society's Rules and Married Indian Princes* (New Delhi: HarperCollins, 2003).

50 Shail Mayaram, *Resisting Regimes: Myth, Memory and the Shaping of a Muslim Identity* (Delhi: Oxford University Press, 1997).
51 Quoted in Caroline Keen, *An Imperial Crisis in British India: The Manipur Uprising of 1891* (London: I. B. Tauris, 2015), pp. 145, 158–9.
52 Keen, *An Imperial Crisis*, p. 2. See also Jyotimoy Roy, *History of Manipur* (Calcutta: Eastlight Book House, 1973 [1958]); Naorem Joykumar Singh, *Colonialism to Democracy: A History of Manipur, 1819–1972* (Guwahati: Spectrum, 2002); and the memoir by Ethel St Clair Grimwood, *My Three Years in Manipur and Escape from the Recent Mutiny* (London: R. Bentley, 1891).
53 Barbara N. Ramusack, 'Incident at Nabha: Interaction beteween Indian States and British Indian Politics', *Journal of Asian Studies*, 28:3 (1969), 563–77.
54 General works are Thant Myint-U, *The Making of Modern Burma* (Cambridge: Cambridge University Press, 2001) and *The River of Lost Footsteps: A Personal History of Burma* (London: Faber & Faber, 2007), and Michael Aung-Thwin and Maitrii Aung-Thwin, *A History of Myanmar since Ancient Times: Traditions and Transformations* (London: Reaktion Books, 2012). A lively account blending history and travel – inspired by the life and work of Sir James George Scott – is Andrew Marshall, *The Trouser People: Burma in the Shadows of the Empire* (Bangkok: River Books, revised edn, 2012). Scott's own account, *The Burman* (New York: W. W. Norton, 1963 [1882]), remains fascinating. More particularly on colonial rivalries see Hla Thein, *Myanmar and the Europeans (1878–1885)* (Yangon: Daw Thinn Thinn Mar Tun Foundation Bank Literary Committee, 2010), which includes many original documents.
55 From Wilhelm Joest, *Ein Besuch beim Könige von Birma* (Cologne: Du Mont-Schauberg, 1882), quoted in Hla Thein, *Myanmar and the Europeans*, p. 71.
56 Notably in a 1924 interview, reprinted in Terence R. Blackburn, *Executions by the Half-Dozen: The Pacification of Burma* (Delhi: APH Publishing Coporation, 2008), p. 80.
57 The French consul in Mandalay Frédéric Haas published a volume on *La France et l'Angleterre en Asie* (Paris: Berger-Levrault, 1892) under the nom de plume of Philippe Lehault.
58 A. T. Q. Stewart, *The Pagoda War: Lord Dufferin and the Fall of the Kingdom of Ava, 1885–6* (London: Faber & Faber, 1972).
59 The following account is taken from Sladen's report and newspaper articles reprinted in Blackburn, *Executions by the Half-Dozen*, pp. 2–12.
60 Blackburn, *Executions by the Half-Dozen*, p. 17.
61 Andrew Ranard, *Burmese Painting: A Linear and Lateral History* (Bangkok: Silkworm Books, 2009), Ch. 2.
62 Quoted in Blackburn, *Executions by the Half-Dozen*, p. 29.
63 Quoted in Blackburn, *Executions by the Half-Dozen*, pp. 47–8.
64 Parimal Ghosh, *Brave Men of the Hills: Resistance and Rebellion in Burma, 1825–1932* (Honolulu: University of Hawai'i Press, 2000), quotation from pp. 89–90.
65 Maitrii Aung-Thwin, *The Return of the Galon King: History, Law, and Rebellion in Colonial Burma* (Singapore: NUS Press, 2011), and 'Genealogy of a Rebellion Narrative: Law, Ethnology and Culture in Colonial Burma', *Journal of Southeast Asian Studies*, 34:3 (2003), 393–419.
66 Sudha Shah, *The King in Exile: The Fall of the Royal Family of Burma* (New Delhi: HarperCollins, 2012).
67 Amitav Ghosh, *The Glass Palace* (London: HarperCollins, 2000).
68 Shah, *The King in Exile*.
69 Marshall, *The Trouser People*, pp. 55–60; Phoebe Kennedy, 'Burmese Dictator Lives Like a King, Laments the Nation's Last Royal', *The Independent* (London), 12 March 2010; 'Lost Kingdom: Myanmar's Forgotten Royals', *Agence France-Press*, 9 November 2013; Poppy McPherson, 'Myanmar's Royal Legacy', *The Diplomat*,

14 March 2015; Rosalind Russell, *Burma's Spring: Real Lives in Turbulent Times* (Bangkok: River Books, 2015), Ch. 5.
70 'President U Thein Sein Visits the Last King's Tomb in India', *The New Light of Myanmar*, 23 December 2012.
71 www.grammar-productions.com. I am grateful to the film-maker, Alex Bescoby, for talking with me about his work.
72 Marshall, *The Trouser People*, p. 43; Donald Stadtner, *Sacred Sites of Burma: Myth and Folklore in an Evolving Spiritual Realm* (Bangkok: River Books, 2011).
73 Ma Thanegi, 'The Thrones of Myanmar Kings', *Enchanting Myanmar*, 2:2 (January–March 2003), www.myanmar-image.com/enchantingmyanmar/enchantingmyanmar2-2/thrones.htm, accessed 25 November 2016.
74 Blackburn, *Executions by the Half-Dozen*, p. 13.
75 Marshall, *The Trouser People*, pp. 43–5.
76 Maitrii Aung-Thwin, 'Remembering Kings: Archives, Resistance and Memory in Colonial and Postcolonial Burma', in Kenneth Hall and Michael Aung-Thwin (eds), *New Perspectives on the History and Historiography of Southeast Asia: Continuing Explorations* (London: Routledge, 2011), pp. 53–82.
77 Stephen L. Keck, '"It Has Now Passed For Ever Into Our Hands": Lord Curzon and the Construction of Imperial Heritage in Colonial Burma', *Journal of Burma Studies*, 11 (2007), 49–82. On recent attitudes towards royal sites, see François Tainturier, 'Of Golden Palaces and Celebrated Rulers: Inventing Traditions in Pre-colonial and Contemporary Myanmar', *Journal of Burma Studies*, 18:2 (2014), 223–58.
78 Susan Conway, *The Shan: Culture, Art and Crafts* (Bangkok: River Books, 2006). See also Scott, *The Burman*; the author coaxed the Shan into accepting British overrule. A classic colonial-era account is Maurice Collis, *Lords of the Sunset* (Bangkok: AVA, 1996 [1938]), a fond portrait of the Shan region and its rulers. See also Sai Aung Tun, *History of the Shan State from its Origins to 1962* (Chiang Mai: Silkworm Books, 2009); Sao Saimong Mangrai, *The Shan States and the British Annexation* (Ithaca: Cornell University Press, 1965); Shona T. S. Goodman, *From Princes to Persecuted: A Condensed History of the Shan/Tai to 1962* ([Seattle]: CreateSpace, 2014); and Elaine Halton, *Lord of the Celestial Elephant* (London: Elaine Halton, 1999).
79 D. R. SarDesai, *Southeast Asia: Past and Present* (Boulder: Westview Press, 2010), Ch. 8.
80 Nigel Barley, *White Rajah* (London: Little Brown, 2002).
81 R. O. Winstedt and R. J. Wilkinson, 'A History of Perak', *Journal of the Malayan Branch of the Royal Asiatic Society*, 12:1 (1934), entire issue.
82 SarDesai, *Southeast Asia*, p. 97.
83 Julien Durup, 'The Innocent Sultan of Perak in the Seychelles', *Seychelles Weekly*, 11 July 2010, www.seychellesweekly.com/July%2011,%202010/top2_sultan.html, accessed 25 November 2016.
84 Quotations from letters printed as an appendix to Cheah Boon Kheng, 'Letters from Exile – Correspondence of Sultan Abdullah of Perak from Seychelles and Mauritius, 1877–1891', *Journal of the Malaysian Branch of the Royal Asiatic Society*, 64:1 (1991), 33–74.
85 Cheah Boon Kheng, 'Letters from Exile'.
86 He later served as governor of the Gold Coast in Africa, and under his administration the Ashanti king Prempeh was deposed and exiled.
87 Quoted in Cheah Boon Kheng, 'Letters from Exile', p. 33.
88 *Oxford Dictionary of National Biography* and, for Henniker Heaton, *Australian Dictionary of Biography*.
89 See J. M. Gulick, 'The War with Yam Tuan Antah', *Journal of the Malayan/Malaysian Branch of the Royal Asiatic Society*, 27:1 (1954), 1–23 (quotation from p. 15), concerning the Negri Sembilan confederacy of chiefs who resisted British incursions. After military skirmishes, the Negri Semilan chief, Antar, fled to Johore in 1876.

He was allowed to return the following year, but with nominal sovereignty over a reduced territory.

90 SarDesai, *Southeast Asia*, p. 97; Cheah Boon Kheng, 'Letters from Exile'.
91 On Abdullah's descendants, see 'Sultan Abdullah's return from the Seychelles, 1894', *Sembang Kuala*, 9 June 2009, https://sembangkuala.wordpress.com/2009/06/09/group-showing-sultan-abdullah-in-uniform-after-his-return-from-the-seychelles-with-some-member-of-his-family/, accessed 25 November 2016.

CHAPTER FOUR

'Dragons of Annam': the French and three emperors in Vietnam

In 1997, the last emperor of Annam died in exile in Paris. Bao Dai had come to the throne of the Nguyen dynasty in 1926, at the age of thirteen, when Annam and neighbouring Tonkin, over which he nominally reigned, were protectorates of France – Cochinchina, the third *ky* or region of Vietnam, had been annexed as a fully-fledged colony by the French. They had carefully groomed Bao Dai for office, both before and after he came to power, with schooling in France, paternalistic watchfulness and ostentatious deference paid to him at the 1931 international colonial exposition in Paris, where the young emperor, arrayed in royal dress, and wearing Vietnamese and French decorations, was given pride of place. In the words of Christopher Goscha, 'Not only did the Nguyen emperor embody the special colonial relationship between France and Vietnam, but at that time he symbolically represented the empire (through the visible intermediary of his person) for the Third Republic ... Bao Dai was the French Republic's colonial monarch'.[1] However, the French vassal showed more interest in automobiles, hunting and the company of attractive women than in ruling and in advancing France's colonial objectives, and he spent much of his time in France or in a new Art Deco mansion in the hill station of Dalat, rather than in the imperial palace in Hué.[2] Meanwhile, nationalists with mounting militancy and increasingly radical ideologies demanded liberation of Vietnam from colonial rule, and modernisers rejected the Nguyen dynasty as a backward relic of the past.

After the German defeat of France in 1940, the Vichy-aligned government of Admiral Jean Decoux in Indochina accommodated the Japanese, who made ever greater demands for concessions from the French.[3] The liberation of Paris in 1944 did not spell the demise of the Decoux government in Hanoi or the end of the war in Asia. Worried that Decoux might turn against them and that the Americans might land in Vietnam, in March 1945 the Japanese occupied Vietnam and ousted the French administration. They persuaded or coerced Bao Dai to proclaim the independence of an 'Empire of Vietnam' affiliated with their Greater East Asian Co-Prosperity Sphere,[4] and over the next three months, the new government began to roll back French colonial rule, in symbolic ways by removing French monuments and renaming streets, and by such measures as nationalising the education system. Meanwhile, Ho Chi Minh, despite the still small size of his Indochinese Communist Party and his own far-from-secure personal position among the unwieldy group of nationalists, quickly began to expand the clandestine presence of the Viet Minh and to wait for an opportune moment to strike. The Japanese capitulated to the Allies on 15 August, and four days later the Viet Minh seized power in Hanoi and northern provincial centres. Bao Dai was in a fateful situation, his pre-war royal powers reduced by the French, his personal reputation hardly glorious, his dynasty considered by radicals as a vestige of 'feudalism', and his position compromised because of collaboration with the Japanese. Not attempting to contest the Viet Minh, on 25 August, Bao Dai abdicated, relinquished his imperial seal and ceremonial sword to Ho, renounced his title to become a simple citizen, and left Vietnam, ostensibly on a mission for Ho to Hong Kong as 'supreme counsellor' of the new government. On 2 September, Ho triumphantly declared the independence of the Democratic Republic of Vietnam.[5]

In the final months of the war, Chinese troops had pushed into northern Vietnam (though without preventing Ho from taking power), while British troops landed in southern Vietnam. Not until 5 October did the Free French forces of General Philippe Leclerc march into Saigon, and the French struggled to re-establish control. After negotiating with Ho, and then repudiating his government, and in the midst of the Indochinese war that had broken out in 1946, the French in 1949 persuaded Bao Dai to return to a unified Vietnam, now an 'associated state' of France, with the hybrid title 'His Majesty, the Head of State'. In 1954, however, the Communists routed the French at Dien Bien Phu, forcing their withdrawal from Southeast Asia. Vietnam was divided, with Ho as leader in the north; Bao Dai remained as nominal head of state of South Vietnam for a year, before his prime minister, Ngo Dinh Diem, engineered a fraudulent referendum that abolished the monarchy.[6]

Bao Dai was the fourth modern ruler of Vietnam to go into exile, but unlike the last emperor, three earlier monarchs were banished by French authorities, two implicated in revolts, the third alleged to be mad. The French nevertheless maintained support for the throne in Hué, though with the sovereign reduced to virtual impotence. The circumstances of the exile of Ham Nghi in the 1880s, Thanh Thai in 1907 and Duy Tan in 1916 illustrate the difficult coexistence of a paramount colonial power and a vassal 'protected' monarchy. As Nguyên Thê Anh has argued in his authoritative study of the colonised monarchy in Vietnam, the guiding principle for the French was to use the Vietnamese emperor to their own purposes, aiming to select and groom incoming rulers to be loyal and docile, steadily reducing their real powers while encouraging performance of ritual and ceremonial duties, and not hesitating to punish those they found uncooperative. From the 1870s until the 1920s the French so weakened the monarchy that it was in effect a dying institution.[7] The cases of the exiled emperors nevertheless show that individual rulers and the monarchy retained some capacity to challenge the French.

The Vietnamese and the French

In the nineteenth century, the French were seeking an outpost in Southeast Asia to compete with the well established British, Dutch and Spanish, and at the end of the 1850s, gunboat diplomacy secured a foothold in Saigon.[8] The French forced the emperor to cede territory around the Mekong delta, which they proclaimed the colony of Cochinchina. Set on further expansion, they moved into central Annam in the following decade and then, despite initial reverses, into Tonkin further north. By the mid-1880s, the French military had secured treaties by which the emperor recognised those regions as French protectorates. Annam remained nominally independent, as did Tonkin, although 'protection' in the northern *ky* was little more than a façade for colonial rule. Cochinchina, Annam and Tonkin – the French refused to use the word 'Vietnam' with its suggestion of a unified nation and people[9] – alongside Cambodia, a French protectorate since the early 1860s, and Laos, taken over in the 1890s, were grouped into the 'French Indochinese Union'. With fertile soil growing ample rice crops, deposits of coal, the manufacture of silk, the later development of rubber production, a strategic location and proximity to the dreamed-of riches of China, Vietnam became a highly prized possession.

Most of the Vietnamese were peasants, tending rice paddies, leading a modest and sometimes impoverished existence sustained by veneration of ancestors and Buddhist beliefs. Administration, based on the model of government derived from China, lay in the hands of mandarins, officials recruited through arduous competitive examinations on the Confucian classics. At the apex stood the emperor, the 'son of heaven', on whose performance of the all-important rites in honour of gods, ancestors and his predecessors rested the welfare of the kingdom.[10] The emperor carried out secular duties as well, issuing and setting his seal on rescripts, appointing officials, receiving foreign embassies, overseeing tax collection and public works, exercising judicial prerogatives. The monarch seldom left the 'purple city' inside the citadel in Hué, where court protocol was rigorous and complex. Homage to the sovereign was marked by officials' repeated prostrations, while the emperor sat impassively on his throne, clothed in silk robes embroidered with dragons and other auspicious symbols. A sacred figure, according to Confucian values and Vietnamese custom, the emperor expected obeisance and obedience.[11]

The authority of the emperor, in practice, was not unlimited. Vietnam had historically been a vassal state of China, the ruler's seal and title accorded by the Chinese emperor in return for tribute. The relationship was often strained, and at times had erupted into warfare. The sovereign also occasionally faced rebellions at home, and struggles between claimants to the throne, as succession was not based on primogeniture. Since emperors fathered numerous children with wives and concubines, competition was bound up with palace intrigues in which dowager empresses and senior consorts, as well as mandarins, manoeuvred on behalf of preferred candidates.

Emperor Tu Duc (r. 1847–83) enjoyed a reputation as a wise and successful ruler, though forced to agree to French demands for territory, trading privileges and permission for missionaries to proselytise. He died with no natural heir, and his immediate successors fared badly. His adopted son Duc Duc reigned for only three days before being deposed by the court, ostensibly for lapses in performance of the rites, and died in captivity. Hiep Hoa, a half-brother of Tu Duc, then lasted for four months, his reign marked by a disastrous military defeat by the French. The two leading mandarins, Ton That Thuyet and Nguyen Van Tuong, opposing his conciliatory attitude towards the invaders, ordered him to abdicate and commit suicide. The poorly fourteen-year-old successor remained on the throne for eight months, his sudden death prompting rumours of assassination. The dynasty was thus further weakened, just when it was buffeted by French military advances that culminated in 1884–85 with the conquest of Tonkin. This state of affairs provided the context for the uneasy relationship between a victorious French colonial state intent on securing control over the new protectorates, a dynasty clinging to the vestiges of its prerogatives, and mandarins and courtiers who jostled for leverage.

France gained great privileges from the treaty with the 'Annamese' in 1884. The imperial seal given by the Chinese emperor to the Vietnamese ruler was smashed, symbolising transfer of authority over the tribute state. French 'Residents' were appointed to Hanoi and Hué, in principle advising the emperor and overseeing French interests, but exercising proconsular powers. In the Hué citadel, a site was set apart for a 'French concession', with a garrison stationed in a neighbouring fortification, the Mang Ca; soon several hundred colonial officials and soldiers were posted to the capital.[12]

Ham Nghi

On 31 July 1884, Emperor Kien Phuc died after little more than six months on the throne, perhaps from smallpox, though possibly poisoned because of his disapproval of an intimate relationship between his stepmother and a senior mandarin. For the fourth time since the death of Tu Duc a year earlier, the imperial family council, dominated by Thuyet and Tuong, chose a new emperor. They settled on the youngest brother of Kien Phuc, who took the reign name of Ham Nghi. For the mandarins, he had the merit of being only thirteen years old, leaving real power in the hands of senior courtiers. It was an inauspicious moment for the start of a reign.[13]

The French objected to the choice of Ham Nghi, worrying he would become the tool of the anti-colonialist mandarin regents, but appeared resigned to his enthronement. Jules Silvestre, the Director of Civil and Political Affairs in Hanoi, nevertheless presciently predicted and planned his downfall. On 19 November, he wrote to the senior French general: 'I suppose that one morning, the Residency will learn of the flight of the king and the Court, who will not have missed issuing a call to arms.'[14] The French were hoping for an occasion when they could get rid of the uncooperative mandarins, and replace Ham Nghi. That turned out to be the case, as Silvestre had foreseen, but the event that triggered changes took the French by surprise.

The battle for Hué

Ham Nghi was installed with pomp in the presence of Pierre Rheinart, the Resident in Hué, who made certain that the French enjoyed pride of place to signify that the ruler, though chosen by an Annamese council, sat on the throne only with French assent.[15] The adolescent Ham Nghi played little immediate role in politics, and power lay with the two regents. Nguyen Van Tuong in 1874 had negotiated an early treaty between Annam and France (for which the French bestowed the Legion of Honour on him), and became Minister of Finances and Minister of Foreign Affairs. His son married a sister of Emperors Kien Phuoc and Ham Nghi. Ton That Thuyet, a distant relative of Ham Nghi, was Minister of War. Thuyet favoured imminent military resistance against the French, while Tuong opposed precipitate armed action. Tuong was considered diplomatic, Thuyet belligerent; personal antipathy brewed between the two men.

Thuyet devised a plan to evict the foreigners without realising he was playing into French hands. He bolstered the citadel's defences, and built an emergency imperial redoubt some distance from Hué, at Tan So. Rumours of a possible attack on the French circulated, but politicians in Paris hesitated to authorise preventive action, as French troops were preoccupied with the Pavillons Noirs, Chinese-supported forces. The pirates, as the French branded them, ignominiously forced the French to evacuate Lang Son; the 'Tonkin Affair' brought down the government of Prime Minister Jules Ferry. Eventually a new French commander and Resident in Annam, General Philippe de Courcy, gained permission to move a contingent from Tonkin to Hué.

When de Courcy arrived, he demanded to be received by the emperor with unprecedented honours, allowed to enter the palace through a central doorway reserved for the sovereign, accompanied by a military escort of soldiers, and pausing for the emperor to come forward. He refused to receive a delegation of mandarins, and unceremoniously dismissed courtiers bringing gifts from the queen mother. De Courcy nevertheless hosted a gala soirée for the French community on the evening of 4 July. Such slights set off Thuyet's plan, for he hoped a surprise attack might force public opinion in France to demand withdrawal from Annam and Tonkin.[16] He was confident that 5,000–6,000 Vietnamese soldiers could successfully face off 1,400 French troopers.

Coordinated Vietnamese attacks on the Mang Ca, the French concession within the citadel and their legation across the Perfume River began just after midnight. Although de Courcy was taken unawares, within hours the French gained the upper hand, and headed for the emperor's 'purple city'. As buildings in the citadel burst into flames from the French counter-attack, the emperor, the queen grandmother (Tu Duc's mother), two queen mothers, the emperor's two brothers and Thuyet fled. De Courcy decided not to pursue the fugitives; securing control of Hué and searching for the royal treasury presented higher priorities. The fighting had left over sixty Frenchmen killed or wounded, and around 1,500 Vietnamese killed, including several of Thuyet's sons. The French looted the imperial city.

The French found a collaborator in Tuong, Thuyet's fellow regent and rival. Declaring that he bore no responsibility for the attack, Tuong pronounced submission to the French, who welcomed his overtures and charged Tuong with 'pacifying' Annam, giving him two months for the task. When Tuong did not succeed, and as the French guessed he was acting with duplicity, the regent was arrested in September 1885 and exiled to Tahiti, where he died a few months later.

French officers blamed Thuyet for the uprising. Captain Gosselin, who took part in the battle, stated that Thuyet 'showed himself to be criminal towards his sovereign, towards his country and towards us'. His initiative was 'the consequence of his hatred for Tuong and for us, and the ultimate sign of his ambition'. Gosselin conceded that Thuyet's rebels had strong convictions: 'One fights such adversaries; one pursues them without mercy; but one cannot but salute them.'[17] 'The principal victim', he added, 'was his young sovereign, dragged in spite of himself away from his capital, in the middle of the battle, condemned for almost four [sic] years to lead the life of an itinerant'.[18]

A Vietnamese perspective comes from a contemporary recitative, whose unidentified author also placed responsibility on an ambitious Thuyet, but saw the action as heroic defence of the fatherland. The work depicts Annam in a state of crisis: 'Outside the brigands [the French] menace us, while inside discord reigns' during the rapid succession of rulers. The French steadily advanced, aided by Vietnamese Christians, who deserve to be wiped out for plotting with 'the Western pirates'. After Ham Nghi's accession Thuyet designed an offensive with a noble cause: 'If the French take over our cities, if we give them all of our wealth, what will we have to leave to our descendants?'[19] The night of the battle brought terror and chaos, French soldiers firing wildly, palaces in flames, people desperately rushing to escape: 'Heaven had clearly deserted the Annamese heroes', and after only four hours, 'already the Nation was lost!'. Meanwhile, 'The King was terrified by the boom of the cannon and the shooting of guns. Sitting on his golden throne, he dissolved in tears, imploring the Emperor of Heaven so that the imperial Family and the whole Nation might continue to live in peace'. Mandarins, advising 'there is no possible tranquillity for Your Majesty', convinced him to take flight. The work closes with the king moving deeper into the countryside, refusing to surrender: 'Adieu the fine palaces with sumptuous rooms where now these damned invaders take their ease.' The poet summoned compatriots: 'Let us follow the King, always before our eyes the character [the written word] of "Loyalty".'[20]

Whether heroes, victims or villains, the emperor and other royals, Thuyet and their band made their way to Tan So, then moved further into the jungle.[21] The queen grandmother, queen mothers and emperor's brothers, on Ham Nghi's command, returned to Hué on 9 July, but the emperor rejected de Courcy and the queen grandmother's injunctions to return as well and remained in hiding.

The Can Vuong movement

French occupation of Hué sparked four years of armed resistance in Annam and Tonkin that targeted the foreigners and Vietnamese Christians, the Can Vuong ('Aid the Emperor') movement. From the emperor's hideout, an imperial edict was issued in Ham Nghi's name and under his seal.[22] It reflected on recent events using Confucian sentiments: 'We came to the throne very young, but have been greatly concerned with self-strengthening and sovereign government. Nevertheless, with every passing day the Western envoys got more and more overbearing. Recently they brought in troops and naval reinforcements, trying to force on Us conditions We could never accept.' Forced into battle, 'We did not have the strength to hold out and allowed the royal capital to fall ... The fault is Ours entirely, a matter of great shame'. However, 'traditional loyalties are strong. Hundreds of mandarins and commanders of all levels, perhaps not having the heart to abandon Me, unite as never before'. With unity and good fortune, 'Heaven will also treat man with kindness, turning chaos into order, danger into peace, and helping thus to restore our land and our frontiers'.[23]

A missive in the emperor's name was also delivered to Tuong asking the regent to negotiate concessions from the French, but reaffirming the sovereign's rights: 'We are inseparable (from Our people) like water and fish: how could We forget each other?'[24] As the months passed, it became clear reconciliation between the Can Vuong movement and the French was impossible, and Tuong's arrest removed a potential intermediary. When Ham Nghi failed to return, the French had the imperial council declare the throne vacant and select a new emperor, Ham Nghi's brother Dong Khanh, although the French were concerned about his 'eccentricity', including mysticism and reports of cruelty.[25] Dong Khanh remained loyal to the French, Gosselin explained forthrightly, because 'he was aware that if we ceased for an instant to back him up, his reign would not last an hour'.[26] The Vietnamese greeted the new emperor with indifference or hostility, and General Prudhomme, the French commander, admitted that 'the ex-king, even having taken flight, is still obeyed everywhere that he can wield influence and where our actions are not backed up by our bayonets'.[27]

As the French battled the Can Vuong resistance, they also sent soldiers in pursuit of Ham Nghi, and tried to extract information on his whereabouts by all means available, including torture. Gosselin led French troops to Than Lang, near where Ham Nghi was eventually captured, and stated that people knew the location of his hideout, but 'when we arrived, all were resigned to support torments, to submit to death, rather than to reveal to foreigners the place of refuge of their king'. 'Our duty', he added, 'imposed such actions on us, we were thus often constrained to go to extremes whose application would have appeared regrettable in any other circumstances'.[28]

Ham Nghi and his party had pushed their way through the jungle of Vietnam and crossed into Laos, hoping to reach Tonkin and rally forces there, though subsequently they drifted back into Annam. Dense vegetation, mountainous terrain and monsoonal rain, combined with fever and dysentery, and increasing desertions, weakened the partisans, though they proved remarkably adept at holding out against the French. In an unexpected move, Thuyet, in early 1887, left Ham Nghi to go to China on the grounds of seeking support from Beijing, which was not forthcoming; he remained in exile until his death in 1913, the Chinese refusing to render him to the French. Thuyet had entrusted Ham Nghi to his own sons, the twenty-four-year-old Ton That Dam, de facto military commander in the emperor's camp, and the sixteen-year-old Ton That Tiep.

The French occasionally held out an olive branch – proposing in October 1886 that Ham Nghi be made viceroy over three provinces – but to no avail. Ham Nghi continued to attract defenders, notably from ethnic Hmong in the highlands, but by late 1888 only a handful remained with him, and he was said to be living on little more than rice.[29] Ham Nghi was finally betrayed by a follower, Truong Quang Ngoc, son of a disgraced mandarin, who, according to Gosselin, was 'made of the stuff of Judas'.[30] Reports of his capture differ, but it seems that Truong moved on Ham Nghi's hideout in the night of 1 November 1888. Two mandarins came outside the hut where Ham Nghi was secreted and were killed before Truong pushed in. Ton That Thiep rushed to the emperor's defence but was fatally speared. The emperor, brandishing a sword, reputedly asked to be killed rather than given up to the French, but was disarmed. With the captured Ham Nghi and an adolescent servant, the conspirators began the two-day journey to a French post, where Ham Nghi was handed over, but nevertheless received with military honours.

Accounts of Ham Nghi's reactions must be read with caution because of lack of corroboration, differing versions and questions of translation. Some remembered that Ham Nghi at first denied he was the fugitive emperor, but others affirmed that he offered no resistance. One French general quoted Ham Nghi: 'You [the French] are enemies and traitors, just as Dong Khanh himself when he follows the French, but as for me, I do not betray my country.' He added, with resignation: 'I must obey the divine will, do with me what you wish. Eat my flesh if that gives you pleasure.' To some Frenchmen, Ham Nghi appeared humble and docile, a youth in need of affection and understanding.³¹ Rheinart, the Resident, found his behaviour insolent, but set his reactions in the context of a fugitive youth taken into custody after seeing his closest friend killed: 'His imagination must have been terrified.' He later stated that if Ham Nghi had embraced the French as 'liberators', he might have been treated 'as a prince whom simple political reasons had momentarily taken away from his country'. However, 'we were received and treated as enemies and Ung Lich [Ham Nghi's birth name] is nothing other than a prisoner'.³²

Meanwhile, Ton That Dam, who was absent from Ham Nghi's camp when he was taken, learned of the emperor's capture. He declared that if the French wanted news of him, they must search for his grave. After writing a farewell letter to Ham Nghi, asking pardon for being unable to defend the emperor, as well as a letter to the French commander proclaiming that 'we only tried to defend ourselves', he committed suicide. Speaking of Thuyet's two sons, Gosselin acknowledges that their 'example of patriotism' earned the 'admiration and esteem of their adversaries'.³³

The French kept Ham Nghi in their camp for several weeks while deciding what to do with him. One official suggested he be returned to the imperial palace, lauded for having 'abandoned' the rebellion and persuaded to submit formally, whereupon he might receive an honorary position. Others expressed concern that he would remain dangerous, or that he might escape. Yet another proposition was that he be kept in internal exile in Saigon.³⁴ The option decided upon, however, was exile overseas. Ham Nghi was informed, to his shock, that he would be deported to Algeria, suitably distant from Indochina and chosen – Gosselin smoothly states – as 'the mildness of its climate could suit [Ham Nghi's] state of health'. A proclamation by Dong Khanh, expressing affection for his deposed brother, euphemistically stated that Ham Nghi's health had been so badly affected in the mountains that he needed to be taken 'to France'; more pointedly, it declared that 'there can no longer be two sovereigns in the same State as there cannot be two suns in the sky'.³⁵ Rheinart wrote to superiors that 'to keep Dong Khanh under our control', it would be good to 'let him understand the possibility of his replacement [by a restored Ham Nghi] should he not remain loyal'.³⁶ Ham Nghi thus would be kept as a monarch-in-waiting who could be returned to the throne if his successors did not bend to French will.

The dethroned emperor never signed an abdication, and was not charged with any crime or put on trial; he had no appeal against the order for his exile. The French did command that Ham Nghi be treated with dignity so as not to inflame what Rheinart called the 'sentimentality' of the public, both in Vietnam and France, where expansion in Indochina was still contested. Ham Nghi was taken in a closed palanquin from the highlands to Saigon, and placed on board a ship bound for North Africa on 12 December 1888. He arrived in Algiers on 13 January 1889; an official, fretting he might hire a boatman to ferry him to the Balearic Islands and catch a British ship back to Vietnam, ordered the exile's close surveillance.[37]

Exile and legacy

Determining the exact role of Ham Nghi during the resistance movement of 1885–89 is difficult. The emperor was only fourteen years old and had been on the throne for less than a year at the time of the battle in Hué. He had not shown himself particularly rebellious or unsettled during his short reign. With the French on one side and the powerful regents and other mandarins on the other, Ham Nghi had little room for manoeuvre, even if he had the capacity. Much of his energy was required for familial and ritual duties, and it is unlikely he was apprised of Thuyet's plans. The French, according to Gosselin's sympathetic memoir, considered that Ham Nghi was virtually a prisoner of Thuyet. He also quoted the emperor as saying that he 'was taken away by force', the court had committed a 'great error' in leaving the palace, and he hoped Catholics would intercede on his behalf.[38] To what extent decisions to flee the citadel, and not return to Hué or surrender, were those of Ham Nghi, or the men around him, remains unclear. The monarch was clearly much distressed at the occupation of Hué, and fled the palace in tears. Perhaps he wished to make peace with the French, and it has been suggested that Thuyet said to the emperor: 'If Your Majesty wants to return to Hué, he must first leave his head here [in the rebels' camp].'[39]

It is unlikely that Ham Nghi had anything to do with the attack in the citadel or with instigating the Can Vuong movement, though he may well have supported its objectives. His proclamations and the Can Vuong manifesto embodied familiar Confucian principles, views of the primacy of the imperial throne that he certainly shared as well as understandable national pride. French invasion and conquest, slights to protocol and arrogance no doubt rankled. His reported statements, if accurately recorded, suggest deeply felt opposition to colonisers. As a fugitive, Ham Nghi cuts a poignant figure, an adolescent removed from his palace to a rough hideout facing the perils of the jungle and insalubrious climate. Caught between the overweening Thuyet and rebels on one side and the French on the other, he had a precarious position. With Dong Khanh invested as emperor, his authority came only from his partisans, and Thuyet seemed to have abandoned him by going to China. A follower betrayed him, and his truest friend was killed before his eyes. He was peremptorily informed he would be deported to a distant country of which he had possibly never heard.

What was significant was not personal initiatives by Ham Nghi in the uprising, but that he was considered by many, before and after deposition, as legitimate emperor. That position made him, for the Vietnamese, in Gosselin's fine words, a 'sovereign, judge, supreme pontiff, father and mother of the people, first mandarin [of the kingdom], holder of the mandate of Heaven, the son of Heaven'.[40] His ouster, implication in a resistance movement and guerrilla warfare, and banishment all enveloped Ham Nghi in a patriotic aura. As Gosselin insightfully remarks, this was 'even more so because, by the nature of things, his name had become the banner of national independence'.[41] Gosselin concedes that 'we applied ... the name of rebels to the partisans of the *ancien régime*',[42] but for the Vietnamese they were defenders of the homeland as well as the regime. Ham Nghi incarnated resistance, the moral and political nationhood represented by the throne, and the bonds between sovereign and people: the 'fish and water' to which he alluded. In the words of General Georges Catroux, a later governor-general of Indochina, 'This young prince ... gradually and fully identified himself as the symbol of the Vietnamese country that he represented'.[43]

The Can Vuong movement continued to unsettle the French for several years after Ham Nghi's capture. According to the historian Charles Fourniau, it primarily mobilised mandarins and other educated members of the elite. They supported the emperor for the lineage and traditions he represented, and saw in the rebellion not only an attack on French colonisers but also a defence of Confucian values, customary social hierarchies and the integrity of the kingdom. The movement was reactionary, in the true sense, an attempt to restore the monarch and the social and cultural system on which the monarchy rested. Though Vietnamese nationalism would evolve, Can Vuong, as Fourniau convincingly argues, represented the initial phase of anti-colonialism.[44]

In 1885, the French might have abolished the Nguyen dynasty and annexed Annam and Tonkin, a measure de Courcy favoured. He reminded superiors that a protectorate implied a dual administration, and Europeans could only hope for resentful cooperation from indigenous monarchs. Prudhomme suggests that the colonial ministry decided against annexation largely because of the opposition it would provoke in a French Parliament where many expressed grave reservations about French expansionism.[45] According to Gosselin, international considerations came into play because of the Tientsen treaty, in which China had recognised French protection over Annam; an attempt to rule directly could have triggered war with China.⁴⁶ The French, furthermore, knew that for the Vietnamese a monarch was vital for their country's wellbeing as intercessor with heaven and guardian of ancestral shrines. They hoped that continuing recognition of a vassal emperor would allow them to draw on the powers of the throne. The colonisers could utilise a willing emperor as executor of policy and an intermediary with the subject population. A suitably brought up Francophile monarch would symbolise and promote acquiescence to French rule.

Ham Nghi in exile

The French treated Ham Nghi with a certain regard, for reasons cogently stated in a letter from the colonial minister almost twenty years after the emperor's exile, the words witnessing the favourable impressions Ham Nghi had made since his ouster. First, the minister 'considered that it was dignified of a nation such as ours that distinguishes itself by its spirit of justice and generosity, to assure a suitable existence to a Prince whom political reasons led us to dispossess and to remove from the throne, but who by the correctness of his attitude, his superior intelligence, the elevation of his character and attachment that he is more and more manifesting for France and our civilisation, and the esteem and goodwill of those who have met him'. The second reason – echoing comments in the 1880s – was that 'It is possible that in the Far East certain eventualities could mean that our sentiments of generosity and justice will match up with our political interests', in other words, that he might be useful, possibly as a restored sovereign.⁴⁷

Ham Nghi was accompanied into exile by an interpreter (who also provided intelligence reports to the French), a servant and a cook from Cochinchina. He arrived in Algeria with the title of Grand Duke (Quan Cong) conferred by his successor, but was generally known as the 'Prince of Annam'. The French provided a generous pension and gave him a residence, the Villa des Pins, at El-Biar, a salubrious and picturesque seaside neighbourhood three kilometres from the centre of Algiers. A Frenchwoman was put in charge of the household, and tasked with keeping the exile under surveillance. Despite his deposition, Ham Nghi retained the prestige and celebrity of a former sovereign, invited to sit in the governor-general's box at the opera soon after his arrival. As he grew older, he was welcomed into Algiers' high society. After first refusing to learn French, he relented, and spent much time reading literary classics. He took art lessons from a local painter, and became an accomplished amateur artist, his European-style works showing the influences of traditional Vietnamese painting. A journalist visiting in

1894, when Ham Nghi was in his early twenties, described him as 'of medium build, slender and supple', dressed in Vietnamese clothing, a young gentleman of 'the right sort and perfect courtesy'. His sitting room contained a picture of a former governor-general of Algeria, and his studio was filled with books, paintings and cameras. He gave the reporter the sense of being 'conscious of his rank', reserved in manner and dedicated to cultural pursuits.[48]

The French found little to complain about Ham Nghi. In 1904, the governor-general of Algeria remarked that over the last sixteen years, there had been 'no effort at conspiracy against his successor in Hué or against the French protectorate', and noted 'the dignity and resignation with which he has accepted during long years the consequences of the errors that he was made to commit, [when he was] almost a child, against our country'.[49] Ham Nghi expressed support for France in the First World War, and by 1919, the Resident in Hanoi stated with satisfaction that 'over [the last] twenty-five years he has learned to know and love France'.[50]

Though officials did not initially want Ham Nghi to visit France, the emperor went to Paris and Vichy as early as 1897. (An official recorded that he never asked to go to Vietnam.[51]) Regular sojourns followed; he took a few sculpting lessons from the great Auguste Rodin, and was received by the president at the Élysée Palace. Gosselin, who had participated in his capture in Vietnam, claimed him as a friend and much later introduced Ham Nghi to the last emperor of Annam, Bao Dai. Another acquaintance was the popular writer Judith Gautier, best known for her fanciful novels set in faraway locations; she wrote a poem about Ham Nghi's exile. The emperor eventually purchased a château in the south of France for his holidays, completing his adaptation to French society.

In Algeria, in addition to reading, painting and sculpting, the ex-emperor occupied his time with violin lessons, practised tennis, gymnastics and fencing, worked in his garden, went hunting, and toured archaeological sites. He took no part in politics, and steadfastly refused to speak about his time as emperor or the Can Vuong movement. In 1904, the thirty-four-year-old married Marcelle Laloë, the nineteen-year-old daughter of a senior magistrate – one picture shows a large crowd on the steps of the cathedral trying to catch a glimpse of the elegant couple, proof of their celebrity status. Another gently caricatures the newlyweds – noticeably pinned to the emperor's gown is a tag of the sort attached to a convict's uniform identifying him as a numbered prisoner of the République Française (see Figure 7).

Two years later, the couple built a Moorish-style house, named the Villa Gia Long after the founder of the Nguyen dynasty. Although Ham

Figure 7 Ham Nghi, emperor of Annam (1872–1943, r. 1884–85), deposed by the French after involvement in a rebellion and exiled to Algeria.

Nghi did not convert, his three children were raised as Catholics. The only son, Minh Duc (1910–80), graduated from the French military academy, fought in France at the outset of the Second World War, and then in the Foreign Legion during the Resistance, and served in Algeria in the 1950s. Nhu Mai (1905–99), the couple's elder daughter, finished at the top of her class at the National Institute of Agronomy in Paris, one of its first women graduates. Neither married or had children. The third child, Nhu Ly (1908–2005), married the Comte de la Besse, with whom she had three children.[52]

There was occasional talk about restoration of Ham Nghi to the throne when the French clashed with his successors. The idea was mooted in the mid-1890s, when the French became concerned about the erratic behaviour of Emperor Thanh Thai, and again in 1907, when he was dethroned. Several French and Vietnamese commentators then argued that Ham Nghi had played no significant role in the 1885 rebellion and affirmed that he had become a loyal supporter of the French, rich with overseas experience, and would make an ideal emperor. Not all were convinced, and some feared his loyalty might not be rock solid.[53] However, General Catroux remarked many years later that had Ham Nghi been returned to the throne, 'he would have symbolised both the soul of the country that he had embodied and the beneficial principle of a fertile union between France and Annam'.[54] It does not seem that Ham Nghi personally ever sought his restoration, and uncertain that he would have agreed to return to Hué.

Ham Nghi died peacefully in January 1943 and was buried in Algiers. In 1965, after the independence of Algeria, his remains were reinterred in the village of Thonac (in the Dordogne), where his elder daughter lived. In the 1990s, his family declined a proposal from the Vietnamese government for the emperor's remains to be repatriated to the imperial tombs in Hué.

'The drama that played out in 1885', according to Catroux, 'proceeded from the same deep-lying causes as that which, in 1953 [sic, referring to the Battle of Dien Bien Phu] brought it to an end. The one and the other were essentially expressions of a revolt opposed to a foreign intervention that came from the national instinct and soul of a people conscious of the value of its civilisation and faithful to its past.'[55] The interpretation is astute. Ham Nghi paid the price not only for his participation in the resistance, whether willingly or under pressure, but also for the opposition to the French occupation and the defence of the homeland that he symbolised. In the 1880s, the French hurried to get rid of a young man whom they judged compromised by, even if not responsible for, resistance. Ham Nghi showed no interest in a nominal viceregal position, and no doubt neither the French nor Dong Khanh were eager for him to stay around as a potential focus for opposition or intrigues. Putting Ham Nghi on trial would have placed the French in the uncomfortable position of having to prove his guilt; if convicted, imprisoning the former ruler would have turned him into a martyr. Exile provided a convenient response to the question of what to do with the deposed monarch. The French would employ the same strategy with two later Vietnamese emperors.

Thanh Thai

After the premature death of Dong Khanh in 1889, another emperor had to be found, and the French choice, to which mandarins agreed, was the ten-year-old Buu Lan, who took the reign name of Thanh Thai.[56] The obscure son of the ephemeral emperor Duc Duc, Thanh Thai had lived with his mother, a minor wife of the emperor, in modest conditions inside the imperial compound. She burst into tears when the French came to take away her son for his enthronement. Thanh Thai showed no desire for the position, and when he arrived at the imperial quarters and was served a cup of tea, he declined to drink it until a mandarin had first tasted the beverage – a not unreasonable fear, with previous emperors in mind, of being poisoned.[57]

The French had selected Thanh Thai largely because he *was* young, unknown and unprepared for the throne, hoping he would be susceptible to their influence, pliable and loyal. Since he was a minor, a regency council was instituted, to which the French appointed two superannuated princes and two others known to be sympathetic to the colonisers. Thanh Thai grew into a slender, well-proportioned man with a handsome face marked by a forthright and insolent-looking gaze, slightly askew because of strabismus (see Figure 8).

A 1902 album of watercolours of the court by Nguyen Van Nhan shows an attractive young Thanh Thai looking suitably regal in multicoloured gowns, surrounded by mandarins and servants holding umbrellas and swords.[58] The monarch displayed interest in such modern technology as bicycles and automobiles, though bemoaning to a visiting journalist that he could not drive his two motorcars as fast as he would like because of crowds of spectators.

During Thanh Thai's reign, the French embarked on a programme of economic development, acquisition of land for commercial agriculture and mining, and urbanism. They remained uncertain as to what degree the emperor and Hué government, still nominally independent, ought to be actively associated with the initiatives. Though the Can Vuong movement had been suppressed, the French knew that many nationalists remained firm monarchists, decrying the weakening of the throne and calling for the emperor to resume the fullness of his old position. The masses retained an emotional attachment to the throne because of its ritual position and time-honoured prestige. The mandarins, for the most part, saw themselves as conservative guardians of tradition. Some in the elite, however, were drawn to new ideas, either resolving to gain what benefits they might from French presence, or 'looking East' for inspiration towards the growing commercial, military and political strength of a rising Japan or towards reformist ideas in China.[59]

Figure 8 Thanh Thai, emperor of Annam (1879–1954, r. 1889–1907), dethroned by the French on charges of 'madness' and sent into internal exile in Vietnam and subsequently to Réunion Island. The monarch, shown here during his reign, wears both Vietnamese and French decorations.

The French soon found cause for concern about the fledging emperor. Less than a year after Thanh Thai's accession, the governor-general wrote to the colonial minister about the 'frail constitution' of the ruler and mooted the question of possible successors if he should die.[60] However, the incipient problem would not be 'frail' physical health. In

1893, the emperor turned fourteen years old and seems to have experienced the early onset of a turbulent puberty, like many adolescents baulking against constraints, especially ones imposed in a hermetic and convention-bound court. Mandarins and French spies reported that he was neglecting his studies, failing to pay expected visits to the queen grandmother and queen mothers, and refusing to attend meetings of the Co Mat (the council of mandarin ministers). Furthermore, he was making nocturnal sorties from the palace, in the company of his brothers, eunuchs, servants or palace women, but not the grand entourage with which an emperor generally left the 'purple city'. The aim of the excursions was to amuse himself, sometimes in dubious quarters of the city, and to find sexual partners, for Thanh Thai developed a precocious and insatiable sexual appetite. The dowagers, mandarins and Resident took the unusual step of roundly scolding the emperor; he issued a *mea culpa* and promised to mend his ways.[61]

Over the next years, however, Thanh Thai proved incapable or unwilling to reform. Escapades outside the palace became an almost daily occurrence, and he sent courtiers to recruit young women for his pleasure. He played practical jokes, such as getting people drunk for his merriment, and engaged in odd games. For instance, he had fifty women he had brought into the palace set up a 'marketplace', and wandered around buying their goods. He sometimes dressed the women in mock military uniforms, distributed fake weapons, and paraded them around the grounds, and once dressed them in pretend nuns' habits.[62]

Some 'games' might have been excused when the emperor was a boy, but he continued playing them in his twenties, to French consternation. Avid sexual interests were neither unusual nor inappropriate for a ruler whose virility was confirmed by a cohort of wives and concubines and numerous progeny, though the French and courtiers expressed concern about Thanh Thai's voracious desire. More worrying was his violence. Thanh Thai was said frequently to strike servants in fits of rage. Some of his games turned deadly – one four-year-old died after his rough play holding her upside down and bashing her head on the floor. With sex partners, his behaviour turned sadistic, with acts the French labelled torture. He kidnapped women and forced them to have sex with him. He was reported to have poured hot oil or boiling water over the genitals of several women, of pricking them with a bayonet, and even of eviscerating one woman. He was alleged to have raped a twelve-year-old sister.

The dowagers and mandarins had repeatedly remonstrated the emperor, inspiring further promises to reform, and his mother brought in what the French called 'sorcerers' to treat her son.[63] In 1893, she had admitted that 'the King is suffering from a capricious malady' produced by 'internal heat in the chest and stomach'; Vietnamese doctors found he had a problem of 'excess excitation'. The French, too, sent in physicians, who found Thanh Thai in good physical shape; they prescribed a 'tonic wine', which the emperor often refused to take. Two years later, an official judged that 'search for sexual pleasures of all sorts had fully absorbed him, and with this permanent excitation he soon arrived at an acute hysterical state that rapidly ravaged a naturally feeble spirit weakened by atavism'. In his *mea culpa* statements, the emperor blamed defects on youth, ignorance and weak character, finding such excuses as the uncomfortable heat that forced him to quit the palace in the evening for relief. He also said enigmatically that he was 'prey to attacks of terror'. He did not seek to deny or justify allegations of sexual abuse and violence.

The reports by Residents, and subalterns charged with keeping tabs on the emperor, spoke of 'reprehensible actions', 'caprices', 'bizarreries', 'eccentricities', and increasingly, the emperor's *'folie'*, or madness. One report suggested that disgruntled eunuchs and servants might exaggerate his behaviour. But so consistent are the reports over an almost eighteen-year period that it is hard to disbelieve that the emperor was persistently engaging in conduct that inflicted injury, distress and perhaps death. Though personal discord existed between Thanh Thai and officials, notably the Resident in office when he was finally deposed, the French had little interest in intentionally blackening the emperor's reputation. Correspondence about his private life was generally marked 'very confidential', indicating the delicate nature of issues that would rebound against both the sovereign and protectorate. The dowagers and mandarins, providing corroboration, discussed the emperor's conduct with the French, and on several occasions formally upbraided him. French doctors treated women who had suffered at the emperor's hands or by his order, and constables interviewed women who had escaped from the palace, as well as a mother who claimed the ruler was holding her daughter captive.

As the emperor's behaviour became more widely known, the French gathered that many in Hué and beyond were losing respect for the monarch. Officials also feared that disesteem for the emperor might become so strong that he would be poisoned by courtiers, like several predecessors. The press in Vietnam and in France were publishing articles about the emperor's antics, and newspapers even further afield – in New Zealand, for instance – were picking up sensationalistic reports about the 'Mad King of Annam'.[64]

Why then did the French for so long tolerate not only Thanh Thai's inattention to duties but scandalous private conduct? Episodic periods of calm reassured the French that Thanh Thai was on the mend, and the emperor was on occasion capable of attending to his obligations, as during state visits to Saigon and Hanoi. He found guarded favour among several officials. Governor-General Paul Doumer, who first met Thanh Thai when he took up his appointment in 1897, thought he had 'a lively intelligence with a great self-possession although he appeared wilful, capricious and bizarre', traits Doumer excused because of youthful age and the indulgences of the harem, 'which was not conducive to intellectual and moral stability'. Moreover, given the short reigns of Thanh Thai's four predecessors, it might have seemed hazardous to dispose of the incumbent in short order.

The issue for the French was not Thanh Thai's morality or palace intrigues; colonial overlords were renowned for turning a blind eye to the foibles of native rulers. The historian Oscar Chapuis remarks, with cold logic, that in general, 'Thanh Thai's insanity ... was of no real concern to the French. Indeed, the deaths at dawn of a few palace maids were trivialities compared with the lofty doctrine of French *"mission civilisatrice"*.'[65] Their priority was consolidation of colonial authority. They had selected Thanh Thai as emperor, with hopes he would be a useful feudatory. The French knew that not all mandarins had been enthusiastic about the choice of ruler in 1889 – some had called for the return of Ham Nghi, or favoured different candidates. Thanh Thai had subsequently failed to win mandarins' affection or allegiance, and a 1902 report from the Resident said that they called Thanh Thai the 'French king'. He acknowledged that 'H.M. Thanh Thai would not reign for an hour if French protection were withdrawn ... I am not just certain of this, but I have such a formal affirmation, though confidentially so, from the women [the queen-mothers] whose duty makes them the proper supporters of the throne'. The implication was that the French could hardly abandon Thanh Thai without loss of face and authority, and implicit recognition of the power of dowagers, mandarins and the public in effecting a change. Having set Thanh Thai on the throne, they could with difficulty kick him off it.

Thanh Thai's recurring misdeeds nevertheless suggested he was incorrigible. By the early years of the twentieth century, officials were canvassing possible replacements, while still reluctant to remove the incumbent. Residents continued to condemn the emperor's excesses, but with no greater action that pleading with him to reform. A new Resident appointed to Hué in 1906, Fernand Lévecque, however, moved in for the kill. The emperor and Resident immediately clashed on funding for the ruler's travels, questions of protocol, renovation of a temple and imprisonment of a member of the royal family. The Resident, perhaps with connivance of others in the administration or court – in particular a mandarin with designs for his son-in-law to become emperor – was looking for justification to dethrone the monarch.

Matters soon came to a head. In June 1906, a constable and French doctors were summoned on reports of the brutalisation by the emperor of four women, aged between sixteen and twenty-two. The women, who had been sexually abused and tortured, required hospitalisation. A constable sent to investigate reported continuing violence. The Resident wrote to the governor-general that 'His Majesty has killed eleven women in three nights', and he added tales of other horrors. The emperor, with his troupe of women 'soldiers', had also staged a mock battle between France and China – a suggestion of political disloyalty not just immorality.[66]

Dramatic as these allegations were, another incident clinched Thanh Thai's fate. Attending a theatrical performance, he shot four times at Ung Huy, vice-president of the royal family council. On questioning, the emperor said that the bullets were blanks, and that he was simply amusing himself and did not foresee any ill effects. Further investigation showed that the bullets were real, as they damaged furniture and grazed two bystanders. A report now remarked that Thanh Thai, fully cognisant of his acts and their repercussions, 'expects one day or another either to be deposed or to be deported outside Asia'.[67] The Resident discussed the issue in the council of mandarins, referring to the 'abominable' acts of the sovereign: 'these are no longer childish play [enfantilllages], but an act of madness or a crime'. The Vietnamese Minister of the Interior informed the meeting that the emperor had admitted that he was taken for a madman, but was not; the Resident retorted that if the emperor was not mad, then he was criminal. The authorities resolved to confiscate a hundred guns that, unaccountably, had been lent to the emperor, and to expel from the palace the 'troupe' of women involved in his theatrics. The emperor was confined to his quarters.

On 22 July 1907, the colonial minister wrote from Paris to say that the government in principle approved deposition of the emperor and the 'necessity to bring an end to the scandalous state of things'. Somewhat precipitately but after years of problems, on 29 July, the governor-general announced that the emperor's powers, on the ostensible grounds of illness, were being transferred to the council of mandarin ministers, transformed into a regency council. This was de facto dethroning, if not de jure deposition, and Thanh Thai was effectively put under house arrest. A Co Mat resolution nevertheless reminded the French: 'In every state of the Far East, there is always a King, who is a chief whose mission is to carry out the dynastic rites of the ancestors and of frontier spirits, and to govern the administrators and the people. All eyes look upon him, destiny – happy or unfortunate – is attached to his person.' It recalled the long history of the Nguyen lineage and stated that 'there is no one who is not profoundly attached to this dynasty'. The regency council 'respectfully notes' that the current king, 'afflicted with illness', 'has committed strange acts' and 'that it will be impossible to hope for his cure, either in a matter of months or years'. It asked that the 'principle of monarchy' be maintained, and a new emperor be chosen, with the approval of the regents. Such a move would provide 'a new proof of our will not to make the protectorate a simple fiction without value for the Annamese' but only an 'instrument of domination'.[68] With real concern, but hoping to regain some of their traditional sway, the council offered persuasive arguments about getting rid of the emperor, but keeping the dynasty.

The transfer of authority to regents, however, caused some concern, according to Governor-General Beau, among Vietnamese feeling that the council had usurped the emperor's powers. He explained to the colonial minister: 'The veritable cause of the very real disquiet that is apparent among all the mandarins ... [is] the fear that the very principle of the monarchy is under threat.' As proof of attachment to monarchy, the French had a letter from mandarins in Thai Binh province: 'Despite changes of dynasty there was not a single day [in the past] when there was not a king at the head of the kingdom.' They asked for restoration of Ham Nghi, whom they argued had been led into rebellion by 'perfidious subjects', and who had since rallied to the French. With strained comparison to the travels of Russia's Peter the Great, they suggested that Ham Nghi's time in Algeria had acquainted him with the benefits of modernity, and that he would return with the wisdom of experience. With a rather more menacing tone, mandarins from Haidoung wrote to the governor-general that Thanh Thai had committed no wrong to his people, and did not deserve the treatment meted out: 'We fear that the day the kingdom is deprived of its king, revolution will break out.' The removal of his powers was a 'grave infraction of the laws of the Protectorate', and if Thanh Thai were not restored, 'revolution will break out ... the consequences your fault'. Neither missive, notwithstanding the alarming prospects they held out, swayed the French.[69]

There was, in fact, little support among mandarins for Thanh Thai, whose behaviour had long aroused opprobrium, especially when it compromised the mandarins' own sense of their status. For instance, they had accused the emperor of humiliating them by holding receptions in ordinary clothing rather than court dress; he once met them, 'wearing a short tunic, like a "boy" [a young servant], holding in his hand a simple cane [rather than a ceremonial staff]', and he failed to respond to their salutations: protocol was a point of honour. Their priority was a respectable and respectful emperor on the throne; they saw nothing unacceptable in removal of Thanh Thai, on condition that he be immediately replaced.

French residents of Vietnam appeared little troubled by the tempests. A government report noted that Hanoi newspapers initially greeted the revocation of the emperor's powers with 'complete indifference'; the press remarked on the 'loyalty' of Vietnamese subjects. One newspaper argued that the action provided an opportune moment for annexation of Annam and Tonkin, while another simply called for enthronement of a new sovereign. Yet another published an article calling Thanh Thai a victim of the 'impunity' of Lévecque. *L'Avenir du Tonkin* said that Thanh Thai's only misdeeds had been 'corporal punishments inflicted on several concubines', which did not violate the Vietnamese penal code, and the emperor had been undone by the 'personal hatred' of the Resident. One letter in particular damned Lévecque: 'If there is one demented person in Hué, it is not the King but his persecutor, M. Lévecque'; M. de Monpezat, the letter-writer, improbably suggested that Thanh Thai had converted to Catholicism in 1905, and that the Freemason Lévecque disapproved. 'With his baptism, the monarch was declared mad, mad enough to be tied up, unworthy to rule, crazily mad ... I will never pardon these Jacobin lackeys who made of an absolute emperor a martyred emperor, nor give up shouting "Vive l'empereur!"'. In the confused conditions in Hué, wild hypotheses could easily circulate.

Although Thanh Thai might have been left as a purely nominal emperor, a permanent regency council established, or his powers delegated to another member of the royal family, a decision was taken to obtain Thanh Thai's abdication and remove him from Hué. As an emperor who did not reign, Thanh Thai was useless to the French, yet the mandarins and populace held that an active emperor was vital. An unoccupied throne (especially with a disempowered emperor hovering in the background) would be an invitation to intrigues. The governor-general thus presented himself in Thanh Thai's quarters on 3 September 1907: 'I explained to him that the French Government, taking into consideration the long period during which he had reigned – a period of peace, tranquillity and progress for Annam – had decided, despite the grave incidents of these last years that would have justified a more rigorous measure, to allow him the possibility of abdicating in favour of one of his sons.' The nature of 'a more rigorous measure' was not spelled out, though the ultimatum was clear. The emperor inquired only what would happen to him, and the governor-general reassured him that the generosity of France would ensure his wellbeing. Thanh

Thai asked to continue to live in Hué but was told this would be impossible, though where he would be sent was not specified: 'He seemed to fear the fate of Ham Nghi and Ranavalo, whose name he repeated several times, and he asked me not to inflict such an exile on him'. (It is interesting that Thanh Thai was acquainted with the fate of the banished queen of Madagascar as well as the former Vietnamese emperor). The governor-general responded that Thanh Thai's feelings would be made known. Hurrying him along, the governor-general stated that the council of mandarins had already convened to await his decision. Thanh Thai wrote out his abdication: 'The Sovereign being master of the Heavens and the Earth, the spirits and men', but with 'limited virtue', had reigned for nineteen years thanks to the 'protection of great France' and the services of devoted mandarins. 'However, [falling] ill as a consequence of the accumulation of cares, it has become overly painful to continue in the exercise of Our exalted duty', and he had therefore decided to give up the throne, name his son as successor and retire to a private palace 'to rest and care for Ourself'.[70] As Nguyên Thê Anh notes, Thanh Thai was not able to affix his seal to the document, as the French had confiscated that instrument of his authority.[71]

'The majority of the [mandarin] council welcomed [the news] with great satisfaction', Governor-General Beau recorded and another official stated that most newspapers had greeted the emperor's removal with 'complete indifference'. The pressing question was who would succeed Thanh Thai.[72] A thirty-page government report in November 1906 had canvassed possible replacements among some 1,800 princes who might have some claim to the throne. One of the most credible, of course, was Ham Nghi, though the author concluded that his loyalty remained in doubt and advised that he should not be considered. The descendants of Dong Khanh, who had reigned to relative French satisfaction, ought to be excluded because of 'brain disorders' in the family. Another possibility was Prince Cuong De,[73] who lived in self-imposed exile in Japan where he had taken part in a nationalist movement that called for restoration of the emperor's powers and regeneration of Vietnamese traditions; that stance and his links with Japan – whose expansionism worried the French – meant he too was eliminated. The report recommended either the eighth son of Hiep Hoa, or the great-grandson of an earlier monarch, Minh Maung; if neither was acceptable, one of Thanh Thai's sons – he had about a dozen offspring – might be selected. In any case, 'the royal prototype' should be 'a being malleable and docile to our instructions who will allow us to assume for our profit the prestige that still attached to the monarchy'.[74]

In the event, the French opted for a son of Thanh Thai, perhaps to establish a principle of direct succession. The eldest was excluded 'because of defects and character flaws' and the youngest ones because of their age. Immediately after receiving Thanh Thai's abdication, a French physician, accompanied by the governor-general, examined the four remaining sons in the presence of the now ex-emperor. They settled on eight-year-old Prince Vinh San, and Thanh Thai wrote his name into the blank space left for designation of his successor on the act of abdication he had already signed. The heir was conducted to the regents, Thanh Thai remarking as the party left the room, 'with the tone of a commandment', as Beau noted: 'I entrust him to you.'[75] He could not foresee that his son, who became Emperor Duy Tan, would also be deposed, and that the two together would be exiled overseas.

'Mad' emperor or rebel?

In addition to words about the emperor's 'perversions', 'caprices' and 'eccentricities', Residents suggested that Thanh Thai suffered from mental debility or outright insanity. For some, this was linked to unbridled libido and a history of mental instability in the ruling family. 'Hysteria', an illness often ascribed to women and connected to sexual behaviour in the late nineteenth century, was one of their non-professional diagnoses. Yet another word used was 'neurasthenia', a term that gained currency in the last decades of the 1800s for a nervous condition with such symptoms as heart palpitations and depression. 'Degeneracy', which also appears in reports, was also a popular diagnosis, often manifested in physical and moral failings, sexual excess or sadism and masochism. One official, referring to the views of doctors who examined the emperor, called Thanh Thai a 'degenerate maniac', suffering from 'cerebral derangement', a condition visible in such physical signs as a shifting gaze, jerky voice, rictus-like smile and stumbling gait.[76] The French thus identified various pathological conditions in contemporary medical theory to explain the emperor's behaviour. However, notions of immoderate sexual urges, vice, perversion and debauchery corresponded with general European fantasies about the wholesale degeneration of Asian civilisation. 'Native' rulers, it was thought, gave free rein to base urges and unbounded pleasures. Violence went hand-in-hand with life-and-death power over potentates' subjects. Accusations of depravity and cruelty provided stock-in-trade in portrayals of native peoples, used to vilify them as uncivilised and in need of Western moralising. Such stereotyping was hardly absent in commentaries on Thanh Thai's behaviour.

For the French, Thanh Thai was of such unstable mind and despicable acts that he must be deposed, notwithstanding their support over eighteen years despite continuing and frequent evidence of his misdeeds.

For some Vietnamese historians, however, not Thanh Thai's mental state but his political opinions led to his downfall. For these writers, and many present-day Vietnamese, he is now regarded, alongside Ham Nghi and Duy Tan, as one of three 'patriotic' emperors who reigned during the colonial period.

An English-language Vietnamese book on the Nguyen dynasty argues that the emperor harboured antipathies for the French and for 'pro-France Vietnamese sycophants'. His incognito sorties outside the citadel were really fact-finding missions to learn about the life of commoners (though, the text concedes, to chat up pretty girls as well). The French tried to forbid the excursions since he used them to give alms to the needy. The emperor was profoundly aware of his responsibilities to his people, and wrote a poem to that effect: 'All mandarins, civil and military alike, wear brocade robes proudly / But only I, the Emperor, carry the burden of ruling the nation'. The rumour that he had courtiers recruit women as concubines was 'a malicious interpretation from the supporters of France with the purpose of devaluing Emperor Thanh Thai, a patriotic king who intended to overthrow the French domination'. The women whom the French saw as amateur thespians and the emperor's sexual partners were in reality 'an army consisting of 50 women. He himself paid for their lodging and eating. The recruitment and training were in secret'. The emperor's creation of an army of amazons was revealed to the French by Truong Nhu Cuong, Minister of the Interior, who hoped to overthrow the emperor and place his son-in-law on the throne. The French and 'sycophants' thus 'spread a rumor [sic] that the Emperor was out of his mind'. The emperor's refusal 'to ratify the appointment of some sycophants' precipitated his deposition.[77]

One present-day Vietnamese commentator elaborates on the notion that the troupe of women dressed in military uniforms formed a brigade being trained in archery, horse-riding and fencing. Four teams of fifty women engaged in military exercises, he adds, some of them scouting for further recruits before the French discovered the manoeuvres. The emperor hired a Paris-trained painter, Le Van Mien, to paint his portrait, but secretly instructed him to provide diagrams of French weaponry, which Thanh Thai used to have guns manufactured. For another writer, the historian Hoang Hien, Thanh Thai's deeply-felt interest in his people inspired him to travel around in disguise to witness their sufferings. Hoang Hien adds that mandarins conspiring against the emperor found ready collaborators among the French, who eagerly awaited an opportunity to dethrone the monarch. That action was much resented among a Vietnamese population that revered the ruler.[78] In these perspectives, therefore, Thanh Thai was secretly and coherently resisting French overlordship.

Some evidence exists of Thanh Thai's episodic criticism of French policies, such as a 1900 message from the mandarins' council bearing his seal that protests against taxes. His random favourable comments about Japan and China disconcerted the colonisers. Non-cooperation – lack of attention to studies, absence at meetings and breach of protocol – could conceivably be interpreted as symbolic tactics of resistance. One Resident's report mentioned concerns about a supposed stockpile of secretly manufactured weapons stored on the palace grounds, though an agent the French infiltrated into the premises found no evidence of an arsenal. It did seem that gunpowder was being produced or had been spirited away from an old royal storehouse, and the agent had been able to buy some; the Resident conjectured that 'rebel bands' might do likewise. He also found it impossible to rule out an eventual plot that might indeed be directed against, rather than carried out by, the emperor: 'King Thanh Thai, just like his predecessor Dhon-Khan [sic], is even less, given his origins, the personification of the monarchy than that of our political victory in Annam.'[79] Thanh Thai certainly possessed weapons, including guns lent by the Resident, but there was no great cache of arms. There is also no convicing indication that Thanh Thai maintained contact with anti-colonialists at home or abroad.

There seems, therefore, no persuasive evidence for supposing that Thanh Thai was actively and intentionally devising an anti-French campaign backed by a military force, and was removed for that reason. If he had been involved in such a plot, it is likely the French would have ousted him far earlier than they did. However, it may safely be assumed that, like many Vietnamese, he was bitter at the French conquest, the leaching away of the monarch's authority, and annoying remonstrations about his personal conduct. It is more the fact of his deposition and exile, rather than his political actions, that have made him into a potent figure in nationalist martyrology, and interpretations that stress his real or supposed anti-colonialism burnish that image.

There have been a few suggestions that Thanh Thai's behaviour was make-believe. The historian Oscar Chapuis, for instance, says that Thanh Thai 'had to plead insanity' in order to resist both the French and mandarins opposed to his authority. Chapuis adds that 'it was not the first time that a member of the Nguyen house chose to play the fool', but hedges his point: 'if he had ever faked then he was probably carried away'.[80] In general, however, most historians accept that Thanh Thai was guilty of behaviour that tended towards violence, sadism and abuse.

Charles Fourniau, while not attempting a psychohistorical analysis, suggests that early developments contributed to Thanh Thai's complex psychological make-up, including heredity, a miserable childhood as marginalised son of a deposed emperor, and the lack of transition between childhood and accession to the throne.[81] Several Frenchmen who knew Thanh Thai accepted some French responsibility in his character flaws. Governor-General Doumer lamented, somewhat curiously: 'The French books that were read to him and that dealt with the life of ancient kings were not always edifying. They excited his imagination and pushed him towards experiments that were dangerous for anyone who was their object.' Hubert Lyautey, a military officer in Vietnam during his reign, and later French elder statesman of colonialism, recounted how the French gave the young emperor 'playthings' such as the insignia of the Legion of Honour, a Gobelins tapestry and musical instruments, 'and they let him grow up as he wished, indolent and all powerful, in this mysterious world of eunuchs, the harem and base servants. And he became royally bored, without any books, without any outside distractions, without any outlet for his instincts. And the sap mounted, and the little fellow became frisky, and those who could satisfy him stood ready, and it was a road from excess to debauchery to cruelty, with all the refinements and to the extent allowed by the absolute exercise of domestic tyranny'. Lyautey concluded with irony, 'We can be proud of having failed with Thanh Thai'.[82]

It is not hard to imagine the adolescent Thanh Thai (with or without books) deeply frustrated by the claustrophobic atmosphere of the court, tiresome performance of rites, overweening influence of dowagers and mandarins, and the demands of the French. His irregular behaviour first became apparent during the most unsettled time of puberty, when refusal to study, disrespect for elders and sexual experimentation are hardly uncommon. The difference between other adolescents and Thanh Thai, of course, was his position as emperor, which he used to satisfy his desires for women, 'games' and luxuries. There was little to stop him inflicting corporal punishment on servants or forcing his attentions on palace women. The origin of his prolonged penchant for 'games' and increasing violence no doubt lay deep in the psyche of a man neither destined nor prepared to be emperor.

After Thanh Thai's abdication, the French kept him for a time in the imperial palace and then sent him into internal exile in Cap Saint-Jacques (Vung Tau), a coastal resort near Saigon. He arrived with four women and nine children, as well as enough baggage to be unloaded at dockside by twenty-five prisoners into six wagons, while a few curious bystanders watched. He pronounced himself satisfied with his lodgings, but questioned the posting of a gendarme outside the house; he was told (not very convincingly) that the policeman was not charged with surveillance but to assure his safety. The ex-emperor was free to move about the local province, but had to ask permission to go to

Saigon. He regularly wrote to officials, without success, to request authorisation for other concubines and children to join him in Cap Saint-Jacques, and for his allowance to be raised.[83] There were occasional reports of sexual excesses and erratic behaviour, such as striking a mandarin, and once parking a new automobile in the salon of his villa.[84] He lived in obscurity for nine years before being sent overseas with his deposed son.

Thanh Thai's history illustrates the way the personal and political became intertwined in a reign and removal of a monarch. As the French reluctantly realised, it proves how they failed in nurturing the sort of vassal monarch they desired. It shows the dilemmas of colonisers maintaining in power a ruler who did not meet their expectations and who compromised their objectives, but whom for many years they would not disavow. It demonstrates the clash between authoritarian monarchy (though one shorn of real authority) and authoritarian colonial power. The long-lasting *affaire* occupied a great deal of time and the energy for colonial officials, and attracted attention from the press, French settlers and the public. It sheds light on the intrigues and sometimes alarming goings-on in the dark recesses of the imperial palace involving royals, mandarins, eunuchs, concubines and servants. The lack of greater and earlier French concern for sexually abused women and girls, as well as eunuchs and servants who had suffered violence at Thanh Thai's hands or instigation, is noteworthy. Though the French provided medical care, and on occasion rescued women from the palace, they made no systematic effort to protect the vulnerable, endangered or abused. The absence of immediate and effective action evidences culpable disregard for the physical and psychological wellbeing of the protectorate's subjects, though no doubt it reflects current attitudes towards native peoples, and native women in general. The priority, so long as possible, was protection of the 'French king'. The precipitant for Thanh Thai's downfall was not his abuses of women but his shooting at a man, the vice-president of the royal family council; not mistreatment of subalterns, but an attack on a highly placed member of the elite. Colonialists preached the *mission civilisatrice* as a campaign against moral outrages and misgovernment, but *raison d'état* – maintenance of French authority and, for many years, support for the king whom they had placed on the throne – was their practice.

Duy Tan

Thanh Thai's successor was the six-year-old Duy Tan[85] (see Figure 9). He looked promising to the colonisers, a cute and clever little boy who could be brought up in French ways – though similar hopes had been

Figure 9 Duy Tan, emperor of Annam (1900–45, r. 1907–16), the son of Thanh Thai. He came to the throne as a boy, was deposed after being implicated in a rebellion, and was banished (with his father) to Réunion Island. General de Gaulle's plan to restore him to the throne in 1945 was thwarted by Duy Tan's death in an aeroplane crash.

expressed for Thanh Thai. As David Pomfret has shown, the French in Indochina invested much interest in children, who embodied innocence and the potential to be shaped by colonisers, but also the danger that upbringing might go wrong and youths go astray.[86]

BANISHED POTENTATES

The boy emperor impressed the French with the dignity he showed at his enthronement,[87] and he settled down to studies and performance of the rites under the regents' watchful eyes. Some particular colonial actions rankled the emperor and court, especially an unsuccessful search in 1912 for buried treasure at the tomb of Emperor Tu Duc, regarded as profanation of the grave. Duy Tan also reacted to slights by mandarins, on one occasion convening the regency council to demand an explanation, indicating an independent streak and defence of the emperor's privileges.

Opposition to the French continued to fester in Vietnam, though with the challenge of articulating an ideology capable of galvanising the populace while avoiding colonial repression. Prince Cuong De, a direct descendant of Gia Long and representative of a 'legitimist' line in the imperial family, lived in self-imposed exile in Japan, and several dozen young anti-colonial activists joined him. One who arrived in 1905 was Phan Boi Chau, a member of the scholar-gentry who was emerging at the forefront of a nationalist movement. Phan Boi Chau had founded the Reformation Society (Duy Tan Hoi) and allied with Cuong De as standard-bearer for a regenerated monarchy though he later become a republican. Their 'Go East' movement hoped for support from the Meiji government, newly victorious in a war against Russia; Japan presented the model of a modernising Asian dynasty that had avoided colonial takeover. A treaty between France and Japan in 1907 resulted in Phan Boi Chau's expulsion, but he regrouped expatriate forces in China and Thailand; Cuong De, too, had been forced to leave Tokyo, but later returned and continued to build the nationalist cause. The other leading figure among nationalists at this time was Phan Chau Trinh; he was dubious about both Japanese assistance and focus on the monarchy as a rallying-point, placing his faith in democracy.[88]

The year 1908 saw dramatic expression of opposition against the French, when, in June, rebels tried to poison the French garrison in Hanoi by adulterating their water supply. They miscalculated the quantity of poison needed, and though two hundred soldiers fell ill, none died; the French guillotined thirteen men involved in the plot. In the meantime protests against taxes and the corvée, and violent attacks against the French, took place around the country. The French responded with summary executions, the razing of villages and thousands of arrests. Phan Chau Trinh was among those convicted, his death sentence commuted to imprisonment; in 1911 he was deported to France.

Although France claimed to have pacified Vietnam, the success of dissident movements in recruiting support, tax revolts and the plot against the garrison revealed cracks in the armour of colonial control.

New ideas were circulating among activists throughout Asia, the example of Japanese modernisation joined after 1911 with that of revolution in China, the overthrow of the Qing dynasty and the reformist and republican ideals of Sun Yat-sen. A new republican organisation, the Vietnam Restoration Society (Viet Nam Quang Phu Hoi), was set up in 1912, with Cuong De as president of a shadow Vietnamese republic. The same year, there was an attempt to assassinate Governor-General Albert Sarraut and, the following year, several French officials were killed. In 1914, the French foiled a plot to construct a bomb factory in Tonkin.

The immediate problem for the French from 1914 was the world war, which created an enormous need in the metropole for troops and workers in strategic industries.[89] Paris looked to the colonies, beginning a campaign that eventually recruited 50,000 Vietnamese soldiers and another 50,000 for French factories. The drives sparked opposition, marked by small uprisings from 1914 to 1916 in various parts of Vietnam. Then, in 1916, in the context of the recruitment effort, mounting anti-colonialism and swirling ideological currents, there was attempted insurrection in Annam, and the emperor was implicated.

Veterans of the 1908 rebellion hatched the plot, with a key role played by Tran Cao Van, whom the French had arrested for inciting tax revolts and deported to the prison island of Poulo Condore (Con Dao), off the southern Vietnamese coast. Freed in 1913, he entered into contact with disaffected mandarins. The time soon seemed propitious for an attack after part of the French army in Vietnam was transferred to European battlefronts. The plotters hoped to raise a mutiny among Vietnamese recruits slated for departure to Europe, which would also provide access to weaponry already distributed to the soldiers.

Duy Tan (in a letter written twenty years after his deposition in which he pleaded for 'amnesty') stated that unnamed conspirators had contacted him in early 1916 – Tran Cao Van bribed a chauffeur to obtain access to the emperor. They alerted him to plans for an uprising and tried to persuade him to join, though the emperor asserted he had attempted to dissuade them: 'My conviction was that a revolt was a folly that could only lead to bloody repression.' They nevertheless continued to seek his endorsement, and in mid-April, arrived at the palace bearing a detailed outline for an attack in Hué and other cities. Nothing could stop the revolt, they informed him, and added (in Duy Tan's words), 'you will be a coward if you are not at the head of those who will die for the independence of a country that is your own and that you have received as the legacy of your ancestors'. Duy Tan argued in 1936 that he again tried to stop the plot, but nonetheless examined the rebels' plan to find that the revolt was to begin in the dark of night with 'the assassination of all the French notables, taken by surprise and if possible in their sleep'. He faced several options: to allow the killing of Frenchmen (some of whom he considered friends) and the repression sure to follow, or 'to denounce my compatriots and thus cowardly betray them [*commettre une lâcheté*]'. Saying that he had no power to halt plans that seemed irreversible, he decided to take command of the revolt, though with the intention to 'give incoherent enough orders and counter-orders to disperse the bands [of rebels] and avoid the killing of Frenchmen'.[90]

The French had intelligence that something was brewing, and had confined troops to barracks and removed their weapons. Tran Cao Van, unaware that the French were on his tracks, went ahead with his plans, and on 3 May, was hiding in a sampan in the Perfume River, ready to ignite the insurrection. Around midnight an interpreter working for the French, who had infiltrated rebel ranks earlier that day, told colonial authorities that the insurrection had gained the emperor's support. Indeed, the interpreter that evening had been introduced to Duy Tan himself, who was aboard another sampan (although it is uncertain in what circumstances he had left the palace for the boat). The emperor told him that at 1:30 the following morning, firecrackers and the trumpeting of elephants would unleash assaults simultaneously in Hué and in provincial cities, and a mutiny would break out in the sixteenth battalion of Vietnamese troops. Duy Tan asked the interpreter for information about French soldiers and arms, swore him to loyalty, and told him to be ready to kill Europeans. Hurrying ashore, the interpreter reported to his French masters, who sprang into action and began rounding up suspected rebels. The planned signal for the uprising was not given, and the only clash involved an attack by a group of 250 to 300 men on a French post in Quang Nam province, which was quickly suppressed.

Duy Tan and the men on his sampan received word that the plot had been uncovered. Though the details remain unclear, they seem to have tried to reach a junk on the lagoon with the intention to flee, but then turned back, on foot, towards Hué. The French sent out a search party, and on 6 May, they tracked the emperor down to a pagoda just outside the city, exhausted but unrepentant. They took him into custody and drove him around Hué in a convertible automobile to show residents he had been apprehended. The French also tried to persuade the emperor, notwithstanding his implication in the failed uprising, to return to the palace, but he refused. The newly appointed Resident, M. Le Marchant de Trigon, convened the Co Mat to discuss the emperor's future, and in lengthy meetings over several days, argued that he should be executed. The Vietnamese ministers adamantly rejected the suggestion, saying that the emperor had been drawn into the conspiracy against his will, that he enjoyed the respect of his subjects, and that his death would turn opinion roundly against the French. They acquiesced in his deposition, in hopes of saving the monarchy rather than seeing it abolished, as some feared the French were considering. Several messages from captured rebels also pleaded for the monarch's life to be spared, including one from Tran Cao Van written just before the French put him to death. Another missive suggested that the young emperor had been hoodwinked by the agitators, and kidnapped on the night of the planned rebellion by plotters disguised as fishermen. The emperor's doctor and tutor also interceded on his behalf.

The final decision, on 13 May, was that Duy Tan would be deposed and exiled, and the French decided to send away his father Thanh Thai for good measure (though he was not at all involved in the plot). Initially held in the French bastion of Mang Ca, Duy Tan on 2 July was transferred by train and ship to Cap Saint-Jacques, and on 3 November, father and son, with their entourages, were placed aboard a ship for Réunion Island. The imperial family council, on French advice, had meantime chosen as new emperor a son of Dong Khanh, who took the reign name of Khai Dinh, and was enthroned on 17 May.

Duy Tan acknowledged in his 1936 letter that the explanation for his actions in 1916 might appear a desperate attempt to excuse him from blame by arguing that only most reluctantly, with the objective of saving French lives, was he drawn into a revolt he considered futile. That does not concord with what the interpreter had quoted him as saying at the time. The French in 1916 found several edicts calling for rebellion that bore the emperor's seal, though they were likely composed by Tran Cao Van. In one account of an interview with French officials after his capture, Duy Tan is recorded as regretting the failure of the rebellion. When questioned by officials including the governor-general and the queen mother, called in to persuade him (despite his involvement in the plot) to return to the throne, Duy Tan stated, in one version of the discussions, that he would do so only if the regency council were abolished and he were immediately given the full powers expected when he reached majority. In another version, he stated: 'If I had wanted to remain emperor, I would only have had to remain safe and sound in my Palace. Why would I have left it to become a "revolutionary"? I will only consent to be king once I no longer see the shadow of a Frenchman [cast] on the land of my country.'

Given varying accounts and lack of corroboration, as in the case of Ham Nghi, it is impossible to ascertain the involvement of the sixteen-year-old monarch in the plot or determine his sympathy for the amateurish rebellion, though it is improbable he played any significant role in actually planning an insurrection. Certain it is that he was apprised of the plans and had not informed the French, and he seems to have left the palace on the night of the insurrection of his own volition. The young, impressionable and naive sovereign had been persuaded into serving as figurehead for the movement, whether or not his prime motivation was protection of French lives; perhaps he hoped that if the uprising improbably succeeded, his kingdom could be freed. His refusal to remain emperor, if indeed he was given that opportunity, remains a puzzling decision, despite his argument that he must bear responsibility for the uprising. Perhaps he felt that, if he resumed the throne, he would be powerless and *persona non grata* to both the French and Vietnamese nationalists.

According to David Marr, the symbolism of his participation was crucial, at the time and afterwards. As the French and the rebels grasped, the emperor, despite intentional dilapidation of the monarchy by colonial authorities, occupied the key position in Vietnamese society. For the last time in the history of the dynasty, Duy Tan was the incarnation of resistance, no matter what he actually did or did not do. His participation 'also represented intimate, direct communication between king and commoner, telling the latter that their seemingly parochial tribulations at the hands of the foreigner were part of a much larger pattern'. Marr concludes: 'a fifteen-year-old king had made a small but spiritually significant gesture'.[91]

Present-day orthodox Vietnamese opinion considers Duy Tan a 'patriotic' emperor, a perspective that withstands variant interpretations about his role in 1916. The image of the emperor, no matter his youth, allying with rebels plotting to overthrow French colonial overlordship, no matter how ill-fated the plans, remains potent in the national narrative, and deposition and banishment add to his aura. Duy Tan's potential involvement with Vietnamese politics, however, was not finished when he boarded the ship for Réunion.

The surveillance of exiled emperors

Thanh Thai (now officially known as Prince Buu Lan), his companions and children, and Duy Tan (known as Prince Vinh San) and his wife, along with several Vietnamese servants, were settled into separate houses in Saint-Denis, the pretty capital of Réunion. Each received a pension from the government of Indochina, and marks of deference (such as being addressed as 'Your Highness' in official correspondence). Thanh Thai took no part in public life and kept mostly to himself, but Duy Tan soon began to find his place in local society. He practised archery, tennis and other sports, on occasion earning pocket money as

'DRAGONS OF ANNAM'

a jockey. He played the violin and joined a Masonic lodge. He contributed a few well-received essays and poems to a literary magazine. He became passionately interested in short-wave radios and successfully operated a radio repair shop (on which more presently). After the return to Vietnam of his wife Mai Thi Vang, he had relationships with three Réunionnais women over the years, and fathered several children. Duy Tan requested naturalisation as a French citizen in 1920 and subsequently, but was refused. Officials also refused his requests, on at least four occasions between 1929 and 1936, to move to France. The presence of a Vietnamese ex-emperor in the metropole, where there lived a growing number of Indochinese students, many of them nationalists, and where political groups such as the Communist Party espoused anti-colonialism, would have created a worry; better he should remain on a small Indian Ocean island. When a visiting South African asked Duy Tan whether he would like to return to Vietnam, he picked up his violin and played 'J'ai deux amours' – the song popularised by Josephine Baker singing of her two loves for 'my country and Paris' – and tearfully mused: 'Why can't I return to Annam? ... Surely I need not go on rotting on this little island, where there are no interests for me ... Why can't they send me home?'[92] That prospect seemed unlikely.

The two former emperors might well have been assimilating into island life, but they were still effectively prisoners, Duy Tan more decidedly a political detainee, even if neither had been sentenced by a court. The French were not convinced of their loyalty, aware they might retain support in Vietnam, and fearful that nationalists could use them to advance causes not in France's interest.

Looking after the royal exiles involved government offices in Vietnam, Réunion and metropolitan France discussing lodging, pension allocations and family matters, and a key part of their management was surveillance. That took a direct form, with policemen posted outside their residences, and mail and visitors monitored. It was also carried out through spies within their households, reports from neighbours, more or less discreet following of their movements and serious consideration of any rumours that reached officials. Though little suggests the French really had much to worry about, vigilance remained intense.[93]

Almost any activity by a political exile could arouse suspicions and prompt inquiries. Attending meetings, joining associations or publishing articles might indicate successful settlement and resignation to banishment, but from a different viewpoint, could provide opportunities for seditious behaviour. Unusual travel hinted at potential efforts at escape. Interest in the short-wave radio (in the case of Duy Tan) provided suspect connections with the outside world. Any encounter with dissidents, foreigners or other Asians among the thousand Chinese and fifty-odd other Vietnamese in Réunion might hint at budding conspiracies. (A small number of Vietnamese indentured labourers had worked on the island before the First World War, though most were repatriated.[94])

Reports by gendarmes reveal officers' assiduity in recording the smallest details, as well as personal observations, hearsay and character judgements, though with surprisingly little 'orientalising' language. In 1922, for instance, a report on Duy Tan branded him 'pretentious' and 'insolent'; he was affected with a 'folly of grandeur' but 'no feeling of humanity', and 'it would be rather dangerous if he returned to his country'. He kept a mistress and was courting women in a theatre troupe, and had joined 'a secret society' of cinema buffs.

The Vietnamese arrived with forewarning about Thanh Thai's character and the rebellion precipitating Duy Tan's deposition. Writing to the governor of Réunion, the governor-general of Indochina expatiated on Thanh Thai's 'acts of authoritarianism, violence, brutality and above all erotomania, [conduct] that raised questions about his sanity'. The governor detailed his misdeeds: 'the king took his sisters as mistresses, gave himself over to orgies, struck, tortured and mutilated palace women, threatened and imprisoned his legitimate wives'. After his deposition, Thanh Thai led a debauched life in Cap Saint-Jacques, and fathered children alleged to be 'the fruit of incestuous relations that he had with certain of his own daughters'.[95] If such unproved comments did not suffice to blacken the former monarch, he warned of Thanh Thai's propensity to spend beyond his means and suggested that Réunionnais merchants be advised not to extend credit to him. Furthermore, in a curious phrase that ironically accorded with the argument that Thanh Thai was faking madness, 'he has always harboured hostile sentiments towards us and his madness was often only a game intended to mask a decided will to ruin the bases of our domination'. The governor-general also commented on Duy Tan: 'Despite the care taken with him and the French upbringing he received, he has not been able to escape the legacy of a heredity whose signs are apparent in his whole physical and moral person.' No details followed, but the impression was that Duy Tan had innate character defects; he might also be prone to escape, vice or subversion.[96]

The exiles were expressly forbidden to go anywhere near ships or docks. When Duy Tan was hired to repair a shipboard radio, police recorded the exact times of his arrival and departure. Duy Tan was permitted to go outside Saint-Denis (often to visit radio clubs) provided he informed the governor's office in advance, but on one occasion was not allowed to take a cruise around the island. In 1919, when he journeyed to the beautiful mountain resort of Hell-Bourg, police reports recorded, with no real evidence, that he was holding public and private political meetings, consorting with dishonourable individuals ('whom he gorges with alcohol') and 'offers an apologia for socialism' – charges that may well reflect French nightmares more than realities.[97] In 1923, the former emperor went to Cilaos, another picturesque mountain village and thermal spa resort, for a two-month holiday. The local police, informed of the impending visit, then sent in weekly reports, noting in which hotel Duy Tan was staying and where he took his meals, and naming companions with whom he went horseback riding and attended the cinema. 'The conversations of the prince reveal nothing suspect from the national point of view', an agent wrote, suggesting that someone was eavesdropping. Another report stated that he no longer talked about hopes of leaving Réunion and wanted to become a naturalised French citizen – a superior official scribbled in the margin 'Beware!'. When Duy Tan took to his bed with a minor illness in 1929, the police invented an excuse to call at his house to make certain he was actually present. Many police reports over the years, however, bear only the one-line statement 'nothing to report'.

Any overtures for escape came from foreigners, not the exiles. Indeed, Duy Tan informed authorities of two proposals he received in the early 1920s. The commander of a small English steamship had met him, presumably by chance, in a restaurant and offered to take him to Durban, South Africa; a couple of years later, a Russian piano-tuner proffered his improbable services to facilitate escape. A decade later, another Russian, a ship mechanic who claimed contacts with an 'Annamese Institute' in the Soviet Union, proposed that the ex-emperor take flight and settle in Moscow. Duy Tan summarily rejected suggestions that would have certainly been doomed to failure. In 1924, the governor-general of Indochina wrote to his counterpart in Réunion that he suspected Thanh Thai was planning an escape, aided by Chinese merchants to whom he owed money. Disguised as a seaman, he would sneak aboard a ship sailing to Mauritius and Hong Kong, where he would organise an attempt to overthrow the reigning Vietnamese emperor. The report did not greatly agitate Réunionnais authorities, one simply penning in the margin that there should be stepped-up surveillance when foreign ships docked in Saint-Denis.[98] In 1938, the government imagined that Duy Tan might be trying to escape with his mistress, who was leaving for Saigon; 'a discreet but tight surveillance' was ordered, to be 'doubled' each time a ship arrived from Vietnam or China. In no case was there evidence of cogent plans to spirit one of the ex-emperors off the island.

Imperial lives on a tropical island

The exile of Duy Tan and Thanh Thai produced the curious circumstance of two deposed emperors, father and son, living on the same small island. They had never enjoyed close relations. Thanh Thai blamed his son's involvement in the 1916 anti-colonial plot for the overseas exile he had desperately wished to avoid in 1907. He also disapproved of his son's efforts at naturalisation.[99] The French identified a particularly thorny issue between the two men. The governor-general of Indochina, mentioning the 'dissension that exists', revealed that on the eve of their departure, Duy Tan accused his wife of having sexual relations with his father: 'Though he provided no evidence for what he said and one should beware of his inventive imagination, such a fact does not appear unlikely given the mores of Prince Buu Lan.' The governor-general surmised, not unreasonably, that such a liaison would 'be of a nature to create grave conflicts between the two princes', and advised that Thanh Thai be made to understand that his status provided no immunity from the law if he abused paternal authority or if his conduct gave rise to 'similar scandals to those that motivated his removal'.[100]

Duy Tan himself wrote to the French in 1916: 'My father and I do not get along, that is to say, he abuses the [filial] submission that I show to him out of respect.' He was temporarily interned in the same compound in Cap Saint-Jacques as Thanh Thai, who expected that he act as an obedient child. He forbade Duy Tan to go out without him, and when they did, 'he slapped me or kicked me when it pleased him'; 'he behaves towards me as to a slave'. Thanh Thai's record made Duy Tan fear that 'he will continue on me his habits of brutality and cruelty'. He complained that although Thanh Thai received a larger pension than he did, his father spent Duy Tan's money. On their journey to Réunion, 'he brutalised me several times and what I say can be attested by the whole ship'. Furthermore, he 'behaved towards me in a fashion impossible to put into a letter' – a discreet reference, perhaps, to Thanh Thai's affair with his wife.

Soon after their arrival a report to the governor-general of Indochina stated that relations between father and son had deteriorated further and forced intervention to 'avoid unfortunate scenes' (of an unspecified nature). Thanh Thai and Duy Tan were no longer on speaking terms. Duy Tan wanted to file an official police complaint against his father about the relations with his wife, as well as to begin divorce proceedings. An official cautioned obedience to French law, but also inquired about Indochinese divorce law, since Duy Tan argued that the French laws were inapplicable to him.[101] A coded telegram from Hanoi failed to clarify the matter, but suggested that the civil code in Cochinchina might be the appropriate legal instrument.[102] The Indochinese government later advised Réunionnais authorities that Duy Tan might formally repudiate his wife, and she could then return, at his expense, to Vietnam. That was done, the ex-empress's departure publicly explained as the result of ill health. Two servants were also repatriated, at Duy Tan's request, but the governor-general remarked that the government 'cannot give in to the fantasies of the two exiled princes'. When Thanh Thai asked that several concubines and servants come to Réunion, the response was: 'In general and to avoid the repetition of the scandalous scenes that too often occurred at Cap Saint-Jacques, it is preferable not to give Prince Buu Lan the means of ... setting up a veritable harem in Réunion.'[103]

By February 1918, Duy Tan had met a young Réunionnaise whom he proposed to marry, and his wish was brought to the attention of the royal family council in Hué – acknowledgement that exiled rulers, in some fashion, were still bound by Vietnamese institutions. It rejected his request on grounds that a Vietnamese could marry only with parental consent, and Duy Tan's mother was opposed; moreover an official divorce had not yet been pronounced between him and his wife. Duy Tan's plans came to nought.[104] The matter of a civil divorce dragged on, and ten years later, the governor-general in Hanoi said that he had received a request from Duy Tan for an official certificate of divorce. He added, in true bureaucratic fashion, that a signed formal repudiation of his wife must first be submitted in triplicate.[105]

For the French, the major worry concerning Thanh Thai continued to be his turbulent private life. He had a family of ten children, most born (to several different women) since his landing in Réunion. Providing for the progeny was a burden given his modest pension, and the government's reluctance to raise his allowance; in 1936, Thanh Thai appealed directly to Emperor Bao Dai, who sent 10,000 francs. Duy Tan also gave money to Thanh Thai's sons. The police wondered how Thanh Thai nevertheless amassed enough money to live as a *petit bourgeois*, and one officer suggested that two of Thanh Thai's concubines were working as prostitutes. Thanh Thai was reported to appear on occasion, 'revolver in hand', to extort extra payments. The policeman acknowledges that no formal complaint had been received, so the law was powerless to intervene. Other reports concerned Thanh Thai's treatment of his women, and several incidents provoked police investigation. One report nevertheless conceded: 'He is an unbalanced and sadistic man who continues to do here what he did in Annam.'

Other occasional contretemps involved the Vietnamese. In January 1920, a neighbour accused Duy Tan of tapping into his electricity cables to power lamps, a radio and a small alembic. The case ended up in court, with Duy Tan fined two hundred francs. Another episode related to the governor. Duy Tan sent a message of welcome to a new governor and asked for an appointment, which was declined on the basis of a busy schedule. Duy Tan fired off a letter complaining of an 'affront', whereupon the police commissioner called him in and administered 'severe remonstrations' for impoliteness.

A month later, the police discovered that Duy Tan had set up a short-wave radio receiver without a licence, and he was again brought in and chastised. This was not the first confrontation concerning Duy Tan's operation of radios, still new-fangled devices at the time. Indeed the radio played an important role in the emperor's life in Réunion. His radio expertise, for someone self-taught, was impressive. He established the first post for short-wave radio reception on the island as early as 1917, championed radio as an important new medium (in particular, for detection of cyclones), and carried out high-altitude experiments on Réunion's mountains. He gave lectures and demonstrations about radio technology to *sociétés savantes*, published several articles on 'radiophony' and set up an association of short-wave radio fans. He opened a shop to repair radios, sometimes on commission for the state.

Duy Tan pursued other interests not always to the administration's liking. In 1936, a Popular Front government of Socialists and Radicals with tacit Communist support came to power in France and foreshadowed substantial changes in colonial policy, including greater rights for indigenous populations (though most proposals were never implemented). Their victory gave Duy Tan the occasion to write the letter requesting 'amnesty' that presented his version of the events of 1916. In an unpublished letter to *L'Humanité*, the Paris newspaper of the Communist Party – which had welcomed Ho Chi Minh into its ranks – he boldly stated: 'Annam claims the right to be an independent and neutral nation in the same way as a European nation.'[106]

On 11 November 1936, celebrated as Armistice Day, Duy Tan was present at a demonstration in Saint-Denis organised by a labour union, and was photographed standing next to a red flag. A newspaper claimed that he 'took the microphone and made an aggressive speech' that 'gravely offended the population'. The governor's council convened to consider the accusation, but it turned out to be a journalistic beat-up, as eyewitnesses interviewed by police said that Duy Tan had made no suspicious comments but only voiced an appeal for peace between peoples and social classes. The gendarme's report remarked on his membership of a human rights association, but concluded that 'he cannot be reproached for any anti-French statements'. Apparently Duy Tan had simply offered help in repairing a malfunctioning microphone, and was asked to speak in impromptu fashion. The governor nevertheless warned him that speaking at such a gathering was inappropriate, forbade him to leave his house for a month, and stepped up surveillance.[107]

Dramatic developments in these years – consolidation of Mussolini's fascist regime, Italian designs on several French colonies and invasion of Ethiopia, Hitler's coming to power in Germany, the Spanish Civil War – raised alarm about any untoward gesture or word. With regard to the exiles, events in Asia were particularly unsettling. In early 1930, Vietnamese soldiers at Yen Bay mutinied and called for overthrow of the French colonial government, and later that year Ho Chi Minh founded the Indochinese Communist Party. In 1931, the Japanese invaded Manchuria and soon installed the deposed Qing emperor as monarch of the puppet state of Manchukuo. In such circumstances, attending a 'leftist' meeting or using an unauthorised short-wave radio could indeed appear subversive to the suspicious.

In March 1936, police monitoring the airwaves had heard Duy Tan on air, raided his house, and seized transformers and a microphone on grounds that he was transmitting without a licence. The governor threatened that if he did so again, he would be incarcerated. In December 1937, when the former monarch asked for permission to transmit on short-wave, the request reached the colonial minister. He sought advice from the governor-general of Indochina, who recommended rejecting the request at least if any messages might reach Indochina or places Indochinese lived. The governor of Réunion was also opposed, and the public prosecutor assured him that, although he could not intervene if Duy Tan did nothing illegal, in case he did broadcast without a licence, the justice system 'would not hesitate for a single instance to intervene with firmness but also with the tact that is appropriate in the circumstances'.

In September 1938, a question again arose about whether Duy Tan was transmitting, though the local radio authority, trying to tune in to the frequency he once used, could hear no transmissions. On being interrogated, Duy Tan stated that since he had been refused a licence, he had made no attempts to use short-wave. Within weeks, police nonetheless searched his house; they spied 'a device which is *perhaps* a transmitter', and suggested to headquarters that a radio technician might invent an excuse to inspect it more closely, though nothing more came of the matter. Meticulous police investigation here meshed with enduring suspicion about the royal exiles and general unease at the international situation.

BANISHED POTENTATES

Vinh San in wartime

As France prepared for war in 1939, Duy Tan twice asked to join the French military, but was turned down. When German armies invaded France in May 1940, he wrote to the governor that 'at a time when France and the totality of its empire must place their material and moral weight into the scales on which the future of the world is being weighed, I do not want it thought that in my country a single one of our able-bodied remains outside the efforts and sacrifice of France for civilisation'. He offered his services as a 'simple soldier or sailor'. He added, slightly obscurely, 'My presence here ... would all too much suggest that there still exist between your country and mine obstacles, certainly negligible ones, but obstacles nevertheless. That is why I wish that they be effaced, by [my] putting on a French uniform'.[108] Nothing suggests that his sentiments were less than genuine, but the French again declined the offer.

In June 1940, France was defeated, and Marshal Pétain agreed to a settlement. Thus began four years of collaboration between the Germans and Pétain's supporters. With very few exceptions, colonial officials pledged loyalty to Pétain, and some colonies, including Indochina, remained under a Vichy-aligned administration throughout the war. On 18 June 1940, General de Gaulle broadcast his famous appeal for continued resistance, the first step in rallying the French and constituting a Free French force, and Pétain's capitulation galvanised nascent support for the Resistance inside France. Efforts also commenced to wrest the colonies from Vichy control.

On 15 June, three days before de Gaulle's broadcast, Duy Tan, who had published several pro-French articles under a nom de plume in the preceding months, wrote his own appeal for resistance, one of the first in the colonies, though it is unclear how widely it was disseminated. 'I wish, through the Governor-General of Indochina, to make my fellow citizens understand and always to have in mind that *only* the grandeur of France can create the grandeur of our country and assure its future; that we cannot live free from slavery except through France, and that we must use all our means to fight for France, without fail, and without taking heed of enemy propaganda.' In a letter to the governor ten days later, he yet again offered his services 'in the hour when the French Empire is going to undertake the immense challenge of saving the Mother Country'. He repeated the offer in September 1940, but the proposals were declined or ignored.

After the capitulation, Réunion remained in the hands of a pro-Vichy administration, even more suspicious than before about possible subversion. In August, police reported on gatherings of men at

Duy Tan's house and radio shop – where his friends could still listen, now illegally, to overseas broadcasts, a vital source of information with newspapers and state radio heavily censored. Presumably relying on a spy in Duy Tan's coterie or on hearsay, the police noted that anti-Vichy comments had been made. No action followed, and radio listening continued until police arrested Duy Tan in 1942. From 7 May to 19 June, he was kept in detention, initially in hospital because of a passing illness. Duy Tan promised that if freed, he would stay at home in the evening and not allow anyone to listen to his radio; at some point in 1942 or 1943, he sold his radio business. The authorities remained on guard, citing the exile's sympathy for the Popular Front, membership of a Masonic lodge, and what was branded his reputation as 'very suspect for the *haute société* and the healthy part of the population', a reference to Vichy adherents. Another, curious reason to beware of him also appeared: since doubt had been cast on the genealogical legitimacy of Emperor Bao Dai (in principle, the son of the preceding emperor), who now cohabited with the pro-Vichy colonial administration, there might be sympathies among a 'legitimist party' for Duy Tan's return.[109]

During the night of 26–27 November 1942, a ship arrived in Réunion bearing Gaullist forces, who liberated the island. In January 1943 Duy Tan made yet another attempt to enlist, stating in a ten-page letter that he felt useless at the moment: 'I am fully conscious that for Free French propaganda in Indochina, I will be of an undoubted usefulness, [and] that is why I want to serve this France that at one time exiled me because I loved liberty too much but which I love passionately, precisely because it is the cradle of liberty, and because in this war it suffers and fights for its liberty as well as for ours.' The statement is an interesting defence of his implication in the resistance movement in 1916, which he tellingly made into a parallel with resistance against the Axis. In being allowed to don a French uniform, 'I will more easily use the authority that attaches to my name. It would not then be an Annamese chief but a French soldier who defends France and its empire ... [not] a former king who wishes to become a soldier, but a soldier who [once] was that'.[110] The text was subtly, indeed eloquently, worded, combining expressions of patriotism with reminders of Duy Tan's former status. He followed up with a telegram directly to de Gaulle, saying that although he had been exiled because of a colonial revolt, 'I love your great country enough that I have wanted to efface the past by volunteering for service since the start of the war'. De Gaulle acknowledged his support in a return telegram, telling Duy Tan: 'France will know how to remember the noble sentiments that you express. I take note of your offer to serve at the moment when circumstances will permit it to be followed up.'

Mixed feelings about the former emperor, however, can still be discerned in Réunion. In commenting on an earlier telegram to de Gaulle in April 1943, the governor of Réunion cabled to the Free French that Duy Tan was 'intelligent [and] intriguing gives me impression he wants to leave La Réunion to undertake political activity in view his re-establishment throne Annam where supposedly still has very numerous partisans'.[111]

Another letter from Duy Tan to the governor, in trying to secure admission into the military, reflected on past events. He claimed he had always been devoted to France but 'social situations create obligations which those who wish to live with honour cannot avoid', a veiled reference to 1916, but with a suggestion that the Vietnamese people had been victims of colonialism. 'The heir of a name [his royal title], I paid the price for this heritage in refusing to submit myself and take the side of the strongest. The record has been enormously blackened, and it has been completely forgotten that the Annamese revolt of 1916, which had a king at its head, did not cost the life of a SINGLE Frenchman. Can anyone say that I am completely foreign to that [fact]? But that is in the past....' Having suggested that he had tempered anti-French actions during the aborted rebellion, Duy Tan continued: 'For thirty years, I have been paying out the debt that I contracted. Is it paid? No, neither to my country, not to France.' Serving France now would be his repayment.

> Your country is spiritually my own and will gain nothing by seeing me die here, whereas my reputation can only gain with proof, in the eyes of the world and of Annam, that even those who have been punished, because they are honourable, were the first to go to its side in its most painful and hardest times. If I should die in doing so, that will be yet another link between our countries because it will be in their common service; if I come out alive, France will know it has a sure friend.[112]

The message was craftily worded, with confession of involvement in the 1916 affair, but affirmations of fealty, and finally, the Free French command agreed to allow Duy Tan to join up.

On 3 January 1944, Duy Tan enlisted in the navy. Though he would have preferred to go to France, the French sent him to Madagascar with the hope that his influence would quell any rising discontent among Vietnamese soldiers whose repatriation to Indochina after the fall of France had been long delayed because of suspension of maritime connections to Vietnam. Duy Tan acquitted himself well of the task, his work noted by de Gaulle's staff. He served in the navy, however, for only twenty-two days, and then was released from duty. Ostensibly the reason was a propensity to sea-sickness, but according to a report to the governor of Réunion, 'the true reason ... is the following: one can never be sure of the feelings of these exiled princes'. There may have been concern that he could take advantage of the passage of his ship through a foreign port to escape.

Duy Tan was brought back to Réunion, where he transferred to the army with the rank of corporal. He worked in radiotelegraphy, and a report noted his 'special competency'. 'I would add', the author wrote, that 'Vinh San energetically proclaims that he does not wish by any means to return to the throne of Annam', but that he wishes to be sent to the battlefront as a simple soldier; when the war ends, 'his dream is that he will be allowed to go to France and acquire a small property where, he says, he will live in the midst of flowers and books'. The report concluded, positively, 'In any case, [he is] a very intelligent and cultivated fellow, who makes agreeable conversation and whose honourable life has commanded the respect of the population. It seems that the ill humour, authoritarianism and base instincts that characterised him in his early youth ... have given way to gravitas, calm and dignity in his life'.[113] A commanding officer, Captain Tibéri, also did not spare laudatory phrases to describe Vinh San: 'always good-spirited', 'very good instructor', 'military spirit: perfect', filled with 'intelligent zeal', 'much liked', 'has authority' 'excellent presentation and conduct'; another officer praised him as 'refined, intelligent, not very communicative; shows his feelings tempered with the reserve innate to his race'.[114]

Enduring French ambivalence about Vinh San nevertheless can be seen in correspondence between the Saint-Denis administration and the Free French Commissioner for the Colonies in Algiers. In January 1944, the governor's office wrote with information on the Vietnamese exiles, implying that Gaullists were considering to which extent they might be either useful or dangerous. Thanh Thai had been deposed for 'violence, brutality and erotomania', and in Réunion 'his life continues to be scandalous', though 'with age his bad instincts have calmed down a little'. As for Duy Tan, his early years were spent in 'debauchery', his behaviour to ministers had been 'insolent and vulgar', and from the age of fourteen, 'he spent whole nights amusing himself and became particularly difficult'. (That comment, however, seems more appropriate for his father: perhaps the misdeeds of the two were confused.) In May 1916, he 'placed himself at the head of a seditious movement', for which he suffered the consequences. Nevertheless, 'it is appropriate to say that his private life is calm and dignified'.[115]

The Free French commissioner, replying to Duy Tan's request to serve in France, opened his letter deferentially with the salutation 'Monseigneur' (a title used for reigning monarchs and, by monarchists, for pretenders) and addressed him in the third person. It acknowledged Duy Tan's stance in 1940 and his regularly expressed devotion to France, and foreshadowed the 'eminent services which our country has the right to expect from Your Highness'. The official conceded that 'the exalted rank that is conferred on Your Highness as a member of the ruling family in Annam creates particular obligations [for the French], the rigour of which we can only deplore', an intimation that Duy Tan could not be set entirely free. Despite the emperor's desire to serve on the frontline, 'it is not possible for us to go back on the decision taken in 1916 in his regard', clearly a reference to his exile. The commissioner asked Duy Tan to fulfil the 'modest role' he had been assigned in Réunion.[116]

Duy Tan's current role might be 'modest', but he reflected ambitiously on the post-war situation of Vietnam and the part he might play in a succinct but remarkable three-page memorandum, 'Views on the Future of the Indochinese Question'. When the Japanese were defeated, the Vietnamese ought to welcome back the French as liberators, not view their return as a re-conquest. The French must make certain that the 'Annamese' did not become involved in intrigues and fall under foreign dominance (probably meaning by the British and Americans, as well as Soviets and Chinese). Duy Tan recommended that the current colonial statute be abolished, with the protectorates of Tonkin and Annam and the colony of Cochinchina unified into an autonomous state of Vietnam, federated with Cambodia and Laos, as protectorates under a governor-general rebadged 'high commissioner'. 'What I want is for all the Annamese to regain a consciousness of being a nation and that this consciousness give them the desire to construct a country worthy of the [French] nation.' The French had long rejected the idea of unifying the three *ky* though anti-colonialists regularly advanced the demand, just as the French persistently avoided the words 'Vietnam' and 'nation', with their connotations of unity, shared identity and self-determination. The possibility of a renewed Indochinese federation was now nevertheless being bandied about by the Free French, as Duy Tan possibly guessed.

The memorandum also commented on the economic and social structure of a future Vietnam. The strength of capitalists, proletarians, and the old and new mandarin groups – the new mandarins those who had benefited from French education and 'superiority gained thanks to the esteem of the French' – must be joined together. 'It does not matter whether this solidarity takes place under the aegis of a Communist, socialist, royalist or monarchical regime; the essential thing is to save the people from Balkanisation', Duy Tan remarked, with a curious use of 'Balkanisation'. The inclusive phrasing alluded to the unwieldy coalition of forces that formed the Resistance and Free French movements, and also the divergent strands of nationalism in Vietnam. Despite the statement that it did not matter under whose aegis a new Vietnam emerged, Duy Tan stated that 'if my intervention proves to be necessary, it is evident that never having been a political figure, never having taken part in political intrigues, I could have influence only as a legitimate king, distanced [*éloigné*] from the throne by circumstances and that circumstances will bring back'. This was as clear a pronouncement as Duy Tan ever publicly made that he was ready and willing to return to the throne, though he quickly added: 'Despite the prestige that my quality [of former ruler] accords me, I would have no power over the masses if my return did not bring to the people a new ideal, a new orientation, a new well-being.' In short, he would reign as a constitutional monarch, at least initially under the paramountcy of the French, for 'I wish for the Annamese people to have enough confidence to retain the French people as a guarantee of their territorial and national integrity'. However, he then introduced, in passing, the explicit notion of 'independence', still anathema to those eager to reassert full French colonial overlordship: 'I want the progress brought by France to Indochina recognised as the cornerstone of the future edifice of our real independence.'

Duy Tan's memorandum went on to outline more clearly what would be the role of a monarch in a post-war period of 'fraternity and solidarity' between the French and Vietnamese. 'I see the crown of Annam linking together all of the dynamic activities of the nation, working for a massive industrialisation of the country which alone can bring to the proletariat the well-being for which it is searching.' With economic development and its benefits, 'I see the monarchical government thus acquiring sufficient popularity to assure the life of the nation and to proceed to an orderly education of the masses. The masses, once educated, will then be led towards a parliamentary government that will be veritably democratic'. Duy Tan was clear that when he was promoting the power of the throne, he was not talking about Bao Dai: 'It is above all as a counterwieght to the anarchic agitation [in Vietnam at the present] that I think I can be useful to the Annamese Nation and the French people.' He ended in stentorian tones: 'In fragile health, I really aspire to calm and rest. However, I will not neglect the payment of the debt that I owe to my Country, to which I owe my rank and my life, and towards France, to which I owe a sense of honour and the notion of total sacrifice to an ideal.'

Duy Tan's text offers an exceptional presentation of his vision for Vietnam and the contribution he could make. The statement is balanced, with phrases intended to speak to various factions, including anti-colonialists ('the nation', 'independence', 'parliamentary government'), the political left ('proletariat'), technocrats planning economic and social development ('industrialisation', 'education'), geostrategists (concern about 'foreign' designs), and French patriots ('honour', 'sacrifice'). While not damning the colonial regime, Duy Tan implies that it had not been fully beneficent though it had brought 'progress'. He foreshadowed a time when Vietnam would be independent, though without suggesting a date or a process for arriving at that goal. Despite averring that the form of regime was of little concern, Duy Tan persuasively defended the idea of a non-political constitutional monarchy, and claimed he was the right man for the throne. His views delivered a powerful message in the midst of the final stage of liberation of a Vietnam fully occupied by the Japanese, perceptions of ulterior designs by Britain and China (whose armies were pushing into the country), rancour between Vichy collaborators and the Free French, and in particular the dramatically increased power and popularity of Ho Chi Minh and the Communist nationalists.

It is unknown how widely Duy Tan's statement was made known or his ideas discussed, and there is almost no reference to his memorandum in contemporary memoirs or historians' accounts. His general views were repeated (in some of the exact words) and made public in what he considered his political testament, issued on 24 March 1945, though that statement took a more moderate form and concentrated on the necessary unification of the *ky*.[117] His perspectives constitute a noteworthy exposition of a plan that at certain points coincided with thinking about the recasting of colonialism among the Free French and even among nationalists and anti-colonialists, and that explicitly broached the eventuality of outright independence. His vision, however, went far beyond what the French were considering at the moment, for their priority remained re-establishment of full dominion in the colonies. A 1944 conference of colonial officials, held in Brazzaville, and chaired by de Gaulle, had indeed ruled out the possibility even of 'self-government' (using the phrase in English) for French territories.

After almost three decades of exile, Duy Tan in the final years of the Second World War, in the context of his *ralliement* to the Free French, was placing himself in a central position. Sentiments of commitment to France fighting to emancipate the country from German occupation and Vichy collaboration, and thoughtful reflections on the future of Vietnam, joined with personal ambition set free in unique and unforeseen circumstances. For the first time there might be a possibility for Duy Tan to return home and even regain some official position. He was aware of the unpopularity of Bao Dai, who had earned a reputation as a

playboy little interested in his duties, and who had been compromised by the Japanese occupation. Duy Tan well knew that the French desperately needed some force to oppose the rising power of the Communists, and that could rally the Vietnamese around the Tricolour while giving some satisfaction to national sentiments. And he hoped that the monarchy, despite its weakening over the past six decades, might serve as the cornerstone in a rebuilt relationship between France and Vietnam. Duy Tan also reckoned that his *ralliement* and wartime service had attracted favourable attention from the Gaullists.

On 5 May 1945, Duy Tan's long hoped for posting to France was ordered, three days before Germany's capitulation. On arrival in Europe in June, he was soon moved with French occupation forces to Germany; the ex-emperor, learning that his battalion would be transferred to Vietnam, gave several talks about Indochina to fellow soldiers. That transfer did not eventuate, and superiors recalled Duy Tan to Paris in October. There he made contacts with other Vietnamese, though sparking little fervour among compatriots.[118]

Vietnam had been in a state of chaos for the past months with the Japanese takeover, Bao Dai's proclamation of an empire of Vietnam under their aegis, then the Japanese capitulation, the Vietnamese emperor's abdication and Ho's declaration of an independent republic.[119] Ho was antagonistic to the French, Bao Dai was seriously compromised because of his the Americans had hinted at a possible international mandate for Vietnam (and provided some aid to the Viet Minh, a friendly gesture reciprocated when Ho quoted from the United States' Declaration of Independence in his proclamation of the independence of Vietnam); the French faced a mighty struggle to re-establish colonial authority. The French nonetheless hoped, so far as possible, to restore the *status quo ante bellum*, and Duy Tan stood in waiting as a possible contributor to that effort. His name was being discussed in Paris, and a strong letter of reference came from Etienne Boulé, a teacher and official in Madagascar, member of the Gaullist Resistance and former German prisoner-of-war. Though hardly an influential *notable*, he put forward the case for Duy Tan. Evoking the compromised position of Bao Dai, he spoke of the exiled emperor as an alternative on the basis that 'his prestige as emperor remains intact'. Furthermore, 'the events that led to his exile are better explained in light of the Resistance' – a recapitulation of the daring argument Duy Tan had made about similar resistance to French colonisers and German occupiers. The establishment of a new Fourth Republic would allow Duy Tan's slate to be wiped clean. De Gaulle, Boulé added, recognised his loyalty and was a 'declared partisan' of Duy Tan. The ex-emperor was a confirmed democrat with advanced ideas, 'the only Annamese personality who has enough moral authority to oppose the claims and the rapacity of the old and new mandarins. He would be ready to serve as a link between the present regime and a liberal one'. Boulé added, oddly, that Duy Tan had no legitimate children, implying the French might in due course exercise a free hand in choosing his successor. The once and perhaps future emperor is 'a sincere friend of France', and believes that if France were to quit Indochina, 'it would be the end of the Annamese Country, which would fall under the yoke of foreigners'. He is of good character, though in fragile health. Finally, he 'has nothing of the puppet about him. He is extremely independent and punctilious about his cultural freedom [liberté spirituelle]', and Boulé questionably asserted, without personal ambitions.[120]

Not all in de Gaulle's camp were won over, though de Gaulle's powerful High Commissioner in Indochina, Admiral Thierry d'Argenlieu, echoed the positive assessments of Duy Tan and possible restoration, as did the governor of Réunion. Officials at the colonial ministry sounded caution about both Duy Tan's personal capacity to live up to expectations and the likelihood of a returned royal rallying the Vietnamese. Some expressed reservations about Duy Tan's proposal for unification of the *ky* and possible demands for real rather than nominal Vietnamese autonomy.[121] Though de Gaulle's and Duy Tan's ultimate objectives did not necessarily coincide, it looked as if they could work together, and Duy Tan might be able to lure compatriots away from the Communists. De Gaulle, whose status in 1945 almost guaranteed that his plans would be implemented, may have felt confident on the basis of the reports that he received and a conversation with Duy Tan that he would prove a malleable vassal. Furthermore, as David Marr has remarked, 'that the prince was completely out of touch with events in his homeland must have been considered an asset by de Gaulle'.[122]

It is unknown how familiar de Gaulle was with the specific views Duy Tan articulated in his memorandum, but the general appears to have decided to cast his lot with Duy Tan. De Gaulle had devised a plan, which he recalled, tersely and rather enigmatically, in his memoirs:

> To whatever ends might be useful, I nourished a secret design. It was to give to the former emperor Duy Tan the means to reappear, if his successor and relative Bao Dai showed himself definitively to be overcome by events. Duy Tan, deposed in 1916 by French authority, become once again Prince Vinh San and transferred to Reunion, had nevertheless through the course of this war determined to serve in our army. He held the rank of *commandant*. Some thirty years of exile had not effaced in the soul of the Annamese people the memory of this sovereign. On 14 December [1945], I received him to see, man to man, what we might accomplish together.[123]

Several days after that meeting, Duy Tan told Pierre Thébault, head of staff of the governor of Réunion, a close friend, that he would be restored to the throne. He would go to Vietnam with de Gaulle in early 1946 and resume his place as emperor; there would be no need for a new enthronement, as he had never abdicated and remained, in fact, the legitimate emperor by virtue of his investiture in 1907. Such was the apparent plan when Duy Tan set off from Paris to visit his family in Réunion in late December.[124] *En route*, his plane crashed in central Africa, with all six passengers and crew killed. Rumours of foul play circulated, but with no real evidence that the accident had been the result of other than natural causes: bad weather, difficult terrain and faulty navigation. De Gaulle remarked that France decidedly did not have good luck.

After the war

Duy Tan left behind six children (from three mothers). Though they had separated by the time of the emperor's death, Fernande Astier, the mother of four of them, inherited few resources; she wrote to the government lamenting her plight, and received some assistance after an inquiry noted that Duy Tan had always dutifully provided for her and the children. However, he had not married any of his companions or legally recognised his children. He could not do so, he had said, without the consent of the imperial family council in Vietnam. Only after his death did a tribunal in Réunion recognise their rights to carry the imperial name. His most notable son, Claude Vinh San, or Nguyen Phuoc Bao Vang, was born in 1934 and educated in Réunion and at the French *lycée* in Saigon. He became an accordionist, composer and leader of the 'Jazz Tropical' band in Réunion, guardian of the family memory and editor of a compendium of biographical documents about Duy Tan that has been invaluable for this chapter.

Thanh Thai, according to the French, sired eight or ten children in Réunion. Growing up in a multi-ethnic society, and speaking Creole, they assimilated into island life. In 1944, a report noted that all but two children (in addition to Duy Tan) still lived with their father. In an unsuccessful plea for an increased pension, Thanh Thai explained the burden of their upkeep, considering the high cost of living and his incapacity to work at the age of sixty-five. One of the sons who lived outside the household was Vinh Kui (Jean), twenty-nine in 1944; according to a government report, he had managed a woodworking shop but 'not having obtained the confidence of the public' – whether because of workmanship, discrimination or poor business management was unexplained – was forced to close the shop. He had since worked irregularly and was a 'vagabond'; though free from run-ins with the law, he had 'a bad reputation' and 'dubious conduct', was uneducated and a suspect in several robberies. Unmarried, he lived on a tiny government pension. The forty-two-year-old Vinh Chuong, the other son who lived on his own, also received a pension plus financial assistance from Duy Tan; he operated a successful bicycle-repair shop. He had lived with a companion for ten years, and they had two children before separating; two other children were born from another liaison. The gendarme investigating the situation of Thanh Thai's progeny reported that despite limited means, Vinh Chuong conscientiously provided for his children. Though his education had not gone past primary school, he was ingenious and intelligent, and had no criminal record. He had never expressed anti-French feelings and professed high regard for the government. His 'conduct and morals have not given rise to any criticism' and 'he enjoys the esteem and consideration of the public'.[125]

After the war and death of Duy Tan, Thanh Thai manifested a desire to return to Indochina, accompanied by two women and various children, and the High Commissioner of Indochina (as the governor-general was now styled) in February 1946 agreed in principle to his repatriation. Unpredictably, the government then asked whether he would not rather prefer to live in France, a proposal to which Thanh Thai replied diplomatically but firmly concerning 'the honour of living in France, in this so generous and so beautiful France which would have my favour if I were still young. But as I am old, I want to die in my native land where I should be laid to rest where the remains of my ancestors lie buried'. His departure kept getting postponed, though both Thanh Thai and the French seemed eager for him to leave, the French perhaps fearing awkwardness if he died in Réunion. Officials were also concerned about the situation in which he lived, described by one gendarme as 'indescribable wretchedness'. Finally, in November, his departure was definitively authorised after he had again written to the governor pleading that declining health made his repatriation urgent. Further delay followed, until, on 24 March 1947, Thanh Thai left Réunion bound for Vietnam; documents refer variously to those who went along as two 'concubines', aged fifty-seven and sixty-two, or one wife or concubine – she is referred to in both ways – and three women over the age of twenty, and children aged ten, five and two.[126] He settled in Cap Saint-Jacques, where he had been kept from 1907 to 1916, and lived quietly. In 1953, he was allowed to visit Hué; photos show an aged, but dignified, figure descending the steps of an aeroplane for a brief sojourn in the city where he had reigned as emperor half a century earlier. Thanh Thai died in hospital in Saigon on 24

March 1954, just several months before the defeat of the French at Dien Bien Phu.

Thanh Thai was buried in Hué though in the most modest of graves, in contrast to the grandiose monumental tombs of some other Nguyen emperors. When the wreckage of the aeroplane in which Duy Tan made his fateful flight was discovered, he was buried in the small cemetery of a Catholic mission. In 1987, thanks to the efforts of Claude Vinh San, Duy Tan began his last journey, to reburial in Vietnam. His coffin was taken from the Central African Republic to Paris for a religious ceremony at the Buddhist pagoda in the Bois de Vincennes (site of the 1931 colonial exhibition), and flown onwards to Vietnam where, in an elaborate ceremony conducted in the presence of family members and Vietnamese officials, the 'patriotic' emperor was entombed next to his father. He had said, in his political testament of 1945, that he wanted his epitaph to be taken from that inscribed on a statue of Marshal Foch, the First World War hero, in London: 'I am conscious of having served England as I served my own country', with the word 'England' changed to 'France'.

Three exiles

The French deposed three Vietnamese emperors of different characters, personal lives and trajectories, and sent them into decades of exile. The first lost his throne after only a year, when as a 'boy-emperor' he was implicated in an insurrection, and the third (also youthful) was toppled after a self-confessed role in another uprising more than thirty years later; the one in-between, toppled after many years on the throne because of grievous private behaviour but with French concern that he was neither fully loyal nor especially useful. The 'patriotic emperors' became prisoners: Ham Nghi a prisoner of war, Thanh Thai forced to abdicate and no less a captive, Duy Tan deposed by fiat and, like his father, transported to an island that served as a favoured prison colony for deported royals and dissidents. They were kept under close surveillance, restricted in their activities, and regarded with varying degrees of suspicion, though the French did provide life-long pensions and treat the 'princes' with certain courtesies. Ham Nghi grew up and aged as an aristocratic gentleman in Algeria, and Thanh Thai lived his turbulent private life in Réunion. Duy Tan invested himself more actively in Réunion society, and seized the opportunity presented by the Second World War to position himself for restoration to the throne. Reinstatement of Ham Nghi had been mooted but not pursued in 1907, and de Gaulle 'devised' a plan for returning Duy Tan to the throne in 1945. The reputation of both men had been largely rehabilitated, though for Duy Tan the transformation took considerable time and effort, and he encountered numerous obstacles along the way. Thanh Thai never managed to wipe his moral copybook clean in the eyes of the colonisers – yet he was the only one of the three to return to Vietnam.[127]

The French, as de Gaulle remarked, did not have luck with Duy Tan in 1945, but they were not particularly fortunate with other emperors. Ham Nghi and Duy Tan, fully cognisant of their decisions or acting under pressure from mandarins and conspirators, were implicated in plots, and Lyautey acidly remarked that the French could be proud of having failed with Thanh Thai. None was the ideal vassal for whom the French wished. The two emperors considered most cooperative ruled for only brief tenures – Dong Khanh for three years from 1885 to 1889, Khai Dinh for nine years from 1916 to 1925. The last emperor, Bao Dai, spent almost two decades on the throne, but dismayed the French with his waywardness and then with his links to the Japanese; he proved incapable of dousing or controlling the flames of nationalism. He was ultimately unable to fulfil the aspirations of either the French or the Vietnamese.

As Nguyên Thê Anh has shown, the French, from the moment of their conquest of Annam and Tonkin onwards, steadily battered the Nguyen throne, hacking away at the powers and prerogatives of the emperors and undermining the social and cultural foundations on which the monarchy rested. Meanwhile, nationalist support for the dynasty also eroded with the failure of the Can Vuong movement and the early restorationist and reformist ideals of Phan Boi Chau. The new ideologies and strategies espoused by Ho Chi Minh's Communists had little room for an emperor and the feudal order he represented, and even when France made a final push to save its Vietnamese empire in the context of the Union Française and the war against the Viet Minh, it did so with Bao Dai only as 'His Majesty, the Head of State'. It is improbable that a repatriated Duy Tan would have been able to keep Vietnam under French overlordship (which he appears not to have envisioned as the long-term goal in any case), to defuse more radical nationalism, or to preserve the monarchy.

Bao Dai abdicated on 25 August 1945 and Duy Tan's death in a plane crash occurred almost exactly four months later, on 26 December. Those coincidences marked not only the end of the dynasty, but the end of the idea of monarchy that had occupied a central position in Vietnamese life for centuries. The death of Thanh Thai came on 24 March 1954, and on 7 May, the Vietnamese nationalists finally defeated the French in battle: the demise of the French empire in Vietnam. When Bao Dai died in Paris in 1997, he was a relic of a dynastic age and a colonial age

'DRAGONS OF ANNAM'

long gone, yet he had also witnessed from afar in the last decades of his life the birth and growth – without French overlords or an 'Annamese' emperor – of an independent, unified and resurgent Vietnam.

Notes

1. Christopher Goscha, *The Penguin History of Modern Vietnam* (London: Allen Lane, 2016), p. 126. See also his 'Bao Dai et Sihanouk: la fabrique indochinoise des rois coloniaux', in François Guillemot and Agathe Larcher-Goscha (eds), *La Colonisation des corps: De L'Indochine au Vietnam* (Paris: Vendémiaire, 2014), pp. 127–75, and 'Bao Dai, monarque colonial', *Les Collections de l'Histoire*, 62 (January–March 2014). Bao Dai, *Le Dragon d'Annam* (Paris: Plon, 1980), is the emperor's own account.
2. Eric Jennings, *Imperial Heights: Dalat and the Making and Undoing of French Indochina* (Berkeley: University of California Press, 2012); ironically, an anti-colonialist cell may have been active among the staff of the palace.
3. Eric Jennings, *Vichy in the Tropics: Pétain's National Revolution in Madagascar, Guadeloupe, and Indochina, 1940–1944* (Stanford: Stanford University Press, 2001).
4. The Japanese had a potential emperor in reserve in the person of Prince Cuong De, who had lived in Japan for several decades, promoted nationalism, and in the complex history of the Nguyen dynasty already had a believable claim on the throne of Hué. See My-Van Tran, *A Vietnamese Royal Exile in Japan: Prince Cuong De (1882–1951)* (New York: Routledge, 2005); and Agathe Larcher-Goscha, 'Prince Cuong De and the Franco-Vietnamese Competition for the Heritage of Gia Long', in Gisele Bousquet and Pierre Brocheux (eds), *Viêt Nam Exposé: French Scholarship on Twentieth-Century Vietnamese Society* (Ann Arbor: University of Michigan Press, 2002), pp. 187–215.
5. Goscha, *The Penguin History of Modern Vietnam*, pp. 203, 209.
6. Jessica M. Chapman, 'Staging Democracy: South Vietnam's 1955 Referendum to Depose Bao Dai', *Diplomatic History*, 30:4 (2006), 671–703.
7. Nguyên Thê Anh, *Monarchie et fait colonial au Viet-Nam (1875–1925): Le crépuscule d'un ordre traditionnel* (Paris: L'Harmattan, 1992). See also Oscar Chapuis, *The Last Emperors of Vietnam: From Tu Duc to Bao Dai* (Westport: Greenwood Press, 2000); and Bruce Lockhart, *The End of the Vietnamese Monarchy* (New Haven: Yale University, 1993), and 'Re-assessing the Nguyen Dynasty', *Crossroads*, 15:1 (2001), 9–53.
8. Recent general histories are Goscha, *The Penguin History of Modern Vietnam*; K. W. Taylor, *A History of the Vietnamese* (Cambridge: Cambridge University Press, 2013); and Pierre Brocheux and Daniel Hémery, *Indochina: An Ambiguous Colonization, 1858–1954* (Berkeley: University of California Press, 2009).
9. On the use of the term 'Annam' (including its use by Vietnamese nationalists) and the relationship of the *ky* and of Vietnam to Indochina, see Christopher E. Goscha, *Going Indochinese: Contesting Concepts of Space and Place in French Indochina* (Copenhagen: NIAS, 2012), esp. pp. 10–11.
10. The Vietnamese titles were translated as both 'emperor' and 'king'; the French used the word 'king' until the 1920s, then began styling the monarch as 'emperor'. For convenience, I have used the latter.
11. On the revealing evolution of court ceremonial under the French, including ways that the emperor used ritual to try to maintain some of the prerogatives and status of the throne, see Nguyen Thi Dieu, 'Ritual, Power, and Pageantry: French Ritual Politics in Monarchical Vietnam', *French Historical Studies*, 39:4 (2016), 717–48.
12. Vu Hong Lien, *Royal Hué: Heritage of the Nguyen Dynasty of Vietnam* (Bangkok: River Books, 2015).
13. One eyewitness account is provided by General Léon Prudhomme: 'Général X', *L'Annam du 5 juillet 1885 au 4 avril 1886* (Paris: R. Chapelot, 1901). Invaluable contemporary sources are two volumes by Captain Charles Gosselin, who served

intermittently in Indochina from 1885 to 1901: *Le Laos et le protectorat français* (Paris: Perrin, 1900), and *L'Empire d'Annam* (Paris: Perrin, 1904). Adolphe Delvaux, 'La Prise de Hué par les Français 5 juillet 1885', *Bulletin des Amis du Vieux Hué* (hereafter *BAHV*), 7:2 (1920), 259–94, and 'Quelques Précisions sur une période troublée de l'histoire d'Annam', *BAHV*, 28:3 (1941), 216–314, provide further details. A later, dramatised account, is Marcel Gaultier, *Le Roi proscrit* (Hanoi: Imprimerie d'Extrême-Orient, 1940), reissued with a preface by General Georges Catroux, as *L'Etrange Aventure de Ham-Nghi, Empereur d'Annam* (Clamecy: La Nef de Paris, 1959).

14 Quoted in François Thierry, *Le Trésor de Hué: Une face cachée de la colonisation de l'Indochine* (Paris: Nouveau Monde Éditions, 2014), 90–1.
15 H. Le Marchant de Trigon, 'L'Intronisation du roi Ham-Nghi', *BAHV*, 4:2 (1917), 77–88.
16 Gosselin, *Le Laos*, pp. 142–3.
17 Gosselin, *Le Laos*, pp. 201, 137.
18 Gosselin, *Empire*, pp. 201–2.
19 E. Le Bris, 'Complainte annamite sur la prise de Hué par les Français', *BAHV*, 29:1 (1942), 1–36.
20 Le Bris, 'Complainte annamite sur la prise de Hué par les Français'.
21 H. de Pirey, 'Une Capitale éphémère: Tan-So', *BAHV*, 1:3 (1914), 211–20.
22 Charles Fourniau, *Annam-Tonkin 1885–1896: Lettrés et paysans vietnamiens face à la conquête coloniale* (Paris: L'Harmattan, 1989).
23 The edict is translated and reproduced in David Marr, *Vietnamese Anticolonialism, 1885–1925* (Berkeley: University of California Press, 1971), pp. 49–51.
24 Gosselin, *Empire*, pp. 269–70.
25 Fourniau, *Annam-Tonkin*, p. 99.
26 Gosselin, *Empire*, p. 325.
27 Prudhomme, *L'Annam du 5 juillet 1885 au 4 avril 1886*, p. 131.
28 Gosselin, *Empire*, p. 289.
29 M. B. Bourotte, 'L'Aventure du roi Ham-Nghi', *BAHV*, 16:3 (1929), 135–58.
30 Ngoc received a bounty for delivering up Ham Nghi; offered administrative positions, he proved so unpopular that he was constrained to move from one posting to another. In December 1893, he was assassinated and decapitated, his head exposed on the site where he had betrayed the emperor.
31 Fourniau, *Annam-Tonkin*, pp. 160–1.
32 Memo by Resident INDO GG 9569, 22 March 1889, Archives Nationales d'Outre-Mer, Aix-en-Provence (ANOM).
33 Gosselin, *Empire*, pp. 202–3.
34 Various documents INDO GG 9569, ANOM.
35 The proclamation of 29 November 1888 is reproduced in Gosselin, *Le Laos*, pp. 326–9.
36 Quoted in Fourniau, *Annam-Tonkin*, p. 162.
37 Unsigned memo, INDO GG 9569, ANOM.
38 Gosselin, *Le Laos*, pp. 142–4.
39 Quoted in de Pirey, 'Une Capitale éphémère', p. 219.
40 Gosselin, *Le Laos*, p. 29.
41 Gosselin, *Le Laos*, p. 239.
42 Gosselin, *Le Laos*, p. 247.
43 Catroux, preface to Gaultier, *Le Roi proscrit*, p. 11.
44 Fourniau, *Annam-Tonkin*, p. 278.
45 Prudhomme, *L'Annam du 5 juillet 1885 au 4 avril 1886*, p. 21.
46 Gosselin, *Le Laos*, p. 210.
47 Colonial Minister to Governor-General, Algeria, 25 June 1904, INDO GG 9569, ANOM.
48 M. de Varigny, in *Le Temps*, December 1894, reproduced in Gosselin, *Le Laos*, pp. 160–6.
49 Governor-Algeria, Algeria, to Colonial Minister, 17 January 1904, INDO GG 9573, ANOM.
50 Resident Hanoi, 3 September 1919, INDO GG 9573, ANOM.

51 Memo, INDO GG 24691, ANOM.
52 Amandine Dabat, 'Le Prince d'Annam, une vie en exil à Alger', *Mémoire – Les Cahiers d'Afrique du Nord* (June 2014), 16–26, and 'Ham Nghi artiste: Le peintre et le sculpteur', *Magazine Good Morning*, August 2012, http://aejjrsite.free.fr/goodmorning/gm136/gm136_HamNghiArtistePeintreSculpteur.pdf, accessed 25 November 2016. Dabat's doctoral thesis, 'Ham Nghi (1871–1944): Empereur en exil, artiste à Alger', defended in 2015, has not yet been published.
53 *La Quinzaine coloniale*, 25 February 1907, pp. 114–15.
54 Catroux, preface to Gaultier, *Le Roi proscrit*, p. 13.
55 Catroux, preface to Gaultier, *Le Roi proscrit*, p. 10.
56 On this period, see Nguyên Thé Anh, *Monarchie et fait colonial au Viet-Nam*, Ch. V.
57 Baille, quoted in Fourniau, *Annam-Tonkin*, p. 147.
58 Phoebe Scott, 'Authority and Anxiety,' in Sara Siew (ed.), *Between Declarations and Dreams: Art of Southeast Asia since the 19th Century* (Singapore: National Gallery, 2015), p. 18.
59 Goscha, *The Penguin History of Modern Vietnam*, esp. Ch. 5; Taylor, *A History of the Vietnamese*, Ch. 11; Brocheux and Hémery, *Indochina*, Ch. 7; Marr, *Vietnamese Anticolonialism*; Truong Buu Lâm, *Colonialism Experienced: Vietnamese Writings on Colonialism, 1900–1931* (Ann Arbor: University of Michigan, 2000).
60 Letter from Governor-General to Secretary of State for the Colonies, 6 December 1890, INDO GG 22137, ANOM.
61 Unless otherwise indicated, this section is based on documents in INDO GG 9575 Dossier: Agissements de Sa Majesté Thanh Thai, and INDO GG 9618 Correspondances diverses, ANOM, without further footnotes except for particularly detailed or significant documents.
62 Rapports du Résident Supérieur en Annam relatifs avec le Roi et le Conseil de Régence, INDO GGI F.03 24692, ANOM.
63 Resident, Hué, to Governor-General, coded telegram, July 1891, INDO GGI 22138, ANOM.
64 'Mad King of Annam', *New Zealand Herald*, 8 December 1906, and 'An Eastern Potentate', *Auckland Star*, 18 September 1909; *L'Illustration*, 14 September 1907, characterised Thanh Thai as a 'real tyrant like a late Roman emperor'.
65 Chapuis, *The Last Emperors of Vietnam*, p. 250.
66 Letters of Resident to Governor-General, 18, 19, 20, 21 June 1906.
67 Report to Governor-General, 25 August 1906.
68 Co Mat resolution sent to colonial minister, 11 August 1907.
69 Governor-General to minister, 20 September 1907, INDO GG 9577.
70 INDO GG 9577, ANOM (all quotations).
71 Nguyên Thê Anh, 'L'Abdication de Thanh-Thai', *Bulletin de l'École française d'Extrême-Orient*, 64 (1977), 257–64.
72 Undated report INDO GG 9577, ANOM.
73 Tran, *A Vietnamese Royal Exile in Japan*, and Larcher-Goscha, 'Prince Cuong De and the Franco-Vietnamese Competition for the Heritage of Gia Long'.
74 Report on candidates to throne, INDO GG 9577.
75 Governor-General to colonial minister, 20 September 1907.
76 Resident to Governor-General, 30 July 1902.
77 Nguyen Viet Ke, *Stories of the Nguyen Dynasty's Kings* (Danang: Danang Publishing House, 2008), pp. 73–83.
78 These Vietnamese arguments are contained in Nguyen Dac Xuan, *Chuyen Ba Vua Duc Duc, Thanh Thai, Duy Tan* (Hué: Thuan Hoa, 1995); and Hoang Hien, *Vua Duy Tan* (Hue: Nha Xuat Ban Thuan Hoa, 1996); and Hoang Trong Thuoc, *Ho so Vua Duy Tan* (1984). I thank Linh Do for reading these works for me, and Nguyen Dac Xuan for a very interesting and revealing conversation with me about the emperors during my visit to Hué in April 2014.
79 Resident to Governor-General, 28 April 1895.
80 Chapuis, *The Last Emperors of Vietnam*, pp. 24–6.

81 Fourniau, *Annam-Tonkin*, p. 147.
82 Quoted by Fourniau, *Annam-Tonkin*, p. 224, and Chapuis, *The Last Emperors of Vietnam*, p. 250.
83 Gactholoc.net/c15/t15-254/bach-dinh-o-cap-saintjacque-vung-tau-dinh-vua-thanh-thai.html.
84 Various documents, INDO GG 9578, ANOM.
85 Nguyên Thé Anh, *Monarchie et fait colonial au Viet-Nam*, Ch. VI; Robert Aldrich, 'Imperial Banishment: French Colonizers and the Exile of Vietnamese Emperors', in Joseph Zizek and Kirsty Carpenter (eds), *French History and Culture: Papers from the George Rudé Seminar (2012)*, Vol. 5, H-France, 2014, 123–33; Pierre Brocheux, 'De l'Empereur Duy Tan au Prince Vinh San: L'Histoire peut-elle se répéter?', *Appoches Asie*, 10 (1989–90), 1–25; E.-P. Thébault, 'Le Tragique Destin d'un empereur d'Annam', *France-Asie*, 200 (1970), 3–40; Nguyen Phuoc Bao Vang (ed.), *Duy Tan, Empereur d'Annam 1900–1945 exilé à l'Ile de la Réunion, ou le destin tragique du prince Vinh San* (Sainte-Marie, La Réunion: Azalées Éditions, 2001). The volume edited by Bao Vang, Duy Tan's son, essentially a compilation of contemporary and later primary documents, has provided the source for much information in this chapter. See also Claude Vinh Sanh and Christian Vittori, *Hommage au prince Vinh San et à l'Empereur Duy Tan* (Saint-Denis: Azalées Éditions, 2000).
86 David Pomfret, *Youth and Empire: Trans-Colonial Childhoods in British and French Asia* (Stanford: Stanford University Press, 2015), Ch. 5.
87 'Notre petit roi d'Annam', *L'Illustration*, 26 October 1907.
88 George E. Dutton, Jayne S. Werner and John K. Whitmore (eds), *Sources of Vietnamese Tradition* (New York: Columbia University Press, 2012), includes pertinent writing by Phan Boi Chau and Phan Chau Trinh. See, also, Phan Chau Trinh, *Phan Chau Trinh and His Political Writings*, ed. Vinh Sinh (Ithaca: Cornell University Press, 2009); and Yves Le Jariel, *Phan Boi Chau (1867–1940): Le Nationalisme vietnamien avant Ho Chi Minh* (Paris: L'Harmattan, 2008).
89 Kimloan Vu-Hill, *Coolies into Rebels: Impact of World War I on French Indochina* (Paris: Les Indes savantes, 2011).
90 Nguyen Phuoc Bao Vang, *Duy Tan*, pp. 83–6.
91 Marr, *Vietnamese Anticolonialism*, pp. 233–4.
92 Julian Mockford, *Pursuit of an Island* (London: Staples Press, 1950), p. 52.
93 The following is fully based on 1 M 4017 Surveillance du Prince Vinh San 1916–1946, Archives départementales de La Réunion (ADR), Saint-Denis.
94 Daniel Varga, 'Les Vietnamiens à La Réunion, de la déportation à l'émigration volontaire (1859–1910)', *Outre-Mers*, 374–375 (2012), 233–74.
95 Governor-General of Indochina to Governor of La Réunion, attachment to letter of 2 November 1916, 1 M 4017, ADR.
96 Governor-General of Indochina to Governor of La Réunion, 2 November 1916.
97 Unnamed gendarme's report, 20 October 1919, 1 M 4017, ADR.
98 Governor-General, Indochina to Governor, Réunion, 18 October 1924, 1 M 4017, ADR.
99 Buu Lann to Governor, Réunion, 7 August 1943, 1 M 4017, ADR.
100 Governor-General, Indochina, to Governor Réunion, 20 November 1916, 1 M 753, subfolder 1914–1917, ADR.
101 Report of (undated) January 1917, signed Duprat, to Governor-General, Indochina, ADR 1 M 753, subfolder 1914–1917, ADR.
102 Unsigned partially coded telegram to Governor-General, Indochina, 15 February 1917, ADR 1 M 753, subfolder 1914–1917, ADR.
103 Governor-General, Indochina, to Governor, Réunion, 10 and 14 May 1917, 1 M 1852, subfolder 1916–1917, ADR.
104 Governor-General, Indochina, to Governor Réunion, 21 February 1918, 1 M 1852, subfolder 1918–1919, ADR.
105 Police report, 24 November 1916, 1 M 1852, subfolder 1916–1917, ADR.
106 Quoted in Brocheux, 'Duy Tan'.

107 Clipping from *Notre Pays*, 16–17 November 1936, unsigned letter from lieutenant to commander of Saint-Denis police; report of Captain Vérines, 19 November; undated order of Governor, 1 M 4017, folder 'Princes Annamites: 1916–1947' ADR. See also Nguyen Phuoc Bao Vang, *Duy Tan*, pp. 83–6.
108 Vinh San to Governor, 21 May 1940.
109 Rapport by Captain Parriaux, 7 December 1943.
110 Vinh San to Governor, 30 January 1943.
111 Governor, Réunion, to de Gaulle, telegram, 10 April 1943, 1 M 4017, ADR.
112 Vinh San to Governor, 10 July 1944, ADR.
113 Unsigned and undated report (with first pages missing), 1 M 4017, ADR.
114 Reports on service by Tiberi and Allegrini, 1944, 1 M 4017, ADR.
115 Letter (incomplete and unsigned) to Commissioner for Colonies, Algiers, 21 January 1944, ADR.
116 Undated letter, Commissioner for Colonies, Algiers, to Vinh San, ADR.
117 Nguyen Phuoc Bao Vang, *Duy Tan*, pp. 152–3.
118 Brocheux, 'Duy Tan'.
119 See Martin Shipway, *The Road to War: France and Vietnam, 1944–1947* (Providence: Berghahn Books, 1996); and Stein Tønnessen, *Vietnam 1946: How the War Began* (Berkeley: University of California Press, 2010).
120 Etienne Boulé to Minister of Colonies, 11 June 1945, ADR.
121 Frédéric Turpin, *De Gaulle, les Gaullistes et l'Indochine, 1940–1956* (Paris: Les Indes savantes, 2005), pp. 190–194; Pierre Journoud, *De Gaulle et le Vietnam (1945–1969)* (Paris: Tallandier, 2011), p. 31; Institut Charles de Gaulle (ed.), *Le Général de Gaulle et l'Indochine, 1940–1946* (Paris: Plon, 1982), esp. pp. 199–201.
122 David Marr, *Vietnam 1945: The Quest for Power* (Berkeley: University of California Press, 1995), p. 547.
123 Charles de Gaulle, *Mémoires de guerre*, Vol. 3 (Paris: Plon, 1959), p. 230.
124 Nguyen Phuoc Bao Vang, *Duy Tan*, p. 160.
125 1 M 4017, folder 'Princes Annamites: 1916–1947', ADR.
126 Subfolder 'Retour en Indochine du Prince Buu-Lam', ADR.
127 Marina Marouda, 'Potent Rituals and the Royal Dead: Historical Transformations in Vietnamese Ritual Practice', *Journal of Southeast Asian Studies*, 45:3 (2014), 338–62.

CHAPTER FIVE

Out of Africa: the British, the French and African monarchs

In Abomey, the capital of the old kingdom of Dahomey, there stands a statue of Béhanzin, who came to the throne in 1889. At the time, France was eager to extend its holdings in West Africa, consolidate a line of trading ports along the Bight of Benin and limit new acquisitions by British, German and Portuguese colonial rivals.[1] In 1890, the French began a war against Dahomey, defended by Béhanzin's ten thousand soldiers, including 'amazon' women warriors. After fighting that lasted through 1893, the French proved victorious, and occupied Abomey the commander proclaimed a French protectorate over Dahomey. Béhanzin fled to the north to regroup, but in January 1894, perhaps hoping for a settlement, he came to the French headquarters. He was taken prisoner, boarded onto a ship with four of his wives, three daughters, a son and a cousin, as well as an interpreter and his wife, and taken to Senegal. The governor there, who was born in Martinique, suggested that the West Indian island would be an appropriate place for Béhanzin's deportation, and soon the prisoner of war was en route to his new home. After twelve years of exile in Martinique, the French transferred Béhanzin to Algeria; now more than sixty years old and in failing health, he died in Blida, after eight months, in December 1906.

Béhanzin stands tall and proud in the Abomey statue, draped in his robes, wearing a regal cap and holding in one hand the symbol of his authority, a staff topped with a shark, his totemic emblem. His other hand is raised in a gesture of salutation, to summon his people or call blessings down upon them. Posed against a portal reminiscent of a triumphal arch, Béhanzin is a hero, and when the light is right, his shadow seems to stride forward. The inscription borrows Béhanzin's own words: 'I will never agree to sign any treaty that might surrender the independence of the land of my ancestors.' Present-day historians from Benin (as Dahomey is now called) speak in the highest terms of

Figure 10 Béhanzin (1844–1906, r. 1889–94), former king of Dahomey in French West Africa, exiled with his family first to Martinique in the West Indies, then to Algeria, where he died.

Béhanzin's 'brave and exemplary battle against the French expeditionary corps', in the words of Joseph Djivo, and Paulin J. Hountondji characterises him as an 'emblematic figure', a 'consummate commander in chief', 'a proud and dignified Prince ... a demanding patriot'.[2]

Béhanzin was the most famous black African leader for the French at the turn of the twentieth century, earning grudging admiration for his valour but also seen as a bar to the spread of the French empire (see Figure 10). He was one of many who suffered a similar fate of defeat, deposition and exile from sub-Saharan Africa at the hands of the French and the British.[3] Béhanzin is now enshrined in the pantheon of indigenous rulers and resisters to European colonialism, and even the French pay tribute to his state-building and the achievements of his court.[4]

The rehabilitation of banished rulers provides a useful entry-point for this chapter on kings from black Africa, who, vilified and toppled by Europeans, now figure on the honour roll of African statesmen. The repatriation and ceremonial interment of exiles' remains constitutes both a reclaiming of the bones of ancestors and acknowledgement of the significance of their actions. Monuments provide 'sites of memory' inscribing heroic figures and achievements on the landscape. Historical and political writings chronicle lives and works for Africans once told by Europeans that the 'dark continent' had no history and that its people were but savages. Outsiders may query certain aspects of the mythification, but ceremonies, memorials and publications bespeak African ownership of an African past.

Several further examples illustrate these perspectives. In 1968, as pride, militancy and optimism swept newly independent African states, the remains of Alfa Yaya were disinterred for reburial in his homeland of Guinea. The French had deposed Alfa Yaya in the 1890s and exiled him to Gabon, then restored him to the throne of the Labé people, only to oust him again in 1911, and send him to Mauritania. A government minister, Camara Damantang, spoke on behalf of Guinea's president in 1968, and noted that the country's national anthem includes a verse in praise of Alfa Yaya. Damantang hailed him as a 'national hero', and branded his reburial a gesture to 'honour the memory of the man who has left us and to permit his soul now to return to the fatherland that he defended with the ultimate sacrifice, since the country has been purged of the defilement of colonisation, thanks to the indefectible will of the people inherited from its most distinguished ancestors'. He concluded that 'there is no more prestigious resistant to French penetration' than Alfa Yaya, one of the 'martyrs to colonialism'.[5]

President Sékou Touré of Guinea, as it happened, was the great-grandson of another sovereign, Samory Touré of the Wassoulou state, who had surrendered to French armies in 1898 and was banished to Gabon.[6] Samory's remains were also returned to Guinea in 1968, reburied on the grounds of the great mosque in Conakry, near where a statue of the nation's founding father was erected. In 2013, Gabon also unveiled a stele dedicated to Samory in the village where he spent his last days, underlining his status across Africa.

Njoya Ibrahim, ruler of the Bamoun country in the Grasslands region of present-day Cameroon, was another remarkable figure in modern African history who has been similarly memorialised with an imposing statue in his capital of Foumban.[7] Born in 1876, he mounted the throne eleven years later and as an adult undertook revolutionary change in his kingdom. With court scholars, he created a new written alphabet and lingua franca, Shumon, based on several African languages but incorporating Arabic and European words. Njoya wrote in Shumon on Bamoun history and customs,[8] a short treatise on medicine and pharmacy, and an exposition of a religion he created in 1915. The creed, with a motto of 'pursuit and attainment', combined elements of traditional animist thought, Islam and Protestant Christianity. Njoya commissioned a geographical survey of his realm and sponsored public works in the capital. He experimented with commercial farming of ostriches and new crops, and invented a machine to grind maize. He revised the Bamoun law code, reduced taxes, moderated sumptuary laws and simplified court protocol. During his reign, the Germans established a protectorate over the Bamoun, but Njoya welcomed the foreigners, and their impact was light. He had an elaborate throne built as a gift for the Kaiser, modelled a new palace on the German headquarters near Foumban, and sometimes wore a German-inspired uniform and eagle-topped helmet.

After the First World War, the Bamoun country passed from German to French hands, and that cohabitation proved less cordial. The new French Resident bluntly told Njoya: 'The sole chief of the Bamoun is the representative of the French government and there is no duality in command. You [*tu*] are my auxiliary whom I have the duty to direct and perfect morally and intellectually for the greater good of your people.' He added: 'The Bamoun will carry out the orders given by me, head of the district, and not those given beneath by you.'[9] The French accused Njoya of trying to regain absolute power and rallied rivals against him; in 1930, they demanded he leave Foumban for retirement at a rural retreat and, when he refused, banished him from his kingdom. The French hesitated whether to deport Njoya to the Congo, Madagascar or another location, but settled on the colonial stronghold of Yaoundé, over four hundred kilometres from Foumban; Njoya died there in 1933.[10]

A conference held at the University of Yaoundé marked the fiftieth anniversary of Njoya's death. Participants were not sparing in praise of a man 'enlightened, even phenomenal' in his achievements, a 'visionary of a Promethean spirit', 'one of the recognised icons of Africa', 'the restorer, the consolidator and the reformer of the Bamoun kingdom', 'an artisan of human rights', a king notable for 'the advancement of the Bamoun woman'. His capital was 'a tropical Parnassus', his reign 'one of the most exalted epochs of black African history', and 'an exhortation to what the "African Renaissance" can do ... for universal well-being'.[11] Such words were effusive, what some might consider hagiographical, but nineteenth-century European commendations of the colonial conquerors of the Bamoun lands were hardly less superlative. Present-day European historians and curators now also recognise the attainments of an African whose realm was subjected to overrule by two colonial regimes.[12]

Europeans colonisers and African sovereigns

Monarchical rulers – with varying titles and differing political and spiritual attributes – reigned over most pre-colonial African polities.[13]

Over the course of culture contact, European relations with these leaders changed dramatically, with powerful African emperors and kings reduced in European minds to the status of mere 'chiefs'.[14] Europeans in colonial times often viewed African rulers as dictatorial, bloodthirsty and corrupt. A particularly denigrating view came from the pen of Robert Baden-Powell, future founder of the Scouts movement. In 1895, he served in a military campaign against Prempeh, the chief of Kumase (in present-day Ghana) and paramount sovereign (*Asantahene*) of the Ashanti confederation. Prempeh had successfully resisted British designs on his kingdom – famous for its gold and textiles – for more than two decades; faced with defeat, he surrendered to avoid bloodshed.[15] Baden-Powell boasts of the fortitude of British soldiers sweltering in tropical heat and suffering from fever, though noting their disappointment that Prempeh had given up so peaceably: 'Their one idea has been to get at the enemy to give him a real good drubbing.' His statements about the Ashanti are uncompromising. 'The brains of the Ashantis are assuredly most non-receptive' to progress, he opined, and 'the stupid inertness of the puzzled negro is duller than that of an ox'; 'blood and loot had for them charms that could not be resisted'. The *Asantahene*'s capital, Baden-Powell continued, was 'a scene of such meanness and squalor'. Prempeh 'looks a regal figure as he sits upon a lofty throne', but 'his flabby yellow face [is] glistening with oil, and his somewhat stupid expression rendered more idiotic by his sucking a large nut like a fat cigar'. On being informed he was deposed and would be exiled, Prempeh manifested his distress, 'bowing himself to the earth for mercy, as doubtless many and many a victim to his lust for blood had bowed in vain to him ... The only "man" among them was the queen'. After Kumase was occupied, the British soldiers went 'poking about in the barbarian king's palace', though Baden-Powell denied (untruthfully) that looting took place. He admitted that Bantama, a necropolis and sacred site in which Ashanti regalia were kept, which he dismissed as a 'fetish village', was set alight, 'and a splendid blaze it made'. As for the fate of Prempeh and fellow prisoners, 'attended as they are by a fair allowance of wives and slaves, and with all their wants supplied, their confinement will in no way be a hardship to them'.[16]

Not all foreigners shared such disobliging opinions and, as will be seen, several defeated rulers attracted support in Europe. There were also more flattering word portraits, though even sympathetic descriptions veered off into racialised stereotypes. For instance, one travelling writer, Jean Vozelle, recounted a visit to Béhanzin in Martinique. He remarked on the sovereign air of this black king, tall, with the muscles of an athlete and powerful hands. He was draped in a long cloth of blue-striped black silk, and through its folds, one divined the force of his being. On his head, a black gold-embroidered silk bonnet that ended in a triangle on his forehead and two horns over his ears, made his mask[-like face] ever more sombre. His feet were at ease in Arab-style slippers, beautifully embroidered like his hat. In his right hand, he held a silver pipe which he regularly brought to his lips and puffed.

Vozelle observed that despite enduring majesty, Béhanzin looked 'vanquished': 'It would seem to be impossible, no matter what might be said, that he does not feel nostalgia for his realm of sand and tents, his amazons, his carnage and orgies of blood, this man who in his exile has retained something royal with his air of a great caged wild beast.' The visitor maliciously added – the remark no doubt intended as humour – that Béhanzin's 'rank of terrifying teeth' frightened Vozelle's daughters, and he referred to one of Béhanzin's women as a 'monkey'. Vozelle did have the courtesy to present two cigarette cases to Béhanzin.[17]

Ideas of racial superiority contributed one rationale for European conquest of black Africa, and for dispensing with rulers deemed resistant or uncooperative in colonisers' quest for territory. Ouster of kings and chieftains became something of a tradition.[18] Among the early dethroned chiefs, the British removed several now obscure rulers in Natal – Fodo, Sidoyi and Matshana – in the 1840s.[19] Then they banished the better known Langalibalele, ruler of the Hlubi, also in southern Africa, in 1873, shipping him off to Robben Island (where Nelson Mandela was imprisoned a century later). He was allowed to return after a year, but not before Hlubi land had been confiscated.[20]

A particularly poignant story from this decade took place in eastern Africa. The British invaded Ethiopia when Emperor Theodore held several Englishmen captive in disgruntlement at lack of British support for the Christian monarch's defence of his country against Muslim neighbours. As the foreigners closed in on his highland redoubt, Theodore committed suicide rather than surrender. The British took into custody the emperor's seven-year-old son Alamayu and decided to take him to Britain; Alamayu's mother died on the journey to the African coast. A British officer and diplomat, Captain Charles Speedy, became Alamayu's guardian and reared him on the Isle of Wight, where he was introduced to Queen Victoria at her estate. The queen took an immediate interest in the young prince and remained solicitous about his welfare as he received the proper education of a young Victorian gentleman – after a brief stay in India when Speedy was posted there – at Cheltenham School and the prestigious Rugby. Alamayu studied Latin and Greek, and excelled at sport. Early photographs by the pioneering

Julia Margaret Cameron show Alamayu in Ethiopian cloak and ornate necklace; in ones from his time at Rugby, the handsome eighteen-year-old wears a fashionable suit and tie. After finishing school, Alamayu went to Leeds for further tutoring to prepare for the British military academy. After an unhappy year at Sandhurst, he returned to Leeds, where in 1879 he came down with a fatal case of pleurisy. Queen Victoria confided to her diary:

> Grieved and shocked to hear by telegram that good Alamayu had passed away this morning, which is too sad, all alone in a strange country without seeing a person or relative belonging to him. So young, so good ... His was no happy life, full of difficulties of every kind, and he was so sensitive thinking that people stared at him because of his colour. But I fear he would never have been happy.

The words expressed sweet and no doubt genuine sentiments, though avoiding the whole issue of the British kidnapping of the Ethiopian prince. The queen ordered Alamayu buried outside St George's Chapel at Windsor Castle.[21]

Two of the most famous depositions in British Africa concerned Zulus, the heirs to King Shaka.[22] Cetshwayo kaMpande came to the throne in 1872, and the British official in charge of native affairs, Theophilus Shepstone, staged a coronation (though it was not sanctioned by Queen Victoria); Shepstone would become Cetshwayo's nemesis. Unlike the Zulus, the British understood the ceremony to represent Cetshwayo's acknowledgement of their paramountcy. Border disputes between Zulus and British settlers in neighbouring Natal soon erupted, and Cetshwayo's refusal to hand over men accused of raids and to agree to other demands concocted by the British sparked an all-out British attack. The Zulus delivered a humiliating defeat to the British at Isandlwana in 1879, but they successfully riposted with a definitive victory at Ulundi, captured Cetshwayo and banished him to the Cape Colony. Only in 1883 was he allowed to return, to be recognised by the British only as head of the Usuthu chieftainship, not king over all the Zulu lands. Warfare then commenced between Cetshwayo and a rival chief, and a wounded Cetshwayo fled to British territory, where he lived in exile until his death in 1884. He was not the last Zulu ruler exiled by the British, as will be seen.

The cases of Alamayu and Cetshwayo show the extent of British intervention in nineteenth-century Africa even outside areas that became their colonies and the French were no different. They witness to the arbitrary treatment of royals (not to mention their commoner compatriots) by the foreigners, aspirations for turning selected and worthy Africans into European gentlemen, and the celebrity of exiled princes and the sympathy they could evoke, but also the challenges of integration inevitably faced by Africans abroad. The fate of the kingdoms they left behind was as fraught with problems as their personal destinies. Consideration of other cases of dethroned African sovereigns in the late 1800s and early 1900s – with a spike in the 1890s during the most aggressive period in European conquest of Africa – allows the entangled motives and circumstances behind their removal to be explored.

The dynamics of deposition

Desire for land, trade and geopolitical influence, and punishment for resistance to European incursions, explained removal and deportation of kings. The weight of the various motives, however, varied according to specific incidents. The role of individual Europeans (such as Shepstone), including businessmen and administrators, also played a major role, and such groups as missionaries occasionally also became involved in disputes.

Military defeat, or the surrender of a ruler, provided one precipitant for banishment of a vanquished leader, especially if he had for long been an intractable enemy of the Europeans, as was the case with Prempeh. The British fought their first war against the Ashanti in the 1820s over questions of slavery and demarcations of the border between the African kingdom and the British outpost in the Gold Coast. A second war occurred in 1874, when the British invaded Kumase after an Ashanti incursion into British territory in pursuit of foes. The British pillaged and dynamited the royal palace, then offered to withdraw in return for 50,000 ounces of pure gold as reparations. The *Asantahene* reluctantly agreed, though only a portion of the payment was forthcoming. In the background was factional dispute in the kingdom with the rapid 'destooling' (dethronement) of two rulers and near civil war. Prempeh came to power in 1888, faced with the still outstanding payment to Britain and the challenge of revivifying the weakened and divided Ashanti state. He declined British demands for a protectorate in 1891, 1894 and 1895, though the colonial office refused to receive a delegation he sent to London to press his case for independence. As British merchants in the Gold Coast agitated for definitive occupation of the Ashanti country, newspapers blackened Prempeh's reputation as a demon and fiend who engaged in slaughter of his subjects, and diplomats worried about other colonisers' interests. The moment for action arrived in 1896, when the Gold Coast governor demanded full payment of the two-decades-old reparations. Receiving no reply, he set out for Kumase with an army detachment.

BANISHED POTENTATES

On arriving, the governor summoned Prempeh out of the palace; surprising the British, he removed his crown and sandals, and knelt before the governor in submission. The governor again demanded full payment, and when Prempeh stated he did not have the funds, pronounced his deposition and exile. The British had simply decided they could no longer treat with Prempeh, and his removal was, they hoped, the end of a long campaign to take over the Ashanti country.

A second circumstance for deposition occurred when Africans who had contracted alliances with Europeans fell out with the colonisers. Samory Touré, master of the Wassoulou state, had signed a treaty with the French in 1887, but that accord soon broke down. Warfare between the expanding foreign and indigenous empires – the French and the Wassoulou – continued for over a decade, with Samory castigated in Paris newspapers, like Prempeh in London, as a cruel despot and bloodthirsty enemy. When the French finally tracked down and captured Samory in 1898, they found him in a remote camp quietly reading the Quran, unwilling to engage in a final battle. He asked the invading soldiers to kill him, but the French commander ordered that his life be spared, though telling him, 'Samory, you [tu] are the cruellest man ever seen in the Soudan. For twenty years, you have not stopped massacring poor blacks'. With two wives, a son, daughter-in-law and servant, Samory was exiled, and died from illness a year later.[23]

In the case of Sidya Ndaté Yalla Diop from the Waalo country on the Senegalese border with Mauritania, rejection of the French combined with betrayal by an African ally. The French had extended recognition to the youthful Sidya as chieftain in the 1850s and sent him for education to Saint-Louis (Senegal) and Algiers. On his return, he was baptised as a Christian and commissioned as a lieutenant in the colonial army. However, Sidya subsequently came under the influence of an Islamic prophet who preached resistance to the French, and the ruler threw his European clothing into a river as a sign of political conversion. His supporters called for a holy war against the foreigners, allying with the powerful ruler of Cayor, Lat Dior. When Lat Dior accepted a strategic compromise with the French in 1875, however, he abandoned Sidya, who was captured by the French and exiled to Gabon.[24]

In the early 1890s, in the Fouta-Djalon federation in the Guinea mountains, the French and another partner turned on each other. Alfa Yaya, who has already been introduced, had found an ally in the French in return for cession of territory; the French indeed obligingly deported one of his rivals. When their relationship soured, and Alfa Yaya sought Portuguese and British aid, the governor of Guinea invited him to a meeting, promptly took him into custody and sent him to Abomey for five years. Allowed to return to Labé in 1910 after swearing fealty to the French, Alfa Yaya again began plotting against the colonisers; they in turn devised a ruse to get him to request weapons, ostensibly for hunting, and then accused him of amassing an arsenal. In October 1911, the French arrested Alfa Yaya and exiled him with a son, this time for ten years, to a desolate outpost in the Sahara, though Alfa Yaya survived for only a year after his arrival.[25]

European desire for access to coveted commercial resources figured in almost all cases of deposition, but business took the central role in British actions against three rulers in the Niger River delta. Palm oil attracted traders to the Oil Rivers region, and they focused on the port of Bonny, where two hereditary chiefly and commercial houses, Manilla Pepple and Anna Pepple, contended for rule. William Dappa Pepple I, of the Manilla dynasty, succeeded to the throne in 1837 and in due course signed treaties giving the British trading rights in return for regular payments; he also agreed to cease slave-trading. When in 1854, Pepple insisted that the British honour payments, which had not been provided as agreed, the British consul forced him to abdicate, on the ostensible grounds of ill health. They deported Pepple to a fort on Fernando Po island (later a Spanish penal colony), where they maintained a consul, then to Ascension Island, but British Quakers took an interest in Pepple's case, and in 1857, brought him to Britain. There he lived until 1861, when he was restored by the British; he reigned until his death five years later.[26]

Meanwhile, a former slave, known to the British as Jaja, had worked his way up to become head of the Anna Pepple house, but after a disastrous campaign against the Manilla Pepple fled upriver, and in 1869 established his own kingdom of Opobo.[27] Jaja and the British started out with cordial relations, and Jaja sent a son to school in Britain. London's consul assured him that 'the queen does not want to take your country or your markets', but Jaja refused to give palm-oil traders a free hand. When the merchants, hard hit by an economic recession in Europe, colluded to fix prices, Jaja imposed a blockade on British trade posts and circumvented middlemen to export oil directly to Europe. He also despatched a delegation to London, unsuccessfully, to seek redress of his grievances. The British representative in Opobo then invited Jaja to a meeting on board a ship to resolve their differences. The ship straightaway set sail and hauled Jaja away to Accra, in the Gold Coast, where he was put on trial for barring trade to inland districts, blocking roadways and failing to honour treaties. Although defended by a solicitor retained by the sole trading company that had not participated in the price-fixing cartel, he was found guilty and exiled to the West Indies, first to St Vincent and then to Barbados.[28]

BANISHED POTENTATES

One of the most famous British colonial campaigns – now regarded as one of the most infamous – was the attack on Benin, the west African kingdom of the Edo people in what is now southwestern Nigeria. The Portuguese initiated trade with the kingdom in the late 1400s, and it became a source for slaves for the Europeans. With the end of legal slave-trading in the early 1800s, attention turned to its rich resources of palm oil, rubber, ivory, kola nuts and timber. Trade, however, was a monopoly of the ruler of Benin, the oba, who opened and closed the door to foreigners and expected tribute for trading privileges; such restrictions riled those hoping for greater profits and further access to the interior of the country. Travellers to Benin, such as Sir Richard Burton in the 1860s, published lurid tales of fetish worship and human sacrifice, providing moral grounds for intervention.[29] In the early 1890s, the British mounted attacks on several territories neighbouring Benin,[30] and tried, unsuccessfully, to secure advantageous treaties with the oba. Pressure mounted for action to take control of what one colonial orator in London called 'the Blackman's garden', hich he said promised 'England's future wealth and greatness'.[31]

In November 1896, the acting British consul-general in the region (stationed in Fernando Po), James Phillips, asked the Foreign Office for 'permission to visit Benin City in February next to depose and remove the King of Benin and to establish a native council in his place, and take such further steps for the opening up of the country as the occasion may require'. With authorisation in hand, as a ruse he solicited an audience with Oba Ovonramwen, but the monarch refused on the grounds that he was secluded for spiritual cleansing and ritual commemoration of his father. The young and inexperienced Phillips nevertheless set out for Benin in January 1897 with a party of British soldiers, in principle to press for an audience but with a stock of weapons at hand. A local chief, acting without the authority of the oba, ambushed the party of nine, and all save two of the British men were killed. The attack provided a *casus belli* and a British punitive expedition set off in February, and soon captured and burned Benin City. The oba escaped, but in August surrendered to the British, and was forced to kneel in submission before colonial officials as he was told that he was deposed. The British exiled the oba and his close family to Calabar, over four hundred kilometres from his capital, where he died and was buried in 1914.[32] The British then permitted the nominal restoration of the throne to Oba Ovonramwen's son, Eweka II, under their colonial authority in the Nigeria protectorate.

A Nigerian-born photographer, Jonathan Adagogo Green, took pictures of the defeated oba on board the *Ivy*, the steam yacht taking him into exile, and later in Calabar. The most poignant photo showed Oba

Ovonramwen seated in a wicker chair aboard the ship, with three armed but barefoot guards from the British Niger Coast Protectorate force standing behind him. The king, with an introspective look on his face, is wearing a rich-looking long chasuble-type garment embroidered with flowers; his hands are not visible, which art historians note breaks with the conventions of portrayal of Benin rulers, and he is stripped of his regalia. Just visible below his garments are the manacles binding his feet, a striking sign of the position to which the British had reduced the deposed king.

The Benin monarchy was not the only casualty in the British conquest of the country. Benin was home to one of the most accomplished traditions of artwork in Africa. Hundreds of carved and richly decorated brass panels (often mistakenly called the Benin 'bronzes') decorated the royal palace, and images of obas and queen mothers were cast as brass heads or full-figure sculptures; court artists also excelled in works of wood and ivory. Much of the artwork was taken as booty by the British, and put on sale to cover the cost of the military expedition to Benin. Three hundred of the brass plaques were displayed at the British Museum in September 1897, only six months after the conquest. Many of the plaques showed the oba, arrayed in a broad neck choker, arm rings and a coral decorated turban, surrounded by attendants bearing shields, sometimes with royal leopards as symbols of the king's power. Other plaques, most dating from the century after 1550, showed Portuguese traders and missionaries, the Edo sculptors manifestly curious about their exotic appearance and dress. Europeans were astounded by the workmanship, and found it difficult to reconcile with notions of African primitivism. Specialists suggested that the works might have been produced by Egyptians (who were given credit for greater skills than sub-Saharan Africans) or Portuguese settled in Benin, but when it was clear that the sculptures were indeed the work of the Edo people, writers used the theory of 'degeneration' (also frequently applied to Asian cultures) to suggest that although the Africans might have produced such remarkable works in an earlier period, Benin culture had degenerated to a savage level by the nineteenth century. The Benin booty was widely coveted in Europe, museums and private individuals buying pieces from the showroom and mail-order catalogue of a British dealer. Many of the pieces remain in overseas collections, including plaques and sculptures in the British Museum, a royal sword in Oxford's Pitt Rivers Museum and the oba's stool (throne) in the Art Institute of Chicago. Demands from Africans for the restitution of the objects have been rebuffed, though the British returned some of the oba's coral regalia to Nigeria in 1938.[33]

While commercial and geopolitical objectives provided the underlying motives for conquest of territory and removal of regalia, individuals such as the ambitious Phillips in Benin or, in the case of the Zulus, Theophilus Shepstone – whether colonial office-holders or private citizens (though boundaries blurred) – played key roles and could act at decisive moments. Men even in relatively subaltern positions could wield great power in the colonies, far away from colonial offices in London and Paris, and left to their own discretion and devices. The evolution of personal relationships could see would-be rulers placed on thrones, and reigning ones kept there or toppled.

The target of one European was Said Ali, sultan of Grande Comore (see Figure 11). The Comoros Islands, lying between Madagascar and the African coast, sparked interest from the French initially because of the fine harbour on Mayotte, which they annexed outright in the early 1840s. (It remains a French overseas outpost.)[34] The other three main islands were still up for grabs by Europeans, who found ample opportunity to intervene as battling sultans contended for hegemony. French weaponry helped win Said Ali's campaign for control of Grande Comore, and in 1885 he signed a contract with Léon Humblot giving him rights to land and trade, and promising recruitment of labour for his plantations. In return Said Ali would receive 10 per cent of the profits from Humblot's company, which produced perfume essences, vanilla and copra. Humblot had first arrived in the Indian Ocean as a botanist in the late 1870s, and later began manufacturing plant essences, all the while promoting to Paris the benefits of acquisition of the Comoros. In 1886, worried about possible British and German designs, the French at last signed a treaty with Said Ali and named a Resident to Grande Comore. When the sultan complained about the Resident's interventions in local affairs, he was replaced in 1889 by none other than Humblot, who arranged for French troops and a warship to aid the sultan in suppressing an insurrection.[35]

Humblot's political position and commercial power made him the strongman of Grande Comore. When the sultan failed to provide the promised labourers, Humblot the businessman demanded compensation, and in his capacity as French magistrate, he ordered Said Ali to pay up. In June 1893, Humblot's house burned, and two months later he survived an attempt on his life; he accused the sultan of being behind the attacks, which Said Ali denied. The governor of Mayotte was brought in to investigate and – perhaps swayed by Humblot's offer to pay off his considerable debts – ordered Said Ali to leave for Mayotte. On the way, whether with persuasion or coercion, he temporarily ceded his powers to the French Resident in Grande Comore. Once Said Ali arrived in Mayotte, the French informed him that he was deposed and,

Figure 11 Sultan Saïd-Ali (?–1916, r. 1886–92), former sultan of Grande Comore (in the Comoros Islands, off the east coast of Africa), who was exiled by the French. Dressed in traditional robes, he also wears the French Legion of Honour medal.

with his family and servants, would be exiled to Madagascar, intimating that his final destination might be New Caledonia; the place of banishment actually turned out to be Réunion Island. Humblot prospered for a few years, but his continued machinations provoked criticism in France and in the Indian Ocean; the French dismissed him as

Resident in 1896, but he remained in business and lived on Grande Comore until his death in 1914.

The antipathy of a French resident towards an African leader was especially blatant for Dinah Salifou, ruler of the Nalou people in the Southern Rivers region of Guinea. French backing had contributed to Dinah's accession to the chieftainship in the midst of warfare between rival claimants, and they gave their protégé a trip to Paris for the 1889 *exposition universelle* and awarded him the Legion of Honour.[36] When Dinah returned home, he found a palace coup in the works, and a new French commissioner, a M. Opigez, suggested he take the head of a key rival, Tocba. In a chance encounter, Dinah duly slew Tocba, whereupon Opigez angrily denied that he had promoted or condoned the killing. Clearly having taken a dislike to Dinah, Opigez compiled a list of the ruler's misdeeds and – in a move reminiscent of British tactics with Jaja – invited him to board a ship to discuss the situation. The ship raised anchor and ferried Dinah to Saint-Louis, where the governor decided to keep him in effective detention. Over the next several years, the government regularly refused Dinah's requests to return home, not so much because he presented a danger to the French as for the administration's desire to cover up for Opigez, who was thought to have badly mishandled the affair. Governor Henri-Félix de Lamothe indeed told the colonial minister that Opigez bore responsibility for Tocba's death, and that the only charge that might be made against Dinah was lack of comprehensive success in the military actions he had been provoked to undertake. He characterised the capture of Dinah as 'kidnapping'. However, *raison d'état* had to prevail, despite the governor's sympathy for the prisoner; natives should not witness the administration disavowing one of its own. Dinah died, in penury and under virtual house arrest, in Saint-Louis in 1897; de Lamothe arranged for the education of his sons in Saint-Louis and Algiers. Thirteen years after Dinah's death, his son Ibrahima journeyed to Paris to seek his father's rehabilitation. A Committee for the Protection and Defence of Natives commissioned an enquiry, which concluded that the action taken against Dinah was unjustifiable and flagrant injustice. The government nevertheless refused to apologise or to provide compensation for Dinah's confiscated assets.[37]

Successors to ousted monarchs, despite being installed with the assent of colonial authorities, were not safe from removal if they did not live up to colonisers' expectations. This happened notably with successors to Béhanzin and Cetshwayo. The French selected Ago-Li-Agbo, Béhanzin's brother, as his replacement on the throne in Abomey, though in the words of Joseph Djivo, this was now only 'a conditional throne, [and] the reign would be consolidated by a protectorate treaty that would alienate both the royal power and authority of a mortgaged throne'. The new king had no legal authority over foreigners, was forbidden to expand his territory or take military action without French approval, and had to promote free trade and French education, as well as protect French-held private property. When Ago-Li-Agbo opposed a capitation tax instituted in 1899, the French subdivided his realm into four districts, further weakening the ruler's authority. Later that year, a delegation led by a son of the late King Gléglé (Béhanzin's father) reported to the French that Ago-Li-Agbo had poisoned four of their brothers and asked them to get rid of the monarch. The governor ordered his arrest and deposition, an official statement saying 'that for several years, Ago-Li-Agbo had not ceased destroying by his bad faith and his intrigues the efforts untaken by the Residents in Abomey for the development of this province'. Furthermore, he was guilty of numerous 'attacks on the life, liberty and property of his subjects'. The king was deported to Njolé, in Gabon. He was allowed to return to Dahomey (but not to live in the capital) ten years later, in 1910, and lived on to 1940; many of his compatriots continued to regard Ago-Li-Agbo as king, though the French abolished the monarchy on his removal. The throne was restored, with a subnational monarch, only after independence.[38]

In southern Africa, the death of Cetshwayo did not end discord in the Zulu lands, nor incursions by British and Boers on their territory. Cetshwayo's son Dinuzulu was installed as his successor (see Figure 12). But his rule was contested by a rival chief, Zibhebhu (another of Cetshwayo's sons). Dinuzulu requested British aid, which was not forthcoming, then appealed to the Boers, who provided soldiers for the defeat of his enemy in return for land concessions. Boer expansionism alarmed the British and eventually disconcerted Dinuzulu, who shifted alliances and accepted British paramountcy in 1887. Dinuzulu nevertheless continued contacts with the Boers, for which he earned a dressing down by the British. He conceded: 'I must know and all Zulu must know that the rule of the House of Shaka [founder of the Zulu kingdom] is a thing of the past. It is dead ... The [British] Queen now rules in Zululand.' Bickering with the British and Zibhebhu continued, then turned into open warfare, and Dinuzulu fled to Boer territory. In November 1888, the British finally captured Dinuzulu and put him on trial.[39]

Despite irregularities in procedures and notwithstanding a muscular defence, the court convicted Dinuzulu of high treason, though dropping a charge of murder. The colonial secretary in London confirmed a sentence of imprisonment for ten years, but decided to exile Dinuzulu along with three other Zulu chiefs to St Helena rather than

Figure 12 Dinuzulu kaCetshwayo (1868–1913, r. 1884–90/1913), Usuthu chief and heir to the Zulu kingdom, exiled by the British to St Helena.

incarcerating them. Nine years later, in 1897, Dinuzulu was repatriated and made head of a now shrunken Usuthu chieftainship. He was also appointed as *induna*, a term that signified 'adviser' to the British, but to the Zulus may well have been understood as 'commander' or 'ruler'. During the Anglo-Boer War, he recruited Zulu soldiers for the

British, which enhanced his reputation with the Europeans, but they disapproved of what they considered an increasingly dissolute personal life. In 1906, after the Natal government had expropriated roughly half of Zulu land and imposed a poll tax on the population, a revolt broke out, the Bambatha Rebellion, led by a minor chief. The rebellion was soon defeated, with two thousand Africans killed (a death toll said to be higher than in the Anglo-Boer War), Bambatha executed and twenty-five participants transported to St Helena.[40]

Though Dinuzulu did not play a major role, he was accused of harbouring rebels. The Natal government agitated for his removal, but London hesitated. Since unrest continued, in December 1907 Dinuzulu was arrested. Once again he came to trial before a specially constituted court, charged on twenty-three counts – including high treason, public violence, sedition, rebellion and being accessory to murder. The court acquitted him on most charges, but convicted him of high treason, ordered him to forfeit his position as Usuthu chief and *induna*, and pay a fine; it also sentenced him to four years of imprisonment. Dinuzulu remained in detention until 1912, when he was freed by Louis Botha, prime minister of the new Union of South Africa, who had once led Boer troops fighting for the Zulu ruler. With the dubious honour of having been twice deposed, once exiled and once imprisoned, Dinuzulu moved to a quiet farm, where he died the following year.

In the case of southern Africa, the British had become bound up in internecine quarrels among Africans and also manoeuvres against competing Europeans, in this case, the Boers. Contests for acquisition of territory with the French had entered into the making and unmaking of kings in western Africa. International disputes similarly set the scene for removal of kings elsewhere, even after the partition of Africa looked to have been resolved by European diplomats and soldiers.

A gentlemen's agreement in 1890 between London and Berlin gave Britain a supposedly free hand on the coveted island of Zanzibar, famed for its spices and valuable position halfway between Cape Town and Bombay, and the island became a British protectorate.[41] When the reigning sultan died in 1896, a fierce contest erupted between two claimants to the throne. When the candidate rejected by the British, Khalid bin Barghash, refused an ultimatum to withdraw, the British sent in gunboats that reduced the sultan's palace to ruin in the fifteen-minute-long Anglo-Zanzibari War (which nevertheless killed five hundred people, mostly in the burning palace). Khalid escaped to the German consulate, and was spirited to German East Africa, where he lived in Dar-es-Salaam for twenty years. In the First World War, British troops attacked German East Africa and a chance for punishment of Khalid presented itself. General Jan Smuts captured Khalid in

1917, and he was exiled to St Helena with several family members and servants. Khalid complained about the weather, lack of mosque and shortness of money, and in 1921 the British agreed to move him to the Seychelles. He continued to lament his fate, writing rather desperately to the colonial secretary: 'I ask you, Sir, why he [the governor] kept me in a strange country without giving me anything, and [he] says I must support myself. I don't know how to earn my living ... I don't like to live in Seychelles ... I don't want to be Sultan of Zanzibar.' Finally, when the pro-British traditional ruler of Mombasa agreed to stand as guarantor for Khalid, the ephemeral Zanzibari sultan was allowed to move to Kenya, where he died after thirty-one years in exile.[42]

Complex local antipathies and coalitions, set against wider issues of international intervention and dominion of the horn of Africa, led to banishment of the Warsangali sultan in northeastern Somalia, Ali Shireh. The British, French and Italians had all staked out territory in the region, but much power was exercised by Muhammad Abdullah Hassan, the 'mad mullah' then considered an outlaw and Muslim fanatic by Europeans though now revered by Somalis as an anti-colonial hero. Ali Shireh was the mullah's brother-in-law, but also episodically his enemy. In a complicated game of alliances, in 1910 Ali Shireh and other 'friendlies' (as the British termed them) joined with the Europeans against Hassan's 'Dervishes'. The British soon doubted Ali Shireh's loyalty and in fact by 1920, he was again making overtures to Hassan. British forces thereupon attacked the fort where Ali Shireh had barricaded himself. Taken to Aden and given a *pro forma* trial, he was exiled, joining others in the Seychelles. The 'mad mullah' died the following year, but the British kept Ali Shireh in the islands for seven years. Finally returning, he lived until after the independence of Somalia in 1960.[43]

Big power politics and local disputes, as these cases show, were instrumental in rulers' winning the favour or inciting the enmity of colonisers, paying the price if they opposed Europeans' attempts to expand or maintain territory. Though the colonisers turned a blind eye to much in the private behaviour and domestic action of the 'protected' rulers, when that conduct became too grievous or Europeans were menaced, the scene was set for a strike against the native chiefs. In the same year as the Zanzibari sultan was forced to flee, the British also exiled Aliyu of Zazau. They accused the Nigerian chieftain of cruelties to subjects, extortions, payments of hired assassins and impressment of girls into his harem, as well as corruption and various other misdemeanours. The British Resident Edward John Arnett, with support from the missionaries eager to proselytise the Muslim ruler's subjects, led the campaign. Matters came to a head when Arnett and his deputy fell ill, with rumours of their being poisoned. (This looked like a replay of an earlier British scenario in India.) Although inquiries failed to substantiate the allegations, and Arnett and his subaltern had meanwhile come under a cloud for imposing excessive taxation, the government sent Aliyu off to a remote provincial town, where he died in 1924. The British looked after Arnett, just as the French had Opigez; he was eventually appointed a Commander of the Order of St Michael and St George, and published a book on western Africa.[44]

The deposition of sub-Saharan monarchs in some cases represented European efforts to defeat the powerful rulers of large states, such as the Wassoulou and Ashanti polities. In others, conflicts occurred in small territories – though some were larger in size and population than several independent European principalities – and, as in the Zazau affair, took on the airs of a comic opera. Yet even the Zazau action revealed major issues involved in colonial governance. Who determined succession to a 'protected' throne and what were the requirements for a ruler? How much autonomy might he retain? What exactly did 'paramountcy' mean and how was feudatory status understood? To what extent were charges of corruption, maladministration and cruelty clashes of different mindsets in colonial situations? Did Europeans have a right to punish those who betrayed alliances? How did personal disputes inflect colonial policy? Whatever the differences of opinion, deposition provided one answer to the questions.

Most cases of African exile came during the early decades of colonisation, though the weapon of deposition continued to be deployed well into the post-First World War period, and it remained in the arsenal even as African nations approached independence. One incident in the British empire dating from near the end of the colonial period took place not in a minor fiefdom, but in Uganda, one of Britain's most prized African possessions. It was not the first time the British had exiled rulers from that country – the Kabaka Mwanga II from Buganda and the Kabalega Chwa II from Bunyoro, defeated in warfare, were banished to the Seychelles in 1899 – but the British hoped Uganda would thereafter be a model for indirect rule.[45] When in 1939 the fifteen-year-old Mutesa II acceded to the throne of Buganda, the most important kingdom in Uganda, the British expected to groom an ideal ruler. Sent to England in his late teens, the Christian 'King Freddie' studied at Magdalene College, Cambridge, and was commissioned as an officer in the Grenadier Guards; in due course, he received a knighthood, and alone among British East African chieftains was accorded the style of 'His Highness'. After returning to Uganda in 1948, however, Mutesa caused consternation because of his prolific intimate relationships – at one time, two sisters were pregnant with his children, and an Englishman threatened to name the king as respondent in a divorce suit.[46]

The British might excuse philandering, but politics caused greater problems. In the context of post-war colonial reform that tended to centralise government at the expense of the Uganda kingdoms, Mutesa became increasingly adamant in defence of royal privileges and Bungandan rights within the Ugandan protectorate. He also opposed the election (rather than appointment) of a majority of members of the Lukiiko, the Bugandan legislature, which would diminish the primacy of chiefs and other notables. Moreover, the future of Uganda itself was at issue, as a British colonial secretary in 1953 suggested formation of a multi-national East African Federation, which raised the spectre of a smaller place for Uganda and domination by Kenya's white elite.

After Mutesa (backed by the Lukiiko) protested the changes, and rejected any future federation, the British governor, Sir Andrew Cohen, formally summoned him to the State House and demanded unconditional compliance from the king and ministers. When Mutesa refused, the governor told him that he was no longer *kabaka*, invoking a clause in the 1900 treaty between Britain and Buganda which specified that Britain would recognise the *kabaka* 'so long as the Kabaka, Chiefs and people of Uganda shall conform to the laws and regulations instituted for their governance by Her Majesty's Government and shall co-operate loyally with Her Majesty's Government'.[47] The governor ordered the king unceremoniously to be bundled into a car and driven to the Entebbe airport, where an aeroplane stood ready to fly him to London.

Mutesa's exile provoked more discontent that Cohen had expected. The Bugandan assembly organised a delegation to Britain to press for his reinstatement, shops in Uganda closed in protest, and prayer services were held at the Kampala cathedral. Indigenous political organisations came out in the king's support, and the queen mother and his wives championed his cause.[48] A court case was mounted, with barristers arguing that the deposition was illegal since Britain had not annulled the 1900 treaty, though the bench ruled that the governor acted within his powers. In Britain, newspapers including *The Times* spoke in Mutesa's favour and a negotiated settlement. The Archbishop of Canterbury charitably warned of further repercussions: 'The continued exclusion of the Kabaka after a constitutional settlement would antagonize Africans all over the continent ... The character of the Kabaka should not be taken into account. Deposition cannot rest upon his marital relations.'[49] Finally, an advisory commission, chaired by the constitutional law expert and historian Sir Keith Hancock, concluded that Buganda should be transformed into a constitutional monarchy under British overrule. It left open the possibility of Mutesa's reinstatement or enthronement of a new *kabaka*. In Britain and Uganda, colonial authorities realised that removal of Mutesa had been counterproductive, and London gave approval for his restoration. On 17 October 1955, Mutesa made a triumphal return to the Entebbe airport; a three-day overland journey took him back to a great welcome in Kampala. The king signed a new agreement with the governor, after which Mutesa and Cohen adjourned together to watch a football match (Buganda versus the Rest of Uganda, which ended with a one-all draw).

There is, however, a further chapter in Mutesa's story, suggesting that independent governments could copy colonial tactics. In 1962, Uganda gained independence, and Mutesa, still reigning as *kabaka* of Buganda, was elected its first president. Political, regional and ethnic troubles festered, and in 1966 Milton Obote staged a *coup d'état*, sending a rising officer, Idi Amin, to attack the king's palace. Mutesa fled to London, where he lived, in straitened circumstances, until his death three years later. As Mutesa wrote in 1967, 'All this has a familiar ring. Obote is behaving much as the British did when they exiled me, and making the same mistakes, though he has added violence and chaos'.[50] Obote abolished the monarchy of Buganda and the other kingdoms, and ruled as dictator until deposed by the eccentric Idi Amin in 1971. Idi Amin curiously authorised repatriation of Mutesa's remains for interment with great ceremony at the royal necropolis.[51] After the re-establishment of democratic government, several Ugandan kingdoms were restored as subnational monarchies in 1993, and Mutesa's son, Muteba II, currently reigns as *kabaka* of Buganda.

Metropolitan opinion about colonial exile

Governing circles in London and Paris generally closed ranks to support, indeed applaud, deposition and exile of men regarded as enemies. Officials and private persons, as happened in the aftermath of Mutesa's removal, however, might express reservations or condemnation. Lord Salisbury bitingly remarked about the way Jaja of Opobo was taken: 'To invite a Chief on board your ship, carefully concealing the fact that you have any designs against his person, and then, when he has put himself in your power, to carry him away is hardly legitimate warfare, even if we had a right to go to war. It is called "deporting" in the papers, but I think that this is a euphemism. In other places it would be called kidnapping.'[52] Governor de Lamothe in Senegal used the same word of 'kidnapping' to refer to French capture of Dinah Salifou.

Deposed rulers might enjoy a considerable degree of European support, none more so than the Zulu rulers. A renegade Anglican bishop in South Africa, John Colenso, and his three formidable daughters, Harriette in particular, became their indefatigable defenders (as they had earlier defended Langalibalele). The Colenso women proved remarkable champions, petitioning ministers, rallying Zulus, and publishing pamphlets and newspaper articles. Harriette journeyed to Britain to publicise Dinuzulu's case through meetings and lectures, and visited the exile in St Helena. The Colenso sisters also offered their house as a meeting place for Zulus; it was in their home that Dinuzulu was arrested in 1906.[53]

Dethroned leaders also spoke for themselves alongside sympathisers in colonial metropoles. For long after his eviction from Grande Comore, for instance, Said Ali proclaimed his innocence in French forums. In a letter to Paris's *Le Figaro* in 1909 Said Ali explained that he held the position of sultan 'by the will of my people, by the grace of God and the Prophet'. He protested that he was now 'ruined, dethroned' and living in 'great penury' despite friendship and loyalty for the French. In pleading for generosity to Said Ali, *Le Figaro*'s correspondent cited the example of the nineteenth-century Algerian Abd el-Kader as a one-time rebel who rallied to the French. He argued that Humblot had hookwinked the sultan into acquiescing to a protectorate, the terms of which he did not fully understand, and cheated him out of payments for exports. The reporter approvingly quoted Said Ali (though it is unknown whether the Comorian composed the letter himself): 'M. Humblot took advantage of both France and of me for his own benefit.' The sultan charged that Humblot had gradually taken over Grande Comore: 'The exchequer of the sultan, the public records, the police, the army, the administration, everything, everything, everything was taken over by him, despite the clear and contrary instructions of … the governor of Mayotte.' Said Ali insisted that Humblot 'took everything from me, in particular … land, slaves, livestock, jewels, women, children, everything was the property of the Resident of France'. In his view, Humblot's was not administration of a protectorate, but the arbitrary reign of 'a pharaoh, the most avaricious, the cruellest, the vilest of men'. Humblot had sought to destroy Said Ali and to 'martyr my people'.[54]

Said Ali and Humblot both found their spokesmen. Humblot's brother-in-law, Charles Legros – his business partner and former secretary-general of the French Residence in Grande Comore – published a pamphlet accusing the sultan of duplicity in using French cooperation to secure his rule, but then trying to assassinate Humblot. Legros vaunted the work done by the Humblot company in setting up plantations, building roads and developing exports. Another author, Annet Lignac, by contrast, wrote about the 'scandals' in a place where 'the white devours the black'; the island of Grande Comore had become 'Humblot Island', and 'His Omnipotence' made the sultan a victim of the 'capitalist hydra'. Humblot had short-changed the sultan in his contractual payments, illegally taken over land, and abused his powers; any evidence against the sultan in the violent attack on Humblot was hearsay.[55] Such diatribes illustrated the lack of consensus in the metropole about colonialism and reflected French fascination with *affaires* of politics, money and personality, though probably few French citizens really had much knowledge of or interest in Comorian issues.

Sympathies for the deposed could be evident in the colonies as well as the metropole. Although Gold Coast and British journalists had demonised Prempeh during his rule, in exile he inspired different emotions. The *Lagos Weekly Record* stated that his fate 'cannot fail but evoke a sentiment of sympathy and regret for an African ruler whose only offence – if he is at all guilty of any – is that he ignored the Governor of the Gold Coast and appealed to the British authorities in London' by going over the head of the governor and sending a delegation to Britain. The newspaper then perceptively addressed the general question of ouster of African rulers who did not suit the British:

> Apart from the merits of this particular case, it may well be questioned as to whether as a general policy, this practice of the deportation of native African rulers, is one which is wise and consistent with the principles of an enlightened and humane civilization. The necessity for an expedient of this kind is hardly obvious, seeing that in cases of this kind, there is not involved the issues and contingencies arising in the case of a deposed European sovereign and which would render his presence in the State in which he has exercised rule, a danger or menace. In the majority of instances in which African rulers have been deposed and deported, after-events have shown that the measure was not only unnecessary but injudicious, and as in the cases of Cetewayo [sic] and Jaja, the act has been followed by an endeavour to make amends by restoring the deposed rulers to their countries.

It added that from the African perspective, deportation 'is invested with a special degree of spite and vindictiveness. The native mind fails to apprehend why the white man whose country is so remote from his own, and whose moral right to exercise rule over him is incomprehensible, would intermeddle to dethrone his king and banish him from his country, and naturally suspicion and distrust become engendered in his mind against the perpetrators of the act'. By contrast, if the native ruler remained in place with curtailed powers and careful supervision, he might become a useful adjunct and 'the native mind gradually becomes reconciled to the situation'. The editorial concluded: 'It is, we opine, not wisdom on the part of the Government to resort to this expedient of deportation, which ... conspires to engender suspicion and disaffection; but rather to endeavour to regulate its policy in such wise as will ensure the confidence and esteem of the natives and thus promote the inseparable interests of both the Government and the people governed.'[56] The astute comments nicely summarise the stakes surrounding 'protected' rulers.

Several of those saddled with colonial sanction, such as Prempeh, sent emissaries to Europe on their behalf, and exiles, such as Said Ali, were occasionally allowed to go to the metropole in person to press their cases or live out part of their banishment. William Pepple's plight attracted the interest of the Aborigines Protection Society, an Irish Member of Parliament and the campaigning editor of the *Pall Mall Gazette*. Jaja of Opobo, thanks to the Quakers, lived in Tottenham until he was allowed to return home. Cetshwayo made a celebrated trip to London, accompanied by three chiefs, two attendants, an interpreter and, as his 'minder', the son of his antagonist, Theophilus Shepstone. The dapper and robust Zulu chief cut a fine figure in European clothes and a traditional Zulu headband. He was granted an audience with Queen Victoria, who told him that she respected him as a brave enemy and hoped he would become a true friend to the British, and he met the Prince of Wales, Prime Minister William Gladstone and other ministers. It was in London that he learned he could return to the Zulu lands, the good impression he had given no doubt linked to confirmation of that decision.[57]

Life in exile

Loss of thrones and banishment to unknown places, not surprisingly, had deleterious effects on many former rulers. The French exile Sidya was so depressed and erratic that a doctor recommended he be taken from Gabon to Senegal for medical treatment. The governor of Senegal, however, refused to let him disembark, and Sidya returned to Gabon, where he soon committed suicide.[58] Several other rulers did not survive long after their deportation, succumbing to age, disease and perhaps the stress of removal and the anomie of exile: Samory Touré and Alfa Yaya lived for only a year, Njoya for two years, Aliyu for four. By contrast, the hardy Said Ali spent twenty-one years in exile, Prempeh twenty-eight, Khalid over thirty. The longer the life in exile, the greater the need to accommodate the colonial order and the circumstances of banishment. Though perhaps without happiness, some appeared to live with resignation and simple pleasures.

Dinuzulu led a relatively gentlemanly existence in St Helena, though he (like other exiles to the island) complained about the climate. He lived in a house furnished with books, pictures and a piano. He attended Anglican services though it is unclear if he formally converted, and took English lessons from a clergyman. He received invitations to gubernatorial functions, and once took part in a tug-of-war against British soldiers. Dinuzulu himself organised a soirée for Queen Victoria's Jubilee in 1897, and he joined Jamestown locals for a lecture given by the visiting Harriette Colenso. One photograph shows Dinuzulu in a three-piece suit and hat, and he sometimes wore spats and carried a riding crop. On his return to southern Africa after nearly a decade, the Zulu chief took several tons of belongings, as well as a menagerie of donkeys, dogs, rabbits, canary, parrot and monkey.[59]

In the Seychelles, Prempeh and the Ashanti lived almost as settlers. Prempeh had a government-provided six-room house on a seventeen-acre property where most of the other exiles resided as well. Each Ashanti chief received an allowance, and they also earned money selling coconuts, vanilla and rubber from the estate. The authorities connected the community to water and electricity lines, and built a football field and cricket pitch for them. A school opened for the rapidly growing number of children (forty-five under the age of fifteen in 1912), and adults as well, including Prempeh, studied English. Prempeh also learned Seychellois Creole and borrowed books from the local library. He and his mother attended St Paul's Anglican Church (where two exiled Ugandan chiefs were also parishioners), and in 1904 were baptised as 'Edward' and 'Victoria'. The governor invited Prempeh to a reception to mark King Edward VII's sixtieth birthday. After one 1912 festivity, Prempeh wrote to thank the governor, enclosing some Ashanti gold jewellery for his daughters. Most enduringly, during his detention Prempeh wrote a history of the Ashanti country.[60]

Prempeh also wrote regular petitions asking for his repatriation. Although Seychelles authorities affirmed that he was thoroughly reconciled to British rule and becoming 'civilised', the British were concerned about possible destabilisation if he returned, and knew that some other chiefs in the colony (many of whom had gained in status with his removal) were less than eager to see him. However, demands for his repatriation were also eventually advanced by fledging organisations of British-educated nationalists, such as the National Congress of British West Africa convened in 1920, the Gold Coast Aborigines' Rights Protection Society and the Wesleyan Mission Synod, as well as the Gold Coast Legislative Council. Finally, in 1924, London relented and allowed Prempeh to return as a private person with no official status, accompanied by any other exiles who wished to go back to Africa. Thousands greeted him when Prempeh arrived in Kumase, and two years later the British reinstated him as chief of the district (though not as *Asantahene*). He restored the damaged and desecrated Golden Stool, which represented Ashanti authority – the whereabouts and ownership of the stool had played a role in a brief 'Golden Stool War' after his departure – and rebuilt the royal mausoleum at Bantama, destroyed by the British in 1896, before his death in 1931.[61]

The exiles were colourful celebrities for their neighbours, though always kept under surveillance in case they might escape or if any anti-colonial sentiments they expressed risked corrupting local people. According to a St Vincent newspaper, Jaja 'is idolised by the coloured population, who treat him with all the honours due to royalty'. As Martinique prepared to receive Béhanzin, the governor assured Paris that 'all precautions compatible with his security will be taken to ease his internment', a local newspaper foreshadowed his arrival with irony: 'Rejoice! Soon, in all probability, we will have a great curiosity and, even more, a distinguished curiosity in our colony.'[62] Béhanzin and his suite were installed two kilometres from the centre of Fort-de-France, the island's capital, in the Fort de Tartenson, and looked after by a cook, two other women domestics and a male servant. Béhanzin's son Ouanilo enrolled as a boarder in a Catholic school in the northern town of Saint-Pierre. Reporters chronicled the Africans' activities, and inevitably commented on the beauty of Béhanzin's wives and daughters. The French authorities, like the British masters of captive royals, included the exile in their guest list; Béhanzin attended a reception aboard a French warship not long after his landing and a commemorative service for the assassinated French president Sadi Carnot. Baptised into the Catholic faith in Martinique, the former king took part in the consecration of Fort-de-France's new cathedral. He regularly travelled to Saint-Pierre to see his son, and the press described townspeople's fascination with the deposed king in colourful robes, smiling and greeting bystanders. (Ouanilo, by fortunate coincidence, was visiting his father in Fort-de-France when the Mont Pêlée volcano erupted in Saint-Pierre in 1902, destroying the city and killing thirty thousand people, the only survivor a prisoner in a gaol cell.) Though interactions with the local black population remained limited, Béhanzin was clearly respected, and a Creole expression gained currency for those behaving above their status: 'Ou ka pran ko-w pou Béhanzin?' (Who do you take yourself for – Béhanzin?).[63]

Surrounded by his family, eternally smoking an elegant long pipe, enjoying champagne and spirits (to excess, gossips muttered), and receiving the occasional visitor, the African king lived quietly. After four years, the governor allowed him to move to an ample Creole residence with veranda and broad lawn. Béhanzin's walks to shop at the fish market, attend mass or wander through the town made him a regular sight, and his friends included a priest, a photographer and a journalist. His daughters, by and by, contracted liaisons, with Béhanzin's first grandson born in 1901 (to an unknown father); a French cavalry officer fathered Andréa, whom Béhanzin affectionately called 'ma petite Blanche'. Despite his tolerant treatment, Béhanzin's petitions to visit France for the 1900 world's fair and to return to Dahomey, though always couched in loyal sentiments, were rejected or ignored.

Béhanzin's views on his life and fate can be discerned from over a hundred chants he composed in Africa and in exile. As king, Béhanzin proudly referred to his grandfather and father as heroes, determined to be worthy of their legacy as rulers and soldiers. Invoking his gods, referencing mythic animals, and recounting forebears' exploits, early chants affirmed his warrior capabilities, as he resolved to suppress rivals, repulse the French and massacre settlers, and as he celebrated his victories. As warfare turned against him, Béhanzin vowed to fight to the end, expressed anger at betrayal, and adamantly rejected any treaty compromising Dahomey's independence. The chants written in exile intimate resentment at his fate and sadness at 'the heritage of the ancestors [now] in shreds'.[64] In another genre, a valedictory speech to troops before his capture – a hallowed pronouncement in Benin's history – Béhanzin claimed the justice of his cause and lauded the bravery of his soldiers, including female warriors, though lamenting that their battlefield achievements had not equalled the ancestors' prowess. He conceded that they could not defeat the white enemies, whose courage and discipline he also acknowledged. The best victory, he concluded, was not over an enemy: 'He who is truly victorious is the man who, alone, continues to fight in his heart. At the entry to the land of the dead, I do not wish for the gatekeeper to find defilement at my feet ... And now let whatever God pleases happen to me.' He urged supporters to return to Abomey, where the conquerors promised safety and, 'so it seems', liberty. To those killed in battle, 'disappeared comrades, unknown heroes of a tragic saga, here is the offering of remembrance: a little oil, a little flower and the blood of a bull ... Farewell, soldiers, farewell!'[65]

Accommodation did not necessarily mean resignation, however, and royal exiles continuously beseeched colonial governments for increased pensions, better living conditions, transfer to more comfortable places of confinement and, in particular, for repatriation if not restoration. As time passed, they pleaded age, ill health and a desire to die at home as grounds for their return. Prempeh, Béhanzin and others fervently stated their loyalty to the colonisers, though whether as genuine sentiments or as strategic ploys cannot be known. Prempeh, sending petitions on a nearly annual basis, pointed out that he had surrendered to the British, a submission that should entitle him to better treatment. In somewhat fractured English, clearly influenced by religious instruction, he conceded that in the 1890s the Ashanti country had been 'in darksome' but that he and his followers had abandoned their 'evil life'. A petition composed by Béhanzin's son Ouanilo in 1906 tried to pull at the emotions of the French colonial minister: 'Though rendered feeble through exile and sorrow, my voice is raised to you today, in an ultimate cry of pain to which your noble French heart cannot remain deaf and insensitive ... Have pity on a father! Have pity on my son! Have pity on two friends of France! Let me see again the longed-for shores of my faitherland.'[66]

Most petitions fell on deaf ears, though for some long-term exiles such as Prempeh, studying English, attending church, living quietly in the Seychelles, and Dinuzulu, similarly diligent in St Helena, official opinions gradually changed. This no doubt improved chances for repatriation and restoration to some nominal status. But before colonial offices could permit such a return, they wanted to be confident not only that a exile posed no danger, but that he might prove of use in cementing the colonial order, serving as a trustworthy feudatory and uniting his people as loyal subjects. Such, unfortunately (from the European standpoint), did not prove the case with the twice deposed Dinuzulu and Alfa Yaya. Governments, in general, did not favour return except for the elderly, such as Jaja and Béhanzin, or in the exceptional case of Khalid, sent to Kenya under surety from a patron. Death in exile, of course, posed the question of repatriation of remains, though that was rarely authorised, since it would have risked inconvenient manifestations of loyalty to a deceased monarch and anti-colonial agitation.[67] Most exiles were fated to bide out their time in modest contentment, resignation or resentment, and to be buried abroad.

A unique denouement occurred in the case of Grande Comore's Said Ali, though it did not result in his restoration. After his deposition, Said Ali's lawyer for years made legal representations on his behalf, slowly working his way through the complex French court system, and as seen earlier, the sultan and others spoke for his cause. In 1910, the French allowed Said Ali to travel to Paris for six weeks, where he visited the sights and liberally awarded his dynastic order and Comorian titles of nobility (making his lawyer a prince). In turn, the president decorated him with the Legion of Honour after Said Ali signed a formal abdication; the accord opened the way for full French annexation of Grande Comore. The former ruler was even permitted to stop in Grande Comore for two months on the way back to Réunion.

Said Ali, through his solicitor, nevertheless pressed on with the court cases. Two pleas from the sultan arrived at the Conseil d'État, France's highest court, in 1911, one concerning royalties owed by Humblot's company. The other asked for annulment of his deposition, which the plaintiff claimed to be illegal. The Conseil d'État decided that it lacked competence concerning diplomatic conventions, but ruled that the governor had been within his powers in deposing the sultan. As for the payments Said Ali claimed, he would need to file suit in a civil court.[68] In 1912, after another case, and despite prosecutors compromising the sultan's reputation by evoking involvement in slave-trade, a civil court ruled in his favour and he was paid the funds owed by Humblot's company.[69] The monies helped provide for his maintenance until his death, in 1916, two years after Humblot's demise.

Most of the exiles left families behind, including sometimes numerous children. The African exiles' progeny pursued their own paths, only a few of which led to fame, fortune or power. Successors of the deposed back at home (where dynasties survived) came to their own arrangements with the Europeans under colonial rule, and some remained notable figures in the post-independence histories of their countries. For instance, one of Njoya's sons, Njimoluh Sédou, installed as nominal king by the French, helped recruit soldiers for France in the Second World War; he became a representative in the Cameroon colonial assembly in 1946 and its Parliament after independence. The heirs of a few, such as the Ashanti and Buganda kings and perhaps most famously the Zulu king Goodwill Zwelithini, the great-grandson of Dinuzulu, today rule as subnational monarchs.[70]

Those descendants who did not possess thrones had varying fates. The children of Béhanzin's daughter Andréa enjoyed notable success as a surgeon, ambassador, midwife, teachers, surveyor and automobile mechanic in France. Béhanzin's distressed son Ouanilo tried to take his own life after his father's death, but managed to re-establish himself. Having completed secondary school in Fort-de-France, he enrolled at the University of Bordeaux, and took a law degree in 1912, though he worked only briefly as a lawyer. Ouanilo volunteered for the French army before the First World War, his service making it possible to gain citizenship. After demobilisation in 1920, he moved between Paris and southwest France, where he worked as an railway administrator and married the daughter of a Chilean consul. Ouanilo visited Dahomey in 1921, hailed by French authorities as a fine example of an *évolué* – a Westernised and 'civilised' African – though he subsequently raised concern by frequenting anti-colonial circles. Ouanilo's efforts to repatriate his father's remains succeeded in 1928, and Ouanilo and his wife escorted Béhanzin's coffin for a low-key burial at the royal necropolis. Relations with local family members and other Dahomeans proved difficult. On the way back to France, Ouanilo fell ill, and died in Dakar.

His unexpected death – according to doctors, from pulmonary and cardiac problems – prompted rumours in Dahomey, and several brothers accused yet another son of Béhanzin of having poisoned Ouanilo. Ouanilo's body, buried in Bordeaux, was returned to Benin in 2006 and interred with state honours and traditional rituals.[71]

Ibrahima, the Nalou prince who had unsuccessfully sought rehabilitation of his father Dinah Salifou, later enlisted in the French Navy, attained the rank of lieutenant and in 1916 was decorated with the Legion of Honour. A son of the Grande Comore's Said Ali joined the French Foreign Legion. The British allowed Sultan Khalid's children to return to Zanzibar from their exile; one collaborated in the compilation of a Swahili–English dictionary, and another graduated from the American University in Beirut and was called to the bar in London. Some of Prempeh's Ashanti relations and companions chose to remain in the Seychelles when he returned to Africa. A granddaughter who left the islands for Ghana in the 1940s returned to live in the Seychelles two decades afterwards and died there in 2005; one of Prempeh's great-granddaughters made a newsworthy visit from Ghana in 2015.

Almost all of the banished African monarchs were men, though accompanied into exile by wives, women relatives and servants. A rare reigning woman to lose her throne had one of the most unpredicted later lives. She came from the small island of Mohéli, in the Comoros archipelago. Just as on Grande Comore, a French trader and adventurer, Jean Lambert by name, had spearheaded French intervention and persuaded Queen Djoumé Fatima to grant him land in 1848. She was overthrown by a rival sultan (from the island of Anjouan), fled to Paris, settled for a time in Zanzibar, then regained her throne when her rival died – Comorian history is nothing if not complex – in the meantime giving birth to a daughter, Salima Machamba, fathered by a Frenchman who was Lambert's plantation manager. The child grew up in the French colony of Mayotte (another of the Comoros Islands, it will be remembered), and was baptised as a Catholic during a convent education. After further ructions in the palace in Mohéli, the fourteen-year-old Salima came to the throne, but following her installation continued her education in Réunion, where she fell in love with a French gendarme. They married, with French blessings, and she abdicated – which solved the problem of what to do with an absentee Christian queen with a French consort reigning over overwhelmingly Muslim subjects. The couple moved to rural Burgundy, in eastern France, where the former queen lived until her death in 1946. Neighbours remembered her as a typical French housewife, though occasionally reminding visitors of her royal heritage. She regularly beseeched French officials for an increase in the allowance she continued to collect, and at one moment of financial difficulty, even wrote (unsuccessfully) to the king of Sweden, as a fellow royal, to ask for a handout. A son, like the scions of several other ex-rulers, served in the French army, and was a German prisoner of war during the Second World War, but the children retained no contacts with Mohéli. Salima's granddaughter, rediscovering her Comorian heritage, has written an account of her life.[72]

African Napoleons

Paris commentators sometimes referred to Samory Touré as the 'Napoleon of the savannahs' (or the 'Black Vercingétorix', with an allusion to the Celtic defender of Gaul defeated by Julius Caesar), which coming from the French suggests at least some admiration. The parallel was not lost on at least one captive or on the British. A British explorer, William Balfour Baikie, visiting William Dappa Pepple of Bonny on Fernando Po, found the African well informed, and they chatted about Wellington and Napoleon: 'Of the latter he was a great admirer, and alluding one day to the fate of that greatest of generals and of politicians, he proceeded ... to sketch a resemblance between his own detention at Fernando Po, and that of the French Emperor at St Helena.' "Why", said he in his peculiar way, and pointing to a print of Buonaparte [sic], "why your gubberment keep me here, I no do bad like he, I be free man, I be King".'[73] After Pepple attempted to escape from the island, the British decided to remove him further away from the African coast – a parallel with Napoleon's trajectory from Elba to St Helena – and transported him to the even more remote South Atlantic island of Ascension. In another reference to the most famous of imperial exiles, London's *Daily Telegraph* irresistibly mused on the fate of Jaja of Opobo banished to a Caribbean island:

> There in the fertile valleys under the 'Soufrière' [volcano], this swarthy smuggler and Royal contrabandist can meditate in peace over his follies, and if he be of a poetical or historical turn of mind, can compare himself to the broad-browed Corsican ... and make it his custom on an afternoon to ... put on a cocked-hat sideways – savage kings as a rule have a penchant for a cocked-hat – and frown at the setting sun in the orthodox posture adopted by deposed monarchs.[74]

Such words were mockery, but they underlined how victorious foreign military and political powers could oust and banish native rulers whom they had defeated in battle, who betrayed them, were accused of placing obstacles in the path of commerce and Christianity, committed foul deeds, or simply fell afoul of antipathetic Europeans. There are, indeed, parallels between the exiled Napoleon and the

Africans, including for several, a second exile after a brief return to power. Napoleon at Longwood House and Dinuzulu in Jamestown, after all, were geographical if not chronological neighbours in St Helena, and such men as Béhanzin and Alfa Yaya presided over courts-in-exile with all the gravitas of the French *ci-devant* emperor. Vilified, but nevertheless accorded a measure of respect from their captors (and, in some cases, support from European partisans), they remained present in the memories, and in the political manoeuvres, of their compatriots. A few such as Pepple and Prempeh lived to return home permanently, fulfilling a desire that escaped Napoleon, but more of them died in their lonely islands. After death, some would be granted heroic repatriations and reburials that recalled the return of Napoleon's remains to Paris in 1840, and in statues, commemorations and panegyrics they now enjoy the fame in their own societies that Napoleon commands in France.

Notes

1 Hélène Joubert and Gaëlle Beaujean-Baltzer, *Béhanzin Roi d'Abomey* (Paris: Fondation Zinzou, 2006); Joseph Adrien Djivo, *Le Refus de la colonisation dans l'ancien royaume de Danxome 1894–1900*, Vol. 2 (Paris: L'Harmattan, 2013).
2 Joubert and Beaujean-Baltzer, *Béhanzin Roi d'Abomey*, pp. 43 and 55.
3 François Michel, *La Campagne du Dahomey, 1893–1894: la reddition de Béhanzin*, ed. Jacques Serres (Paris: L'Harmattan, 2001).
4 This is evident in the displays on Benin at the Musée du Quai Branly, Paris. There was also an exhibition in Martinique in 1995, 'Béhanzin: l'exil d'un roi 1894–1906', Bibliothèque Schoelcher, Fort-de-France. *L'Exil du roi Béhanzin*, directed by Guy Deslauriers, script by Patrick Chamoiseau (Organisation internationale de la Francophonie, 2012), and *Béhanzin, le rêve inachevé* (directed by André-Marie Johnson) are filmed homages.
5 Thierno Diallo, *Alfa Yaya, roi du Labé (Fouta-Djallon)* (Paris: ABC, 1976); Robert Cornevin, 'Alfa Yaya Diallo fut-il un héros national de Guinée ou l'innocente victime d'un règlement de comptes entre gouverneurs?', *Revue française d'histoire d'outre-mer*, 57:208 (1970), 288–96.
6 Touré had led the campaign for independence of Guinea in 1958, radically separating himself from other colonial leaders by promoting immediate and full separation from France.
7 Alexandra Loumpet-Galitzine, *Njoya et le royaume bamoun: les archives de la Société des Missions Évangéliques de Paris, 1917–1937* (Paris: Karthala, 2006); Bachair Ndam, *De Njoya Ibrahim à Mbombo Njoya Ibrahim: Histoires et incompréhensions d'une dynastie qui survit* (Saint-Denis: Edilivre, 2014); Eugène Désiré Eloundou and Arouna Ngapna, *Un Souverain bamoun en exil: le roi Njoya Ibrahima à Yaoundé (1931–1933)* (Paris: L'Harmattan, 2011); Christraud Geary and Adamou Ndam Njoya, *Mandou Yenou: photographies du pays bamoun, royaume ouest-africain* (Munich: Trickster Verlag, 1985). Denys Ferrando-Durfout, *Njoya le réformateur* (Yaoundé: EdiSavana, 1989), a children's book, testifies to present-day respect for the king in Cameroon.
8 Sultan Njoya, *Histoire et coutumes des Bamum* (Yaoundé: IFAN, 1952).
9 Quoted in Eloundou and Ngapna, *Un Souverain bamoun en exil*, p. 27.
10 Eloundou and Ngapna, *Un Souverain bamoun en exil*, based on interviews with elderly Cameroonians who knew of his exile at first hand, provides a comprehensive account.

11 Colloque international Roi Njoya, *Le Roi Njoya: créateur de civilisation et précurseur de la renaissance africaine* (Paris: L'Harmattan, 2014).
12 The Musée du Quai Branly in 2015 had a small exhibition on Njoya and the art of his court, including paintings of the Bamoun sovereigns, royal decrees and examples of Shomun writing, and a photograph of Njoya working at his desk, his study decorated with carvings, elephant tusks and textile wall-hangings. (Author's notes; there was unfortunately no printed catalogue.)
13 See, e.g., Daryll Forde and P. M. Karberry, *West African Kingdoms in the Nineteenth Century* (Oxford: Oxford University Press, 1967); and Jean-Pierre Chrétien, *The Great Lakes of Africa: Two Thousand Years of History* (New York: Zone Books, 2003), esp. Chs II–III.
14 Tarikhu Farr, 'When African Kings Became "Chiefs": Some Transformations in European Perceptions of West African Civilization, c. 1450–1800', *Journal of Black Studies*, 23:2 (1992), 258–78.
15 Standard sources on the nineteenth century are T. J. Lewin, *Asante before the British: The Prempean Years, 1875–1900* (Lawrence: Regents Press, 1978); T. C. McCaskie, *State and Society in Precolonial Asante* (Cambridge: Cambridge University Press, 1995); W. Tordoff, *Ashanti under the Prempehs, 1888–1935* (Oxford: Oxford University Press, 1965); and I. Wilks, *Asante in the Nineteenth Century: The Structure and Evolution of a Political Order* (Cambridge: Cambridge University Press, 1989).
16 R. S. S. Baden-Powell, *The Downfall of Prempeh: A Diary of Life with the Native Levy in Ashanti, 1895–96* (London: Methuen, 1896), quotations from pp. 142, 64, 57, 41, 115, 117, 126, 110, 131 and 150.
17 Jean Vozelle, 'Béhanzin à la Martinique', *Revue de Paris*, 1 May 1898, 220–4. Cf. the views of another visitor, Albert Londres, 'Terre d'ébène', in *Oeuvres complètes* (Paris: Arléa, 1992), pp. 587–91.
18 This chapter does not seek to provide a comprehensive discussion about all of the numerous rulers deposed by the British and French. For some examples not covered here, see, e.g., P. A. Roberts, 'The Sefwi Wiawso Riot of 1935: The Deposition of an Omanhene in the Gold Coast', *Journal of the International African Institute*, 53:2 (1983), 25–46; Anshan Li, 'Asafo and Destoolment in Colonial Southern Ghana, 1900–1953', *International Journal of African Historical Studies*, 28:2 (1995), 324–57; Meredith Terretta, 'Chiefs, Traitors, and Representatives: The Construction of a Political Repertoire in Independence-Era Cameroun', *International Journal of African Historical Studies*, 43:2 (2010), 227–53; and Tunde Oduwobi, 'Deposed Rulers under the Colonial Regime in Nigeria: The Careers of Akarigbo Oyebajo and Awujale Adenuga', *Cahiers d'études africaines*, 171 (2003), 553–71.
19 Thomas McClendon, 'You Are What You Eat Up: Deposing Chiefs in Early Colonial Natal, 1847–58', *Journal of African History*, 47 (2006), 259–79.
20 Norman Herd, *The Bent Pine: The Trial of Chief Langalilabele* (Johannesburg: The Ravan Press, 1976).
21 Elizabeth Laird, *The Prince Who Walked with Lions* (London: Macmillan, 2012); BBC Radio 4, 'Alamayu', broadcast 21 December 2012; 'C. C.', *Anecdotes of Alamayu, the Late King Theodore's Son* (London: William Hunt, 1869).
22 Stephen Taylor, *Shaka's Children: A History of the Zulu People* (London: HarperCollins, 1994), provides good background. The key works on the two exiled rulers are Jeff Guy, *The Destruction of the Zulu Kingdom: The Civil War in Zululand, 1879–1884* (London: Longman, 1979), and *The View Across the River: Harriette Colenso and the Zulu Struggle against Imperialism* (Oxford: James Currey, 2002). See also C. T. Binns, *The Last Zulu King: The Life and Death of Cetshwayo* (London: Longmans, 1963) and *Dinuzulu: The Death of the House of Shaka* (London: Longmans, 1968), and Donald R. Morris, *The Washing of the Spears: The Rise and Fall of the Zulu Nation* (New York: Simon & Schuster, 1964).
23 Julie d'Andurain, *La Capture de Samory (1898): l'achèvement de la conquête de l'Afrique de l'Ouest* (Paris: L'Harmattan, 2012). See also Yves Person, *Samori: une révolution dyula* (Dakar: IFAN, 3 vols, 1968–75).

24 Boubacar Barry, *Le Royaume du Waalo: Le Sénégal avant la conquête* (Paris: Karthala, 1985); Mamadou Diouf, *Le Kajoor au XIXe siècle: pouvoir ceddo et conquête coloniale* (Paris: Karthala, 2014); Ababacar Fall-Barros, ' "Histoire cachée": Il y a 136 ans, le 17 janvier 1877, Sidya Diop fût jugé, condamné par un tribunal colonial et déporté au Gabon', Ndarinfo, 16 January 2013, www.ndarinfo.com/Histoire-cachee-Il-y-a-136-ans-le-17-janvier-1877-Sidya-Diop-fut-juge-condamne-par-un-tribunal-colonial-et-deporte_a4586.html, accessed 25 November 2016.
25 Diallo, *Alfa Yaya*, and Cornevin, 'Alfa Yaya Diallo'.
26 E. J. Alagoa, *A Chronicle of Grand Bonny* (Ibadan: Ibadan University Press, 1972).
27 Sylvanus Cookey, *King Jaja of the Niger Delta: His Life and Times, 1821–1891* (New York: NOK, 1974); E. J. Alagoa, *Jaja of Opobo: The Slave Who Became a King* (London: Longman, 1970); Anthony Esenswa, *Jaja: King of Opobo* (Central Milton Keynes: Author House, 2009); E. J. Jaja, *King Jaja of Opbo (1821–1891)* (Lagos: Opobo Action Council, 1977).
28 Edward L. Cox, *Rekindling the Ancestral Memory: King Jaja of Opobo in St Vincent and Barbados, 1888–1891* (Cave Hill: University of the West Indies and the Barbados Museum and Historical Society, 1998).
29 For Burton's and later writers' views, see Osarhierne Benson Osadolor and Leo Enahoro Otoide, 'The Benin Kingdom in British Imperial Historiography', *History in Africa*, 35 (2008), 401–18.
30 Among other peoples who suffered attacks were the Itsekiri, whose chief, Nana (or Nanna) Olomu, held the post of Governor of Benin River (a position established by the British in 1851 and in principle alternating between two families). Despite treaties between the Itsekiri and the British, relations deteriorated, and the upshot was the ouster of Olomu in 1894 and his exile first to Calabar, and then to the Gold Coast (Ghana); he returned to his homeland in 1906 and died ten years later. A statue of Olomu was erected in his capital of Koko, and in 2016, ceremonies were held in his old palace (now a museum containing his treasures) on the centenary of his death and he was hailed as a hero of resistance against colonialists. See Obaro Ikime, *Merchant Prince of the Niger Delta: The Rise and Fall of Nana Olomu, Last Governor of the Benin River* (London: Heinemann, 1968), and Egufe Yafugborhi, '100 Years of Nanna of Itsekiri's "Living History" ', *Vanguard*, 10 July 2016, www.vanguardngr.com/2016/07/100-years-nanna-itsekiris-living-history/.
31 Thomas Uwadiale Obinyan, 'The Annexation of Benin', *Journal of Black Studies*, 19:1 (1988), 29–40; for a fuller account, see Alan Ryder, *Benin and the Europeans, 1485–1897* (London: Longman, 1969).
32 Oba Ovonramwen has been the subject of several plays; see Ifeanyi Ugwu, 'Deconstructionist Interpretations of Rotimi's *Ovonranwen Nogbaisi* in [sic] Yermina's *The Trials of Oba Ovonramwen*', *Research on Humanities and Social Sciences*, 3:13 (2013), 86–94.
33 Annie C. Coombes, catalogue entries in Alison Smith, David Blayney Brown and Carol Jacobi (eds), *Artist and Empire: Facing Britain's Imperial Past* (London: Tate Publishing, 2015), pp. 78–81. See also the British Museum dossier at britishmuseum.org/PDF/Benin_art_Nov2015.pdf.
34 Jean Martin, *Comores: Quatre îles entre pirates et planteurs* (Paris: L'Harmattan, 1983).
35 The following account is based on Jean-Louis Guébourg, *La Grande Comore: Des Sultans aux mercenaires* (Paris: L'Harmattan, 1993).
36 Philippe David, 'Villages, sujets et visiteurs coloniaux à l'Exposition universelle de Paris (1889)', in Papa Sama Diop and Hans-Jürgen Lüsebrink (eds), *Littérateurs et sociétés africaines: Regards comparatistes et perspectives interculturelles* (Tübingen: G. Narr, 2001), pp. 187–98.
37 Thierno Diallo, *Dinah Salifou, roi des Nalous* (Paris: ABC, 1977); Baba Ibrahima Kake, 'A propos de l'exil de Dinah Salifou, roi des Nalous', *Présence africaine*, 3 (1964), 146–58.
38 Joseph Adrien Djivo, *Le Protectorat d'Abomey: Ago-Li-Agbo, 1894–1900* (Abomey: Université Nationale du Bénin, 1985), quotations from p. 25.

39 *The Trial of Dinuzulu on Charges of High Treason* (Pietermaritzburg: Times Printing, 1910).
40 P. S. Thompson, 'Dinizulu and Bhambatha, 1906: An Invasion of Natal and an Uprising in Zululand That Almost Took Place', *Historia*, 58:2 (2013), 40–69.
41 See Sarah K. Croucher, *Capitalism and Cloves: An Archaeology of Plantation Life on Nineteenth-Century Zanzibar* (New York: Springer-Verlag, 2015).
42 Ian Hernon, *Massacre and Retribution: Forgotten Wars of the Nineteenth Century* (Stroud: Sutton, 1998), Ch. 16; P. J. L. Frankl, 'The Exile of Khalid Bin Barghash Ali-Busa'Idi: Born Zanzbar C. 1291 AH/AD 1874 Died Mombasa 1845 AH/AD 1927', *British Journal of Middle Eastern Studies*, 33:2 (2006), 161–77; Julien Durup, 'The Exile Sayyid Khalid bin Barghash Al-Basaidi in the Seychelles', *Seychelles Weekly*, www.seychellesweekly.com/September5,2010/top6a_The Exile Sayyid Khalid bin.html, accessed 25 November 2016.
43 Patrick Kitaburaza Kakwenzire, 'Colonial Rule in the British Somaliland Protectorate, 1905–1939' (PhD dissertation, University of London, 1976); Robert L. Hess, 'The "Mad Mullah" and Northern Somalia', *Journal of African History*, 5:3 (1964), 415–33.
44 Edmund M. Hogan, *Berengario Cermenati among the Igbirra (Ebira) of Nigeria: A Study in Colonial, Missionary and Local Politics, 1897–1925* (Ibadan: HEBN, 2011).
45 D. A. Low, *Fabrication of Empire: The British and the Uganda Kingdoms, 1890–1902* (Cambridge: Cambridge University Press, 2009); M. S. M. Kiwanuka, 'Bunyoro and the British: A Reappraisal of the Causes of the Decline and Fall of an African Kingdom', *Journal of African History*, 9:4 (1968), 603–19; Justin Willis, 'A Portrait of the Mukama: Monarchy and Empire in Colonial Bunyoro, Uganda', *Journal of Imperial and Commonwealth History*, 34:1 (2006), 105–22.
46 This account is based on Low, *Fabrication of Empire* as well as the Kabaka's own account, *The Desecration of My Kingdom* (London: Constable, 1967), the memoir of his former prime minister, Paulo Kavuma, *Crisis in Buganda, 1953–55: The Story of the Exile and Return of the Kabaka, Mutesa II* (London: Collins, 1979), and Uganda Protectorate, *Withdrawal of Recognition from Kabaka Mutesa II of Buganda (report presented by the Secretary of State for the Colonies to Parliament)* (London: Colonial Office, 1953). Kevin Ward, 'The Church of Uganda and the Exile of Kabaka Mutesa II, 1953–55', *Journal of Religion in Africa*, 28:4 (1998), 411–49, provides insight into the role of churchmen.
47 Uganda Protectorate, *Withdrawal of Recognition*.
48 Carol Summers, 'All the Kabaka's Wives: Marital Claims in Buganda's 1953–5 Kabaka Crisis', *Journal of African History*, 58:1 (2017), 107–17.
49 Quoted in Ward, 'The Church of Uganda', p. 435.
50 *Withdrawal of Recognition from Kabaka Mutesa II of Buganda*, p. 194.
51 Letter of George Jones to 'Mr. Nolte', 15 May 1971, Institute of Current World Affairs, iewa.org/wp-content/uploads/2015/09/Gj-12.pdf, accessed 25 November 2016.
52 Quoted in Cookey, *King Jaja*, p. 127.
53 Guy, *The View Across the River*.
54 *Le Figaro*, 17 February 1909, commentary on letter of Said Ali by Charles Davenant.
55 Charles Legros, *La Grande-Comore, 1884–1909* (Paris: n.p., 1909); Annet Lignac, *Les Scandales de la Grande Comore* (Paris: n.p., 1908).
56 Georgia McGarry (ed.), *Reaction and Protest in The West African Press: A Collection of Newspaper Articles on Five Nineteenth Century African Leaders* (Leiden: Afrika-Studiecentrum, 1978), pp. 81–2.
57 Bridget Theron, 'King Cetshwayo in Victorian England: A Cameo of Imperial Interaction', *South African Historical Journal*, 56 (2006), 60–87.
58 Fall-Barros, '"Histoire cachée": Il y a 136 ans, le 17 janvier 1877'.
59 St Helena National Trust, 'St Helena National Trust Education Packs, 4.1. Island Prisoners – Dinuzulu', www.nationaltrust.org.sh/publications/the-historical-education-pack/, accessed 25 November 2016.

60 Otumfuo, Nana Agyema Prempeh I, *'The History of Ashanti Kings and the whole country itself' and Other Writings*, ed. A. Adu Boahen, Emmanuel Akyeampong, Nancy Lawler, T. C. McCaskie and Ivor Wilks (Oxford: Oxford University Press, 2003), which includes several essays on Prempeh before his exile, in the Seychelles and after his return, as well as Prempeh's own writings. See also W. Tordoff, 'The Exile and Repatriation of Nana Prempeh I of Ashanti (1896–1924)', *Transactions of the Historical Society of Ghana*, 4:2 (1960), 33–58; and Tony Mathiot, 'The King of Ashanti – 24 Years of Exile in Seychelles', Virtual Seychelles website, www.pfsr.org/history-of-seychelles/the-king-of-ashanti-24-years-of-exile-in-seychelles/, accessed 25 November 2016. On the cohort of royal exiles in the Seychelles, see Uma Kothari, 'Contesting Colonial Rule: Politics of Exile in the Indian Ocean', *Geoforum*, 43 (2012), 697–706.
61 Christopher Bayley and Tim Harper, *Britain's Forgotten Wars* (London: Allen Lane, 2007), Ch. 9.
62 Quoted in Patrice Louis, *Le Roi Béhanzin: Du Dahomey à la Martinique* (Paris: Arléa, 2011), p. 31, whose book provides details on Béhanzin in Martinique.
63 Louis, *Le Roi Béhanzin*, p. 55.
64 Albert Bienvenu Akoha and Apollinaire Medagbe, *Chants de Béhanzin, le résistant* (Paris: L'Harmattan, 2015), quotation from p. 169.
65 https://afrolegends.com/2012/05/14/sans-parole-sans-honneur-la-loi-du-materialisme-behanzin-one-of-the-last-african-resistant-to-colonization/.
66 Quoted in Louis, *Le Roi Béhanzin*, p. 100.
67 A British exception was the repatriation of the remains of the Ugandan chief Mwanga from the Seychelles in 1910. The report from the *Uganda Notes* of September 1910 is reprinted in Philip Briggs with Andrew Roberts, *Uganda* (London: Bradt, 2013), pp. 164–5.
68 *Recueil des arrêts du Conseil d'État*, Series 2, Vol. 81 (1911), pp. 848–9.
69 'Le Sultan Saïd-Ali contre MM. Humblot et Legros, Tribunal civil de la Seine', *Revue des grands procès contemporains*, 1 October 1912.
70 Because of factional disputes and fears for his safety, when in his twenties, Goodwill lived for three years in self-imposed exile in, of all places, St Helena. Some of the reigning subnational kings in Africa are profiled (and photographed) in Daniel Lainé, *African Kings* (Berkeley: Ten Speed Press, 2000). See also the images of Alfred Weidinger at www.flickr.com/photos/a-weidinger/sets/72157629895167757/ , accessed 25 November 2016.
71 Djivo, *Le Protectorat d'Abomey*, pp. 91–102. Didier Samson, 'Bénin: Ouanilo de retour à Abomey', RFI, 28 September 2006, www1.rfi.fr/actufr/articles/081/article_46428.asp, accessed 25 November 2016.
72 Anne Etter and Raymond Riquier, *À Salima de Mohéli, dernière reine comorienne, la fidélité d'une petite-fille* (Moroni, Comores: Komedit, 2012); Julienne Nivois, *A Pesme, en Franche-Comté...une reine oubliée par l'histoire* (n.p.: Dominique Guéniot, 1995).
73 William Balfour Baikie, *Narrative of an Exploring Voyage up the Rivers Kwóra and Binue – commonly known as the Niger and Tsádda – in 1854* (London: John Murray, 1856), p. 332.
74 Quoted in Cookey, *King Jaja*, p. 144.

CHAPTER SIX

The French and the queen of Madagascar: Ranavalona III, 1897

Madame,
Since the Government of the French Republic has declared Madagascar a French colony, the institution of the Monarchy has become of no use in Imerina.

I had hoped that your influence over your people would have aided me to bring an end to the insurrection that afflicted the country several months ago. But such was not the case and the pacification that is spreading little by little in Imerina was only achieved thanks to the unceasing efforts of French troops.

In consequence, I invite you to resign from your functions.

Furthermore, since your presence in Madagascar could create a certain inconvenience for some further time, I desire that you leave Tananarive tomorrow morning, going to Tamatave where you will be taken to Réunion Island, and where you will receive the most generous hospitality from French authorities.

All arrangements will be made so that your voyage will take place in the best conditions and so that you will be treated with all the respect due to your situation and your sex.

Please accept, Madame, the assurance of my great consideration.

Gallieni[1]

In that rather curt letter, dated 27 February 1897, General Joseph Gallieni, commander-in-chief of French forces in Madagascar, deposed and exiled Queen Ranavalona III, who had reigned as monarch on the Indian Ocean island since 1883. She would live in exile, briefly on Réunion Island then in Algeria, until her death in 1917. The French continued to control Madagascar until it regained independence in 1960.[2]

Ranavalona III counted among a very small number of reigning women monarchs anywhere in the world in the late nineteenth century. She was also one of few female sovereigns to be exiled after the invasion, occupation and annexation of their countries by imperialists.

Ranavalona's reign, removal and life in exile thus present interesting perspectives on gender, monarchy and colonialism. Her story also gives insight into a cult of royal celebrity in the *fin de siècle* and *belle époque* that encompassed even a deposed queen.

The French conquest of Madagascar

Madagascar, larger in area than metropolitan France, boasted good harbours, a strategic position and fertile soil.[3] The Merina majority of the population (which encompassed seventeen ethnic groups among 2.5 million people in the 1880s) descended from Southeast Asian migrants; others had arrived from eastern Africa. Merina society included a small class of nobles (the *Andriana*), commoners (*Hova*), and around 500,000 slaves (at the time of the French conquest) from lower-status and minority ethnic backgrounds. Madagascar largely escaped Portuguese and Dutch colonisation during the 1600s and 1700s. French adventurers endeavoured to establish a colony there in 1643; they abandoned the settlement after thirty years, but set up an enduring outpost on the off-shore island of Sainte-Marie in 1750. The British, increasingly masters of the Indian Ocean, dissuaded French activities, while Protestant missionaries gained influence, and in 1817, Britain signed a treaty with King Radama I. His widow and successor, Queen Ranavalona I (r. 1828–61), proved less friendly to foreigners, earning notoriety as a 'female Caligula' blamed for 200,000 deaths, many of them Christian converts.[4] She expelled Europeans, a notable exception a Frenchman, Jean Laborde, who produced weaponry and textiles, and was rumoured to be her lover. The next sovereign, Radama II (r. 1861–63), lifted the ban on Europeans, though assassination cut short his reign. Under his widow, Rasoherina (r. 1863–68), who assumed the throne, Madagascar continued its opening to the outside world. More missionaries arrived, Catholics as well as the Protestants who converted the next monarch, Queen Ranavalona II (r. 1868–83), another widow of the polygamous Radama II. Mervyn Brown compares the court of relatives, officials and servants to a 'minor Balkan country of the same period'.[5]

Real political power lay with the prime minister, Rainilaiarivony. A *Hova*, born in 1828, Rainilaiarivony rose to power at the side of his father and elder brother, chief ministers from 1833 onwards, and took command of the Merina army. In 1864, Rainilaiarivony and Rasoherina ousted his brother, and Rainilaiarivony stepped into his shoes as prime minister, a position he held until 1895. Rainilaiarivony consolidated power, and domination of the monarchy, by marrying Rasoherina, and he subsequently wed her two successors, Ranavalona II and Ranavalona III, the latter when she was widowed just before becoming queen.

Rainilaiarivony was at the time over thirty years older than the monarch he effectively placed on the throne. They produced no offspring together, and the queen remained childless.

Rainilaiarivony enjoyed respect overseas as a hesitatingly modernising premier of a nominally Christian country, and European states as well as the United States maintained diplomatic relations with Madagascar.[6] Foreigners, ranging from Protestant pastors to merchants, and the British and South African officers who led the Malagasy army, had a prominent presence. Attired in starched white uniform, sword, richly embroidered cape and bicorne hat, Rainilaiarivony looked the model of the late nineteenth-century statesman as he partnered queens dressed in European floor-length gowns, bustles and fancy hats. Even critics credited the prime minister with effective state-building, establishment of a modern bureaucracy, public works projects and extension of Merina rule over coastal populations. Yet the government refused to allow the construction of roadways from the coast to the capital, fearing invasion (rightly, as it turned out), and most transport was by porters. Slavery persisted, as did unpaid compulsory labour service. Brown nevertheless judges the country considerably more advanced than most in Africa.

On 22 November 1883, her twenty-second birthday, the beautiful niece of the previous monarch was enthroned as Queen Ranavalona III[7] (see Figure 13). She affirmed her Protestant Christian faith, intoning biblical injunctions that it is 'righteousness that exalteth a nation' and the 'fear of God is the beginning of wisdom'. She proclaimed her duty to subjects: 'It is I who am your protection, the refuge of the poor, and the glory of the rich; and when I say "Rest in confidence," you should really be confident. For my desire from God is to benefit you, to make you prosperous, and to govern you in righteousness.' She also promised to defend the country: 'Should anyone dare to claim even a hair's breadth, I will show myself to be a man, and go along with you to protect your fatherland.' 'Is it not so, O people?', she asked, raising her sceptre, as her subjects brandished guns, spears and shields.[8]

Great problems faced Ranavalona and her prime minister: a large government debt, decline in law and order, increasing demands from foreigners for commercial and extra-territorial privileges, lack of up-to-date weaponry for the army, and territorial disputes between Merina and other ethnic groups. For the French colonial historian Marc Michel, 'on the eve of French intervention, both the Malagasy society and state were in the midst of a major crisis – a ripe fruit was ready to fall'.[9] For Gwyn Campbell, an authoritative economic historian of Madagascar, a tripartite confluence of circumstances allowed for French takeover. First, and most crucially, the Merina state was in a terminal decline.

Figure 13 Queen Ranavalona III (1861–1917, r. 1883–97) of Madagascar, exiled by the French in 1897, first to Réunion Island and then to Algeria, dressed as a French gentlewoman.

By the late 1800s, efforts at industrialisation, modernisation and the development of an autarkic economy pioneered at mid-century had largely failed. Attempts by the Merina monarchy to secure control over the multiple ethnic groups and coastal regions of the island – a kind of indigenous sub-imperialism or what Campbell labels 'secondary imperialism' – had not succeeded in making the monarch in Tananarive sovereign of all of the island. Both the aristocratic class and the commoners were disaffected and increasingly alienated from the regime. The Merina state, in effect, imploded. Meanwhile, the British, despite their predominant influence in Madagascar as traders and missionaries, by the last decades of the nineteenth century had decided that Madagascar was expendable in their plans, for they had greater interests on the eastern coast of the African mainland and in other islands, and already enjoyed fine port facilities throughout the Indian Ocean region in South Africa, Mauritius, India and Ceylon. Relative British disinterest opened the way for the French; though Campbell discounts French determination to seize the island until very late, he identifies their aggressiveness as the third contributor that led to the extinction of Malagasy sovereignty.[10]

By the 1880s, the metropolitan French and residents of Réunion set their sights on Madagascar. For inhabitants of the small island of Réunion, the near-by 'Grande Ile' loomed as a kind of Eldorado for settlement, trade and military engagement, and the Réunionnais lobbied Paris for expansion in Madagascar (and elsewhere in the Indian Ocean, as in Djibouti).[11] The French navy saw the potential of having new port facilities. In the climate of the 1880s, when France was extending its empire in Southeast Asia but with considerable criticism at home and some marked reverses in the Far East, Madagascar appeared to the colonial lobby a large and easy target. Using the trumped-up excuse of aggression against settlers, the French sent in an expeditionary force. In 1885 it forced Ranavalona to sign a treaty that in all but name made Madagascar a French protectorate under the authority of a Resident-General, but left the monarchy and indigenous government largely intact. That situation endured for a decade. The British meanwhile retained great influence thanks to Protestant missionaries.[12]

Imperial rivalries grew ever stronger in the western Indian Ocean, and in 1890, Britain and France concluded an arrangement giving Britain free rein in Zanzibar, and France carte blanche in Madagascar. The French did not immediately move to secure dominion, but in 1894, on the predictable grounds of threats to French citizens and national interests, Paris issued an ultimatum to the queen to accept a new treaty conceding enhanced privileges. When her government refused, the French invaded, bombarded and occupied the eastern port of Tamatave, then took Majunga in the west, and marched to the capital of Tananarive. As the French advanced, the queen tried to rally her people, declaring, 'Are there no men among you who will fight? ... I am but a woman; but I would far rather die in my palace than yield to the French'. Though the French lost few soldiers in fighting, a third died from tropical diseases, the highest death toll in any colonial campaign. The Malagasy prime minister, referring to the dense jungle that impeded French progress, and the malaria and dysentery that felled soldiers, remarked: 'I have two generals to defend me, Hazo and Tazo (forest and fever).'[13]

The survivors of the invasion force occupied Tananarive on 1 October 1895. With little choice, Ranavalona signed yet another treaty, but the French arrested Prime Minister Rainilaiarivony and exiled him to Algeria, where he died within months. This left Ranavalona to fend on her own in a struggle that led to the end of the Merina dynasty.

The French general and the Malagasy queen

The pomp and defiant stance of the monarch at her coronation in 1883 had weakened into impotence by 1895, and Ranavalona could do little but acquiesce to French demands. After the French took Tananarive, she granted an audience to General Frédéric Metzinger. The meeting was cordial, but the queen, according to Alfred Durand – who wrote an account of her last days on the throne and her journey into exile – 'seemed embarrassed, not having ever received [a visitor like the general] in an audience without the prime minister'. Also present were three female members of the queen's family, Ramazindrazana, Rasindranoro and Razafindrazaka. Durand commented, with reference to the French officers there: 'These gentlemen compared this line of women to the figurines in innocent games at public fairs.'[14] The gendered perspective would continue to inflect French views.

Soon a *kabary*, a public ceremony, inaugurated the protectorate, attended by the French commander and the queen, Ranavalona, wearing a Legion of Honour decoration and an elaborate cape presented by the French. Bands played the queen's anthem and the 'Marseillaise'. The queen's standard still flew over the royal palace, and for the moment, relations appeared promising, the virtually powerless queen long to reign over the Malagasy under French paramountcy. A new civilian Resident-General, Hippolyte Laroche, a Protestant like the queen, treated her with deference, and courted favour by offering her dresses and perfume from Paris.

The relatively amicable relationship between sovereign and colonisers did not last. In Paris, military and colonial lobbyists agitated to transform the protectorate into annexation. Resistance to European invaders meanwhile persisted in Madagascar, and on the night of the national holiday, 22 November 1895, a rebel in the north, claiming the queen had ordered him to kill all Europeans, massacred the family of a British missionary. This ignited the *menalamba* revolt, which burned with intensity for two years and rekindled sporadically until 1899. The name, meaning 'red shawls', came from the colour – signifying the Malagasy earth and the monarchy – of the scarf donned by the rebels. The *menalamba*, who targeted and killed Europeans and Malagasy Christians, and burned their churches, aimed to drive out foreigners and restore the pre-colonial Merina religion and state. The attacks spread panic among the French, who responded with strong-arm military and political tactics.

The Europeans implicated Ranavalona in the insurrection. However, Stephen Ellis, the authoritative scholar of the uprising, remains sceptical about direct connections between the queen and the rebels. Kept under close French surveillance, Ranavalona would have found it near impossible to maintain close contact with insurgents though she may well have sympathised with some of their objectives, though not their anti-Christian violence. Rebels regularly invoked the queen's name to give the insurrection legitimacy; according to Ellis, a rebellion without the queen as symbol would have been considered only brigandage. Some swore loyalty to the monarch; others felt her association with the Europeans and treaty-signing, even if under duress, had compromised the monarch.[15]

In 1896, the French Parliament would annex Madagascar as a fully-fledged colony, and it emancipated slaves there; trumpeted as a humanitarian gesture, the latter action also intended to secure support from the freed Malagasy. Paris appointed a new Resident-General and commander-in-chief, General Joseph Gallieni, a forty-seven-year-old officer, who had served in West Africa, and won plaudits for 'pacifying' Tonkin.[16] He came to Madagascar with a two-pronged strategy of colonial conquest: the establishment of effective French rule as a *'tâche d'huile'*, an oil stain in which the military gradually spread its effective control, and a *'politique des races'*, a strategy of divide-and-rule in which the colonisers set one ethnic one group against the other. Gallieni also possessed conviction about the need to *'franciser'* (make French) the natives.[17] A republican and anti-clerical, Gallieni had little sympathy for monarchists or missionaries.[18] In his private life, he had little interest in women.

Gallieni arrived in Tananarive in September, entering the capital in an almost royal procession with honour guard, musicians and standard-bearers.[19] He pointedly declined to meet the queen straightaway. Instead, he issued a decree demoting Ranavalona III from 'Queen of Madagascar' to 'Queen of the Imerina' (the Merina lands), the first in a series of steps to undermine her power and to implement his *politique des races*. When they finally met, formally but cordially, the encounter was manifestly one between colonial master and native subject. With earlier French administrators, Ranavalona had sat on a throne raised on a dais, but Gallieni made certain that he and the queen were seated on identical chairs on the same level. Gallieni also had the French flag hoisted over her palace, and soon he confiscated the royal seal. Brought down to his level, without flag or seal, the queen was deprived of the insignia of rule. Gallieni also ordered the arrest and execution of several officials, including one of the queen's uncles, and the arrest of her aunt, Princess Ramazindrazana, both royals accused (with scant evidence) of complicity with rebels. Ramazindrazana was sent into internal exile on Sainte-Marie.[20]

Gallieni had hoped, according to Durand, that the queen 'would keep her promises', presumably, submission to the French, and 'would succeed through "*kabarys*" in calming discontent'. Gallieni wrote to an associate in October 1896: 'I have kept the queen in Imerina, because she has real prestige among the Hovas and she must serve me as an instrument, but she no longer has the right to do anything by herself.' He reported to the minister of colonies: 'I must recognise that if the queen does not love us – which for me is without doubt – at least she does what I prescribe without the least objection.' Thus she was paraded around various localities to give addresses: according to Durand, 'Ranavalo[na] made her "kabary", exhorting the people to calm and obedience, but the tone said the opposite of the words'.[21] The moment when Gallieni decided to depose the queen is not known, though Michel suggests that it came in November.[22]

On 23 November, the Merina realm's most sacred traditional ceremony took place: the annual *fandroana*, when after various rituals, the queen (secluded behind a curtain) took a bath, with the water then sprinkled over her people. Normally a time of great celebration, in 1896 the ceremony took place in a subdued atmosphere, with some of the French openly making fun of the most solemn of royal rituals. Gallieni did not see fit to attend, his absence evidencing lack of regard for the monarchy and provoking the French Protestant pastor Benjamin Escande to confide to his journal: 'It is a shame for France, I was humiliated, sickened with this.'[23]

Five weeks later, Gallieni's anti-royal sentiments had hardened, but he still hesitated to act. On 28 December, he wrote to Paris: 'All of the troublemakers [the *menalamba* rebels] have constantly invoked the orders of the queen in order to carry along the people, which proves that, especially in the countryside, she retains prestige.' He conceded that 'If as in Tananarive, this prestige is greatly diminished, it would not be less dangerous to think straightaway of deposing her'. However when that happened, he predicted, 'The name of the queen will be quickly forgotten outside Imerina'. On 5 January 1897, Gallieni sent a message to his field officers highly critical of the queen, clearly preparing for her overthrow. Paris, however, did not throw its full support behind the general, and the same day, the colonial minister, Albert Lebon, wired Gallieni 'that nothing should be done to hasten the deposition, unless her conduct gives us proof of justified new reproaches. It is in our interest to use her ascendancy until the last moment, no matter how minimal it has become, all the while underlining, as you have taken care to do at every public opportunity, that she now has a role subordinate to your great influence'.

The admonition may have cooled the general's impetuosity, but he moved to isolate the queen further, restricting outside access to her palace largely to clergyman given advance permission. Gallieni also commissioned construction of a closed sedan-chair in which the queen might be transported away. On 13 January, he wrote to the colonial minister: 'I am preparing little by little her deposition.' Gallieni felt that 'in two or three months, I hope that I shall have the villages safely in hand enough so that I simply depose her without the leaders of the insurrection or the Malagasy partisans of the British being able to use that fact to create a new uprising'. Shortening the time frame, even days later, he wrote to the governor of Réunion, inquiring whether that colony would be willing to take in the queen.

Gallieni needed more evidence before his plan could be enacted. So he sent to commanders of the French military districts a circular letter, asking whether the queen retained popularity among her countrymen, whether her deposition and abolition of the monarchy were opportune, and if such moves would provoke heightened unrest. Gallieni's subordinates told the general what he wanted to hear. One stated that 'the queen no longer enjoys great prestige', and that she was regarded with 'indifference'. Another stated uncompromisingly that the queen had 'no authority'; the people viewed her with 'neither fear nor affection'. She was discredited as too close to the French and responsible for the warfare that had brought great suffering. An officer reported from Antsirabé: 'I reckon that the disappearance of the queen and of the royalty would pass unnoticed in the province', adding that in any case, the change would be a fait accompli to be accepted willingly or by force. For another, 'the name and title of the queen are no longer invoked'; any residual loyalty he judged an expression of anti-French feeling rather than pro-Ranavalona allegiance. The district commander of Babay noted that the queen's status had steadily been eroded since the mid-1880s; he, too, found little for the French to fear, though troops should stay vigilant. He suggested that the French might even provoke a native movement against the queen, soliciting petitions from 'notables and petits fonctionnaires tending towards the abolition of the monarchy and the establishment of direct French administration'. Many Malagasy, he opined, already accepted France as the 'sole master' of the country.

Gallieni had specifically asked whether the French might rely on native support, and commanders assured him it would come from freed slaves, as they had hoped. Moreover, the officers advised, even nobles had lost faith in the queen and were rallying to the French. Petty officials, though with no love for the French, would see practical advantages to joining the winning side. Many soldiers fighting against the French had already deserted. There was nevertheless a concern that Protestants, with links to the British, might resist French suzerainty. One unsigned statement among the commanders' replies, not very convincingly, hinted at a conspiracy between British officials and Protestants to keep the French from gaining full control of Madagascar. Several commanders thought that most Malagasy were little concerned by politics at all – a statement somewhat belied by the *menalamba* uprising – and were preoccupied by problems of everyday life; several ventured unsurprising comments concerning the credulity and simple spirit of the people. In any case, one advised that in case of opposition, 'only terror will bring down the *Andriana* and the *Hovas*, [while] good procedures [and] affection will forever rally the freed slaves to us'. Only a few responses to Gallieni's circular voiced reservations about the upcoming deposition, one officer advising that it would be preferable to await pacification of the provinces. Several mentioned possible pretenders to the throne as a menace, with one or two suggesting the replacement of Ranavalona with a monarch loyal to the French.

Largely supportive views from the field provided Gallieni with his desired mandate. On 26 February, he wrote to the colonial minister: 'I would have persisted in keeping Ranavalona as sovereign of Imerina, but I see that she cannot submit to her new situation, and in view of new troubles that we foresee in the spring, I have decided to depose her in order to finish with a situation that cannot continue any longer without considerably troubling our work of pacification.'[24] He carried out the plan smoothly and effectively, the following day deposing the queen. Her exile must be 'worthy of her former rank and worthy of us'[25] – an admission that as important as the comfort and dignity of the queen was the perception that the French were acting as civilised gentlemen to an ex-queen under their guardianship.

Gallieni reported to Paris that the deposition had been an 'indispensable' measure of 'urgency' to show that the French were 'true masters' of the country. He affirmed that he would have taken action earlier if it had been possible, and added with a touch of overstatement that his commanders' advice promoting deposition had been 'unanimous'. He enumerated issues that forced his hand: the hostility of the 'noble castes', persistence of 'rebel bands whose chief always acted in the name of the Queen', intrigues of 'certain foreigners', and Malagasies' uncertainty about who really ruled Madagascar. Gallieni also played the nationalist card, signalling the influence over the queen of an indigenous Protestant pastor who, he alleged, was in the pay of British missions and had spread anti-French propaganda. Dispensing with the queen, in short, allowed Gallieni to secure French hegemony. He confirmed to the colonial minister that provisions had been made for Ranavalona in Réunion, with a pension charged to Madagascar's budget, and that she would be treated 'with all of the respect and all the goodwill due to a woman'. (He did not add, however, 'to her situation', as he had written in his letter to Ranavalona.)

When the news reached Paris, Members of Parliament questioned whether the deposition had received ministerial approval. The colonial minister informed senators that, in a telegram of 20 February, Gallieni forewarned Paris it was impossible to retain the monarchy. The minister avowed his ignorance of any actual precipitant that triggered the timing of Gallieni's move, but conceded that a telegram advising the general that deposition would be premature had not arrived before Gallieni proceeded with the ouster. André Lebon nevertheless expressed full confidence in Gallieni, though he cabled the general apprising him of the Senate debates, and 'regretted that the circumstances had forced General Gallieni to take this decision without having been able to receive the prior authorisation of the government'. 'Incident closed', the cable concluded.

Gallieni provided an extensive reply, complaining of his discomfiture about the questioning of his authority. In the staccato style of cables, and with the occasional euphemistic phrase, he wrote:

> Your instructions concerning pacification, destruction Hova hegemony confederation separate states, abolition slavery unachievable with maintenance monarchy. Suppression Queen thus principal objective for me over six months. If had dared would have deposed Ranavalo[na] on my arrival but dangerous then because insurrection at gates of Tananarive. Thus began to speak energetically to her then confined her to her palace after having tried without success to make use of Her. Finally well-prepared moment invited Queen to leave.

As long as the queen remained, Gallieni argued, France's enemies would invoke her support. The palace had remained a centre of 'intrigues' because Ranavalona was 'secretive, prideful and show-off, unable to forget her past grandeur, welcoming all influences hostile [to] France', such as her pastor's machinations. He also repeated the unsubstantiated rumour of a Protestant and British conspiracy. 'Thus contrary your supposition maintenance royalty not only not useful, but detrimental because nurtured hopes nobles hostile, irreducible, ruined by suppression slavery and drove away from us Malagasy ready to rally.' Since Gallieni feared a new bout of insurgency, the situation had turned critical. If it had degenerated with a grand anti-French plot in Ranavalona's name, moreover, he would have been forced to arrest the queen – and, he stated, transport her as prisoner to Djibouti or elsewhere.

Gallieni again defended his actions in answering a separate private inquiry from Lebon. He also made disobliging comments about the Malagasy: local people were liars, and 'the Malagasy has no religious convictions; he is simply a fetish-worshipper in the depths of his being'. Rather gratuitously, Gallieni added that not a single Malagasy woman would not take up with a French man, perhaps even with the approval of her husband, father or brother, 'from the Queen and the princesses all the way to the daughters of the lowest porters'. He impugned the morals of the queen's aunt, Princess Ramazindrazana, whom some had portrayed as saintly but whom the French thought a pro-British troublemaker. In her possessions his soldiers found 'an instrument that is generally only encountered in the establishments of our celebrated *hétaïres* [high-class prostitutes] of the boulevards' – a dildo. Moreover, 'In the queen's [palace], in making an inventory of objects left in her room, a packet of obscene photographs was discovered that almost brought a blush to the experienced old trooper helping to classify all this material'.

Such comments betray Gallieni's underlying feelings about the population of Madagascar, ones no doubt shared with many colonisers. The second-hand tittle-tattle about the queen's dirty pictures and her aunt's sex-toy provided useful ways to blacken the reputation of the royal women whom he had dispossessed and exiled. Although the morals of 'native' men were never above reproach, the salacious rumours personalised his generic views about the lubriciousness of indigenous women.

Gallieni's cable to Lebon also detailed measures taken to efface the monarchy. Gallieni decreed Malagasy crown lands to be French state property, and ordered court rulings be made in the name of the French Republic rather than the queen. He took over the Rova, the royal fortress, where he garrisoned French troops, and made plans to turn the royal palace into a French school and commercial museum. He replaced the queen's standard with the Tricolour, and declared 14 July rather than the date of the queen's ritual bath as the national holiday; the sanguinary call to arms in the chorus of the 'Marseillaise' was

altered, however, to 'Because France is our mother, the object of our pride, let us cry: Bravo! Bravo! Acclaim her, O Malagasy!'[26] France now assumed the role of the monarchy.

In one of the most potent gestures, Gallieni undertook what was, in effect, desecration of the royal tombs. Madagascar's sovereigns had been interred in the former capital of Ambohimanga, twenty-four kilometres from Tananarive. Gallieni, noting that for Malagasy, 'the master of the land has in his possession the remains of the former kings', ordered the Merina monarchs exhumed and transferred to a new burial site inside the French-occupied Rova in Tananarive. This constituted an attempt to desanctify the site most sacred to the Merina dynasty, to 'remove from Ambohimanga its character as a sacred city', as Gallieni himself put it, and to 'museumify' the remains of the old rulers. Not only the reigning queen must be captured and displaced; so, too, must the bones of her ancestors.

The end of the monarchy and the dynamics of colonial conquest

Marie-France Barrier, Ranavalona's biographer, characterises her deposition and banishment as 'kidnapping'. No formal accusations were proffered against Ranavalona, let alone presented to her except in the opaque language of Gallieni's 'invitation' to leave the throne. She was never arrested, charged or put on trial. She signed no act of abdication or otherwise renounced her rights or those of her heirs to the throne. She possessed no real avenue of appeal against her ouster, though it should be noted that she never wrote to the colonial minister to protest her treatment or demand reinstatement. Given the force of French arms, and the apparent loss of the monarchy's credibility, she had no possibility of rallying compatriots, and her forced rapid departure from Tananarive left no time to try. The senators who questioned Gallieni's actions, and commentators who wrote sympathetically about Ranavalona's plight, lacked the influence or inclination to contest her overthrow, and their reservations focused on unauthorised initiatives by a military commander rather than the fate of his victim. French Protestants showed disquiet, but their priority was evangelisation, with hopes of replacing British pastors in Madagascar. French colonialists championed the bravery and acumen of Gallieni and the troops; their achievements struck a resonant chord in the context of 1890s imperialism, jingoism and international rivalry. In a France where defence of the military had become near synonymous with patriotism since the trial of Alfred Dreyfus in 1894, criticism of the general, despite less than unanimous approbation for colonialism, remained muted. The British (and other foreign Protestants) in principle objected to removal of a Christian queen and, in a more general sense, to the French conquest, but London was bound by the 1890 agreement dividing up the Indian Ocean and unwilling to intervene.

In the midst of all this, Ranavalona cuts a sad figure, and that perhaps helps explain why the French dispensed with her so easily. She was not to the monarchy born, and had been placed on the throne by Rainilaiarivony, who for twelve years had dominated the government and his wife. Ranavalona had indeed proved capable of calling her people to resistance at her coronation and again in 1895, but without successful efforts by the Malagasy. Her position had become largely symbolic, though as Gallieni well knew, her prestige was not negligible, at least until the last phase of her reign. The queen had firmly embraced Christianity, but, as the *menalamba* revolt showed, not all Malagasy accepted the imported religion, and some feared she was, willingly or involuntarily, an ally of the French. Furthermore, many coastal, non-Merina groups had always contested the hegemony of Tanananarive.

Ranavalona was little prepared in the difficult art of statecraft, certainly when her country faced the military might and imperialist will of the French. The overthrow of Rainilaiarivony left her without a powerful advocate. Lack of fluency in French limited direct negotiation with the foreigners; though Laroche had been sympathetic to her, Gallieni clearly was not. Without a designated heir, a loyal prime minister or effective military forces, she lacked powerful champions, and if the French reports were true, nobles, commoners and freed slaves increasingly saw their future lying with the French rather than with the Merina monarch. She proved unable to resist the virtual French protectorate of 1885 or the formal protectorate a decade later. Kept effectively as a prisoner by the French throughout 1896, she had little room for last-minute manoeuvres. The French showed no interest in finding a replacement as monarch – as they had done in Vietnam in 1885 – and there was no obvious candidate. Gallieni had decided that the Imerina monarchy no longer commanded great loyalty, that it could not be used (as the French continued to hope in Vietnam) to marshal support for the colonial state by preserving certain hierarchies and traditions, and that it was, thus, of no use to the French. If they installed another sovereign, they would have to concede privileges and treat with a potential adversary. It was easier to dispense with the dynasty altogether along with the incumbent monarch.

The gendered perspective of the French on Ranavalona is manifest. She was not only a woman, but a widow before the age of twenty-two, then married to a man old enough to be her father. She bore no children,

a problem for any monarch, crucially responsible for continuing the lineage, but also perhaps perceived as a failure of the maternal role of a woman, monarch or not. Commentators when Ranavalona was on the throne and after her exile described the queen as delicately built, mild-mannered, soft-spoken, dreamy, sometimes coquettish, almost doll-like in appearance; they noted her fascination with French fashion and perfumes, pleasure in donning elegant Parisian gowns and opening gifts. Such descriptions, even if objectively true, served to feminise and even infantilise the queen. And against the line of female 'figurines' at the court, the French arrayed uniformed men, bristling with swords and guns, the personification of a conquering masculinity. At the end, Gallieni's assurance of French consideration for Ranavalona's situation and sex bespoke the triumph, the patriarchalism and paternalistic *noblesse oblige* of the victor towards a woman now dependent on men who had occupied her country and taken her throne.

The queen in exile

So it was that on the last day of February 1897, Ranavalona III headed into permanent exile, leaving behind the ruins of her dynasty.[27] The diaries of Alfred Durand, delegated to take her away from Tananarive, provide eyewitness insight into the journey out of Madagascar.[28] The thirty-four-year-old Durand, who had served on the island for eight years, had first met the thirty-six-year-old queen in early October 1896. Over the next weeks, 'the Queen, the princesses and the court took me as a confidante', Ranavalona probably happy to meet someone, even a member of the occupying forces, of similar age, who spoke Malagasy fluently, and who treated her with kindness. The queen indeed soon sent Durand a present of twenty kilos of sugar, two bottles of champagne and two dried zebu tongues, a local delicacy. The queen also opened her heart: 'She told me that she was very afraid, because she feared being exiled.'[29] At the start of the next year, Gallieni indeed alerted Durand to Ranavalona's imminent overthrow. Ranavalona started down the path into exile only several hours after, late in the evening, she received her letter of dismissal from Gallieni, with just time for servants to pack what turned out to be a considerable number of trunks.[30]

Walking out of the palace in tears, Ranavalona took Durand's arm. 'I myself felt moved and sad', he wrote, as 'for the last time she left this Palace surmounted by a raptor with spread wings – the royal raptor – "Voromahery", the bird of strength, symbol of Radama's dynasty. We were leaving for exile!'. The queen climbed into the sedan-chair Gallieni had commissioned, at the centre of a procession of 700–800 porters and soldiers. As the trip continued across rough terrain, Ranavalona experienced 'violent crises of nerves', and comforted herself by drinking from a bottle of rum as 'each stage distanced her from her palace, her power, her people and she began to suffer cruelly from her isolation'. When the convoy crossed a turbulent river in a storm, Durand lent the queen his spare shirt and raincoat. She took fright at boarding a steam-powered vessel for the first time, but cheered up with the novelty of the voyage. They all suffered from heat and mosquitoes, and the porters once went on strike for supplementary rations. Along the route, they passed historic ruins and temples, and came across Malagasy peasants and Chinese road-workers, who were shooed away. Durand had been instructed always to keep the queen in his sights. At one stop, Durand remarked to her that early in the French invasion, at that very spot, he had learned that she had placed a price on Frenchmen's heads. 'Yes, and today, the Queen is your prisoner; these are the vagaries of war!', she replied.[31]

The convoy arrived in Tamatave on 7 March, joined the following day by the queen's sister Rasendranoro, who Durand reported had 'a very marked penchant for strong drink'; she had given five francs to a porter for a bottle of rum, which Durand confiscated and poured out, telling her that she could have redcurrant cordial and seltzer water. Also joining the royal party were Rasendranoro's daughter Razafinandriamanitra, heavily pregnant to a French soldier. The queen was happy to see her relatives, but 'very emotional' as she climbed aboard a ship, still wearing the insignia of the Legion of Honour. Captain Le Dô welcomed her on board but had been instructed not to pay her military honours. The ship departed a day in advance of schedule, a ploy to avoid any demonstrations in the queen's favour. It stopped at Sainte-Marie to pick up her aunt, Ramazindrazana, whose tears Durand ascribes to disappointment, as she had somehow imagined being collected to become queen in place of her niece.

The ship thence set sail for Réunion, arriving on 14 March, with small crowds turning out, some shouting 'Vive Gallieni! Vive l'armée!' The royals boarded a small train into Saint-Denis, the queen frightened at her first experience of rail travel until Durand provided reassurance. The governor greeted her in person, though again without military honours. When the royal party arrived at their lodgings, Ranavalona fretted until her jewellery cases were brought, no doubt as much because of the financial security the jewels represented as for their ornamental and sentimental value.

Almost immediately, Razafinandriamanitra went into labour and gave birth, though the mother died within hours. The queen requested that the infant be baptised as a Catholic with the name Marie-Louise;

Durand served as godfather as a crowd of 1500 massed around the church. (The queen had received a Catholic baptism and converted to Protestantism on becoming monarch; the Catholic christening might have been intended to win sympathy from the largely Catholic French.) This was the last of Durand's duties; the ex-queen enjoined him never to forget his goddaughter, his fellow officers hosted a dinner, and Gallieni sent a testimonial of commendation. Years later, Ranavalona wrote to Durand to congratulate him on his marriage, and the soldier and queen eventually had a friendly meeting in Paris.[32]

Gallieni, with evident satisfaction, summed up the queen's trip to the colonial minister, emphasising that she had been well treated, and downplaying any support for her. On the journey to the coast, there was 'no emotion' at her passage, and in Saint-Denis only 'the curious' turned up at the dock. 'Several noisy demonstrations took place at the exit of the rail station', he added somewhat vaguely, noting that the governor of Réunion would make certain that no 'suspect agitation' would take place. Soon after she settled in Réunion, Ranavalona addressed a letter to Gallieni. Composed in Malagasy, the sentiments express resignation, but she wrote almost as a young person reporting to a parent, or a holiday-maker recording in bland terms a trip that must have inspired tumultuous emotions. The queen was grateful to Gallieni for arranging her departure in a manner that allowed her to save face.[33] The reception given aboard the *Lapérouse* had been very good; the captain and his officers 'treated myself and my entourage like their children'. The queen charted the boat's course and the reunion with her aunt. When she landed, the governor and his wife 'received me very well, and I was very content and thank you infinitely'. She spoke with generosity about Durand. She wrote sadly about her niece's death, but noted with appreciation that the governor, Captain Le Dô and Durand had attended the funeral. The letter closes: 'I have the honour to assure you once again that I am an obedient servant with joy to all the orders and wishes of France.' The letter is signed 'Your servant, Ranavalona III'. There is no reason not to assume the sentiments genuine, though she may have realised that remonstration about her fate would be in vain and hoped that an accommodating attitude might could prove more beneficial. Ranavalona's lack of open rancour then or later, however, is noteworthy.

The ex-queen lived quietly for almost two years on Réunion, occasionally attending official receptions and other events. Her sister, aunt and infant great-niece provided companionship. Also accompanying her to Réunion was her pastor, who had earlier aroused Gallieni's suspicions. She employed two Malagasy secretaries, a cook and four servants. She in no way behaved in a fashion unacceptable to the French, or had contacts or activities that raised their concerns.

BANISHED POTENTATES

Meanwhile, imperial rivalries reached boiling point with British and French forces coming head to head at Fashoda in 1898, British and Boers moving towards war in South Africa, and Germans and Italians pursuing territorial gains in eastern Africa. The *menalamba* rebellion, combined with a new millenarian movement, rekindled in opposition to increased taxes and corvées, and in the midst of rumours that Britain and France were at war. Such developments made the French fear that Réunion lay too close to Madagascar and to British Mauritius as a permanent residence for Ranavalona. The colonial minister, approached by Gallieni (who remained governor-general of Madagascar), on 23 November 1898 – just two months after the Fashoda incident – authorised the removal of Ranavalona to Algiers. Among other benefits, mechanisms of surveillance were well developed in the city that already hosted the deposed Emperor Ham Nghi.

The Réunion governor called on Ranavalona to announce her move only on the very day that she would have to leave, 1 February 1899. The journey to Algeria took twenty-four days, the longest sea voyage made by the now thirty-seven-year-old. The ship stopped briefly in Marseille, where the queen put up at the aptly named Hôtel des Colonies, but authorities denied her request to visit Paris. Curious crowds gathered in Algiers on her arrival on 5 March. The government had rented a three-storey house for Ranavalona and her entourage near a park in the Mustapha quarter on the heights of the city, ironically situated near the lodgings where her consort had spent the brief exile before his death.

The Algerian colonial government designated as the official looking after Ranavalona the same man responsible for her late husband. A French subaltern accommodated in her house had orders to report any suspicious activity. Several servants attended Ranavalona and her family, although the staff quarrelled among themselves and indulged in bouts of drinking and rowdy behaviour, especially when Ranavalona was not at home; her sister Rasendranoro, who enjoyed dancing, earned a parlous reputation. Gossip about their activities tarnished the household, though not touching Ranavalona; several changes in employees eventuated.

The French allowed the queen to attend Protestant worship services, go for walks and ride around in her carriage. She studied French, played the piano and received visitors. One of her closest friends was her doctor, who was also Denmark's consul in Algiers. On occasion, Ranavalona petitioned for an increase in her allowance. The governor-general of Algeria was often sympathetic, writing to Paris that 'The dignity of the colony of Madagascar, I would say even that of France, is implicated in this question', and stating at another time: 'I think that it is a question of the renowned generosity of France that the sight of an unmerited reduction in the circumstances of an unfortunate woman and a sovereign worthy of full respect, which would be visible to the eyes of all and in particular in the eyes of foreigners, be avoided.' Gallieni, who paid the bills until 1905, remained intransigent, and only after his retirement as governor-general was her pension raised.[34] In 1910, Gallieni called on Ranavalona in Algiers; according to Barrier, Gallieni said she first appeared upset, but then happy to see him.[35]

Few momentous incidents troubled the queen's life, though in 1901 her sister Rasendranoro died; Ranavalona adopted her great-niece Marie-Louise, who along with her aunt shared the queen's house. Ranavalona also had a *dame de compagnie*, named in a government report as Mme Howey: 'a foreign woman with little experience [in budget matters]', but someone 'who employs herself usefully in directing and restraining the workings of the household'.[36] In 1908, the entourage moved to a larger and more modern residence, thereafter called the 'Villa Tananarive' or the 'Villa des Princesses'.

The Malagasy queen in republican France

In 1900, authorities thwarted Ranavalona's desire to visit the *exposition universelle* in Paris, and a decade later, they turned down her request to visit Madagascar. However, they had relented concerning her wish to see France, and the ex-queen began to travel there about once every two years.[37] In 1901, she visited Paris and the Ile de France (where the city of Fontainebleau commissioned a plaque to commemorate the visit), before going to Arcachon, on the Atlantic seacoast. Two years later, the Auvergne offered her principal destination. In 1905, she stayed in Saint-Germain-en-Laye on the outskirts of Paris before moving on to Cabourg, Houlgate and Trouville in Normandy. Later trips took her to La Baule and Quiberville, also in Normandy, and, on her last journey, in 1913, to the eastern spa town of Aix-les-Bains. The itineraries were inspired, in part, by the travel pages of periodicals Ranavalona read in Algiers, and such magazines undoubtedly featured spa towns as attractive destinations. 'Taking the waters' was touted as bringing both medical and recreational benefits, and spa towns were popular holiday spots in the colonies and the metropole.[38] Not surprisingly, some of Ranavalona's destinations, including Aix-les-Bains, Arcachon and Vic-sur-Cère, were spa resorts.

The celebrity status of touring royals is hardly unknown today, but in the years before the First World War, they enjoyed particular popularity. Queen Ranavalona was one of these royal celebrities, though a deposed monarch reliant on colonial officials for permission to travel and for funds to cover the cost. The loss of her status as a reigning sovereign did not diminish the interest of the press and spectators.

Le Petit Journal, though only a few pages in length, and with somewhat random reporting and short news briefs, claimed the highest print-run of any newspaper in the world, and it took enduring interest in Ranavalona's comings and goings. A front-page headline on 1 June 1901 announced simply 'Ranavalo[na] à Paris', the title implying she was well enough known not to require further identification. Articles followed her movements in almost obsessive detail, noting on one day that she left her accommodation after a morning lie-in and lunch '*à l'européenne*', stating approvingly that she 'naturally' only ate French dishes. The journalist took care to specify that she went for an outing at 3 p.m., accompanied by her aunt and great-niece, and said that the queen wore a dress of black silk decorated with violet flowers, her aunt a yellow outfit and the little girl a white dress. The writer mused that such vivid colours might be normal in Tananarive, but were not '*très parisienne*' in the eyes of those gathered to see the 'exotic queen and her relatives'. The royal party, their landau flanked by policemen on bicycles, was 'much noticed and very well received' as it proceeded along the *grands boulevards* to the Champs-Élysées, and on to the Madeleine church and the Opéra, then drove to the Place de la République and back to Notre-Dame. The royal party alighted to visit the cathedral, where Ranavalona admired a statue of Marguerite de Valois, which she found showed an appropriately serious gaze for a queen. On they went to the Luxembourg Gardens, where Marie-Louise, the journalist stated, longingly contemplated other children at play until a mother lent her a jumping-rope, and she joined in, 'neither more nor less than a pure-blooded French girl' – it will be remembered that her father was a French soldier – while the queen waited patiently and chatted with bystanders.

The piece is rather charming, and not unlike reports published nowadays recording every minute, gesture and article of clothing of a touring princess. Yet the words bear heavily the stereotypes of the colonial age: the 'exotic' queen whose tastes in fashion and food suggest assimilation and appreciation of French life, though perhaps not entirely so, and the *métisse* Marie-Louise, who came close to being a real French girl. Underlying those traits only emphasises that Ranavalona was not like contemporary visitors such as the reigning queens of Sweden or Spain, nor like the mothers in the Luxembourg Gardens. Paris nevertheless spread out its beauties for their delight, with wide streets and grand buildings suggesting a contrast to ramshackle towns and malarial jungles that readers might recall from descriptions of Madagascar. No mention, unsurprisingly, is made that Ranavalona was a queen dethroned by the French, visiting Paris only with their leave, a royal ward of the republican state.

In provincial cities, the visit of even an ex-queen became a notable civic event, her stay in Arcachon a prime example. Ranavalona satisfied a long-held wish to visit the resort near Bordeaux that attracted fashionable *belle époque* tourists, though she had another curious reason for going there. In 1896, a school in Arcachon had performed a children's play, entitled 'Les rapatriés de Madagascar ou la reine Ranavalo[na] à Arcachon', on the French conquest of the island, and the return of the victorious soldiers to France. Ranavalona figured as a minor character. Knowing of her interest, the mayor vaunted the charms of his city to Ranavalona, and her visit fortuitously coincided with his campaign for re-election. The *Avenir d'Arachon* followed her one-month visit closely, describing her every dress, and noting at what hour she took tea and dined. She arrived, as customary, with aunt and great-niece, Marie-Louise's governess, a Malagasy medical student from Paris who served as interpreter, and a French officer deputised to accompany her. Ranavalona went for walks on the beach and took boat rides, and she received a French general and a countess whose acquaintance she had made in Algeria. She did the rounds of hotels for meals or refreshments, and accepted invitations to private homes. She attended choral and orchestral concerts. She inspected an oyster farm and the local aquarium. She worshipped at the Protestant church in the company of the British vice-consul. And she had a day's outing to Bordeaux. She was presented with a synopsis of the 1896 play that had sparked her interest. A local woman penned a poem saying how welcome Ranavalona was and what a relief it must be to lay down the burden of a sceptre, counselling her to 'be forever French!'. Ranavalona departed Arcachon in a train carriage filled with flowers from well-wishers, her visit little different from a tour by a still-reigning queen.[39]

Journalists' efforts to get copy, no matter how minor the story, were in evidence again during Ranavalona's 1903 visit to Vic-sur-Cère in the Auvergne.[40] A reporter from *Fémina* – it is not coincidental that a women's magazine gave particular attention to the Malagasy queen – showed up at her hotel, to be told that Ranavalona had been put out with another article and was not receiving members of the press. Little Marie-Louise, playing in the garden, was less shy, and ran up to the journalist, who recorded their conversation. 'Do you like little French boys?', Marie-Louise was asked. 'Not always ... They are mean. When I hit them ... they hit back ... So I hit the big ones', she announced with aplomb. Photographs showed the six-year-old, impeccably attired in a frilly white dress and hat, alongside French companions, in one picture with a wheelbarrow, in another with sticks balanced on their shoulders like guns at a military parade. Obviously, Marie-Louise's play was not confined to dollies, though the journalist asked if she had a doll. The princess responded that she did, but that its head was broken. (*Fémina* proudly recorded that it sent her a new one, since 'little Malagasy girls like the same games as their French contemporaries'.) Finally, the queen appeared, elegant in a full-length skirt, long necklace and boa. A photo also showed her in an automobile, above the caption 'the little queen is not hostile to progress'; the wording speaks for itself.

In 1905, *Le Petit Parisien*, on the front page, announced that the queen had arrived fatigued in Marseille after a rough crossing of the Mediterranean but, with only a brief rest, took the train to Paris, where she stayed at a 'boarding-house' (the phrase in English), to the curiosity of fellow Japanese guests.[41] On her visit to Saint-Germain-en-Laye, another periodical, *L'Illustration*, published a short piece informing readers that the royal exiles lodged in a simply furnished five-room apartment near the train station; a photo shows a rather melancholy ex-sovereign flanked by the aunt and great-niece and ensconced in a musty bourgeois sitting-room.[42]

L'Illustration reported on photogenic subjects, and *Le Petit Parisien* exhibited a penchant for human interest stories, scandals and *mondanités*, but the venerable and conservative *Le Figaro* also published articles on the former queen. *Le Figaro* was well known for empathy with *le tout Paris*, and a special affection for those bearing *particules* and noble titles. Like its more *populaire* counterparts, a 1901 article detailed Ranavalona's departure for a tour in France, from her fears of sea-sickness to the cost (with a substantial 10,000 francs allocated by the colonial ministry). Another article provided background on the queen's name, appearance and character. As was always the case, she was described as tiny in build, with a charming face, looking like 'an exotic Tanagra'. She was invariably well groomed, a real *Parisienne*, shy and soft-spoken; the journalist said she smiled 'like a child'. She enjoyed music and was immensely fond of her great-niece. Significantly, *Le Figaro* wrote sympathetically of her exile, exonerating her of anti-French manoeuvres before her deposition, which it blamed on the actions of Rainilaiarivony. Indeed, said the journalist, 'elle voulait le plus possible se franciser': she wanted to make herself as French as possible.

When Ranavalona visited in 1907, *Le Figaro*'s reporter was again hot on her heels, or at least watching from a respectful distance. A long article, describing a visit to Cabourg, provided an opportunity to criticise the meagre allowance provided by the Malagasy government. A highlight was a reception at the Grand Hôtel, where the queen arrived in a decorated automobile, welcomed by the mayor and presented with a bouquet by the daughter of a *député*. Twenty people, including government officials, joined her for dinner. The queen apologised for not being more elegantly attired, though her jewels included a necklace presented by President Émile Loubet, while her aunt wore a brooch presented by President Sadi Carnot. A gala performance of 'Lakmé' followed the meal; the journalist called Léo Délibes's opera, set in India, 'appropriate' as entertainment.

Two particular events figured on the agenda in 1907. Ranavalona went to Versailles to enrol her ten-year-old great-niece in the school where she would spend the rest of her childhood, returning to Algiers for holidays. Ranavalona's visit to a colonial exhibition at the Jardin Botanique Colonial in the Paris suburb of Nogent-sur-Marne provided a poignant moment in her stay. The queen was said to be taken with emotion as she toured the Madagascar pavilion, and quietly shed a few tears while listening to a performance by musicians from Tananarive. Her spirits revived with tea at the Indochinese pavilion after what *Le Figaro* called this 'excursion to the little Madagascar in Nogent'.

Ranavalona was only one in a procession of reigning, superannuated, and deposed sovereigns visiting Paris to the delectation of reporters and readers. Her tourist activities were hardly atypical, even for non-royals; in 1907, for example, in addition to the *exposition coloniale*, she visited the Louvre, the Gobelins tapestry factory and Sèvres porcelain works, Versailles, and the châteaux of Compiègne and Fontainebleau. Going to Arcachon or the Auvergne and taking the waters were standard upper-class pursuits, and the queen spent time shopping in Paris, one visit to the provinces delayed until she finished the round of her providores. The details in the press reinforced the status of Ranavalona as a celebrity, but also a gendered view about the genteel lady traveller.

Each time Ranavalona arrived in Marseille, an official from the colonial ministry, bearing flowers, welcomed the former queen, and mayors turned out wherever she travelled; even deposed, Ranavalona enjoyed rights to official courtesies and perhaps provided a particular pleasure for those who met royalty. A policeman or soldier went along to ensure her safety but no doubt also to keep an eye out for any inappropriate activities or contacts. On one visit, the president received the deposed queen, and on another, she attended a session of the Chambre des Députés, suggesting that any past wrongdoings had been forgiven. The visits to the Élysée and the Palais Bourbon also implied that the French were rewarding Ranavalona for docility in exile and trying to assure her future fidelity. Press reports on her tours usefully helped to popularise France's rule in Madagascar, cordial relations between conquerors and conquered, and the kindly way the French treated those they ousted. Ranavalona was now harmless, of scant political importance, though of curiosity to the public as a minor celebrity and not devoid of a certain propaganda value; the cute great-niece provided an extra asset that offset her childlessness. Fathered by a French solider (though born out of wedlock), Marie-Louise showed the benefits of French blood and upbringing. France's *mission civilisatrice*, newspapers implied, had worked well on native royals who appreciated *haute cuisine* and *haute couture* (and dolls and jumping ropes), attended Christian worship and the opera, visited museums, promenaded in parks and took the waters at spas. In line with Gallieni's hopes, Ranavalona looked fully *francisée*. Crowds, though small, gathered enthusiastically to see the ex-queen become French subject 'with the most respectful and benevolent curiosity'.[43] The deposed ruler was presented, in short, as a colonial success story, the model of a Francophile native under imperial dominion.

In her last years Ranavalona no longer travelled to France, increasing age, a tight financial situation and the world war making such journeys unfeasible. During the First World War, she donated to the Red Cross, but seems to have taken no further part in the war effort. Those who knew her late in life remarked on her pleasures and the occasional reminder of her reign. For Pastor Frank Puaux, one of her closest associates: 'Judging by misleading appearances, one could believe that she did not have a clear consciousness of her destiny, but sometimes a gesture or a word could lead one to believe that she was living again in a vanished past.' He remembered that 'one day I introduced to her one of our colonial administrators who had served with distinction in Madagascar, and he showed her a decoration that she had awarded him. The queen found it hard to hide her emotion, but overcame it with a simple dignity. Like all women, she loved jewels and clothing, [and] the flowers that she adored and that decorated the Villa Tananarive in Mustapha'.

Ranavalona died at home, of an aneurysm, at the age of fifty-six, on 23 January 1917, her death briefly noted in newspapers preoccupied by the war. Her funeral, two days later, was attended by the governor-general of Algeria, the mayor of Algiers, the French navy commander, several consuls, members of her church and acquaintances. A detachment of soldiers rendered military honours – a courtesy not extended since her deposition – as she was buried in the Saint-Eugène cemetery next to her sister. But the French had not seen the last of the queen, nor were they absolved of responsibility for her surviving relatives.

The royal family

During the queen's lifetime, authorities had to address questions relating to other members of the royal family: the finances of the exiles, their accommodation and travels, and the education of Marie-Louise. For instance, in 1902, Gallieni noted that of 205,000 francs worth of assets confiscated when the queen was deposed, he had kept aside 25,000 francs for her sister. With Rasendranoro's death, Ranavalona wanted the money divided equally between a nephew, Rakotomena, who remained in Madagascar, and Marie-Louise. In agreeing, Gallieni rather smarmily mentioned that he had decided to 'allow a measure of generosity and extreme goodwill to benefit individuals and families who, by their origins and their interests in a despotic and brutal regime, had at a certain time misunderstood our authority and had combated our influence'. He firmly told the queen that the money represented an 'allocation' not an 'indemnity'.[44]

Ramazindrazana and Marie-Louise outlived Ranavalona.[45] Marie-Louise spent her entire life outside of Madagascar, first in Réunion, then in Algeria, but mostly in France. She attracted attention from the press, as already seen, perhaps because of her paternity, partly because she was an attractive and engaging child. She was raised as a proper French girl, and studied English, the piano, drawing and dress-making. When enrolled at school in Versailles, she boarded with a private family. Her guardian, Raoul Allier, an honorary professor of Protestant theology, delivered regular reports to the authorities on her welfare. In 1913, when Marie-Louise was sixteen, he stated she was 'of extremely lively intelligence' and applied herself with dedication to schoolwork (though she was not very good in mathematics). He worried that, since she suffered from nosebleeds and colds, the French weather was bad for her health, but she at least got away to Algiers for holidays.

When she finished secondary schooling, Marie-Louise studied pharmacy. The French continued to pay her pension after the queen's death; she occasionally requested extra benefits. Around 1924, Marie-Louise married a Monsieur Bossardt (or Bosshart), an agricultural engineer of no great fortune; his circumstances inspired the governor-general of Madagascar to raise her pension. Marie-Louise Bosshart became a nurse, and was awarded the Legion of Honour for service during the Second World War. She died obscurely in Le Havre in 1948, without children.

After Ranavalona's death, her aunt, Ramazindrazana, nearing the age of seventy and suffering from eye problems, successfully requested permission to move to Nice, a city with good climate that was a favourite of retired colonials. Like Marie-Louise she continued to draw a government pension. Ramazindrazana's household was not without intrigue. Mrs Howey, the late queen's *dame de compagnie*, accompanied Ramazindrazana to Nice, where she served as counsellor, comptroller and head of her staff. There was, however, a new arrival at the residence, a Miss Herbert, a British missionary who had worked in Madagascar. Howey was suddenly dismissed or retired on the grounds of age. In 1920, Ramazindrazana requested authorisation to go to Reading, England, with Herbert, a friend of more than thirty years, she said. The French, learning that settlement of an insurance policy provided one of the motives for the trip, became concerned about Herbert's influence. Though a police investigator reported that Ramazindrazana was lucid and the friendship genuine, permission was denied. Howey, for her part, contacted the French, alleging that Herbert was taking advantage of Ramazindrazana; she characterised Ramazindrazana and Herbert's journey to Chamonix (a replacement for Reading) as 'kidnapping'. She explained:

> Ten years ago I was appointed by the Government to serve the queen; at her death, I remained with the princess. In order to console her in her grief, and so that she might speak her own language, I suggested bringing Miss Herbert to spend some time with us ... However, the very day of her arrival, this English woman ensconced herself in the same bed as the princess, leaving her neither by day nor by night!

The exclamation point suggested irregular intimacy, and Howey said that Herbert had persuaded Ramazindrazana to rewrite her will to make Herbert sole beneficiary. Furthermore, the Englishwoman had already taken many of her possessions: 'The poor old princess was completely hypnotised by this woman.' Howey played both moral and nationalist cards, in one missive alleging that Herbert 'like the other missionaries, had engaged in propaganda against France and Galieni [sic]'. The French decided that Howey was simply disgruntled, and intervention was not warranted. The dispute went into abeyance, or at least the archives go silent, but questions arose on Ramazindrazana's death. Herbert was indeed her sole beneficiary, other than for a thousand francs left to two relatives in Madagascar. Marie-Louise, signing herself as Princess Razafinandriamanitra – the use of a title and Malagasy name noteworthy – wrote to complain that it had been Ranavalona's wish that her great-niece receive an inheritance after the death of Ramazindrazana, but that Herbert had kept almost everything.

It is difficult to know what was happening behind the scenes. Was Ramazindrazana in possession of her faculties, or being cruelly manipulated by Herbert and perhaps also Howey? Was Howey simply angry at being displaced? The intrigues in Nice are the stuff of *petite histoire*, but they precipitated correspondence between the Nice police, the prefect of the Alpes-Maritimes, the governors-general in Algiers and Tananarive and the colonial minister in Paris: a large network centred on the unfortunate relative of a deposed queen, touching on finance, law, morality and even nationalism. The tempest in a teacup reveals the after-effects of exile of a ruler. For twenty years, France bore responsibility for the welfare of the queen whose throne they had taken, and for some years after her death for her family members. Though the burden on the Malagasy budget was not heavy, there lingered expectations of maintaining royal exiles in modest comfort, including a pension for Marie-Louise that lasted for half a century after her great-aunt's ouster.

Ranavalona's return to Madagascar

In 1925, the year following Ramazindrazana's death, the governor-general of Algeria wrote to his counterpart in Madagascar about a complaint received concerning the sorry state of Ranavalona's tomb in Algiers.[46] He blamed the poor upkeep on lack of funding from the government of Madagascar, and commented that the French, in taking away Ranavalona's throne, had 'contracted a moral obligation at least to preserve for her a situation worthy of her former rank'. Not doing so would lower France's esteem. The letter sparked little reaction from Tananarive, and in 1926, the governor-general wrote again, sending two photos of the neglected tomb. The governor-general of Madagascar replied, rather testily: 'The sepulchre seems to be sufficiently appropriate to me, and I have decided not to undertake any modification.'[47]

Moves to repatriate Ranavalona's remains date from around 1935, when Raoul Dalais, a former colonial administrator, published an article in *Bordeaux colonial et maritime* about her tomb. This inspired a letter from a Malagasy man who reminisced about a visit to the gravesite: 'I felt strongly how France's having forgotten about the mortal remains of the Queen had something distressing [about it] and that it was inhumane to prolong this twenty-year exile still longer.' He recalled that the body of Prime Minister Rainilaiarivony had been repatriated in 1900 and reburied in Gallieni's presence, as it happened, and wondered why the queen could not follow.

In January 1936, Dalais entered into contact with the colonial ministry, and the bureaucratic wheels slowly began to turn. Léon Cayla, the governor-general of Madagascar, advised Paris that he did not find the moment right for repatriation of the queen's remains. Indeed, his opinion was dismissive:

> this question is of interest only to the natives of the highlands of the Grande Ile [the Merina]. And even so, one must add that until recent times the opinion of the Hova has been little preoccupied by the matter. Their attention was drawn to the subject several months ago, when they

became aware of overtures made to the Department [of political affairs at the ministry] by a former functionary of the Colony. In certain milieus in the central region, the idea was favourably received, the return of the remains of Ranavalona III being considered as a sort of recognition of the old Hova hegemony.

For Cayla, therefore, concern about the queen's remains was relevant only to a particular group and region. He continued, distancing himself from Gallieni's *politique des races*: 'French policy is indeed intending to associate more and more in our efforts the diverse elements of the population and to avoid as much as possible the predominance of one race over the others.' Though not explicit in this response, however, the official was concerned about contemporary political agitation in Madagascar (on which more presently).

The matter languished until mid-1938, when a new colonial minister, Georges Mandel, again sought Cayla's views. The governor-general simply reproduced much of his letter from two years earlier, but nevertheless appeared more sympathetic to the queen's reburial. Malagasy, he noted, had been very touched when Cayla arranged for return of the body of a musician who died in Paris during the 1931 Exposition Coloniale. Since conditions were now quieter in Madagascar than two years before, he had no opposition to the proposal, 'so long as can be avoided, by press information, any inexact interpretation that might be given'. Repatriation of Ranavalona's body would be only an acknowledgement of 'an honourable old custom' of ceremonial burial of ancestors' remains, and that might in fact be 'good policy'. In short, with appropriate publicity, the government could attract goodwill. Perhaps in Cayla's mind, as well, was the thought that rehabilitating the precolonial dynasty, or at least giving proof of French regard for the last queen and for Merina sensibilities, would wither the nationalist ideas taking root in Madagascar.

Mandel gave his approval, and the decision won applause from both French veterans of military campaigns in Madagascar and Malagasy residents in the metropole. An old soldier, now living in Oran, wrote to the minister with 'respectful felicitations', and a retired colonel who had fought on the island posted his article on Malagasy death customs. A decorated former army nurse in Madagascar, who recalled serving refreshments to the queen when she visited a hospital, expressed pleasure at the 'enlightened idea' of returning Ranavalona's remains. Les Anciens et les Amis de Madagascar, on letterhead emblazoned with a map, wrote in similar terms from Paris, and a letter arrived on Mandel's desk from a Malagasy association in Marseille. A Malagasy dentist in Paris requested details of the reburial arrangements, and another letter-writer asked to go to Algeria for the exhumation.

Georges Bousserot, former *député* of Réunion, member of the Conseil Supérieur des Colonies, and promoter of the repatriation plan, saluted a 'decision that responds to the wishes of the elite among the population of the Grande Ile'.

A group of Malagasy students in Paris called on Mandel in person to express their appreciation, with a Dr Raherivelo pronouncing a 'Homage to the Government of the French Republic and declaration of loyalty to the Mother Country, in the name of the Malagasy of France'. The undoubtedly heartfelt, but obsequious, words called the planned return of Ranavalona's remains humane, noble and liberal: 'By this decision, the Government of the Republic shows to the whole world the true face of immortal France in its relationships with its protected people and children.' He voiced Malagasy joy, gratitude and respect at a gesture that would count as one of the government's 'historic acts' and a 'mark of confidence' in the Malagasy people. More practically, Raherivelo asked for a subvention for Malagasy to travel to Marseille, where Ranavalona's casket would transit en route to Tananarive. He concluded, rousingly, 'Vive la France! Vive la République! Vive Madagascar! Vive le Ministre des Colonies!'

All went according to plan, though one clipping in the archives, described as from the 'colonial press' but otherwise unidentified, complained that the plans had been made in such 'precipitation and discretion' that many Malagasy had only heard the news through press reports; it referred, enigmatically, to 'a certain resistance which at the moment we will have the courtesy not to denounce'. Meanwhile, the governor-general of Algeria remarked that Ramazindrazana had asked to be buried in Algiers alongside Ranavalona, but that it was not proposed to repatriate the aunt's remains. The archive folders retain no record of correspondence between officials and Marie-Louise, Ranavalona's closest living relative.

The government intended reburial ceremonies to remain dignified, but low key, not wishing to turn Ranavalona into a hero or martyr. The departure of her body from Algiers and its arrival in Marseille were nevertheless saluted with military honours. Representatives of the colonial ministry and the prefecture attended the ship's landing in Marseille, as indeed did Malagasy delegations from Paris. Ranavalona's coffin arrived in Tamatave on 29 October, met by the regional French governor, in the first stage of ceremonies carefully choreographed by the governor-general's staff. Army musicians played the traditional 'Aux morts', the crowd observed a minute of silence and soldiers presented arms, before the coffin, covered in a red and gold flag, was placed onto a special train heading for the highlands. The train pulled in to Tananarive the following afternoon, after an overnight stop, the population alerted to its arrival with cannon fire. Governor-General and Madame Cayla waited at the station, alongside other authorities, foreign consuls and unnamed 'relatives of Ranavalona'. As troops again presented arms, the coffin was borne to a station hall decorated with violet and black drapery, when until almost midnight, visitors filed by the catafalque to pay respects.

The next afternoon the queen's body was moved to the Rova, the fortress encompassing the French-occupied royal palaces and Gallieni's new necropolis for the Merina monarchs. A military honour guard surrounded the bier, decorated with roses and chrysanthemums, in front of an audience that had gathered since early morning. Cayla gave a short but meaningful speech, the only one of the day. He began by recalling that sacred tradition held that a Malagasy should be buried in the land of the ancestors, a custom that France now honoured. In reburying Ranavalona in the royal tombs, 'She thus gives to the Malagasy, whose loyalty has been recently affirmed in such a moving fashion, a new testimony to her maternal solicitude. How could she not answer to the call of local tradition, she who in the gravest hours of its history, knew how to remain true to her ideal of human comprehension and fraternity?' From that rather sibylline remark, Cayla turned to the last decades of the queen's life: 'Ranavalona III in her exile learned to know the depths of the French soul and the creative genius of an old nation which had resolved to make of Madagascar one of the finest provinces of its immense empire.' From 'Alger-la-Blanche', he conjectured, she had been able to imagine the 'work that was pursued, in an atmosphere made peaceful', in 'Tananarive-la-Rouge' – a reference to the white architecture of Algiers and the red soil of Madagascar, but also to urban projects undertaken in the Malagasy capital. He neatly avoided mention of French refusal to allow Ranavalona to revisit her homeland. She knew, Cayla intoned, that eventually 'French voices' would unite with the echo of the mountains of the Merina country to lay her to rest, lying among the kings 'like the most humble of her former subjects'. He concluded by hoping that those in the *mère-patrie* and Algeria who had brought about this 'pious gesture' would receive 'the homage of Malagasy gratitude'. A Protestant pastor prayed, a band played Chopin's funeral march, and the queen's coffin was carried by 'ten indigenous guards' to its tomb, there placed, according to custom, facing the setting sun.

The ceremony indeed appears simple and dignified, but Cayla's speech was a masterwork of colonialist spin. He said nothing about French conquest of Madagascar, Gallieni's arbitrary deposition and exile of the queen, and the sometimes mean-spirited way she was afterwards treated. The governor-general made no reference to the aunt, sister or niece whose bodies were not repatriated, nor to the great-niece who outlived her. He contrasted a peaceful and modernising Madagascar with a country of disorder and poverty before the arrival of the French. Madagascar was a 'province' of an 'immense' empire, its traditions honoured though its independence was taken away and its dynasty abolished.

Perhaps the late queen, seemingly reconciled with French rule, might not have objected to Cayla's statements. The prayers offered for a Christian queen and her entombment in Malagasy tradition suggests that some compatriots had accommodated themselves with the changes wrought by foreign influence. Cayla's words were not surprising, though with notes of hypocrisy and self-satisfaction. It would be anachronistic to expect expressions of regret at the fate of the queen or an apology for the way she and her country were treated. Lauding her 'maternal' role and docility reinforced the image of the queen as a powerless woman now lying in peace 'like the most humble of her subjects'.

Malagasy reaction was largely positive, though with some differences of opinion. One leftist newspaper in Tananarive contrasted royal gestures under the old monarchy, when the sovereign distributed food to the poor and slaves, with those of the French Republic, which primarily benefited the wealthy. A Communist newspaper, *Le Prolétariat malgache*, stated that 'young Malagasies are far from desiring the return of a past that they abhor and they are very attached to France and its democratic institutions by conviction and from gratitude'. Such words were perhaps strategic testimony to the promise of an international Communism encompassing France and its empire, as well as a critique of pre-colonial feudalism. Remarks in another issue nevertheless charged that the Malagasy, denied French citizenship, were little more than 'foreigners in their own country'. More conservative papers nostalgically evoked an idealised and folkloric royal past. Meanwhile, *Le Colon de Madagascar*, its title indicative of readership, dismissed the ceremony: 'We have the impression that too much noise is being made about the return to Madagascar of the mortal remains of the Hova ex-Queen Ranavalona III.' The colonialist paper pointedly added: 'It would seem that they [French officials] want to move to a sort of rehabilitation which would be a tacit disavowal of the measures taken by the French government on [sic] February 1897.' Ranavalona had 'paid her debt' through exile, but the journalist wondered why such a big fuss was being made about a monarch whose dynasty incurred the opposition of non-Merina peoples in Madagascar: 'Do they want ... to give to the Hova population a particular acknowledgement of satisfaction that nothing justifies and that risks being interpreted as an expression of partiality?'[48]

The *retour des cendres*, in the short term, scored a guarded success for the French, but without long-lasting effects in galvanising support. Solofo Randrianja argues convincingly that the aim was 'recuperation of popular emotion for the greater glory of the colonial regime'. Rendering homage to the Malagasy heritage and last occupant of the throne, but one rendered impotent, represented a continuation of a policy followed since Gallieni. Randrianja also sees the reburial as the last gasp of the royalists in Madagascar, the 'old Hova' elite and its identity, to be succeeded by new nationalist ideologies.[49] Furthermore, the potential benefits to the colonial order could not make up for the failure of colonial reforms mooted, but not delivered, by the Popular Front in 1936–37. The theatre of colonialism – ceremonies, rituals and symbolic gestures, no matter how powerful – could not solve the material and cultural problems of the colonised. The Malagasy might applaud the French gesture, and pledge fealty to the Republic, but disappointed expectations would fuel anti-colonial nationalism.

Ranavalona's remains dwelt in the Rova cemetery during the remaining decades of French colonial rule, through a rebellion in 1947 put down with bloodthirsty severity by the French,[50] in the years leading to independence in 1960, and during the decades of misguided political and economic projects, poverty and political corruption that were Madagascar's more recent fate. In 1995, a massive fire broke out at the Rova, with arson suspected, and the palaces and fortress burned. The heat caused the tombs of the Merina monarchs to explode; only the body of one was recovered, and there is disagreement about whose remains they were. Other salvaged items are on display in the palace of Rainilaiarivony, the grandeur of which rivalled the queen's palace, while the Malagasy government gradually attempts to rebuild the Rova.[51]

Monarchism, republicanism and nationalism after Ranavalona

After the removal of Ranavalona, the French tried to replace monarchical panoply with republican pageantry and power. They relegated one of the queen's golden crowns, throne, palanquins, banners inscribed with the cypher 'R.M.' (Ranavalona Manjaka), gifts from presidents and monarchs to a museum in Tananarive, and sent another crown to the army museum in Paris. Taking over the Rova, transferring the remains of the Merina monarchs, and placing regalia in historical museums appropriated the old order.⁵² Though the Rova architecturally dominated the cityscape of Tanananarive, the governor-general's palace loomed as the real seat of power, situated on an aptly named Avenue de France leading to the Square Jean Laborde.⁵³ On the Place Poincaré in 1923 the French erected a towering equestrian statue of Gallieni, inscribed in honour of 'the pacifier and organiser' of Madagascar. Near the base, standing in front of a zebu, a smaller figure of a Malagasy, a shawl around his shoulders, doffs his hat and looks up admiringly at Gallieni.

The following year, colonial authorities decided to build a war memorial to the 3,101 Malagasy killed in battle during the Great War (out of 41,355 conscripted men and 34,386 sent to Europe). They chose as the site an island on Lake Anosy, the 'Lac de la Reine', where a small royal chalet had stood; they selected the location, according to Eric Jennings, largely because of the royal associations. Figures of a Malagasy and a French soldier stood in front of a monument, dedicated 'to the memory of French and Malagasy soldiers *morts pour la France*'. A tall column rose above a base decorated with bas-reliefs of zebus, a figure of Victory at its summit (though in concrete rather than bronze since subscriptions failed to meet expectations). The monument is resolutely French, but with allusions to Malagasy funerary monuments.⁵⁴ It still stands in Tanananarive; the statue of Gallieni was pulled down after independence, replaced by a column dedicated to those who died in the 1947 insurrection. There is no statue of Queen Ranavalona.

The *idea* of the indigenous monarchy survived during the course of the *menalamba* rebellion, and references to the Merina polity and its dynasty did not completely disappear after the death of Ranavalona.⁵⁵ In the inter-war years monarchism returned to political debate in terms of what Randrianja sees as a mythification of the pre-colonial monarchy. Critics of colonialism encompassed progressives arguing for amelioration of the colonial order, assimilationists calling for full integration of the colony into the French Republic, and nationalists campaigning for autonomy or independence. Trade unions and a new Communist Party added to the ideological ferment. Commentators from various points of the spectrum wrote about the merits of the pre-colonial Merina state, contrasting it with the colonial regime. Jean Ralaimongo, in the first issue of *Le Prolétariat malgache*, in May 1937, lauded the pre-colonial Merina rural communities as proto-soviets that managed the social ownership of land when 'Malagasy society was a veritable communist society'. (That judgment, for Randrianja, nevertheless goes against the historical record; the rural communities enshrined class inequalities to the benefit of nobles.) Another nationalist, Ramananjato, wrote in panegyric fashion about pre-colonial Merina education, including the sending of scholarship boys to England by Radama I, which he juxtaposed to the spare funds the French spent on schooling. Ramananjato presented his arguments at a meeting of the Union des Travailleurs Nègres, which was close to the Communist Party, and the Congrès International des Noirs et des Arabes, held in Paris in 1936 to protest against the Italian conquest of Ethiopia – the conference certainly one of the reasons Governor-General Cayla judged repatriation of Ranavalona's remains untimely that year. Other nationalists stressed the role of Rainilaiarivony in establishing state institutions and consolidating Merina administration. Though an idealised monarchy might still provide a reference, nationalists did not demand the return of the Merina dynasty. L'Avenir, a group of twelve intellectuals formed in 1937 in opposition to the Communists, called for restoration of the regime of 'the ancestors', though more radical demands drowned out the call.[56]

At the time of Ranavalona's death and reinterment, few in the colonial elite realised the import of rising nationalism, imagined that the British would undertake an unsuccessful attempt to wrest Madagascar from a Vichy-aligned colonial government during the Second World War,[57] or predicted a rebellion far more violent, and one put down with far greater bloodshed by the French, just after the war. Few, too, foresaw the independence of Madagascar, along with most other French African colonies, in 1960. Two years before independence, Charles de Gaulle, newly installed as president of the Fifth Republic and head of the recently created French *Communauté*, visited Tananarive. He spoke near the sacred Mahamasina stone, on which monarchs' thrones stood for coronations, and which the French had incorporated into a football stadium. Always one for grand gestures and carefully chosen words, de Gaulle turned towards the Rova, which looked down on the stadium from the hillside, and declared: 'In the future you will once again be a state, as you were when this palace was inhabited.'[58] That came to pass, but no monarch ruled from the Rova.

Gender and exile

A key difference between Ranavalona and other banished monarchs was her gender, and the issue of her 'femaleness', and that of her exiled relatives, shows up in every act of her life's drama. She succeeded two other queens on the throne and, like them, was married – without enthusiasm, one surmises – to her prime minister, who effectively ruled Madagascar. French descriptions of the queen as slight, shy and much taken with foreign luxuries draw on notions of femininity. The kindly Durand betrayed many commonplace gendered sentiments in saying that her favourite avocation was 'reverie and the contemplation of the stars', that she was a 'coquette', and 'crazy (folle)' with pleasure at receiving a new canopy for her throne, but also that she was 'a real plaything in the hands of the powerful grasp of her husband'.[59] The French played on these stereotypes by offering Ranavalona gowns and perfumes from Paris. However, when they turned against Ranavalona, she was portrayed as conspiring and treacherous – traditional negative qualities attributed to women. Galllieni's comments about dirty pictures supposedly found among her belongings, and the suspected sex toy in her aunt's affairs, added a stroke of immorality to the portrait of women who had failed to fulfil the prime duty, in nineteenth-century visions of womanhood, of producing children. Durand's comments about the queen breaking down in tears as she left her palace and country – a perfectly understandable reaction in the circumstances – and swigging from a rum bottle further added to an image of womanly frailty and moral laxity. Somewhat contradictorily, Ranavalona was thought capable of inspiring a rebellion against the French. These perspectives endured after Ranavalona's death. A 1946 novel by Danika Boyer sympathetically depicts Ranavalona as 'charming' and 'dreamy', though with 'the heart of a savage'. The novel concludes that 'the queen lost the island with feminine weakness'.[60] Gallieni would perhaps not have disagreed, though he may have been relieved that 'feminine weakness' meant he did not face a more obdurate opponent.

Those who banished Ranavalona made a point of directing that she be treated with regard for her sex, a statement of contemporary attitudes, and not just policy. Male military officers, governors and ministers decided the fate of the queen and female royals in her close family. A photograph of Ranavalona getting out of her sedan chair to board the ship to Réunion shows a tiny, stooped figure in a long dark dress and a very large hat that obscures her face. Surrounding her, in addition to Malagasy porters, are no fewer than a dozen sturdy-looking Frenchmen in white uniforms and pith helmets, looking relaxed but curious, with more men staring at the scene from the background. The *Lapérouse* stands imposingly, its hardware and rigging further affirmation of naval and colonial machismo.

For the remainder of her life, Ranavalona was a minor celebrity in Algiers, Paris and the provincial centres where she holidayed. Spectators and the press focused on her as woman as well as former queen. Reporters dwelt on her clothing and evaluated how successfully she imitated a *Parisienne*. They described her as the caring foster-mother of a charming little girl (who was becoming a 'real' French girl), the cultured lady who visited museums and attended worship services, the sentimental exile who shed a tear at a Malagasy exhibition, the loyal and obedient subject who even entertained in her drawing-room the man who had dethroned her. The comings and goings of such a woman contributed to the 'people' pages of newspapers and such magazines as *Fémina*, and appealed to their largely female readership. Meanwhile Ranavalona was kept under surveillance by governors and prefects, policeman and spies; she depended on the men who ran the French state for her pension, housing and permission to travel. At Ranavalona's reburial, Cayla referred to the queen's 'maternal solicitude'; safely in death, under the French, she again became the mother of the nation.

Ranavalona largely played the gendered role assigned to her, perhaps with little choice or inclination to do otherwise. However, it is worth recalling the strong affirmations of her rights and duties as sovereign in her coronation address and her later defiant comments to would-be aggressors: 'And should anyone dare to claim even a hair's breadth [of the realm], I will show myself to be a man.' That very Elizabethan comment, of course, itself bespeaks gender expectations, but it reveals a different side of the character of the queen than the one the French highlighted.

We do not really know what Ranavalona made of her life or her fate, and what options she had. Did she instigate resistance to the French or acquiesce to their conquest? Did she desire to keep her throne or was she in some measure relieved to give it up after a difficult reign? In her private life, was she the victim of a forced marriage and perhaps undesired sexual relations with her prime minister, or was their relationship companionate or loving? Did she yearn for a married life and children with a spouse of her choosing? Did she disapprove of 'loose living', or did she want to break out of the constraints of royalty and religion? Should she be characterised as fearful in the wake of French invasion, brave in her efforts to face up to colonialisers, or resigned to the inevitable? With a different strategy, might she have been able to retain her throne? How happy was she in exile? Did she truly believe French rule beneficial to her country? What were her hopes for Madagascar? Whatever the answers, in photographs the queen almost invariably wears a sad expression.

Ranavalona's exile occurred in the same year as the diamond jubilee of Queen Victoria, one monarch's fall a reversed image of the apotheosis of the other. A year later, the Habsburg empress Sisi was assassinated. In 1890, Queen Wilhelmina acceded to the throne of the Netherlands, beginning a fifty-eight-year rule as suzerain over the Dutch East Indies and Holland's other colonies. Meanwhile, the tsarina and the kaiserin reigned as imperial consorts, little knowing that their dynasties had only two more decades on the throne, and in faraway China, Cixi acted as the power behind the ill-fated Qing throne. Ranavalona never possessed the authority of these other female royals.

Another peer of the Malagasy queen was Lili'uokalani, who became queen of Hawaii in 1891; two years later, she was deposed in a coup led by Europeans and Americans, backed by the US government.[61] Issuing a statement damning 'any and all [actions] done against myself and the constitutional government of the Hawaiian Kingdom', Lili'uokalani nevertheless yielded to superior force. As the foreigners and their Hawaiian allies proclaimed a republic, Lili'uokalani was placed under detention. After being implicated in an uprising aimed at restoration of the monarchy, in 1895, she was arrested, convicted and sentenced to five years of hard labour and a fine, a sentence commuted to house arrest at the 'Iolani Palace. The former queen continued to protest her treatment, despoliation of royal property, and annexation of the Hawaiian Islands by the United States in 1898. Lili'uokalani died, in Honolulu, in November 1917, just five months after the death of Ranavalona in Algiers. The deposed queens of Madagascar and Hawaii may or may not have known about each other, or reflected on their parallel destinies at the hands of the foreign men who took over their countries.

Notes

1 Joseph Gallieni to Queen Ranavalona, 27 February 1897, ANOM FR ANOM 44 PA 5/29.
2 Malagasy was transcribed into a written language by missionaries in the early 1800s, but the spelling continued to vary. Both 'Ranavalo' and 'Ranavalona' are used. (The fact that the last letter or syllable of Malagasy names is generally silent explains some of the variation.) The polity of the dominant Merina ethnic group is usually given as Imerina ('Émyrne' in nineteenth-century French). 'Hova' has variously applied to the class of commoners and the whole Merina ethnic group. On the complex question of ethnonyms, see Pier M. Larson, 'Desperately Seeking "the Merina" (Central Madagascar): Reading Ethnonyms and Their Semantic Fields in African Identity Histories', *Journal of Southern African Studies*, 22:4 (1996), 541–560. I have used the French names for localities, thus Tananarive (now Antananarivo), Tamatave (Toamasina), Majunga (Mahajanga) and Sainte-Marie (Nosy Baraha).
3 General works in English are Mervyn Brown, *A History of Madagascar* (London: Damien Tunnacliffe, 1995); and Solofo Randrianja and Stephen Ellis, *Madagascar: A Short History* (London: Hurst and Company, 2009). In French, see the older Hubert Deschamps, *Histoire de Madagascar* (Paris: Berger-Levrault, 1965).
4 See the rather sensationalised biography by Keith Laidler, *Female Caligula: Ranavalona, The Mad Queen of Madagascar* (Chichester: John Wiley, 2005). See also Arianne Chernock, 'Queen Victoria and the "Bloody Mary of Madagascar"', *Victorian Studies*, 55:3 (2013), 425–49.
5 Brown, *A History of Madagascar*, p. 216.
6 The daughter of the United States consul in Tananarive in the 1890s, an African American, married a member of the royal family and moved to Washington. Their son, under the name of Andy Razaf, became a jazz composer and musician, famous for the song 'Ain't Misbehavin''.

7 Marie-France Barrier's biographical *Ranavalo, dernière reine de Madagascar* (Paris: Éditions Balland, 1996), is based on archival material and contemporary documentation. However, in addition to verbatim quotations from original materials (given without specific references), Barrier includes imagined conversations, narrates incidents and ascribes emotions in a way that historians refrain from doing.
8 J. Richardson, 'The Coronation of Ranavalona III', *The Antananarivo Annual and Madagascar Magazine*, 7 (1883), 102–10.
9 Marc Michel, *Gallieni* (Paris: Fayard, 1989), p. 179. See also Joseph-Simon Gallieni, *Lettres de Madagascar, 1896–1905* (Paris: Société d'éditions géographiques, maritimes et coloniales, 1928), though it has surprisingly little on the queen.
10 Gwyn Campbell, *An Economic History of Imperial Madagascar, 1750–1895: The Rise and Fall of an Island Empire* (Cambridge: Cambridge University Press, 2005).
11 Claude Bavoux, 'Les Réunionnais de Madagascar de 1880 à 1925' (Dissertation, University of Paris-7, 1997).
12 J. P. Daughton, *An Empire Divided: Religion, Republicanism, and the Making of French Colonialism, 1880–1914* (Oxford: Oxford University Press, 2006), Part IV.
13 Quoted by Michel, *Gallieni*, p. 183. The phrase has also been credited to King Radama I, who boasted that his island was defended by two generals, 'General Hazo, forest, and General Tazo, fever'. William Ellis, *Three Visits to Madagascar during the Years 1853, 1854, 1856* (London: John Murray, 1858), p. 319.
14 Alfred Durand, *Les Derniers Jours de la cour Hova: l'exil de la reine Ranavalona* (Paris: Société de l'histoire des colonies françaises, 1933), p. 73. Lieutenant Durand became a colonial administrator, French senator, professor of Malagasy at the École nationale des Langues orientales in Paris, and author of several works on Madagascar.
15 Stephen Ellis, *The Rising of the Red Shawls: A Revolt in Madagascar 1895–1899* (Cambridge: Cambridge University Press, 1985).
16 Michel, *Gallieni*.
17 Michael P. M. Finch, *A Progressive Occupation? The Gallieni-Lyautey Method and Colonial Pacification in Tonkin and Madagascar, 1885–1900* (Oxford: Oxford University Press, 2013).
18 Michel, *Gallieni*, p. 231.
19 The following section on the last months of the queen's reign and her deposition and exile is based, unless otherwise indicated, on material in the Archives Nationales d'Outre-Mer, FN ANOM 44 PA/5/29.
20 Finch, *A Progressive Occupation*, p. 207.
21 Durand, *Les Derniers jours*, p. 108.
22 Michel, *Gallieni*, p. 193.
23 Quoted in Brown, *A History of Madagascar*, p. 234.
24 Quoted in Barrier, *Ranavalo, dernière reine de Madagascar*, pp. 236–9.
25 Quoted in Durand, *Les Derniers jours*, p. 111.
26 Michel, *Gallieni*, p. 202.
27 A succinct non-academic account is Roland Barraux, *Ranavalo III: Une reine malgache en exil* (Paris: L'Harmattan, 2013).
28 These are contained in ANOM FR ANOM 61 APC 1 and used here.
29 Quoted in Durand, *Les Derniers jours*, p. 80.
30 The quotations come from Durand's report to Gallieni, written from Saint-Denis on 17 March 1897.
31 Durand, *Les Derniers jours*, p. 114.
32 ANOM FR ANOM 61 APC 1. The file contains several clippings about Ranavalona's visits to France, suggestive of Durand's continued interest in the queen.
33 Michel, *Gallieni*, p. 196.
34 Criticism had followed Gallieni throughout his tenure in Madagascar. Among his most vocal critics were Gabriel Laffaille, private secretary to Hippolyte Laroche during his brief period as Resident-General, who wrote (under the penname Jean Carol) impassioned critiques of Gallieni's methods, collected as *Chez les Hovas: au pays rouge* (Paris: Paul Ollendorff, 1897), and the radical deputy and writer Paul Vigné

THE FRENCH AND THE QUEEN OF MADAGASCAR

d'Octon, whose novel *La Gloire du sabre* (Paris: Flammarion, 1900), blamed Galllieni for a massacre.

35 Barrier, *Ranavalo, dernière reine de Madagascar*, p. 249.
36 Quoted in Barrier, *Ranavalo, dernière reine de Madagascar*, p. 342.
37 Other Malagasy visitors included official delegations, students, pastors and soldiers. See Jean-Michel Bergougniou, Rémi Clignet and Philippe David, *'Villages Noirs' et autres visiteurs africains et malgaches en France et en Europe (1870–1940)* (Paris: Karthala, 2001), pp. 86–91.
38 Eric Jennings, *Curing the Colonizers: Hydrotherapy, Climatology, and French Colonial Spas* (Durham, NC: Duke University Press, 2006).
39 Noël Courtaigne, 'La presse sur les traces de la Reine Ranavalo', Arcachon, cartes postales anciennes, leonc.fr/histoire/ranavalo/index.html, accessed 25 November 2016; and Aimé Nouailhas, 'Ranavalo à Arcachon', *Bulletin de la Société historique et archéologique d'Arcachon et du Pays de Buch*, 123 (2005), 90–9.
40 Digitised material from Archives départementales du Cantal, sous-série 10 PH, http://archives.cantal.fr/ark:/16075/a011350284478FAXYA9/1/1 and a0113502844785xFDZD.
41 *Le Petit Parisien*, 28 September 1905.
42 *L'Illustration*, 7 October 1905.
43 61 APC Papiers Durand, ANOM.
44 GS Mad 373/1014, ANOM.
45 This section is fully based on FM 37 MAD c. 373 d. 1013 Situation des members de l'ancienne dynastie hova, ANOM.
46 This section is based on FM 37 MAD c. 334 d. 882 and FM SG Mad/334/882, ANOM. Transfert des restes mortels de la reine; my account largely accords with Solofo Randrianja, *Société et luttes anticoloniales à Madagascar (1896 à 1946)* (Paris: Karthala, 2001).
47 Randrianja, *Société et luttes anticoloniales*, p. xx.
48 Randrianja, *Société et luttes anticoloniales*.
49 Randrianja, *Société et luttes anticoloniales*, p. 107.
50 Jacques Tronchon, *L'Insurrection malgache de 1947: Essai d'interprétation historique* (Paris: Karthala, 1986).
51 Jean Frémigacci, 'Le Rova de Tananarive: Destruction d'un lieu saint ou constitution d'une référence identitaire?', in Jean-Pierre Chrétien and Jean-Louis Triaud (eds), *Histoire d'Afrique: les enjeux de mémoire* (Paris: Karthala, 1999), pp. 421–44.
52 On the importance (and fate) of Malagasy regalia, see Marie-Pierre Ballarin, *Les Reliques royales à Madagascar: source de légitimation et enjeux de pouvoir (XVIIIe-XXe siècles)* (Paris: Karthala, 2000).
53 See Gwendolyn Wright, *The Politics of Design in French Colonial Urbanism* (Chicago: University of Chicago Press, 1991), on urbanism in colonial Tananarive.
54 Eric Jennings, 'Madagascar se souvient: Les multiples visages du monument aux morts du Lac Anosy, Antananarivo', *Outre-Mers*, 350–1 (2006), 123–40. There is also a monument to the Malagasy war dead – a tall column surmounted by a black eagle – in the former Jardin Botanique Colonial in Nogent-sur-Marne – site of the 1907 exposition that Ranavalona visited.
55 There were, of course, many aspects of social continuity between the pre-colonial and colonial regime. See Faranirina V. Rajaonah, 'Prestige et métier dans la société malgache: A Tananarive aux XIXe-XX siècles', *Le Mouvement social*, 204 (2003), 65–79.
56 Françoise Raison-Jourde (ed.), *Les Souverains de Madagascar: l'histoire royale et ses resurgences contemporaines* (Paris: Karthala, 1983); see also Stephen Ellis, 'The History of Sovereigns in Madagascar: New Light from Old Sources', in Didier Nativel and Faranirina V. Rajaonah (eds), *Madagascar revisité: en voyage avec Françoise Raison-Jourde* (Paris: Karthala, 2009), and Gwyn Campbell, *David Griffith and the Missionary History of Madagascar* (Leiden: Brill, 2012). On urban changes in the region, see Faranirina V. Rajaonah (ed.), *Cultures citadines dans l'Océan Indien occidental (XVIII-XXI siècles): pluralisme, échanges, inventivité* (Paris: Karthala, 2011).

57 See Martin Thomas, *The French Empire at War, 1940–1945* (Manchester: Manchester University Press, 1998), pp. 139–54; and Eric T. Jennings, *Vichy in the Tropics: Pétain's National Revolution in Madagascar, Guadeloupe and Indochina, 1940–1944* (Stanford: Stanford University Press, 2001), Chs 2–3.
58 Quoted in Frémigacci, 'Le Rova de Tananarive', p. 429.
59 Durand, *Les Derniers jours*, pp. 135, 136, 138.
60 Danika Boyer, *Sa Majesté Ranavalo III, ma reine* (Paris: Fasquelle, 1946); quotation from p. 178.
61 Neil Thomas Proto, *The Rights of My People: Liliuokalani's Enduring Battle with the United States, 1893–1917* (New York: Algora, 2009).

CHAPTER SEVEN

From conquest to decolonisation: exile from French North Africa

By the 1920s and 1930s, nationalist movements were gathering force around the colonised world, as shown by manifestos, conferences and debates occurring at the time of the repatriation of the remains of Queen Ranavalona to Madagascar. Over the next years, the Second World War, efforts by Europeans to regain control of their possessions and remould their overseas empires, and independence movements brought about profound changes and ultimately led to emancipation of most European colonial territories. The prospect of the restoration of Duy Tan to the throne of Annam in 1945 and the failure of his successor Bao Dai either to satisfy the French or forestall the radical nationalists, discussion about the place of the princely states in independent India and Pakistan, and the British deposition and reinstatement of King Mutesa in Uganda were part of the seismic transformation from a colonial to a post-colonial world. These issues also provided evidence that indigenous monarchs still played a role, or might do so, in the evolution of their countries, under European paramountcy or liberated from colonial overrule.

The question of revamped colonialism, autonomy or independence also played out, though in varying ways, in French North Africa: Algeria, Tunisia and Morocco. The French had invaded Algeria in 1830, on the pretence of a slight to their consul by the *dey*, ruler of the Regency of Algiers; elected by local elites for life, the *dey* ruled autonomously, but nominally represented the Ottoman sultan. Hussein Dey surrendered to the French conquerors; denied permission to move to France, although he was later allowed to visit Paris, he went into voluntary exile first in Naples, and then Alexandria; he regularly petitioned the French for various benefits, and according to the French, intrigued against them, before his death in 1838.[1] (Ironically, the French king who ordered the invasion of Algeria, Charles X, also lost his throne, in the revolution of 1830, and spent the rest of his life in Britain and the Habsburg empire.) Abolishing the office of *dey*, the French ruled Algeria directly, ultimately dividing it into three *départements* (the administrative divisions of the metropole) fully integrated into France – as much a part of the mainland, in constitutional terms, as Burgundy or Provence – as well as a military territory in the Sahara. It took several decades, however, for the French to secure control over the vast country, and in doing so, they had to defeat one of the most prominent and powerful Algerian leaders. He became (at least before Béhanzin) their most famous nineteenth-century colonial exile.

Emir Abd el-Kader came from a distinguished political and religious lineage, and was often referred to as a 'prince' by the press. After the French invasion, he joined his father as military commander in a holy war against the foreigners. In 1834, Abd el-Kader and the French agreed a treaty, though fighting broke out again five years later. In 1843, the French took Abd el-Kader's *smala*, or camp, but he eluded them as a fugitive until he surrendered in 1847.[2] The French exiled Abd el-Kader and his family to France, ultimately housing them in the grand Renaissance château at Amboise. When Louis-Napoleon made himself Emperor Napoleon III in 1852, he resolved to free the Algerians – perhaps mindful of the years he himself had spent as a political exile in Britain – and journeyed to the Loire château to announce their release in person. Abd el-Kader and his entourage, after a visit to Paris, left for Turkey, then settled in Damascus in 1855. Three years later, he published a book-length *Letter to the French* expounding his political and religious views in a spirit of reconciliation and ecumenism.[3] When anti-Christian riots erupted in Syria in 1860, Abd el-Kader intervened, providing information to the French consul about the attacks and sheltering a thousand Christians in his compound. The French lauded his actions, and there was talk of his becoming a French-sponsored 'King of Arabia', governor of a French territory in the Middle East or even 'King of Algiers'. A triumphal tour of Europe (where he was received by both Napoleon III and Queen Victoria), award of the Legion of Honour, and an honoured position alongside Napoleon's wife Empress Eugénie at the opening of the Suez Canal in 1869 completed his rehabilitation. During the last years of his life, and after his death in 1883, Abd el-Kader has been honoured, though not always with the same perspectives by Europeans and Arabs, as a 'hero of the two shores': a remarkable trajectory for an enemy become friend of the colonisers.[4]

The French meanwhile turned Algeria into a settler colony, with *colons* arriving from Italy, Spain, Malta and France itself, leaving no room for pre-colonial indigenous rulers, and very little space for Algerian participation in politics. After more than a century, safeguarding the rights of the *Français d'Algérie* led the French into a bloody and fratricidal war against the nationalists that concluded only in 1962, with the independence of Algeria.

Though France did not have to treat with a monarch in Algeria, the situation was different in the two protectorates of Tunisia and Morocco, and indeed, several dramatic incidents of royal deposition and exile played out in these countries of the Maghreb. The 'problems' the French faced with the *bey* of Tunis and the sultan of Morocco recall challenges of cohabitation with indigenous dynasties in other colonies, but also the new nexus provided by the Second World War and the nationalist movements of the 1950s.

France established control over Tunisia in 1881, with the intention of protecting the eastern flank of Algeria, taking advantage of good ports and wealthy natural resources, and curbing Italian designs on the country. Following an invasion, the Treaty of Bardo left in place the *bey*, head of a dynasty that had ruled – in principle, under the aegis of the Ottomans – from 1705 onwards. The French agreed to protect the throne of the *bey*, respect Islam and allow a measure of self-government under a watchful and often interventionist French Resident-General. The arrangement, at least from the French perspective, seemed to work out relatively well for some decades.[5]

In the case of Morocco, the establishment of a French protectorate was bound up with the deposition of two sultans. At the start of the twentieth century, French commercial interests already had footholds in Morocco, a large and independent state that was outside the Ottoman orbit, attracted by its prime geopolitical position straddling the Atlantic and the Mediterranean, fertile land and mineral wealth. Other powers, however, had their eyes on Morocco, and confrontations with an expansionist Germany over influence there, in 1906 and 1911, almost brought the two European powers to war though the conflicts paradoxically led the way for French takeover.

While regional rulers remained strong in Morocco, the sultan, head of the Alaouite dynasty (which dated back to the 1600s), descendant of the Prophet and 'Commander of the Faithful', held enormous political and spiritual prestige. The French, however, considered his regime theocratic, feudal and backward. The reigning sultan at the beginning of the twentieth century, Moulay Abdelaziz, faced foreign incursions, domestic rebellions and financial difficulties. Gradualist reforms, rather than buttressing his authority, aggravated opposition from conservatives and regional power-brokers. The Algeciras conference of 1906 forced concessions on the sultan, and in the next years, the French occupied Oujda on the Algerian frontier and bombarded the Atlantic port of Casablanca. After an armed challenge from his older half-brother, Abdelhafid, the viceroy in Marrakesh, Abdelaziz lost his

Figure 14 Sultan Moulay Abdelhafid (1875–1937, r. 1908–12) of Morocco and his minister, Kaddour Ben Ghabrit, in the company of a uniformed French official.

throne in 1908. Taking flight and rescued in part by French assistance, he found refuge in the internationalised city of Tangier.[6]

The great powers, including France, recognised Abdelhafid as new sultan, but according to the contemporary journalist Walter Harris, he 'was not the man to restore the dying Morocco back to health'[7] (see Figure 14). A rebellion provided an excuse for French occupation of Fez, one of the sultan's several capitals, in 1911; that provoked the Germans to send a gunboat, the *Panther*, and British ships also steamed towards Morocco. German backdown ended the 'Agadir crisis' and gave France a free hand. Abdelhafid was left in a precarious position, frightened by the foreign spectres, as well as a mutiny, a general uprising and the appearance of a rival claimant to the throne who portrayed himself as having supernatural powers. His offer to the French to abdicate, under pressure at home and internationally, was gratefully received by the new French Resident-General, General (later Marshal) Hubert Lyautey, who had been stationed in Madagascar at the time of the deposition of Ranavalona. Presented with a handsome cheque, Abdelhafid left for Europe, though not before ordering his crimson parasol and palanquin burned, for (in Harris' words), 'he realised that he was the last independent Sovereign of that country, and was determined that with its independence these historical emblems should disappear too'.[8] Though Abdelaziz thought that the French might imprison him, he received a gala reception in Marseille and travelled on to the spa town of Vichy and to Paris, before eventually settling in Tangier. The city now hosted two former sultans of Morocco, though they studiously avoided contact with each other. They both died in Tangier, Abdelhafid in 1937, his predecessor Abdelaziz six years later.

With a fresh sultan on the throne, Yusef, a brother of Abdelaziz and Abdelhafid, the French could proceed with setting up their new regime in Morocco. Lyautey – an admirer of North African culture, and a royalist by sympathy – hoped to restore the Alaouite dynasty to an active partnership as he pursued programmes of economic development and urban renewal.[9] Despite a good relationship between sultan and Resident during Lyautey's tenure, Morocco was not 'pacified', and the French faced a revolt in the 1920s.

Abd el-Krim's movement started in Spanish Morocco, a broad coastal strip neighbouring the French protectorate. The son of an Islamic judge, Abd el-Krim worked as a teacher, journalist, translator and employee of the Spanish colonial administration in Melilla, but became involved in nationalist and anti-colonial activities. Accused of conspiring with the Germans during the First World War, he was imprisoned from 1916 to 1918, but escaped to lead a rebellion in the Rif Mountains with the aim of forcing the Spanish and French out of Morocco. In 1925 he invaded the French protectorate, and Paris sent in troops under the command of a wartime hero, Marshal Philippe Pétain. The combined Spanish and French forces defeated Abd el-Krim, and the French exiled him to Réunion, home to banished Thanh Thai, Duy Tan and Said Ali (and for a time Ranavalona). There he lived for over two decades, another famous if non-royal political exile transported from one colony to another.[10]

By the late 1920s, the French hoped to have secured their positions in Tunisia and Morocco, which were being ruled as near colonies despite the deference paid to the *bey* and sultan. However, that rule was being undermined, particularly in Tunisia, where a political party, Destour, calling for eviction of the French and a return to an 1863 constitution, was set up in 1920. Two yeas later, Moncef, the son of Nasir, the reigning *bey*, organised a meeting between his father and leaders of Destour. The French manipulated the *bey*'s remarks on the occasion into condemnation of the reformers, which so angered Nasir that he threatened to abdicate, although the disagreement was resolved. The nationalists did not disappear, and a more radical faction, led by Habib Bourguiba, split from the Destour in 1934 to form the Néo-Destour– the party that eventually led Tunisia into independence and Bourguiba to the presidency. That was some time in the future, and the French meanwhile cracked down on dissidents with censorship and imprisonment. Bourguiba, indeed, was serving time in prison when Nasir's son Moncef succeeded a cousin as *bey* in 1942.

The downfall of Moncef Bey

Moncef, born in the year of the Treaty of Bardo, came to the throne as an energetic sixty-two-year-old, but at an inauspicious moment (see Figure 15). Germany had defeated and occupied much of France in 1940, and the remainder of the country was under Pétain's Vichy regime. The Vichy government was determined to hold on to France's overseas empire, but the Free French and Allies were equally determined to wrest it away from Pétain's control.[11] As the Free French pursued the war against the Axis, Mussolini voiced irredentist intentions about Tunisia, and opinion in the empire divided between supporters of Pétain and de Gaulle, the stage was set for dramatic developments. Pétain had appointed as Resident-General Admiral Jean-Pierre Estéva, a man eager to combat nationalist tendencies, keep the protectorate in the Vichy orbit, and implement aspects of Pétain's 'national revolution'.[12]

At a ceremony attended by Estéva, Moncef's formal speech on assuming the throne made reference to Pétain as a great man who had saved France. Over the next months, however, his gestures provoked French concern and then alarm. A tour of the country that took Moncef to poor communities heightened his popularity, and he made welcome changes in protocol, for instance, by abolishing the practice of subjects kissing the *bey*'s hand. More worryingly for the Vichy authorities, he affirmed to indigenous officials that 'you are my own representatives in the country ... Do not forget that you are my representatives and that I am the king', making it clear that Tunisian public servants took pride of place over French administrators.[13]

In August 1942, the *bey* presented to Estéva a memorandum of sixteen recommended reforms. He said that the French, who had been steadily appropriating greater powers, should adhere punctiliously to the Bardo treaty. There should be moves towards a 'Tunisification' of the administration with equal pay for local and French appointees. A consultative council should be established. Arabic should serve as the primary language in schools. Public utility companies should be nationalised. Estéva forwarded Moncef's memorandum to Vichy, which unsurprisingly showed little inclination to adopt the measures.

The following month, Moncef publicly swore an oath 'to act in the interests of the Tunisian people', a symbolic message to both his

Figure 15 Moncef Bey (1881–1948, r. 1942–43), the ruler of Tunisia, in court dress before his deposition in 1945.

subjects and the French. A few weeks later, at a ceremony marking the end of Ramadan, he decorated the secretary-general of the protectorate, who was considered pro-Tunisian, remarking that he would have refused a beylical honour to a *fonctionnaire* who had not shown such loyalty to the kingdom; the comment raised French eyebrows. As one Frenchman followed another in the reception queue, Moncef pointedly asked Estéva why no Tunisians appeared among high-ranking officials. Accounts of the conversation differ, but it appears the Resident suggested that none was capable of holding senior office, and added that French officials enjoyed his full confidence. That prompted Moncef to write to Pétain, unsuccessfully asking for Estéva's recall.

On 8 November, Allied troops landed in Algeria, and within days forty thousand Axis soldiers occupied Tunisia. Though this violated the 1940 Franco-German armistice, the protectorate authorities acquiesced, while the Free French called for resistance. Remaining officially neutral in public, Moncef expressed pro-Allied sentiments in a meeting with the American consul-general and wrote directly to President Franklin Roosevelt. However, opinion in Tunisia generally leant towards the Axis; resident Italians openly supported Mussolini, and Moncef Bey's son Raouf, married to an Italian, headed a pro-German faction. Hoping to win nationalists' endorsement, the Axis arranged for the release of Bourguiba from French detention in December 1942. Hustled to Rome, he nevertheless refused to give a speech in favour of the Axis, though they hinted at possible independence for Tunisia. Moncef stayed out of the limelight, but he received visiting German and Italian military commanders and, at Estéva's instigation, awarded them decorations – an action later held against him.

Moncef increasingly rankled the Vichy Resident-General. In January 1943, he appointed a reformist as chief minister without seeking prior approval. Stating that Tunisia's 90,000 Jews were as much his subjects as Muslims, he opposed anti-Semitic measures, including requirements that Jews wear yellow stars and be excluded from certain professions; despite his efforts, most Jews were deported to German concentration camps. The *bey* similarly resisted conscription of Tunisian labourers by the occupation armies. He also refrained from condemning Allied bombing of Tunisia.

By April 1943, the Allies had secured control of most of the country. The occupying Axis troops made a last stand at Hammam-Lif, where Moncef was ensconced in one of his palaces; the Germans asked the *bey* to move to La Marsa (close to Tunis) or to come to Germany, but he refused, and weathered the battle that took place around him. The Allies gained a victory, and British troops took over the palace and escorted the *bey* to La Marsa, though accounts differ as to whether he was treated with dignity or manhandled. The Free French were already debating his fate, with the preferred option being to get rid of the *bey*, because of alleged collaboration with the Axis, anti-French actions and pro-nationalist sympathies.

The French hoped that a fatigued and humiliated Moncef would quietly retire, but his chief minister, M'hamed Chenik, strengthened the *bey*'s resolve. Moncef and Chenik held a fateful meeting with the French commander, General Alphonse Juin, on 13 May 1943. When Juin suggested abdication, Moncef indignantly retorted: 'I hold my throne from God, who has preserved my life and who can take it away ... I have sworn to defend my people until my last breath. I will not leave unless my people demand it of me.'[14] The *bey* defended himself against charges of collaboration, which Juin implicitly conceded were shaky, and remarked that the French were subjecting him to greater pressures than had the Germans. After further verbal jousting, Juin blurted out that if Moncef refused to go, he would be deposed, and gave him several hours to consider his decision. When Moncef had Juin informed that he would not abdicate, the general, accompanied by a cohort of soldiers, proceeded to the *bey*'s palace and forcibly packed him into a car, which sped to the airport. He was flown to Laghouat in the Algerian desert and lodged in a rundown hotel, where he suffered from terrible heat, poor food and French surveillance. Meanwhile in Tunis, General Henri Giraud, on behalf of the Free French, formally proclaimed Moncef's deposition, and invested his cousin Amin as the new and, as it turned out, last *bey* of Tunis.[15] As Jean Martin argues, 'the bey of Tunis found himself dethroned much less because of collaboration, which in any case remained unproved, but because of his attitude of bringing into question the protectorate'.[16]

Recognising the fait accompli, Moncef issued a formal abdication, ostensibly justified by fragile health, and he was moved to more comfortable conditions in Ténès, also in Algeria. In Tunisia, the French cracked down on support for the former ruler and anti-colonial agitation by arresting over nine thousand people. In spite of the repression, a loose movement and ideology, *moncéfisme*, emerged, with adherents demanding reinstatement of Moncef.[17] Bourguiba, the leading nationalist, was at first wary, but ultimately rallied to the *bey*, perhaps hoping to win support from traditionalist Tunisians for his Néo-Destour movement.

The end of the war did not resolve the situation, as Moncef's defenders continued to demand his rehabilitation, and Amin failed to win public support. A 'Congress of the Night of Destiny' adopted a resolution branding Moncef's deposition a violation of the Bardo treaty and an affront to Islam. Tunisian nationalists also gained endorsement from the new Arab League in Cairo, where Bourguiba lived in voluntary exile. In August 1945, fearful of Moncef's continued presence in North Africa, the French transferred the *bey*, his wife, son and a faithful aide-de-camp to Pau (where Abd el-Kader had been temporarily confined decades earlier).[18]

France was now facing anti-colonial unrest throughout the empire. A riot in the Algerian city of Sétif in May 1945, with the death of French *colons*, had been put down with great bloodshed, which only further stimulated the nationalist movement. The Indochinese War broke out the following year, and in 1947, the French confronted and suppressed an insurrection in Madagascar. A provocative speech by the sultan of Morocco (to be discussed presently) in April of that year emboldened nationalists there. Newly organised trade unions in Tunisia sponsored strikes, and there took place a major confrontation between protesters and French police in Sfax in August. Also in 1947, the French authorised Abd el-Krim to leave Réunion for France, thinking he was resigned to French rule in the Maghreb, but he escaped en route and headed for Egypt, where he was given asylum and became an intractable opponent of French colonialism in North Africa.

After the escape of the Rif leader, Paris tightened restrictions on Moncef. However, seeing in him a more appealing ally than the radical Bourguiba, the French intimated that he might be restored to the throne if he condemned the activities of North African nationalists, and formally agreed to Tunisia joining the new Union Française, an umbrella 'commonwealth' of France and its overseas territories. Moncef refused: 'Even if I spend the rest of my life in a cage, nourishing myself [only] on bread and olives, I will not give in.'[19] Nevertheless, he asserted that, as a true friend of France, he stood ready for negotiations leading to his country's emancipation. Discussions continued, but there was apparently also a half-baked plot by *moncéfistes* for the *bey* to flee Pau in a hired aeroplane, in the dead of night, and return to Tunisia; the *bey* finally declined to take part in a plan that stood little chance of success.

By mid-1948, the French were amenable to Moncef's return to Tunisia, initially as a private citizen, with possible restoration to the throne if Amin could be accommodated. However, the health of the sixty-seven-year-old was rapidly deteriorating, and he died on 1 October 1948. The French allowed burial of his remains, with honours, at the necropolis of the *beys*; large crowds turned out to pay their respects. Amin Bey continued to reign as the nationalist cause under Bourguiba finally secured Tunisian independence in 1956. The following year, Bourguiba proclaimed a republic, brought to an end the rule of King Amin (as he was now titled) and abolished the monarchy. Amin remained in Tunisia under virtual house arrest until his death in 1962.

Moncef's position during the war, like that of many in France itself, had been difficult and his stances contingent on the circumstances he faced. His political views clearly favoured reform, autonomy and maintenance of the *bey*'s rights. This alienated him from both the

Vichy regime and the Free French – the colonial policy of Vichy and Free France shared many principles, particularly opposition to self-government or independence for the possessions and protectorates. De Gaulle's provisional authorities were happy to be rid of Moncef in 1943, but within several years, he appeared a more acceptable option than Bourguiba as France countered the immense challenges from nationalists in Africa, Madagascar and Indochina, and as it tried to recast its old empire into a new model Union Française. However, France had failed to recognise the potential value of Moncef in time, or much earlier to enact the reforms he proposed, which might have at least defused or delayed some of the nationalist ardour. Moncef's death, like that of the exiled Vietnamese Duy Tan, in whom de Gaulle had placed his hopes, left no one capable of buttressing French rule against the *indépendantistes*. Amin Bey, France's man in Tunis, ultimately paid the price for the inability of the beylical dynasty to bring about a transition from colonial subjection to liberation. The story would be different in France's other North African protectorate.

The fall and rise of the sultan of Morocco

Mohammed V, the eighteen-year-old third son of Sultan Yusef, came to the throne in Morocco in 1927, and initially acceded to the advice and demands of the French Resident-General. In 1939, Mohammed issued a statement of resounding support for France at the start of the Second World War, and the following year lamented that France's defeat affected him as if his own lands had been occupied. He placed Morocco's resources at the disposal of the Free French, and Moroccan soldiers played a valiant role in the liberation of France. In 1943, however, the sultan met with Franklin Roosevelt during an Allied conference in Casablanca, a meeting that disconcerted the French because of the American president's perceived anti-colonial inclinations. De Gaulle also met the sultan and recorded a favourable impression, though the Free French leader suspected that Mohammed was willing to cooperate with any individual or group to further his known objective of self-government. De Gaulle invited the sultan to Paris for the 14 July celebrations in 1945, and made him a Compagnon de la Libération, the highest honour for those who had rendered service against the Axis. Such consideration, the French hoped, would help retain Mohammed's loyalty.[20]

By this time, however, opposition to the French in Morocco had swelled. A National Party critical of foreign overlordship was founded in 1937, and in 1943, metamorphosed into the Istiqlal Party, the name, meaning independence, manifest indication of its programme. Paris promised reforms, but ruled out independence. Although sympathetic to the aims of Istiqlal, Mohammed nevertheless stated, probably at French insistence, that the word 'independence' should disappear from Moroccans' vocabulary. The French arrest of notable Istiqlal leaders in the late 1940s and subsequently – some exiled, others imprisoned – only fuelled Istiqlal's popularity, especially in the cities, though less so in the conservative countryside. Provincial chiefs, who retained great influence, remained opposed to establishment of a more centralised state and to Istiqlal's secularism. In particular, the Berber-backed Pasha of Marrakesh, Thami el-Glaoui, nurtured hereditary antipathy towards the sultans, and benefited from the French *politique des races*. The French considered Berbers the original population of Morocco who had been taken over by Muslim Arabs, and thought them more amenable to French cultural and political influence. An alliance of convenience between the Glaoui and the French developed into a bulwark against both the sultan and Istiqlal.

In April 1947, rioting broke out in Casablanca after a fight between French African soldiers and Moroccans over a woman, an indication of incendiary tensions in the country. In a scheduled speech in Tangier soon afterwards, the sultan spoke pointedly of the proud Arabic and Islamic heritage of Morocco, departing from the text approved in advance by the French, and leaving out the expected obsequious references to the good work France was accomplishing. The French took the omission as an insult, and in May they ominously replaced a conciliatory Resident-General with a hard-line one, General Alphonse Juin, the man who had deposed the *bey* in Tunisia only a few years before. The scenario in Morocco would unfold with many similarities to the earlier saga in Tunisia.

Already the French were considering the future of the sultan, and instructions from Paris to Juin noted that if the palace raised obstacles to his policy, 'either a voluntary abdication, or a deposition provoked by the French authority itself' could be envisaged. The sultan was to be apprised of this eventuality.[21] Relations between Mohammed and Juin began coldly. Juin spoke weighted words about 'co-sovereignty' and reform, while Mohammed talked about democracy and repeal of the treaty that established the protectorate. Then the sultan began to decline to affix his seal to certain French-devised decrees. Relations grew so hostile by 1950 that, according to Anthony Clayton, Juin was 'increasingly convinced that the deposition of the Sultan was inevitable'.[22] After the sultan, on a visit to Paris that year, expressly called for repeal of the 1912 protectorate treaty, Juin allied more closely with the Glaoui. The Glaoui lambasted Mohammed in person in December: 'You are no longer the sultan of Morocco, you are the sultan of the Communist and atheist Istiqlal' – a comment that got him banished from the sultan's palace.[23] Clashes continued, as when Juin ordered two members of the government council to leave a meeting after criticism of the French; the men immediately went to the palace, where the sultan's reception of them provoked Juin's ire. When the sultan refused Juin's demand that he disavow Istiqlal, Juin threatened to depose him. Indeed, if the sultan had not under duress signed a reform protocol presented by Juin, or if Paris had given Juin the go-ahead, the sultan may well have lost his throne in 1951. President Vincent Auriol, however, opposed such action and disapproved of Juin's aggressive approach.

Juin, in the event, was replaced as Resident (and consoled by elevation to the dignity of Marshal of France), though he continued to wield great influence behind the scenes in Paris and in Morocco, where administrators who shared his views still occupied key positions. Nationalist unrest had not abated, however, and reached new heights in December 1952, when a hundred people were killed in a riot; the French responded with renewed arrests of Istiqlal and trades union members. The nationalists' opponents placed blame for the situation on the sultan, perceiving him as leagued with anti-colonialists. In March 1953, the Glaoui, while touring the country, openly called for the sultan's deposition, his views applauded by *colons*. Opinion in Paris, even among ministers, remained divided; one minister, the future president François Mitterrand, resigned from the government because of its North African policy, astutely predicting that even if the sultan were removed, he would continue to personify Moroccan dynastic traditions and nationalist aspirations to the detriment of France.

With further violence and another provocative speech by Mohammed, the pendulum was nevertheless swinging against him. The Glaoui convened his allies among the regional chiefs, and the assembly passed a resolution calling for the sultan to leave the throne. Despite lobbying by Juin, the Glaoui and *colons*, the government still hesitated to move, with Paris hoping the sultan could be persuaded to relinquish most of his remaining powers and remain as a figurehead. A new Resident-General, Auguste Guillaume, warned Mohammed about the possibility of deposition, but also tried to calm the Glaoui. Yet in August, the Glaoui and his supporters withdrew recognition of the sultan as spiritual leader of Morocco, an unparalleled attack on the Commander of the Faithful. Riots soon broke out, and the French again held the sultan responsible for the unrest. Meetings between Mohammed and Guillaume produced no compromise, as the sultan still refused to condemn Istiqlal. Finally on 20 August, after heated debate, the *conseil des ministres* in Paris agreed to the sultan's removal.

BANISHED POTENTATES

In Rabat, Guillaume – in a replay of the dethroning of Moncef – took an escort of machine-gun-armed soldiers to the sultan's palace, arriving just after lunch and interrupting his siesta. Summoning Mohammed, the Resident-General told him: 'The French government, for reasons of security, requests you to abdicate. If you do it of your free will, you and your family will be able to live in France, and be very well treated (*hautement considéré*).' The sultan refused: 'Nothing in my actions or words would justify abandoning the duties which have been legitimately vested in me. If the French government considers the defence of liberty and of the ordinary people a crime that merits punishment, I hold this defence as a virtue worthy of honour and glory.' Guillaume retorted: 'If you do not abdicate immediately of your free will, I have been charged with removing you from the country so that public order can be maintained.' Then Mohammed: 'I am the legitimate sovereign of Morocco. Never will I betray the mission with which my trusting and faithful people have assigned me.'[24] Guillaume thereupon declared that Mohammed and his two sons would be deported, and at gunpoint, they were marched to a waiting car and on to the airport, bound for an unrevealed destination. The aeroplane landed in Corsica, where the sultan and princes were sent to a dilapidated hotel in the village of Zonza. The sultan protested, and his party, which now included further family members, was shifted to a more agreeable but remote hotel in Ile Rousse, where they spent several months, courteously treated but kept under close guard, and billed a large sum per day for their detention.

In Morocco, the Glaoui and his supporters, even before Mohammed's forced departure, had recognised Mohammed Ben Arafa, an aged cousin of the sultan, as spiritual leader, and the French proclaimed him the new sultan. Arafa enjoyed no real popularity, and political conditions worsened further, marked by attempts to assassinate the newly installed sultan and the French Resident. In another echo of the deposition of Moncef, the French feared that Corsica was perilously close to Morocco should Mohammed try to escape, and determined to send him further away; after mooting Tahiti and New Caledonia, they chose Madagascar.

The sultan and his entourage were settled into a wing of the grand Hôtel des Thermes in the colonial spa town of Antsirabé, the sultan charged 80,000 francs a day for lodging, maintenance and food. (The Hôtel Crillon in Paris sent cooks and waiters, in appreciation for the sultan's patronage of that luxurious institution.) The sultan promised to refrain from political activity or intervention in Moroccan affairs from afar, though he again refused to abdicate. Mohammed, his wives and concubines, two sons and a daughter born soon after his arrival – among an entourage of more than thirty – lived at the hotel for twenty-one months. Security services kept the sultan and princes under close surveillance, but left them relatively free in their daily lives. The sultan worshipped at the local mosque, sat in cafés reading newspapers, traded at local shops for presents for his infant daughter, and became a familiar sight, clad in a djellaba, walking around the marketplace. His sons – aged seventeen and twenty-five – played tennis and football, went hunting and frequented nightclubs and restaurants, reputedly enjoying liaisons with several young ladies. Occasional incidents occurred, as when a fight broke out at a club after a patron took offense at the princes' flirtations. Otherwise, the sultan's family lived as contentedly as possible. Local newspapers paid little attention to the North African royals, though the Moroccan nationalist press published occasional articles critical of the sultan's treatment.[25]

Mohammed maintained contact, directly and through intermediaries, with the Istiqlal Party at home, where the situation was becoming dire. His banishment and the installation of Arafa, rather than quelling discontent, had aggravated unrest and stoked anti-colonialism. Armed attacks, explosions and arson took place with increasing frequency, and with several hundred killed after Mohammed's exile. The colonial government reacted with torture of suspects, widened arrests and collective punishments of villages. In Paris, the government, in the final throes of the disastrous war in Indochina, spared relatively little time for Morocco until after the final defeat at Dien Bien Phu in early 1954; it was then confronted with the start of the war in Algeria. In any case, the revolving-door ministries of the Fourth Republic reflected lack of a coherent approach to Moroccan affairs other than continued opposition to Mohammed's return.

Only gradually did the French acknowledge that there could be no solution to the Moroccan problem that did not include or at least gain the approbation of Mohammed. The government began overtures to the exiled sultan, sometimes through the good offices of his doctor and lawyer, and then more officially through a military officer, but persistently refused the sultan's request to come to France for discussions.[26] In 1955, the French made the rather extraordinary suggestion that a new sultan – neither Mohammed nor Arafa – be established on the throne. Mohammed rejected the idea, but agreed to a regency council in place of Arafa, pending resolution of his status. The French, however, by happenstance in the midst of yet another domestic crisis, now had to confront Arafa's reluctance to give up his position. Finally, the Glaoui, the major power-broker and heretofore a firm French ally, decided his interests would be better served by ending opposition to Mohammed. He agreed formally to submit to the sultan's authority, thus defusing the campaign against return of the exile among regional leaders and Berbers.

Thanks largely to Mohammed's intransigence, and with the turn of the Glaoui, the French finally accepted that the sultan must be restored. He was flown to Paris, after being accorded full military honours on his departure from Madagascar, a change from his unsaluted arrival. (The Moroccans' ten tonnes of luggage followed in a second plane.) At a chateau outside Paris, Mohammed met with the president, a procession of ministers, and his nemesis, the Glaoui, who famously prostrated himself before the sultan. On 16 November 1955, after twenty-seven months in exile, Mohammed made a triumphal return to Morocco and his throne. In a speech two days later, he announced that Morocco would become independent the following year, a statement ecstatically welcomed by compatriots. In 1956, Morocco duly regained independence and the sultan took the title of King Mohammed V.

The French strategy in Morocco had proved an absolute failure. They had been unable to seduce the sultan away from his nationalist sympathies, and then failed to secure his abdication. Arafa, who replaced him, proved dramatically incapable of convincing the population of his legitimacy. The French had misjudged Mohammed's resolve and underestimated his popularity; they had incautiously cast their lots with the Glaoui and wrongly dismissed Istiqlal as a minority movement sometimes branded a band of terrorists. According to a contemporary diplomat, officials in Rabat, behind-the-scenes operators in Paris, and the Glaoui's faction had intentionally conspired against the sultan in a 'Machiavellian' manner as a 'camarilla of plotters'.[27] In removing the sovereign without consultation with the *makhzen*, the sultan's government, they contravened the 1912 treaty. The Glaoui's withdrawal of recognition of the sultan as spiritual leader was irregular without endorsement from Muslim elders (and provoked a *fatwa* against the Glaoui by the rector of Cairo's Al-Azhar University). The spiriting away of the sultan and his sons amounted to no less than kidnapping. His removal sparked militancy among anti-colonialists in France, where the distinguished novelist François Mauriac chaired a support committee. Mohammed's banishment greatly enhanced his reputation among nationalists, and among promoters of decolonisation in France and internationally in general, and it underlined the sultan's place as the keystone in Moroccan politics.

The Alaouite dynasty was indeed greatly buttressed by Mohammed V's efforts in favour of independence and his leadership after 1956. His son, Hassan, who had served a political apprenticeship as Mohammed's spokesman in exile, succeeded him as king in 1961. Under Mohammed V's grandson, Mohammed VI, the present king, Morocco survived the

'Arab spring' of 2010-12 without the convulsions felt elsewhere in North Africa. Despite the bitter conflicts of the mid-1950s, France and Morocco have remained fast friends politically and commercially since independence (though with criticism by some of neo-colonialism and a too cosy relationship), particularly strong links developing between its sovereigns and French presidents. On one visit to Paris, Mohammed VI took part in the naming by the Paris city government of the square outside the Institut du Monde Arabe as the 'Place Mohammed V'.

As for Arafa, he was convinced by the French (in return for a considerable payout) to leave Rabat in October 1955 for Tangier, still an international city – and a tried and true destination for ex-sultans – where he formally abdicated. After Morocco resumed administration of Tangier the following year, Arafa moved to Nice, later living for a time to Beirut, but returning to France after his house in Lebanon was burgled (and the royal seal he had taken into exile was stolen). He died in 1976, and his coffin was kept for two years in the Paris mosque until King Hassan agreed to a discreet burial of his remains in an ordinary grave in Fez.

From colonialism to decolonisation

The French imperium in North Africa, from the defeat of Abd el-Kader to the banishment of Mohammed V, was marked by the exile of opponents, both ordinary men (such as Bourguiba, among many others) and royals, including Moncef Bey from Tunisia and, in varying circumstances, no fewer than four sultans of Morocco. There were remarkable parallels with the British empire. Mohammed V's triumphal return to Morocco coincided with the return of Kabaka Mutesa II in Uganda – Mutesa arrived home on 17 October 1955 and Mohammed on 16 November. The coincidence showed the enduring use of deposition and exile as a strategy by the French and the British to maintain suzerainty over protectorates, but also the ultimate failure of that strategy and acceptance of restoration of dethroned rulers. Ouster and banishment had looked good ways of dispensing with resistant leaders, in the mid-twentieth century just as in the early 1800s, but times had changed. Nationalist movements were stronger, much better organised and much more adept at recruiting support from the elite and masses. Citizens and subjects were more politicised and ready to be mobilised. Ministers and others in the public arena in the metropoles were more divided about arbitrary colonial measures than they had usually been decades before. In the post-Second World War period, the incrimination of the racialist foundations of colonial expansion in the wake of Nazi atrocities, international commitments to human rights, the anti-colonialism (in principle) of the Soviet Union and the United States, and the spread of ideologies of liberation had altered colonial situations. The colonial powers tried to remake their empires in the forms of the British Commonwealth and the Union Française, offering greater investments and grand development projects, and promising devolution of political power (in the case of the British) and expanded representation in Parliament (for the French). Nationalists, however, as had been dramatically proved to the British in India and the French in Vietnam, and as the French in the 1950s were refusing to accept in Algeria, were no longer content with such measures. For many, independence, not reform or self-government, was increasingly becoming the goal. The exile of Mutesa and Mohammed had been a latter-day reprise of a veteran colonial tactic, but if it had sometimes – although only on occasion – worked in the past to 'pacify' an overseas outpost, the strategy could no longer do so.

Notes

1 On the the exile of the *dey*, see Victor Dermontès, 'Trois ans d'exil, trois ans d'intrigues: le Dey Hussein en Italie', *Bulletin de la Société de géographie d'Alger*, 9:1 (1905), 120–43, and Gustave Gautherot, *La Conquête d'Alger 1830* (Paris: Payot, 1929), as well as the novelised K. Bouguerre, *La Première Mort de Hussein-Dey* (n.p.: En.A.P. Editions, 1990). The ironic parallel of the exile of Hussein Dey and of the French king, Charles X, just after the conquest of Algiers, is nicely encapsulated in an anonymous satirical poem, 'Hussein-Dey, ex-dey d'Alger, à Charles X, ex-roi de France': 'Charles, Christian dog, what comic misfortune, after having ravished my African kingdom, sees you repulsed by your incensed people, and constrained by force to quit your capital? ... I am revenged, Capet: in good faith, I pardon you'. (Bibliothèque nationale de France YE06252.)
2 Jacques Frémeaux, *La Conquête de l'Algérie: la dernière campagne d'Abd el-Kader* (Paris: CNRS Éditions, 2016).
3 Abd el-Kader, *Lettre aux Français*, trans. René Khawam (Paris: Phébus, 2007).
4 John W. Kiser, *Commander of the Faithful: The Life and Times of Emir Abd el-Kader* (Rhinebeck: Monkfish, 2008); and Bruno Étienne, *Abdelkader* (Paris: Hachette, 1994). On the Algerians' exile in the Loire Valley, Amel Chaouati, *Les Algériennes du château d'Amboise: la suite de l'émir Abd el-Kader* (Ciboure: La Cheminante, 2013). There is also a novel by Martine Le Coz, *Le Jardin d'Orient* (Paris: Michalon, 2008). For present-day views, see Musée de l'Histoire de France, *Un Héros des deux rives, Abd el-Kader, l'homme et sa légende* (Paris: Archives nationales, 2003), the catalogue of an exhibition.
5 Jean-François Martin, *Histoire de la Tunisie contemporaine: De Ferry à Bourguiba, 1881–1956* (Paris: L'Harmattan, 1993); and Mary Dewhurst Lewis, *Divided Rule: Sovereignty and Empire in French Tunisia, 1881–1938* (Berkeley: University of California Press, 2014).
6 C. R. Pennell, *Morocco since 1830: A History* (New York: New York University Press, 2000); Daniel Rivet, *Lyautey et l'institution du protectorat français au Maroc, 1912–1925* (Paris: L'Harmattan, 3 vols, 1996). See also a work on a key player at the time of the establishment of the protectorate: Hamza Ben Driss Ottmani, *Kaddour Benghabrit: un Maghrébin hors du commun* (Rabat: MARSAM, 2011).
7 Walter B. Harris, *Morocco That Was* (Edinburgh: William Blackwood, 1921), p. 122.

FROM CONQUEST TO DECOLONISATION

8   Harris, *Morocco That Was*, p. 124.
9   See Barnett Singer and John Langdon, *Cultured Force: Makers and Defenders of the French Colonial Empire* (Madison: University of Wisconsin Press, 2004), Ch. 5.
10 David S. Woolman, *Rebels in the Rif: Abd El Krim and the Rif Rebellion* (Stanford: Stanford University Press, 1968); Zakya Daoud, *Abdelkrim: Une épopée d'or et de sang* (Paris: Séguier, 1999); Thierry Malbert, *L'Exil d'Abdelkrim El Khattabi à La Réunion 1926–1947* (Saint-Denis: Orphie, 2016).
11 Eric Jennings, *Vichy in the Tropics: Pétain's National Revolution in Madagascar, Guadeloupe and Indochina, 1940–1944* (Stanford: Stanford University Press, 2001); Martin Thomas, *The French Empire at War, 1940–1945* (Manchester: Manchester University Press, 2007).
12 The following account largely follows Said Mestiri, *Moncef Bey, Tome 1: le règne* (Tunis: Arc Éditions, rev. edn, 1998), and *Moncef Bey, Tome 2: chronique des années d'exil* (Tunis: Arc Éditions, 1990); Mestiri, a medical doctor and historian, was related to the *bey*'s minister M'hamed Chenik.
13 Mestiri, *Moncef Bey*, Vol. 1, p. 63.
14 Quoted in Mestiri, *Moncef Bey*, Vol. 1, p. 232.
15 Quoted in Mestiri, *Moncef Bey*, Vol. 1, p. 229.
16 Martin, *Histoire de la Tunisie contemporaine*, p. 151.
17 Juliette Bessis, 'Sur Moncef Bey et le moncéfisme: La Tunisie de 1942 à 1948', *Revue française d'histoire d'Outre-Mer*, 70:260–1 (1983), 97–131.
18 Mestiri, *Moncef Bey*, Vol. 2.
19 Quoted in Mestiri, *Moncef Bey*, Vol. 1, p. 269.
20 My account is based on Rivet, *Lyautey et l'institution du protectorat français au Maroc*; Pennell, *Morocco since 1830*; Jean Lacouture, *Cinq hommes et la France* (Paris: Seuil, 1961), pp. 181–263; Guy Delanoë, *Lyautey, Juin, Mohammed V: Fin d'un protectorat – mémoires historiques* (Paris: L'Harmattan, 1988); the memoirs of the sultan's doctor, Henri Dubois-Roquebert, *Mohammed V, Hassan II, tels que je les ai connus* (Casablanca: Tarik, 2003); and Anthony Clayton, 'Emergency in Morocco, 1950–56', in Robert Holland (ed.), *Emergencies and Disorder in the European Empires* (London: Routledge, 1994), pp. 129–47. There is also a historically firmly grounded novel about Mohammed's exile by François Salvaing, *818 Jours* (Paris: Éditions du Sirocco, 2014).
21 Quoted in Delanoë, *Lyautey, Juin, Mohammed V*, p. 205.
22 Clayton, 'Emergency in Morocco', p. 134.
23 Quoted in Delanoë, *Lyautey, Juin, Mohammed V*, p. 211.
24 Delanoë, *Lyautey, Juin, Mohammed V*, pp. 170–8 (quotation, p. 178); the scene is also recounted by the future King Hassan in his memoirs.
25 Frédéric Garan, 'Un Sultan à Madagascar', *Expressions*, 33 (2009), 59–117.
26 Henri Dubois-Roquebert, *Mohammed V, Hassan II*, provides a sympathetic portrait of the sultan, who told Dubois-Roquebert that he would never be content to be a puppet of the French. The doctor, not surprisingly, is highly critical of Guillaume and Juin.
27 Delanoë cites a 1953 report written by Léon Marchal, director of the 'Africa-Levant' section of the Ministry of Foreign Affairs tracing the development of plans to depose the sultan from 1947 onwards, instigated in particular by Juin.

Conclusion

The ouster of monarchs continued after colonies obtained independence, though now by successor regimes rather than colonial governments.[1] Among those forced off their thrones in ex-colonies, in addition to King Mutesa in Uganda, were the kings of Egypt, Tunisia, Iraq, Libya and Laos.[2] Afghanistan and Iran were among other countries that ousted their monarchs. The princely states of South Asia were incorporated into India and Pakistan in the late 1940s, though not always with the enthusiasm of the maharajas; in 1971, the Indian prime minister, Indira Gandhi, did away with their privy purses and withdrew recognition of their princely titles. The chogyal, traditional ruler of Sikkim, had kept his crown under the British, but lost it and fled his country in 1975 when India assimilated the Himalayan state.[3] The Republic of Indonesia removed the privileges of the sultans and rajas when it gained independence from the Dutch in the 1940s, though allowing the sultan of Yogyakarta, who had supported the independence movement, to keep his position; he now also serves as hereditary provincial governor. Only after a *coup d'état* in Burma in 1962 were the rights of the Shan princes, which had been preserved under the British after the overthrow of King Thibaw and in the early years of independence, abolished by the new military dictators. A special case of deposition occurred after the Chinese invasion of Tibet in 1959 and the flight of the Fourteenth Dalai Lama from Lhasa to refuge in the Indian city of Dharamsala.[4] In the 1970s, a revolution overthrew Emperor Haile Selassie, who had earlier returned to the throne of Ethiopia after fleeing Italian colonisation in the 1930s. The most recent sovereign to be toppled was the king of Nepal in 2008. The newly deposed Asians and Africans joined European ex-sovereigns, though since the late 1940s the Greek king has been the only European monarch to lose his crown, and indeed the throne of Spain was restored in 1975. The global cohort of monarchs has shrunk markedly since the heyday of royalty a century ago.

CONCLUSION

The circumstances of latter-day removals and those of the colonial era, of course, differ greatly. However, there are parallels concerning regime change and the eviction of compromised rulers – including, in Africa and Asia, several tainted by association with colonial masters – as well as rhetoric about replacement of bad government with good government, and destruction of 'feudal' orders. Similarities also manifest themselves in the lived experiences of European and non-European, colonial and post-independence sovereigns in voluntary exile or forced banishment: concerns about finances and status, debates over their deeds and misdeeds, occasional though vain efforts to regain crowns, and the question of their place in historical narrative and collective memory. To what extent were they impotent potentates?

The history of deposed royal rulers in the colonies, just like that of later exiles, has a dramatic, even cinematic quality. Before their downfall, one pictures Njoya Ibrahim inventing a new alphabet and syncretic religion, Jaja of Opobo promoting palm oil trade, Samory Touré building an empire, Oba Ovonramwen ensconced in a palace decorated with brass plaques reflecting his majesty and also depicting the exotic Europeans who came to his court. When rulers crossed the colonisers, the scene cuts to a frightened Sri Vikrama Rajasinha dragged out of a hut and bound with vines, King Thibaw and Queen Supayalat conveyed out of the royal palace in Mandalay past ranks of kowtowing Burmese subjects and British soldiers standing to attention, and Prempeh and Béhanzin surrendering with dignity. Then there is the journey into exile, with tearful Ranavalona carried on a palanquin through the jungles of Madagascar, the king of Kandy on board the *Cornwallis* and the oba of Benin on the *Ivy*, kept under watch by guards and curious members of the crew. There is a poignancy to images of rulers during their years in exile, the last Mughal emperor on his deathbed in Rangoon and Dinuzulu biding his time in chilly St Helena, and drama in pictures of Duleep Singh and his redoubtable children engaging in their various pursuits around Europe. In Calcutta, the king of Oudh presides over his court-in-exile, Ham Nghi reads and paints in Algiers, Duy Tan tinkers with radios in Saint-Denis. The maharaja of Coorg, King Cetshwayo and Sultan Said Ali in metropolitan capitals struggle to gain redress for their grievances, and Queen Salima Machamba busies herself with housework in provincial France.

The colourful and often melancholy situations of the deposed rulers, however, should not be overly romanticised. Many sovereigns had dramatically used, and abused, the considerable powers vested in them. They claimed god-given privileges, and sometimes enjoyed the status of demi-gods. They exacted onerous taxes and harsh forced labour, and reinforced hierarchies and privileges that kept many of their subjects in poverty. They lorded it over their people from ornate palaces and strongly defended citadels, expending much effort to gain or retain power for themselves and their heirs. Monarchs tried to extend their domains by the conquest of neighbouring countries, the exploitation of their resources and sometimes the enslavement of their populations. Like all political figures, they hard-headedly and often deftly negotiated and manoeuvred for best advantage, not forgoing violence in contests against compatriots and foreigners. Some committed heinous acts, both in their political dealings and in their private lives.

The Europeans who deposed Africans and Asians were rapacious invaders and occupiers, with capacities for violence in conquest and rule at least equal to their victims, and with long traditions of arbitrary governance that were unashamedly transposed to the colonies even after they had been challenged at home. They made it clear that 'protected' rulers left in place were vassals, enjoined to obedience and obeisance to the paramount colonial masters, and left on the throne at the sufferance of the foreigners. They could be installed and supported, or rejected and removed by the colonisers. Even when Europeans ostentatiously addressed those they dethroned with deference and attended solicitously to their needs, the colonisers had reduced the ousted monarchs to captives, prisoners of war or political prisoners, wards of the state whose fate depended on decisions taken in London or Paris.

The removal of the native sovereigns, even ones of dubious character and doubtful local allegiance, represented an intentional and occasionally premeditated attack on indigenous institutions and cultures. Protectorate treaties and decrees of annexation promised protection for Buddhism, Islam and other religions, respect for local customs, and in many cases recognition of the rights of pre-colonial elites. However, one of the historical hallmarks of monarchical systems is the near inextricable interlinking of the crown with other domains of public life: the monarch as religious figure, law-giver and ultimate judge, military commander, commissioner of public works and patron of artists. The removal of a sovereign, and even more the abolition of a dynasty, thus knocked out the capstone in a country's or a people's culture. That culture could be maintained and rebuilt, as the resilience of colonial societies showed, but the effects of the change were also evident and, in places, disastrous. So, too, was the opening it provided for the colonial states, with their own potentates and rituals, to put themselves in the place of the old monarchies.

Some in the colonised societies, of course, had little regard for particular local rulers or whole dynasties. Rivals contested succession to

CONCLUSION

thrones, and cabals intrigued against reigning or potential monarchs and chiefs. Minority or peripheral ethnic or religious groups chafed at the imperialism of dominant elites and regimes, before and after the arrival of the Europeans. Those favouring rapid modernisation regarded veteran dynasties as relics of the past, exemplars of feudalism and obstacles to change. Some accommodated colonial regimes well, taking advantage of new opportunities offered in administration and business, seeking out European education and employment, wearing European fashions and adopting aspects of European lifestyle, sporting the insignia of knighthoods and the Legion of Honour. Meanwhile, nationalists increasingly (though not everywhere) espoused republicanism, rather than monarchism, as the principle of governance once independence was regained. Europeans themselves, after all, showed growing doubts about monarchy, both at home – as seen, in particular, by the overthrow of the Bourbon, Orleanist and Bonapartist dynasties in France – and in regards to foreign monarchies that came under their 'protection'.

Nevertheless, from the revolutionary decades that saw the deposition of Napoleon and Sri Vikrama Rajasinha on opposite sides of the globe down to the years of decolonisation that witnessed the removal and restoration of the sultan of Morocco and the king of Buganda, monarchism endured. It is worthwhile recalling that some of the first significant movements of national resistance, such as the Can Vuong movement in Vietnam (and the efforts of figures such as Prince Cuong De and Phan Chu Trinh) and the *menalamba* insurrection in Madagascar, summoned supporters to rally round the monarchy and restore the powers of the throne usurped by foreigners. Nationalists later demanded the release and reinstatement of the Ashanti and Zulu kings, and several other exiles. Renegade members of royal families promoted themselves as candidates for thrones, and pretenders with few if any familial claims to crowns continued to pose as would-be kings, from Ehelepola in post-conquest Ceylon (and a succession of rebels over the next thirty-odd years) to Saya San in 1930s Burma. The doctrine that had allowed the East India Company to annex states with empty thrones before 1857 was thereafter abjured by the British government. Queen Victoria's sympathy for reigning monarchs, the dethroned and their kin was manifest in her private writings and her public interventions, seen in the cases of Duleep Singh and his family, the maharaja of Coorg and his daughter, the orphaned son of the emperor of Ethiopia and rebellious ruler of Manipur whose execution she cautioned would be unseemly. For the British, monarchy was the natural order of things, so long as Indian maharajas, Shan princes and Malay sultans recognised the paramountcy of the British Crown. Even in republican France, colonial leaders such as Marshal Lyautey and Governor-General Paul Doumer were sympathetic to the idea of monarchy and to the men who reigned under their proconsulship, and colonisers saw the benefits of keeping kings on thrones, though under their control. The potential re-enthronement of Duy Tan in Vietnam in 1945 and the actual return of Sultan Mohammed to Morocco a decade later are reminders of the persistence of belief in monarchy in the colonial world, even when colonialism and monarchism had both come under attack.

Clashes between colonisers and kings, perhaps inevitably, erupted with regularity, and the strategy of ousting a monarch (and sometimes ending a dynasty) was ever an option to be deployed: in Ceylon in 1815 and Burma in 1885, in the removal of fathers and sons who reigned as Zulu kings and maharajas of Indore, and in the treatment of successive sultans of Morocco. At several moments, the tactics essayed seemed almost to be taken from a manual: luring an African chieftain on board a European ship and whisking him to exile, blackening the reputation of a monarch so dark that his removal seemed a legitimate defence of the martyred subjects, promising emoluments to a ruler who agreed to go quietly or overturning the verdict of a trial that unexpectedly found against the expectations of the colonisers. And the rulebook by the nineteenth century stated that, except in the case of a death on the battlefield, a troublesome monarch could not be executed. A crowned head might be chastised, denied courtesies and emoluments, stripped of powers, ousted from the throne and deposed, but not sent to the scaffold or the guillotine.

Deposition might occur at the outset of conquest, as part of the consolidation of imperial territories or as a later response to resistance or perceived misbehaviour. Often it was a last resort, after attempts to seduce or coerce a monarch into cooperation had proved unsuccessful, or after efforts to discipline and reform a disobedient or wayward monarch had failed. The final moves were sometimes precipitated by particular incidents (such as insurrections or alleged plots to poison Europeans) but could also represent the building-up, over years and decades, of designs for colonial expansion or of tensions between Europeans and indigenous 'protected' rulers in countries the Europeans had already occupied. The role of individuals – Gallieni and Shepstone, and many subalterns, as well as adventurers such as Humblot – was decisive, their initiatives enthusiastically or resignedly approved by superiors in Paris or London. Deposition and exile were nonetheless often arbitrary, even metropolitan commentators critical of the lack of due process, fair trials and right of appeal. Those driven from their thrones served out their exile 'at the king's pleasure', their release,

CONCLUSION

repatriation and eventual restoration as seemingly arbitrary as their removal had been.

A few deposed maharajas enjoyed the pleasures of gilded exile in European cities. Other exiles consoled themselves in relative comfort in their new abodes elsewhere, their families, religions, traditions and avocations providing consolation. Many defeated rulers lived in conditions materially superior to those of their countrymen and the populations among whom they were confined in St Helena and the Seychelles, Algeria and Réunion. They collected pensions, resided in roomy houses, accepted gestures of courtesy, and had direct access to viceregal officials in ways unavailable to commoners. Most had champions at home and in Europe who continued to press cases for compensation, repatriation or restoration. Their *ci-devant* status accorded a degree of celebrity, with attention (though not always laudatory) from royal-watchers and journalists. Among the crowds of political exiles, the ex-monarchs' situation was exceptional, in large part because of their royal status, one that both British monarchists and French republicans still allowed their prisoners.

By the end of the colonial period, in many countries around the globe, monarchism – kingship, in one form or another, is arguably the oldest and most widespread form of the state – had lost its old potency, though it has not disappeared. By the late twentieth century, ten monarchs in Europe survived, though as the hallowed expression goes, they reigned rather than ruled. Elsewhere, and with greatly differing prerogatives, there is still in Asia an emperor in Japan, kings in Thailand, Cambodia and Bhutan, a reigning sultan in Brunei and a hereditary sultan elected as head of state in Malaysia. There are kings in Morocco, Lesotho and Swaziland in Africa; in the Middle East there are the kingdoms of Jordan, Saudi Arabia and Bahrain, and the other emirates and sultanates of the Gulf.[5] Countless pre-colonial polities, ruled over by what Europeans derogatorily termed 'kinglets' (*roitelets*), however, were incorporated into independent states whose boundaries were largely drawn by the colonisers, with democracy sometimes honoured in the breach in their annexation. Republicanism, and more radical ideologies, meant that few colonies gaining independence opted to restore old dynasties or have kept them down to the present day,[6] though some new hereditary dynasties have also appeared.[7] Morocco, where no fewer that four sultans had suffered exile, provides an exception, as does Cambodia, notwithstanding its convoluted post-colonial history. There is as little likelihood of heirs to the Nguyen dynasty in Vietnam or the Konbaung lineage in Burma regaining their ancestral thrones as there is of French Bourbons, Russian Romanovs or Austrians Habsburgs being restored in Europe.

BANISHED POTENTATES

Colonialism, in Europe and conquered territories, embodied a certain type of statecraft in which the government, frequently of a monarchical sort, of one country imposed overrule on another country, commonly one also governed under hereditary principles. Exceptions existed, of course, in the colonial endeavours of republican France and the United States, and in the continuation of the Portuguese empire long after the overthrow of the kings in Lisbon. Moreover, not every pre-colonial polity in Africa, Asia and Oceania was ruled in monarchical fashion. However, the clash of monarchical systems and what they represented – conquest as a strategy for establishing new governing lineages, the inheritance of the right to rule, the sacred nature of kings, an alliance of 'throne and altar', expectations of subjects' deferential fidelity, the roles and privileges of extended royal families and the court in public life, the spectacle of majesty – formed a key part of the dynamics of many colonial situations, even in the republican French overseas empire. Deposing and banishing sovereigns provided a practical strategy for the conquerors, though it ultimately failed to secure long-lasting pacification: the French imperium in Annam lasted about seventy years, the protectorate over Morocco only forty-odd years. European monarchs still reign over a few distant domains, but these are but the remnants of once great colonial empires.[8]

For decades under European rule, as their successors manoeuvred around colonial overlords, deposed and exiled native monarchs lived on, several for forty or fifty years, a few until after the independence of their countries.[9] They reminded compatriots of foreign occupation, and cautioned colonisers about the strength of indigenous resistance. Some waited in reserve, hoping to be restored, their return to power occasionally envisaged or, rarely, decreed by imperial authorities. Their heirs persisted over generations, with diminishing vigour, to advance claims to succession or compensation. Roving journalists from time to time still discover descendants guarding the flame of their patrimony, sighing in resentment or resignation at the loss of ancestral thrones, quarrelling with rival pretenders, trying to maintain an appropriate standard of living or sometimes living in outright penury.

In the former colonies, the legacies of deposed monarchs and abolished dynasties endure. In Vietnam 'patriotic kings' are enshrined in the national pantheon. African rulers who resisted Europeans are heralded as heroes and monumentalised in bronze and stone statues. Post-independence governments have tried to channel the glory of ancient kings in Sri Lanka and Myanmar. Sub-national monarchs such as the Ashanti king and the oba of Benin still wield influence and enjoy respect, and traditional rulers such as the Zulu king have gained formal recognition in South Africa's post-apartheid constitution. In

CONCLUSION

India, scions of maharajas hold positions of prominence in government and society, and faithfully serve as custodians of princely lines. Their splendid palaces attract tourists, as do the imperial tombs in Hué, the world heritage site in the royal capital of Abomey, and the reconstructed Konbaung compound in Mandalay. Museum collections – the repatriated thrones of the Kandyan king in Colombo and the Burmese king in Rangoon – are treasures of national history and art, while artefacts in overseas collections – the Benin plaques in London, a Malagasy crown in Paris – are mementos of a culture appropriated by the colonisers. By removing monarchs, Europeans might end individual reigns and abolish dynasties, but they could not thereby forever rule colonies. Nor could they efface the power, prestige and spectacle that native rulership embodied or the heritage the sovereigns left behind.

Notes

1 Many non-royal rulers, some of whom had acceded to power under colonial rule or with the support of former colonial masters, also took the path of exile, later to be forced out of office. Critics of 'neo-colonialism' point out that European countries have continued to intervene to prop up, and overthrow, rulers in their former colonies. (Stephen Smith, *Voyage en postcolonie: le nouveau monde franco-africain* (Paris: Grasset, 2010.)
2 On Iraq, see Gerald de Gaury, *Three Kings in Baghdad: The Tragedy of Iraq's Monarchy* (London: I. B. Tauris, 2008 [1961]).
3 Andrew Duff, *Sikkim: Requiem for a Himalayan Kingdom* (Edinburgh: Birlinn, 2015); Sunanda K. Datta-Ray, *Smash and Grab: Annexation of Sikkim* (Chennai: Tranquebar, 2013); and the memoirs of the last chogyal's consort, Hope Cooke, *Time Change: An Autobiography* (New York: Simon & Schuster, 1980).
4 Sam Van Schaik, *Tibet: A History* (New Haven: Yale University Press, 2011). The Thirteenth Dalai Lama was an earlier Tibetan exile. After a British invasion of Tibet, in 1904 he fled to Mongolia; China announced his deposition and asserted sovereignty over Tibet. The Thirteenth Dalai Lama nevertheless lived in China until 1909. He subsequently returned to Tibet, but fled again when Chinese troops invaded in 1910. He then lived for two years in British India. On his final return to Lhasa in 1913, he declared the independence of Tibet. See Charles Bell, *Portrait of a Dalai Lama: The Life and Times of the Great Thirteenth* (New Delhi: Munshiram Manoharlal, 2000 [1946]).
5 Benedict Anderson's research on surviving monarchies was cut short by his untimely death, but is featured in his 2013 lecture on 'Why have monarchies survived in Southeast Asia?', Centre d'études de l'Asie de l'Est, Université de Montréal, 2013, viewable online at www.youtube.com/watch?v=RqjE8dR8wlk, accessed 25 November 2016.
6 There is also the curious history of Jean-Bedel Bokassa, a former officer in the French colonial army who became president of the Central African Republic in 1966; in 1976, he proclaimed himself Emperor Bokassa I and nearly bankrupted his country on an elaborate Napoleonic-style coronation. He was overthrown by French military intervention in 1979, and fled to France, but was tried and sentenced to death *in absentia* in Bangui. Bokassa returned to the Central African Republic in 1986 and was again convicted. After several years in prison, he was freed and died in Bangui. (Geraldine Faes and Stephen Smith, *Bokassa Ier, un empereur français* (Paris: Calmann-Lévy, 2000)).

7 The three generations of Kims who rule North Korea provide a glaring example.
8 Robert Aldrich and John Connell, *France's Overseas Frontier: Départements et Territoires d'Outre-Mer* (Cambridge: Cambridge University Press, 1992), and *The Last Colonies* (Cambridge: Cambridge University Press, 1998). In the French Pacific territory of Wallis and Futuna, three kings still reign.
9 In October 2016 the former King Kigeli V, deported from Rwanda in 1961 after a referendum abolished the monarchy – just before the country gained independence from Belgium – died in exile in the United States. (Sam Roberts, 'Kigeli V, the Last King of Rwanda, Dies at 80', *New York Times*, 21 October 2016.)

BIBLIOGRAPHY

'Letter of George Jones to "Mr. Nolte"', *Institute of Current World Affairs* (15 May 1971), iewa.org/wp-content/uploads/2015/09/Gj-12.pdf.

n.a., The Colonial Prisoners Removal Act, 1869 – 32 & 33 Vic. c. 10. (Imperial) Amended by Statute Law Revision Acts, 1883, 46 & 47 Vic. c. 39 and 1893 (No. 2) 56 & 57 Vic. c. 54 (www.legislation.gov.uk/ukpga/Vict/32–33/10).

n.a., 'Exhibition: Béhanzin: L'exil d'un roi 1894–1906' (brochure), Bibliothèque Schoelcher, Fort-de-France, Martinique, 1995.

n.a., 'La Réunion, Terre d'exil', in Daniel Vaxelaire (ed.), *Le Mémorial De La Réunion* (Saint-Denis: Australe Éditions, 1979), 284–91.

n.a., 'Le Sultan Saïd-Ali contre MM Humblot et Legros, Tribunal Civil de la Seine', *Revue des grands procès contemporains*, 1 October 1912.

n.a., 'The Last King's Jail Cell', www.yamu.lk/place/the-last-kings-jail-cell/review-41889.

n.a., *Recueil des arrêts du Conseil d'État*, 2:81 (1911), 848–9.

n.a., 'Sultan Abdullah's return from the Seychelles, 1894,' Sembang Kuala, 9 June 2009, https://sembangkuala.wordpress.com/2009/06/09/group-showing-sultan-abdullah-in-uniform-after-his-return-from-the-seychelles-with-some-member-of-his-family/.

Abd el-Kader, *Lettre aux Français*, trans. René Khawam (Paris: Phébus, 2007).

Abeyasinghe, Tikiri, 'Princes and Merchants: Relations between the Kings of Kandy and the Dutch East India Company in Sri Lanka, 1688–1740', *Sri Lanka Archives*, 4 (1984), 35–59.

Agence France-Press, 9 November 2013.

Akoha, Albert Bienvenu and Apollinaire Medagbe, *Chants de Béhanzin, le résistant* (Paris: L'Harmattan, 2015).

Alagoa, E. J., *A Chronicle of Grand Bonny* (Ibadan: Ibadan University Press, 1972).

Alagoa, E. J., *Jaja of Opobo: The Slave Who Became a King* (London: Longman, 1970).

Aldrich, Robert, 'Imperial Banishment: French Colonizers and the Exile of Vietnamese Emperors', in Joseph Zizek and Kirsty Carpenter (eds), *French History and Culture: Papers from the George Rudé Seminar*, vol. 5, H-France, 2014, 123–33.

Aldrich, Robert, 'Out of Ceylon: The Exile of the Last King of Kandy', in Ronit Ricci (ed.), *Exile in Colonial Asia: Kings, Convicts, Commemoration* (Honolulu: University of Hawai'i Press, 2016), pp. 48–70.

Aldrich, Robert, 'The Return of the Throne: The Repatriation of the Kandyan Regalia to Ceylon', in Robert Aldrich and Cindy McCreery (eds), *Crowns and Colonies: European Monarchies and Overseas Empires* (Manchester: Manchester University Press, 2016), pp. 139–62.

BIBLIOGRAPHY

Aldrich, Robert and John Connell, *France's Overseas Frontier: Départements et Territoires d'Outre-Mer* (Cambridge: Cambridge University Press, 1992).

Aldrich, Robert and John Connell, *The Last Colonies* (Cambridge: Cambridge University Press, 1998).

Aldrich, Robert and Cindy McCreery (eds), *Crowns and Colonies: European Monarchies and Overseas Empires* (Manchester: Manchester University Press, 2016).

Aldrich, Robert and Cindy McCreery (eds), *Royals on Tour: Politics, Pageantry and Colonialism* (Manchester: Manchester University Press, 2018).

Alexander, Michael and Sushila Anand, *Queen Victoria's Maharajah: Duleep Singh, 1838–93* (London: Weidenfeld & Nicolson, 1980).

Anand, Anita, *Sophia: Princess, Suffragette, Revolutionary* (London: Bloomsbury, 2015).

Anderson, Benedict, 'Why Have Monarchies Survived in Southeast Asia?', Centre d'études de l'Asie de l'Est, l'Université de Montréal, 2013, www.youtube.com/watch?v=RqjE8dR8wlk.

Anderson, Clare, *Subaltern Lives: Biographies of Colonialism in the Indian Ocean World, 1790–1920* (Cambridge: Cambridge University Press, 2012).

d'Andurain, Julie, *La Capture de Samory (1898): l'achèvement de la conquête de l'Afrique de l'Ouest* (Paris: L'Harmattan, 2012).

Appuhamy, A. D., *The Rebels, Outlaws and Enemies to the British* (Colombo: M. D. Gunasena, 1990).

Arasaratnam, S., *Ceylon and the Dutch, 1600–1800* (Aldershot: Ashgate, 1996).

Aronson, Theo, *Queen Victoria and the Bonapartes* (London: Thistle, 2014).

Arris, Michael, *The Raven Crown: The Origins of Buddhist Monarchy in Bhutan* (Chicago: Serindia Publications, 1994).

Arunachalam, Ponnambalam, *Light from the East, being Letters on Gnanam, the Divine Knowledge*, ed. Edward Carpenter (London: Allen & Unwin, 1927).

Asserate, Asfa-Wossen, *King of Kings: The Triumph and Tragedy of Emperor Haile Selassie I of Ethiopia* (London: Haus Publishing, 2015).

Atugoda, Satharathilaka Banda, 'Tomb of King Wickrama Rajasinhe in Vellore – India', http://amazinglanka.com/wp/tomb-of-sri-wickrama-rajasinhe-2/.

Auckland Star, 18 September 1909.

Aung-Thwin, Maitrii, 'Genealogy of a Rebellion Narrative: Law, Ethnology and Culture in Colonial Burma', *Journal of Southeast Asian Studies*, 34:3 (2003), 393–419.

Aung-Thwin, Maitrii, 'Remembering Kings: Archives, Resistance and Memory in Colonial and Postcolonial Burma', in Kenneth Hall and Michael Aung-Thwin (eds), *New Perspectives on the History and Historiography of Southeast Asia: Continuing Explorations* (London: Routledge, 2011), pp. 53–82.

Aung-Thwin, Maitrii, *The Return of the Galon King: History, Law, and Rebellion in Colonial Burma* (Singapore: NUS Press, 2011).

BIBLIOGRAPHY

Aung-Thwin, Michael and Maitrii Aung-Thwin, *A History of Myanmar since Ancient Times: Traditions and Transformations* (London: Reaktion Books, 2012).

Baden-Powell, R. S. S., *The Downfall of Prempeh: A Diary of Life with the Native Levy in Ashanti, 1895–96* (London: Methuen, 1896).

Baikie, William Balfour, *Narrative of an Exploring Voyage up the Rivers Kwóra and Binue – Commonly Known as the Niger and Tsádda – in 1854* (London: John Murray, 1856).

Ballantyne, Tony, 'Maharajah Dalip Singh, Memory, and the Negotiation of Sikh Identity', in *Between Colonialism and Diaspora: Sikh Cultural Formations in an Imperial World* (Durham, NC: Duke University Press, 2006), pp. 86–120.

Ballarin, Marie-Pierre, *Les Reliques royales à Madagascar: source de légitimation et enjeu de pouvoir (XVIIIe-XXe siècles)* (Paris: Karthala, 2000).

Bance, Peter, *The Duleep Singhs: The Photograph Album of Queen Victoria's Maharajah* (Stroud: Sutton, 2004).

Bance, Peter, *Sovereign, Squire and Rebel: Maharajah Duleep Singh and the Heirs of a Lost Kingdom* (London: Coronet House, 2009).

Bandaranayake, Raja C., *Betwixt Isles: The Story of the Kandyan Prisoners in Mauritius* (Colombo: Vijitha Yapa, 2006).

Bandaranayake, Senake and Albert Dharmasiri, *Sri Lankan Painting in the Twentieth Century* (Colombo: The National Trust Sri Lanka, 2009).

Bangash, Yagood Khan, *A Princely Affair: The Accession and Integration of the Princely States of Pakistan, 1947–1955* (Oxford: Oxford University Press, 2015).

Bao Dai, *Le Dragon d'Annam* (Paris: Plon, 1980).

Barley, Nigel, *White Rajah* (London: Little Brown, 2002).

Barraux, Roland, *Ranavalo III: une reine malgache en exil* (Paris: L'Harmattan, 2013).

Barrier, Marie-France, *Ranavalo, dernière reine de Madagascar* (Paris: Éditions Balland, 1996).

Barry, Boubacar, *Le Royaume du Waalo: Le Sénégal avant la conquête* (Paris: Karthala, 1985).

Bavoux, Claude, 'Les Réunionnais de Madagascar de 1880 à 1925' (Dissertation, University of Paris-7, 1997).

Bayley, Christopher and Tim Harper, *Britain's Forgotten Wars* (London: Allen Lane, 2007).

BBC Radio 4, *Alamayu, Great Lives Series*, broadcast 21 December 2012.

Beer, Daniel, *The House of the Dead: Siberian Exile under the Tsars* (London: Allen Lane, 2016).

Bell, Charles, *Portrait of a Dalai Lama: The Life and Times of the Great Thirteenth* (New Delhi: Munshiram Manoharlal, 2000 [1946]).

Belliappa, C. P., *Victoria Gowramma: The Lost Princess of Coorg* (New Delhi: Rupa, 2014).

Bergougniou, Jean-Michel, Rémi Clignet and Philippe David (eds), *'Villages Noirs' et autres visiteurs africains et malgaches en France et en Europe (1870–1940)* (Paris: Karthala, 2001).

BIBLIOGRAPHY

Bessis, Juliette, 'Sur Moncef Bey et le moncéfisme: La Tunisie de 1942 à 1948', *Revue française d'histoire d'Outre-Mer*, 70:260–1 (1983), 97–131.

Binns, C. T., *Dinuzulu: The Death of the House of Shaka* (London: Longmans, 1968).

Binns, C. T., *The Last Zulu King: The Life and Death of Cetshwayo* (London: Longmans, 1963).

Blackburn, Anne M., *Locations of Buddhism: Colonialism and Modernity in Sri Lanka* (Chicago: University of Chicago Press, 2010).

Blackburn, Terence R., *Executions by the Half-Dozen: The Pacification of Burma* (Delhi: APH Publishing Corporation, 2008).

Blackburn, Terence R. (ed.), *Justice for the Raja of Sattara?* (New Delhi: APH Publishing Corporation, 2007).

Bouguerra, K., *La Première mort de Hussein-Dey* (n.p.: En.A.P. Éditions, 1990).

Bourotte, M. B., 'L'Aventure du Roi Ham-Nghi', *Bulletin des Amis du Vieux Hué*, 16:3 (1929), 135–58.

Boyer, Danika, *Sa Majesté Ranavalo III, ma reine* (Paris: Fasquelle, 1946).

Boyle, Richard, 'British Royal Encounters with Sri Lanka', *Explore Sri Lanka*, November 2013, http://exploresrilanka.lk/2013/11/british-royal-encounters-with-sri-lanka/.

Boyle, Richard, 'A Right Royal Tour', *Himal Magazine*, June 2009, http://old.himalmag.com/component/content/article/539-a-right-royal-tour.html.

Briggs, Philip (with Andrew Roberts), *Uganda* (London: Bradt, 2013).

Brocheux, Pierre, 'De L'Empereur Duy Tan au Prince Vinh San: L'histoire peut-elle se répéter?', *Approches Asie*, 10 (1989–90), 1–25.

Brocheux, Pierre, and Daniel Hémery, *Indochina: An Ambiguous Colonization, 1858–1954* (Berkeley: University of California Press, 2009).

Brown, Mervyn, *A History of Madagascar* (London: Damien Tunnacliffe, 1995).

Burton, Antoinette, *The Trouble with Empire: Challenges to Modern British Imperialism* (New York: Oxford University Press, 2015).

C. C., *Anecdotes of Alamayu, the Late King Theodore's Sons* (London: William Hunt and Co., 1869).

Calwell, Robert G., 'Exile as an Institution', *Political Science Quarterly*, 58:2 (1943), 239–62.

Campbell, Gwyn, *An Economic History of Imperial Madagascar, 1750–1895: The Rise and Fall of an Island Empire* (Cambridge: Cambridge University Press, 2005).

Campbell, Gwyn, *David Griffith and the Missionary History of Madagascar* (Leiden: Brill, 2012).

Cannadine, David, *Ornamentalism: How the British Saw Their Empire* (London: Allen Lane/The Penguin Press, 2001).

Capper, John, *The Duke of Edinburgh in Ceylon: A Book of Elephant and Elk Sport* (London: Provost & Co., 1871).

Carey, Peter, *The British in Java, 1811–1816: A Javanese Account* (Oxford: Oxford University Press, 1992).

Carey, Peter, *Destiny: The Life of Prince Diponegoro of Yogyakarta, 1785–1855* (Bern: Peter Lang, 2014).

BIBLIOGRAPHY

Carey, Peter, *The Power of Prophecy: Prince Dipanagara and the End of an Old Order in Java, 1785–1855* (Leiden: KITLV Press, 2007).
Carol, Jean, *Chez Les Hovas: Au Pays Rouge* (Paris: Paul Ollendorff, 1898).
Chaouati, Amel, *Les Algériennes du Château d'Amboise: la suite de l'émir Abd El-Kader* (Ciboure: La Cheminante, 2013).
Chapman, Jessica M., 'Staging Democracy: South Vietnam's 1955 Referendum to Depose Bao Dai', *Diplomatic History*, 30:4 (2006), 671–703.
Chapuis, Oscar, *The Last Emperors of Vietnam: From Tu Duc to Bao Dai* (Westport: Greenwood Press, 2000).
Cheah Boon Kheng, 'Letters from Exile – Correspondence of Sultan Abdullah of Perak from Seychelles and Mauritius, 1877–1891', *Journal of the Malaysian Branch of the Royal Asiatic Society*, 64:1 (1991), 33–74.
Chernock, Arianne, 'Queen Victoria and the "Bloody Mary of Madagascar"', *Victorian Studies*, 55:3 (2013), 425–49.
Choksey, R. D. (ed.), *Raja Pratapsingh of Satara (1818–1839): Select Documents from the Satara Residency Papers, Peshwa Dafter, Poona, and the Elphinstone Papers, India Office Library, London* (Poona: Bharata Itihasa Samshodhaka Mandala, 1970).
Choksey, R. D. (ed.), *Raja Shahji of Satara, 1839–1848* (Poona: self-published, 1974).
Chrétien, Jean-Pierre, *The Great Lakes of Africa: Two Thousand Years of History* (New York: Zone Books, 2003).
Clayton, Anthony, 'Emergency in Morocco, 1950–56', in Robert Holland (ed.), *Emergencies and Disorder in the European Empires* (London: Routledge, 1994), pp. 129–47.
Codrington, H. W. (ed.), *Diary of Mr. John D'Oyly* (New Delhi: Navrang, 1995 [1917]).
Collis, Maurice, *Lords of the Sunset* (Bangkok: AVA, 1996 [1938]).
Colloque international Roi Njoya, *Le Roi Njoya: Créateur de civilisation et précurseur de la renaissance africaine* (Paris: L'Harmattan, 2014).
Conradi, Peter, *The Great Survivors: How Monarchy Made it into the Twenty-First Century* (Richmond: Alma Books, 2012).
Conway, Susan, *The Shan: Culture, Art and Crafts* (Bangkok: River Books, 2006).
Cooke, Hope, *Time Change: An Autobiography* (New York: Simon & Schuster, 1980).
Cookey, Sylvanus, *King Jaja of the Niger Delta: His Life and Times, 1821–1891* (New York: NOK, 1974).
Coomaraswamy, Ananda K., *Mediaeval Sinhalese Art* (New York: Pantheon Books, revised edn, 1956 [1907]).
Rajah of Coorg, *Coorg and Its Rajahs* (London: John Bumpus, 1857).
Copland, I. F. S., 'The Baroda Crisis of 1873–77: A Study in Governmental Rivalry', *Modern Asian Studies*, 2:2 (1968), 97–123.
Copland, Ian, *The British Raj and the Princes: Paramountcy in Western India, 1857–1930* (Bombay: Orient Longman, 1982).
Copland, Ian, *The Princes of India in the Endgame of Empire, 1917–1947* (Cambridge: Cambridge University Press, 1997).

BIBLIOGRAPHY

Cornevin, Robert, 'Alfa Yaya Diallo fût-il un héros national de Guinée ou l'innocente victime d'un règlement de comptes entre gouverneurs?', *Revue française d'histoire d'outre-mer*, 57:208 (1970), 288–96.

Courtaigne, Noël, 'La presse sur les traces de la Reine Ranavalo', leonc.fr/histoire/ranavalo/index.html.

Cox, Edward L., *Rekindling the Ancestral Memory: King Jaja of Opobo in St Vincent and Barbados, 1888–1891* (Cave Hill: University of the West Indies and the Barbados Museum and Historical Society, 1998).

Croucher, Sarah K., *Capitalism and Cloves: An Archaeology of Plantation Life in Nineteenth-Century Zanzibar* (New York: Springer-Verlag, 2015).

Dabat, Amandine, 'Ham Nghi (1871–1944): Empereur en exil, artiste à Alger' (PhD dissertation, Université Paris-Sorbonne, 2015).

Dabat, Amandine, 'Ham Nghi artiste: Le peintre et le sculpteur,' *Magazine Good Morning*, August 2012, http://aejjrsite.free.fr/goodmorning/gm136/gm136_HamNghiArtistePeintreSculpteur.pdf.

Dabat, Amandine, 'Le Prince d'Annam, une vie en exil à Alger', *Mémoire – Les Cahiers d'Afrique du Nord* (June 2014), 16–26.

Daily Mail, 1 February 2016.

Daily Telegraph, 8 April 2009.

Dalrymple, William, *The Last Mughal: The Fall of a Dynasty, Delhi, 1857* (London: Bloomsbury, 2006).

Dalrymple, William, *Return of a King: The Battle for Afghanistan* (London: Bloomsbury, 2013).

Dalrymple, William and Anita Anand, *Koh-i-Noor: The History of the World's Most Infamous Diamond* (London: Bloomsbury, 2017).

Daoud, Zakya, *Abdelkrim: Une épopée d'or et de sang* (Paris: Séguier, 1999).

Datta-Ray, Sunanda K., *Smash and Grab: Annexation of Sikkim* (Chennai: Tranquebar, 2013).

Daudet, Alphonse, *Les Rois en exil* (Paris: Dentu, 1879).

Daughton, J. P., *An Empire Divided: Religion, Republicanism, and the Making of French Colonialism, 1880–1914* (Oxford: Oxford University Press, 2006).

David, Philippe, 'Villages, sujets et visiteurs coloniaux à l'Exposition Universelle de Paris (1889): Dinah Salifou et sa "caravane"', in Papa Samba Diop and Hans-Jürgen Lüsebrink (eds), *Littératures et sociétés africaines: Regards comparatistes et perspectives interculturelles* (Tübingen: G. Narr, 2001), pp. 187–98.

David, Saul, *The Indian Mutiny: 1857* (London: Penguin, 2002).

Davy, John, *An Account of the Interior of Ceylon* (London: Longman, 1821).

De Bruijn, Max and Remco Raben, *The World of Jan Brandes, 1743–1808* (Amsterdam: Waanders and Rijksmuseum, 2004).

De Garis, B. K., 'Heaton, Sir John Henniker (1848–1914)', *Australian Dictionary of Biography* (Canberra: National Centre of Biography, Australian National University, 2006).

De Gaulle, Charles, *Mémoires de guerre*, Vol. 3 (Paris: Plon, 1959).

De Gaury, Gerald, *Three Kings in Baghdad: The Tragedy of Iraq's Monarchy* (London: I. B. Tauris, 2008 [1961]).

BIBLIOGRAPHY

De Silva, Colvin R., *Ceylon under the British Occupation, 1795–1833* (New Delhi: Navrang, 1995 [1941]).

De Silva, K. M., *A History of Sri Lanka* (Colombo: Vijitha Yapa, 2008 [2005]).

Delanoë, Guy, *Lyautey, Juin, Mohammed V: Fin d'un protectorat – Mémoires historiques* (Paris: L'Harmattan, 1988).

Delvaux, Adolphe, 'La Prise de Hué par les Français, 5 Juillet 1885', *Bulletin des Amis du Vieux Hué*, 7:2 (1920), 259–94.

Delvaux, Adolphe, 'Quelques Précisions sur une période troublée de l'histoire d'Annam', *Bulletin des Amis du Vieux Hué*, 28:3 (1941), 216–314.

Dermontès, Victor, 'Trois ans d'exil, trois ans d'intrigues: le Dey Hussein en Italie', *Bulletin de la Société de géographie d'Alger*, 9:1 (1905), 120–43.

Des Cars, Jean, *Le Sceptre et le sang: Rois et reines en guerre, 1914–1945* (Paris: Perrin, 2014).

Deschamps, Hubert, *Histoire de Madagascar* (Paris: Berger-Levrault, 1965).

Des Forges, Alison Liebhafsky, *Defeat is the Only Bad News: Rwanda under Musinga* (Madison: University of Wisconsin Press, 2011).

Despagnet, Frantz, *Essai sur les protectorats: Étude de droit international* (Paris: Larose et Forcel, 1896).

Dharmadasa, K. N. O., 'The Sinhala Buddhist Identity and the Nayakkar Dynasty in the Politics of the Kandyan Kingdom, 1739–1815', in Michael Roberts (ed.), *Sri Lanka: Collective Identities Revisited* (Colombo: Marga Institute, 1997), pp. 79–104.

Diallo, Thierno, *Alfa Yaya, roi du Labé (Fouta-Djallon)* (Paris: ABC, 1976).

Diallo, Thierno, *Dinah Salifou, roi des Nalous* (Paris: ABC, 1977).

Dias Bandaranayaka, William, 'How the Last King of Kandy was Captured by the British: An Eye-Witness's Account, Rendered from the Sinhalese', *Journal of the Royal Asiatic Society (Ceylon)*, 14:47 (1896), 107–11.

Diouf, Mamadou, *Le Kajoor au XIXe siècle: pouvoir ceddo et conquête coloniale* (Paris: Karthala, 2014).

The Diplomat, 14 March 2015.

Dirks, Nicholas, *The Hollow Crown: Ethnohistory of an Indian Kingdom* (Cambridge: Cambridge University Press, 1988).

Dirks, Nicholas, *The Scandal of Empire: India and the Creation of Imperial Britain* (Cambridge, MA: Harvard University Press, 2006).

Disanayaka, J. B., *Lanka: The Land of Kings* (Maharagama: Sumitha Publishers, 2007).

Djivo, Joseph Adrien, *Le Protectorat d'Abomey: Ago-Li-Agbo, 1894–1900* (Abomey: Université Nationale du Bénin, 1985).

Djivo, Joseph Adrien, *Le Refus de la colonisation dans l'ancien royaume de Danxome 1894–1900*, Vol. 2 (Paris: L'Harmattan, 2013).

Dolapihilla, Punchibandara, *In the Days of Sri Wickramarajasingha, Last King of Kandy* (Ratmalana: Vishva Lekha, 2006 [1959]).

Dubois-Roquebert, Henri, *Mohammed V, Hassan II, tels que je les ai connus* (Casablanca: Tarik, 2003).

Duff, Andrew, *Sikkim: Requiem for a Himalayan Kingdom* (Edinburgh: Birlinn, 2015).

BIBLIOGRAPHY

Dumons, Bruno, *Rois et princes en exil: une histoire transnationale du politique dans l'Europe du XIXe siècle* (Paris: Riveneuve, 2015).

Duncan, James S., 'The Power of Place in Kandy, Sri Lanka: 1780–1980', in John A. Agnew and James S. Duncan (eds), *The Power of Place: Bringing Together Geographical and Sociological Imaginations* (Boston: Unwin Hyman, 1989), pp. 185–201.

Durand, Alfred, *Les Derniers jours de la cour Hova: L'Exil de la reine Ranavalona* (Paris: Société de l'histoire des colonies françaises, 1933).

Durup, Julien, 'The Exile of Sayyid Khalid Bin Barghash Al-Basaidi in the Seychelles', *Seychelles Weekly*, www.seychellesweekly.com/September5, 2010/top6a_The Exile Sayyid Khalid bin.html.

Durup, Julien, 'The Innocent Sultan of Perak in the Seychelles', *Seychelles Weekly*, 11 July 2010, www.seychellesweekly.com/July 11, 2010/top2_sultan.html.

Dutton, George E., Jayne S. Werner and John K. Whitmore (eds), *Sources of Vietnamese Tradition* (New York: Columbia University Press, 2012).

Duyker, Edward and Coralie Younger, *Molly and the Rajah* (Sydney: Australian-Mauritian Press, 1991).

The Economic Times, 30 January 2011.

Edwards, Penny, *'Watching the Detectives: The Elusive Exile of Prince Myngoon of Burma'*, in Ronit Ricci (ed.), Exile in Colonial Asia: Kings, Convicts, Commemoration (Honolulu: University of Hawai'i Press, 2016), pp. 248–278.

Eliséef, Danielle, *Puyi* (Paris: Perrin, 2014).

Ellis, Stephen, 'The History of Sovereigns in Madagascar: New Light from Old Sources', in Didier Nativel and Faranirina V. Rajaonah (eds), *Madagascar revisitée: En voyage avec Françoise Raison-Jourde* (Paris: Karthala, 2009), pp. 405–31.

Ellis, Stephen, *The Rising of the Red Shawls: A Revolt in Madagascar 1895–1899* (Cambridge: Cambridge University Press, 1985).

Ellis, William, *Three Visits to Madagascar during the Years 1853, 1854, 1856* (London: John Murray, 1858).

Eloundou, Eugène Désiré and Arouna Ngapna, *Un Souverain bamoun en exil: le roi Njoya Ibrahima à Yaoundé (1931–1933)* (Paris: L'Harmattan, 2011).

Ernst, Waltraud and Biswamoy Pati (eds), *India's Princely States: People, Princes and Colonialism* (London: Routledge, 2007).

Esenswa, Anthony, *Jaja: King of Opobo* (Central Milton Keynes: Author House, 2009).

Étienne, Bruno, *Abdelkader* (Paris: Hachette, 1994).

Etter, Anne and Raymond Riquier, *À Salima de Mohéli, dernière reine comorienne, la fidélité d'une petite-fille* (Moroni, Comores: Komedit, 2012).

Evans, Grant, *The Last Century of Lao Royalty: A Documentary History* (Chiang Mai: Silkworm Books, 2004).

Faes, Geraldine and Stephen Smith, *Bokassa Ier, un empereur français* (Paris: Calmann-Lévy, 2000).

Fall-Barros, Ababacar '"Histoire cachée": Il y a 136 ans, le 17 janvier 1877, Sidya Diop fût jugé, condamné par un tribunal colonial et déporté au Gabon', *Ndarinfo*, 16 January 2013, www.ndarinfo.com/Histoire-cachee-Il-y-a-136-ans-le-17-janvier-1877-Sidya-Diop-fut-juge-condamne-par-un-tribunal-colonial-et-deporte_a4586.html.

BIBLIOGRAPHY

Farooqui, Amar, *Zafar and the Raj: Anglo-Mughal Delhi, c. 1800–1850* (New Delhi: Primus Books, 2013).

Farr, Tarikhu, 'When African Kings Became "Chiefs": Some Transformations in European Perceptions of West African Civilization, c. 1450–1800', *Journal of Black Studies*, 23:2 (1992), 258–78.

Fasana, Enrico, 'Pratap Singh a Satara: "Rise and Fall" di un principe indiano (1818–1848)', *Annali della Facoltà di Scienze Politiche, Università di Studi di Trieste* (1980), 759–814.

Fernando, P. E. E., 'The Deportation of King Sri Vikrama Rajasimha and His Exile in India (Based on Archival Documents in Madras)', *University of Ceylon Review*, 20:3–4 (1962), 163–87.

Ferrando-Durfout, Denys, *Njoya le réformateur* (Yaoundé: EdiSavana, 1989).

Le Figaro, 17 February 1909.

Finch, Michael P. M., *A Progressive Occupation? The Gallieni-Lyautey Method and Colonial Pacification in Tonkin and Madagascar, 1885–1900* (Oxford: Oxford University Press, 2013).

Forde, Daryll and P. M. Karberry, *West African Kingdoms in the Nineteenth Century* (Oxford: Oxford University Press, 1967).

Forrest, Denys, *Tiger of Mysore: The Life and Death of Tipu Sultan* (London: Chatto & Windus, 1970).

Fourniau, Charles, *Annam-Tonkin 1885–1896: Lettrés et paysans vietnamiens face à la conquête coloniale* (Paris: L'Harmattan, 1989).

Frankl, P. J. L., 'The Exile of Khalid Bin Barghash Ali-Busa'idi: Born Zanzbar c. 1291 AH/AD 1874 Died Mombasa 1845 AH/AD 1927', *British Journal of Middle Eastern Studies*, 33:2 (2006), 161–77.

Frémeaux, Jacques, *La Conquête de l'Algérie: La dernière campagne d'Abd El-Kader* (Paris: CNRS Éditions, 2016).

Frémigacci, Jean, 'Le Rova de Tananarive: Destruction d'un lieu saint ou constitution d'une référence identitaire?' in Jean-Pierre Chrétien and Jean-Louis Triaud (eds), *Histoire d'Afrique: les enjeux de mémoire* (Paris: Karthala, 1999), pp. 421–44.

Fujitani, T., *Splendid Monarchy: Power and Pageantry in Modern Japan* (Berkeley: University of California Press, 1998).

Galbraith, John S., 'The Trial of Arabi Pasha', *Journal of Imperial and Commonwealth History* 7:3 (1979), 274–92.

Gallieni, Joseph-Simon, *Lettres de Madagascar, 1896–1905* (Paris: Société d'éditions géographiques, maritimes et coloniales, 1928).

Ganière, Paul, 'L'embarquement de Napoléon pour Sainte-Hélène', *Le Souvenir napoléonien*, 51 (1988), 8–20.

Garan, Frédéric, 'Un Sultan à Madagascar', *Expressions*, 33 (2009), 59–117.

Gaultier, Marcel, *L'Etrange Aventure de Ham-Nghi, Empereur d'Annam*, preface by General Catroux (Paris: La Nef de Paris, 1959).

Gaultier, Marcel, *Le Roi proscrit* (Hanoi: Imprimerie d'Extrême-Orient, 1940).

Gautherot, Gustave, *La Conquête d'Alger 1830* (Paris: Payot, 1929).

Geary, Christraud and Adamou Ndam Njoya, *Mandou Yenou: photographies du pays bamoun, royaume ouest-africain* (Munich: Trickster Verlag, 1985).

BIBLIOGRAPHY

Geiger, Wilhem (ed.), *Culavamsa, Being the More Recent Part of the Mahavamsa, Part I*, trans. C. Mabel Rickmers (London: Pali Text Society, 1973).

Ghosh, Amitav, *The Glass Palace* (London: HarperCollins, 2000).

Ghosh, Parimal, *Brave Men of the Hills: Resistance and Rebellion in Burma, 1825–1932* (Honolulu: University of Hawai'i Press, 2000).

Girindrawardani, A. A. A. Dewi, Adrian Vickers and Rodney Holt, *The Last Rajah of Karangasem: The Life and Times of Anak Agung Agung Anglurah Karangasem (1887–1966)* (Denpasar: Saritaksu, 2014).

Glencross, Matthew, *The State Visits of Edward VII: Reinventing Royal Diplomacy for the Twentieth Century* (London: Palgrave Macmillan, 2016).

Goodman, Shona T. S., *From Princes to Persecuted: A Condensed History of the Shan/Tai to 1962* ([Seattle]: CreateSpace, 2014).

Gooneratne, Brendon and Yasmine Gooneratne, *This Inscrutable Englishman: Sir John D'Oyly (1774–1824)* (London: Cassell, 1999).

Gopalakrishnan, S., *The Nayaks of Sri Lanka, 1739–1815: Political Relations with the British in South India* (Madras: New Era, 1988).

Goscha, Christopher, 'Bao Dai et Sihanouk: la fabrique indochinoise des rois coloniaux', in François Guillemot and Agathe Larcher-Goscha (eds), *La Colonisation des corps: De l'Indochine au Vietnam* (Paris: Vendémiaire, 2014), pp. 127–75.

Goscha, Christopher, 'Bao Dai, monarque colonial,' *Les Collections de l'Histoire*, 62 (January–March 2014), pp. 70–1.

Goscha, Christopher E., *Going Indochinese: Contesting Concepts of Space and Place in French Indochina* (Copenhagen: NIAS, 2012).

Goscha, Christopher, *The Penguin History of Modern Vietnam* (London: Allen Lane, 2016).

Gosselin, Charles, *L'Empire d'Annam* (Paris: Perrin, 1904).

Gosselin, Charles, *Le Laos et le protectorat français* (Paris: Perrin, 1900).

Government of the Central Provinces and Berar, *Collection of Correspondence Relating to the Escape and Subsequent Adventures of Appa Sahib, Ex-Raja of Nagpur 1818–1840* (Nagpur: C. P. & Berar, 1939).

Granville, William, 'Deportation of Sri Vikrama Rajasinha', Part I, *The Ceylon Literary Register*, 3:11 (1936), 487–504.

Granville, William, 'Deportation of Sri Vikrama Rajasinha', Part II, *The Ceylon Literary Register*, 3:12 (1936), 543–50.

Grimwood, Ethel St Clair, *My Three Years in Manipur and Escape from the Recent Mutiny* (London: R. Bentley, 1891).

Groenhout, Fiona, 'Debauchery, Disloyalty, and Other Deficiencies: The Impact of Ideas of Princely Character Upon Indirect Rule in Central India, c. 1886–1946' (PhD dissertation, University of Western Australia, 2007).

Groenhout, Fiona, 'Educating Govind Singh: "Princely Character" and the Failure of Indirect Rule in Colonial India', in Peter Limb (ed.), *Orb and Sceptre: Studies on British Imperialism and Its Legacies in Honour of Norman Etherington* (Clayton, Victoria: Monash University Press, 2008), pp. 1–23.

Groenhout, Fiona, 'The History of the Indian Princely States: Bringing the Puppets Back onto Centre Stage', *History Compass*, 4:4 (2006), 629–44.

BIBLIOGRAPHY

Groenhout, Fiona, 'Loyal Feudatories or Depraved Despots? The Deposition of Princes in the Central India Agency, c. 1880–1947', in Waltraud Ernst and Biswamoy Pati (eds), *India's Princely States: People, Princes and Colonialism* (London: Routledge, 2007), pp. 99–117.

Guébourg, Jean-Louis, *La Grande Comore: Des Sultans aux mercenaires* (Paris: L'Harmattan, 1993).

Gulick, J. M., 'The War with Yam Tuan Antah', *Journal of the Malayan/Malaysian Branch of the Royal Asiatic Society*, 27:1 (1954), 1–23.

Gunasinghe, Newton, *Changing Socio-Economic Relations in the Kandyan Countryside* (Colombo: Social Scientists' Association, 2007).

Gunawardena, C. A., *Encylopedia of Sri Lanka* (New Delhi: New Dawn Press, 2006).

Gunawardena, R. A. L. H., 'Colonialism, Ethnicity and the Construction of the Past: The Changing "Ethnic Identity" of the Last Four Kings of the Kandyan Kingdom', in Martin van Bakel, Renée Hagesteijn and Pieter van de Velde (eds), *Pivot Politics: Changing Cultural Identities in Early State Formation Processes* (Amsterdam: Het Spinhuis, 1994), pp. 197–221.

Gunesekera, Romesh, *The Prisoner of Paradise* (London: Bloomsbury, 2012).

Gupta, Bunny and Jaya Chaliha, 'Exiles in Calcutta: The Descendants of Tipu Sultan', *India International Centre Quarterly*, 18:1 (1991), 181–8.

Guy, Jeff, *The Destruction of the Zulu Kingdom: The Civil War in Zululand, 1879–1884* (London: Longman, 1979).

Guy, Jeff, *The View Across the River: Harriette Colenso and the Zulu Struggle against Imperialism* (Oxford: James Currey, 2002).

Halton, Elaine, *Lord of the Celestial Elephant* (London: Elaine Halton, 1999).

Harris, Walter B., *Morocco That Was* (Edinburgh: William Blackwood and Sons, 1921).

Hazareesingh, Sudhir, *The Legend of Napoleon* (London: Granta Books, 2004).

Herd, Norman, *The Bent Pine: The Trial of Chief Langalilabele* (Johannesburg: The Ravan Press, 1976).

Hernon, Ian, *Massacre and Retribution: Forgotten Wars of the Nineteenth Century* (Stroud: Sutton, 1998).

Hess, Robert L., 'The "Mad Mullah" and Northern Somalia', *Journal of African History*, 5:3 (1964), 415–33.

Hien, Hoang, *Vua Duy Tan* (Hué: Nha Xuat Ban Thuan Hoa, 1996).

The Hindu, 16 February 2001; 6 May 2007; 8 February 2009.

Hogan, Edmund M., *Berengario Cermenati among the Igbirra (Ebira) of Nigeria: A Study in Colonial, Missionary and Local Politics, 1897–1925* (Ibadan: HEBN, 2011).

Holt, John Clifford, *The Religious World of Kirti Sri: Buddhism, Art, and Politics in Late Medieval Sri Lanka* (New York: Oxford University Press, 1996).

Holt, John Clifford (ed.), *The Sri Lanka Reader: History, Culture, Politics* (Durham, NC: Duke University Press, 2011).

Howe, Stephen (ed.), *The New Imperial Histories Reader* (London: Routledge, 2009).

BIBLIOGRAPHY

Ikime, Obaro, *Merchant Prince of the Niger Delta: The Rise and Fall of Olomu, Last Governor of the Benin River* (London: Heinemann, 1968).

L'Illustration, 7 October 1905; 14 September 1907; 26 October 1907.

Independent (London), 12 March 2010.

Institut Charles de Gaulle (ed.), *Le Général de Gaulle et l'Indochine, 1940–1946* (Paris: Plon, 1982).

Ivarsson, Søren and Christopher E. Goscha, 'Prince Petsarath (1890–1959): Nationalism and Royalty in the Making of Modern Laos', *Journal of Southeast Asian Studies*, 38:1 (February 2007), 55–81.

Jackson, Anna and Amin Jaffer with Deepika Ahlawat (eds), *Maharaja: The Splendour of India's Royal Courts* (London: V&A Publishing, 2009).

Jaffer, Amin, 'Indian Princes and the West', in Anna Jackson and Amin Jaffer with Deepika Ahlawat (eds), *Maharaja: The Splendour of India's Royal Courts* (London: V&A Publishing, 2009), pp. 194–227.

Jaja, E. J., *King Jaja of Opbo (1821–1891)* (Lagos: Opobo Action Council, 1977).

Jayawardena, Kumari, *Nobodies to Somebodies: The Rise of the Colonial Bourgeoisie in Sri Lanka* (Colombo: Social Scientists' Association and Sanjiva Books, 2000).

Jayawardena, Kumari, *Perpetual Ferment: Popular Revolts in Sri Lanka in the 18th and 19th Centuries* (Colombo: Social Scientists' Association, 2010).

Jennings, Eric, *Curing the Colonizers: Hydrotherapy, Climatology, and French Colonial Spas* (Durham, NC: Duke University Press, 2006).

Jennings, Eric, *Imperial Heights: Dalat and the Making and Undoing of French Indochina* (Berkeley: University of California Press, 2011).

Jennings, Eric, 'Madagascar se souvient: les multiples visages du monument aux mort du Lac Anosy, Antananarivo', *Outre-Mers*, 350–1 (2006), 123–40.

Jennings, Eric, 'Remembering "Other" Losses: The Temple du Souvenir Indochinois of Nogent-sur-Marne', *History and Memory*, 15:1 (2003), 5–48.

Jennings, Eric T., *Vichy in the Tropics: Pétain's National Revolution in Madagascar, Guadeloupe and Indochina, 1940–1944* (Stanford: Stanford University Press, 2001).

Joest, Wilhelm, *Ein Besuch beim Könige von Birma* (Cologne: Du Mont-Schauberg, 1882).

Johnson, André-Marie, *Gbêhanzin, le rêve inachevé*, documentary film, 2007.

Joubert, Hélène, and Gaëlle Beaujean-Baltzer, *Béhanzin Roi d'Abomey* (Paris: Fondation Zinzou, 2006).

Journoud, Pierre, *De Gaulle et le Vietnam (1945–1969)* (Paris: Tallandier, 2011).

Kaartinen, Timo, 'Exile, Colonial Space, and Deterritorialized People in Eastern Indonesian History', in Ronit Ricci (ed.), *Exile in Colonial Asia: Kings, Convicts, Commemoration* (Honolulu: University of Hawai'i Press, 2016), 139–64.

Kake, Baba Ibrahima, 'A propos de l'exil de Dinah Salifou, roi des Nalous', *Présence africaine*, 3 (1964), 146–58.

Kakwenzire, Patrick Kitaburaza, 'Colonial Rule in the British Somaliland Protectorate, 1905–1939' (PhD dissertation, University of London, 1976).

Kavuma, Paulo, *Crisis in Buganda, 1953–55: The Story of the Exile and Return of the Kabaka, Mutesa II* (London: Collins, 1979).

BIBLIOGRAPHY

Keck, Stephen L., '"It Has Now Passed for Ever into Our Hands": Lord Curzon and the Construction of Imperial Heritage in Colonial Burma', *Journal of Burma Studies*, 11 (2007), 49–82.

Keen, Caroline, *An Imperial Crisis in British India: The Manipur Uprising of 1891* (London: I. B. Tauris, 2015).

Keen, Caroline, *Princely India and the British: Political Development and the Operation of Empire* (New Delhi: Viva Books, 2012).

Kemper, Steven, *The Presence of the Past: Chronicles, Politics, and Culture in Sinhala Life* (Ithaca: Cornell University Press, 1991).

Kemper, Steven, *Rescued from the Nation: Angarika Dharmapala and the Buddhist World* (Chicago: Chicago University Press, 2015).

Kershaw, Roger, *Monarchy in South-East Asia: The Faces of Tradition in Transition* (London: Routledge, 2001).

Kipling, Rudyard, 'On the City Wall', in *Soldiers Three and Other Stories*, originally published in *Soldiers Three and Other Stories* (1892), online at https://ebooks.adelaide.edu.au/k/kipling/rudyard/soldiers/chapter27.html.

Kiser, John W., *Commander of the Faithful: The Life and Times of Emir Abd El-Kader* (Rhinebeck: Monkfish, 2008).

Kiwanuka, M. S. M., 'Bunyoro and the British: A Reappraisal of the Causes of the Decline and Fall of an African Kingdom', *Journal of African History*, 9:4 (1968), 603–19.

Knight, Ian, *With His Face to the Foe: The Life and Death of Louis Napoleon, the Prince Imperial, Zululand 1879* (Stroud: Spellmount, 2007).

Kothari, Uma, 'Contesting Colonial Rule: Politics of Exile in the Indian Ocean', *Geoforum*, 43 (2012), 697–706.

Kulkarni, Sumitra, *The Satara Raj (1818–1848): A Study in History, Administration and Culture* (New Delhi: Mittal Publications, 1995).

Kumarasingham, Harshan, *A Political Legacy of the British Empire: Power and the Parliamentary System in Post-Colonial India and Sri Lanka* (London: I. B. Tauris, 2013).

Lacouture, Jean, *Cinq hommes et la France* (Paris: Seuil, 1961).

Laidler, Keith, *Female Caligula: Ranavalona, the Mad Queen of Madagascar* (Chichester: Wiley, 2005).

Lainé, Daniel, *African Kings* (Berkeley: Ten Speed Press, 2000).

Laird, Elizabeth, *The Prince Who Walked with Lions* (London: Macmillan, 2012).

Lâm, Truong Buu, *Colonialism Experienced: Vietnamese Writings on Colonialism, 1900–1931* (Ann Arbor: University of Michigan Press, 2000).

Lamant, Pierre L., *L'Affaire Yukanthor: Autopsie d'un scandale colonial* (Paris: Société française d'histoire d'Outre-Mer, 1989).

Larcher-Goscha, Agathe, 'Prince Cuong De and the Franco-Vietnamese Competition for the Heritage of Gia Long', in Gisele Bousquet and Pierre Brocheux (eds), *Viêt Nam Exposé: French Scholarship on Twentieth-Century Vietnamese Society* (Ann Arbor: University of Michigan Press, 2002), pp. 187–215.

Larson, Pier M., 'Desperately Seeking "the Merina" (Central Madagascar): Reading Ethnonyms and Their Semantic Fields in African Identity Histories', *Journal of Southern African Studies*, 22:4 (1996), 541–60.

BIBLIOGRAPHY

Le Bris, E., 'Complainte annamite sur la prise de Hué par les Français', *Bulletin des Amis du Vieux Hué*, 29:1 (1942), 1–36.

Le Coz, Martine, *Le Jardin d'Orient* (Paris: Michalon, 2008).

Le Marchant de Trigon, H., 'L'Intronisation du roi Ham-Nghi,' *Bulletin des Amis du Vieux Hué*, 4:2 (1917), 77–88.

Lee, Christopher, *Seychelles: Political Castaways* (London: Elm Tree Books, 1976).

Legros, Charles, *La Grand-Comore, 1884–1909* (Paris: n.p., 1909).

Lehault, Philippe, *La France et l'Angleterre en Asie* (Paris: Berger-Levrault, 1892).

Le Jariel, Yves, *Phan Boi Chau (1867–1940): Le Nationalisme vietnamien avant Ho Chi Minh* (Paris: L'Harmattan, 2008).

Lester, Alan, 'Place and Space in British Imperial History Writing', in Robert Aldrich and Kirsten McKenzie (eds), *The Routledge History of Western Empires* (Abingdon: Routledge, 2014), 300–14.

Lewin, T. J., *Asante before the British: The Prempean Years, 1875–1900* (Lawrence: Regents Press, 1978).

Lewis, Mary Dewhurst, *Divided Rule: Sovereignty and Empire in French Tunisia, 1881–1938* (Berkeley: University of California Press, 2014).

Li, Anshan, 'Asafo and Destoolment in Colonial Southern Ghana, 1900–1953', *International Journal of African Historical Studies*, 28:2 (1995), 324–57.

Lignac, Annet, *Les Scandales de la Grande Comore* (Paris: n.p., 1908).

Llewellyn-Jones, Rosie, *The Last King in India: Wajid 'Ali Shah* (London: Hurst, 2014).

Llewellyn-Jones, Rosie (ed.), *Lucknow: City of Illusion* (Munich: Prestel, 2006).

Lockhart, Bruce, *The End of the Vietnamese Monarchy* (New Haven: Yale University Press, 1993).

Lockhart, Bruce, 'Re-assessing the Nguyen Dynasty', *Crossroads*, 15:1 (2001), 9–53.

Londres, Albert, 'Terre d'ébène', in *Oeuvres Complètes* (Paris: Arléa, 1992), pp. 587–91.

Louis, Patrice, *Le Roi Béhanzin: du Dahomey à la Martinique* (Paris: Arléa, 2011).

Loumpet-Galitzine, Alexandra, *Njoya et le royaume bamoun: les archives de la Société des Missions Évangéliques de Paris, 1917–1937* (Paris: Karthala, 2006).

Low, D. A., *Fabrication of Empire: The British and the Uganda Kingdoms, 1890–1902* (Cambridge: Cambridge University Press, 2009).

Major, Andrea and Crispin Bates (eds), *Mutiny at the Margins: New Perspectives on the Indian Uprising of 1857* (Los Angeles: Sage, 2013).

Malbert, Thierry, *L'Exil d'Abdelkrim El-Khattabi à La Réunion, 1926–1947* (Chavagny-sur-Guye: Éditions Orphie, 2016).

Mangrai, Sao Saimong, *The Shan States and the British Annexation* (Ithaca: Cornell University Press, 1965).

Mansel, Philip and Torsten Riotte (eds), *Monarchy and Exile: The Politics of Legitimacy from Marie de Médicis to Wilhelm II* (London: Palgrave Macmillan, 2011).

BIBLIOGRAPHY

Margana, Sri, 'Caught between Empires: Babad Mangkudiningratan and the Exile of Sultan Hemengkubuwana II of Yogyakarta, 1813–1826', in Ronit Ricci (ed.), *Exile in Colonial Asia: Kings, Convicts, Commemoration* (Honolulu: University of Hawai'i Press, 2016), pp. 117–38.

Marks, Sally, '"My Name is Ozymandias": The Kaiser in Exile,' *Central European History*, 16:2 (1983), 122–70.

Marouda, Marina, 'Potent Rituals and the Royal Dead: Historical Transformations in Vietnamese Ritual Practice', *Journal of Southeast Asian Studies*, 45:3 (2014), 338–62.

Marr, David, *Vietnam 1945: The Quest for Power* (Berkeley: University of California Press, 1995).

Marr, David, *Vietnamese Anticolonialism, 1885–1925* (Berkeley: University of California Press, 1971).

Marshall, Andrew, *The Trouser People: Burma in the Shadows of the Empire* (Bangkok: River Books, revised edn, 2012).

Marshall, Henry, *Ceylon: A General Description of the Island and Its Inhabitants* (London: William H. Allen, 1846).

Martin, Jean, *Comores: Quatre îles entre pirates et planteurs* (Paris: L'Harmattan, 1983).

Martin, Jean-François, *Histoire de la Tunisie contemporaine: de Ferry à Bourguiba, 1881–1956* (Paris: L'Harmattan, 1993).

Mathiot, Tony, 'The King of Ashanti – 24 Years of Exile in Seychelles', www.pfsr.org/history-of-seychelles/the-king-of-ashanti-24-years-of-exile-in-seychelles/.

Matthew, H. C. G., 'Heaton, Sir John Henniker, First Baronet (1848–1914)', in *Oxford Dictionary of National Biography* (Oxford University Press, 2004; online edn 2008).

Mayaram, Shail, *Resisting Regimes: Myth, Memory and the Shaping of a Muslim Identity* (Delhi: Oxford University Press, 1997).

McAteer, William, *To Be a Nation, being the third part of The History of the Seychelles, 1920–1976* (Mahé, Seychelles: Pristine Books, 2008).

McCaskie, T. C., *State and Society in Precolonial Asante* (Cambridge: Cambridge University Press, 1995).

McClendon, Thomas, 'You Are What You Eat Up: Deposing Chiefs in Early Colonial Natal, 1847–58', *Journal of African History*, 47 (2006), 259–79.

McGarry, Georgia (ed.), *Reaction and Protest in the West African Press: A Collection of Newspaper Articles on Five Nineteenth Century African Leaders* (Leiden: Afrika-Studiecentrum, 1978).

McPherson, Poppy, 'Myanmar's Royal Legacy', *The Diplomat*, 14 March 2015.

Mendis, G. C. (ed.), *The Colebrooke-Cameron Papers* (Oxford: Oxford University Press, 1956).

Mendis, Vernon L. B., *The Rulers of Sri Lanka* (Colombo: S. Godage & Bros, 2000).

Mestiri, Saïd, *Moncef Bey, Tome 1: le règne* (Tunis: Arc Éditions, rev. edn, 1998).

BIBLIOGRAPHY

Mestiri, Saïd, *Moncef Bey, Tome 2: Chronique des années d'exil* (Tunis: Arc Éditions, 1990).

Michel, François, *La Campagne du Dahomey, 1893–1894: La reddition de Béhanzin*, ed. Jacques Serres (Paris: L'Harmattan, 2001).

Michel, Marc, *Gallieni* (Paris: Fayard, 1989).

Michelland, Antoine, *Marie Ier, le dernier roi français: la conquête d'un aventurier en Indochine* (Paris: Perrin, 2012).

Mills, Lennox A. *Ceylon under British Rule, 1795–1833* (New Delhi: n.p., 1995 [1941]).

The Milwaukee Sentinel, 12 January 1936.

Mizzima News, 28 July 2005.

Mockford, Julian, *Pursuit of an Island* (London: Staples Press, 1950).

Morris, Donald R., *The Washing of the Spears: The Rise and Fall of the Zulu Nation* (New York: Simon & Schuster, 1964).

Morris, Jan, *The Spectacle of Empire: Style, Effect and Pax Britannica* (London: Faber & Faber, 1982).

Mulhar Rao Gaekwar, Maharaja of Baroda, *The Great Baroda Case: Being a Full Report of the Proceedings of the Trial and Deposition of His Highness Mulhar Rao, Gaekwar of Baroda for Instigating an Attempt to Poison the British Resident at His Court* (Calcutta: R. Cambray & Co., 1905).

Mulhar Rao Gaekwar, *The Trial and Deposition of Mulhar Rae Gaekwar of Baroda* (Bombay: Bombay Gazette Steam Press, 1875).

Müller, Frank Lorenz and Heidi Mehrkens (eds), *Sons and Heirs: Succession and Political Culture in Nineteenth-Century Europe* (London: Palgrave Macmillan, 2016).

Musée de l'Histoire de France, *Un Héros des deux rives: Abd el-Kader, l'homme et sa légende* (Paris: Archives nationales, 2003).

Mutesa, King of Buganda, *The Desecration of My Kingdom* (London: Constable, 1967).

de Naurois, Etienne Jacobé, *Le Protectorat: Théorie générale et application aux Protectorats français* (Toulouse: Rousseau, 1910).

Ndam, Bachair, *De Njoya Ibrahim à Mbombo Njoya Ibrahim: Histoires et incompréhensions d'une dynastie qui survit* (Saint-Denis: Edilivre, 2014).

Newbury, Colin, *Patrons, Clients, and Empire: Chieftaincy and Over-rule in Asia, Africa, and the Pacific* (Oxford: Oxford University Press, 2003).

The New Light of Myanmar, 23 December 2012.

New York Times, 21 October 2016.

New Zealand Herald, 8 December 1906.

Nguyen Dac Xuan, *Chuyen Ba Vua Duc Duc, Thanh Thai, Duy Tan* (Hué: Thuan Hoa, 1995).

Nguyen Phuoc Bao Vang (ed.), *Duy Tan, Empereur d'Annam 1900–1945 exilé à l'Ile de la Réunion, ou le destin tragique du Prince Vinh San* (Sainte-Marie, la Réunion: Azalées éditions, 2001).

Nguyên Thê Anh, 'L'abdication de Thanh-Thai', *Bulletin de l'Ecole française d'Extrême-Orient*, 64 (1977), 257–64.

Nguyên Thê Anh, *Monarchie et fait colonial au Viet-Nam (1875–1925): Le crépuscule d'un ordre traditionnel* (Paris: L'Harmattan, 1992).

BIBLIOGRAPHY

Nguyen Thi Dieu, 'Ritual, Power, and Pageantry: French Ritual Politics in Monarchical Vietnam', *French Historical Studies*, 39:4 (2016), 717–48.

Nguyen Viet Ke, *Stories of the Nguyen Dynasty's Kings* (Danang: Danang Publishing House, 2008).

Nivois, Julienne, *A Pesme, En Franche-Comté ... une reine oubliée par l'histoire* (n.p.: Dominique Guéniot, 1995).

Njoya, Sultan, *Histoire et coutumes des Bamum* (Yaoundé: IFAN, 1952).

Nouailhas, Aimé, 'Ranavalo à Arcachon', *Bulletin de la Société historique et archéologique d'Arcachon et du Pays de Buch*, 123 (2005), 90–9.

Obinyan, Thomas Uwadiale, 'The Annexation of Benin', *Journal of Black Studies*, 19:1 (1988), 29–40.

O'Brien, Patricia, *Tautai: Samoa, World History, and the Life of Ta'isi O. F. Nelson* (Honolulu: University of Hawai'i Press, 2017).

Oduwobi, Tunde, 'Deposed Rulers under the Colonial Regime in Nigeria: The Careers of Akarigbo Oyebajo and Awujale Adenuga', *Cahiers d'études africaines*, 171 (2003), 553–71.

Ondaatje, Christopher, *Woolf in Ceylon: An Imperial Journey in the Shadow of Leonard Woolf, 1904–1911* (London: HarperCollins, 2005).

d'Orléans, Charles-Philippe, *Rois en exil: Quand les Cours d'Europe trouvaient refuge au Portugal* (Paris: Express Roularta, 2012).

Osadolor, Osarhierne Benson and Leo Enahoro Otoide, 'The Benin Kingdom in British Imperial Historiography', *History in Africa*, 35 (2008), 401–18.

Osborne, Milton E., *Sihanouk: Prince of Light, Prince of Darkness* (Sydney: Allen & Unwin, 1994).

Osterhammel, Jürgen, *The Transformation of the World: A Global History of the Nineteenth Century* (Princeton: Princeton University Press, 2014 [2009]).

Ottmani, Hamza Ben Driss, *Kaddour Benghabrit: un Maghrébin hors du commun* (Rabat: Marsam, 2010).

Peleggi, Maurizio, *Lords of Things: The Fashioning of the Siamese Monarchy's Modern Image* (Honolulu: University of Hawai'i Press, 2002).

Peleggi, Maurizio, *Thailand: The Worldly Kingdom* (London: Reaktion Books, 2007).

Pennell, C. R., *Morocco since 1830: A History* (New York: New York University Press, 2000).

Person, Yves, *Samori: une révolution dyula* (Dakar: IFAN, 3 vols, 1968–75).

Phan Chau Trinh, *Phan Chau Trinh and His Political Writings*, ed. Vinh Sinh (Ithaca: Cornell University Press, 2009).

Phuntsho, Karma, *The History of Bhutan* (London: Random House, 2013).

Pieris, Anoma, 'The "Other" Side of Labor Reform: Accounts of Incarceration and Resistance in the Straits Settlements Penal System, 1825–1873', *Journal of Social History*, 45:2 (2011), 453–79.

Pieris, P. E., *Ceylon and the Portuguese, 1505–1658* (Delhi: Sri Satguru Pub., 1986 [1920]).

Pieris, P. E., *Tri Sinhala: The Last Phase, 1796–1815* (New Delhi: Asia Educational Services 2001 [1939]).

Pilimatalavuva, Ananda S., *The Chieftains in the Last Phase of the Kandyan Kingdom (Sinhalé)* (Pannipitiya: Stamford Lake, 2008).

BIBLIOGRAPHY

Pilimatalavuva, Ananda S., *The Pilimatalavuvas in the Last Phase of the Kandyan Kingdom* (Pannipitiya: Stamford Lake, 2008).

de Pirey, H., 'Une Capitale éphémère: Tan-So', *Bulletin des Amis du Vieux Hué*, 1:3 (1914), 211–20.

Pohath-Kehelpannala, T. B., *The Life of Ehelapola, Prime Minister to the Last King of Kandy* (Colombo: The Observer, 1896).

Pomfret, David, *Youth and Empire: Trans-Colonial Childhoods in British and French Asia* (Stanford: Stanford University Press, 2015).

Powell, Geoffrey S., 'Brownrigg, Sir Robert', *Oxford Dictionary of National Biography*, www.oxforddnb.com/index/3/101003718/.

Prematilleke, Leelananda and Ranjith Hewage, *A Guide to the National Museum, Colombo* (Colombo: Department of National Museums, 2012).

Prempeh I King of Ashanti (Otumfuo, Nana Agyeman), *'The History of Ashanti Kings and the Whole Country Itself' and Other Writings*, ed. A. Adu Boahen, Emmanuel Akyeampong, Nancy Lawler, T. C. McCaskie and Ivor Wilks (Oxford: Oxford University Press, 2003).

Proto, Neil Thomas, *The Rights of My People: Liliuokalani's Enduring Battle with the United States, 1893–1917* (New York: Algora, 2009).

Prudhomme, Général Léon, *L'Annam du 5 juillet 1885 au 4 avril 1886* (Paris: R. Chapelot, 1901).

Purdue, A. W., *Long to Reign? The Survival of Monarchies in the Modern World* (Stroud: Thrupp Publishing, 2005).

Quinzaine coloniale, 25 February 1907.

Rafiqi, A. S., *Inversion of Times*, ed. Yehya En-Nasr Parkinson (London: Luzac, 1911).

Raison-Jourde, Françoise (ed.), *Les Souverains de Madagascar: l'histoire royale et ses résurgences contemporaines* (Paris: Karthala, 1983).

Raja, Siddharth, 'Tipu Sultan: The Forgotten Connection with India's First Sepoy Mutiny', *The Wire*, 30 July 2016, http://thewire.in/54776/tipu-sultan-forgotten-connection-indias-first-sepoy-mutiny.

Rajaonah, Faranirina V. (ed.), *Cultures citadines dans l'Océan Indien occidental (XVIIIe-XXIe siècles): Pluralisme, échanges, inventivité* (Paris: Karthala, 20110.

Rajaonah, Faranirina V., 'Prestige et metier dans la société malgache: à Tananarive aux XIXe-XXe siècles', *Le Mouvement social*, 204 (2003), 65–79.

Ramusack, Barbara N., 'Incident at Nabha: Interaction between Indian States and British Indian Politics', *Journal of Asian Studies*, 28:3 (1969), 563–77.

Ramusack, Barbara, *The Indian Princes and Their States*, The New Cambridge History of India, Vol. III:6 (Cambridge: Cambridge University Press, 2004).

Ranard, Andrew, *Burmese Painting: A Linear and Lateral History* (Bangkok: Silkworm Books, 2009).

Randrianja, Solofo, *Société et luttes anticoloniales à Madagascar (1896 à 1946)* (Paris: Karthala, 2001).

Randrianja, Solofo and Stephen Ellis, *Madagascar: A Short History* (London: Hurst and Company, 2009).

Ray, Satyajit, *The Chess Players*, film, 1977.

BIBLIOGRAPHY

Reed, Susan A., *Dance and the Nation: Performance, Ritual, and Politics in Sri Lanka* (Madison: University of Wisconsin Press, 2010).

Rees, Neil, *A Royal Exile: King Zog and Queen Geraldine of Albania* (London: Court of King Zog Research Society, 2010).

Rey, Matthieu, 'The British, the Hashemites and Monarchies in the Middle East', in Robert Aldrich and Cindy McCreery (eds), *Crowns and Colonies: European Monarchies and Overseas Empires* (Manchester: Manchester University Press, 2016), pp. 227–44.

Ricci, Ronit, 'From Java to Jaffna: Exile and Return in Dutch Asia in the Eighteenth Century', in Ronit Ricci (ed.), *Exile in Colonial Asia: Kings, Convicts, Commemoration* (Honolulu: University of Hawai'i Press, 2016), pp. 94–116.

Richardson, J., 'The Coronation of Ranavalona III', *The Antananarivo Annual and Madagascar Magazine*, 7 (1883), pp. 102–10.

Rivet, Daniel, *Lyautey et l'institution du protectorat français au Maroc, 1912–1925* (Paris: L'Harmattan, 3 vols, 1996).

Robbe, Emilie (ed.), *La Conquête de la mémoire: Napoléon à Sainte-Hélène* (Paris: Gallimard/Musée de l'Armée, 2016).

Roberts, Michael, *Sinhala Consciousness in the Kandyan Period, 1590s–1815* (Colombo: Vijitha Yapa, 2003).

Roberts, P. A., 'The Sefwi Wiawso Riot of 1935: The Deposition of an Omanhene in the Gold Coast', *Journal of the International African Institute*, 53:2 (1983), 25–46.

Rogers, John D., 'Early British Rule and Social Classification in Lanka', *Modern Asian Studies*, 38:3 (2004), 625–47.

Rolland, Louis and Pierre Lampué, *Précis de législation coloniale* (Paris: Dalloz, 1936).

Roy, Jyotimoy, *History of Manipur* (Calcutta: Eastlight Book House, 1973 [1958]).

Russell, Garth, *The Emperors: How Europe's Rulers Were Destroyed by the First World War* (Stroud: Amberley, 2004).

Russell, Rosalind, *Burma's Spring: Real Lives in Turbulent Times* (Bangkok: River Books, 2015).

Ryder, Alan, *Benin and the Europeans, 1485–1897* (London: Longman, 1969).

Sai Aung Tun, *History of the Shan State from its Origins to 1962* (Chiang Mai: Silkworm Books, 2009).

St Helena National Trust, 'St Helena National Trust Education Pack, 4.1. Island Prisoners – Dinuzulu', www.nationaltrust.org.sh/publications/the-historical-education-pack/.

Salvaing, François, *818 Jours* (Paris: Editions du Sirocco, 2014).

Samaraweera, Vijaya, 'Arabi Pasha in Ceylon, 1883–1901', *Islamic Culture*, 50:3 (1976), 219–27.

Samson, Didier, 'Bénin: Ouanilo de retour à Abomey', RFI, 28 September 2006, www1.rfi.fr/actufr/articles/081/article_46428.asp.

Santhanam, Kausalya, 'Lankan Legacy', *The Hindu*, 6 May 2007, www.thehindu.com/todays-paper/tp-features/tp-sundaymagazine/lankan-legacy/article2275191.ece.

SarDesai, D. R., *Southeast Asia: Past and Present* (Boulder: Westview Press, 2010).
Sargent, Inge, *Twilight over Burma: My Life as a Shan Princess* (Chiang Mai: Silkworm Books, 1994).
Raja of Satara, *A Letter to the Right Hon. Sir Henry Hardinge* (London: Alex Munro, 1845).
Sauer, Walter, 'Austria-Hungary: The Making of Central Europe', in Robert Aldrich (ed.), *The Age of Empires* (London: Thames & Hudson, 2007), pp. 196–219.
Schrikker, Alicia Frederika, 'Dutch and British Colonial Intervention in Sri Lanka, c. 1780–1815: Expansion and Reform' (PhD dissertation, University of Leiden, 1976).
Schultz, Kirsten, *Tropical Versailles: Empire, Monarchy and the Portugal Royal Court in Rio de Janeiro, 1808–1821* (London: Routledge, 2001).
Scott, James George, *The Burman* (New York: W. W. Norton, 1963 [1882]).
Scott, Phoebe, 'Authority and Anxiety', in Sara Siew (ed.), *Between Declarations and Dreams: Art of Southeast Asia since the 19th Century* (Singapore: National Gallery, 2015), pp. 8–29.
Seelmann, Hoo Nam, *Lautloses Weinen: Der Untergang des Koreanischen Köninghauses* (Würzburg: Königshauses & Neumann, 2011).
Seneviratne, H. L., 'The Alien King: Nayakkars on the Throne of Kandy', *Ceylon Journal of Historical and Social Studies*, 6:1 (1976), 55–61.
Sévilla, Jean, *Zita, impératrice courage, 1892–1989* (Paris: Perrin, 2003).
Sévilla, Jean, *Le Dernier Empereur* (Paris: Perrin, 2009).
Shah, Sudha, *The King in Exile: The Fall of the Royal Family of Burma* (New Delhi: HarperCollins, 2012).
Shipway, Martin, *The Road to War: France and Vietnam, 1944–1947* (Providence: Berghahn Books, 1996).
Silber, G., 'Rois déchus et pensionnés,' *Le Monde illustré*, 12 October 1912, pp. 236–7.
Singer, Barnett and John Langdon, *Cultured Force: Makers and Defenders of the French Colonial Empire* (Madison: University of Wisconsin Press, 2004).
Singh, Naorem Joykumar, *Colonialism to Democracy: A History of Manipur, 1819–1972* (Guwahati: Spectrum Publications, 2002).
Sivasundaram, Sujit, *Islanded: Britain, Sri Lanka and the Bounds of an Indian Ocean Colony* (Chicago: University of Chicago Press, 2013).
Smith, Alison, David Blayney Brown and Carol Jacobi (eds), *Artist and Empire: Facing Britain's Imperial Past* (London: Tate Publishing, 2015).
Smith, Stephen, *Voyage en postcolonie: le nouveau monde franco-africain* (Paris: Grasset, 2010).
Sonbol, Amira (ed.), *The Last Khedive of Egypt: The Memoirs of Abbas Hilmi II* (Cairo: American University in Cairo Press, 2006).
Souvannaphouma, Mangkra, *Laos: Autopsie d'une monarchie assassinée* (Paris: L'Harmattan, 2010).
Stadtner, Donald, *Sacred Sites of Burma: Myth and Folklore in an Evolving Spiritual Realm* (Bangkok: River Books, 2011).

BIBLIOGRAPHY

Stengs, Irene, *Worshipping the Great Moderniser: King Chulalongkorn, Patron Saint of the Thai Middle Class* (Singapore: NUS Press, 2009).

Stewart, A. T. Q., *The Pagoda War: Lord Dufferin and the Fall of the Kingdom of Ava, 1885–6* (London: Faber & Faber, 1972).

Strathern, Alan, *Kingship and Conversion in Sixteenth-Century Sri Lanka: Portuguese Imperialism in a Buddhist Land* (New Delhi: Cambridge University Press, 2010).

Stroud, Patricia Tyson, *The Man Who Had Been King: The American Exile of Napoleon's Brother Joseph* (Philadelphia: University of Pennsylvania Press, 2015).

Summers, Carol, 'All the Kabaka's Wives: Marital Claims in Buganda's 1953–5 Kabaka Crisis', *Journal of African History*, 58:1 (2017), 107–17.

Sunday Times (Colombo), 11 March 2012.

Suwannathat-Pian, Kobkua, *Palace, Political Party and Power: A Story of the Socio-Political Development of Malay Kingship* (Singapore: NUS Press, 2011).

Tainturier, François, 'Of Golden Palaces and Celebrated Rulers: Inventing Traditions in Pre-Colonial and Contemporary Myanmar', *Journal of Burma Studies*, 18:2 (2014), 223–58.

Taylor, Jean Gelman, 'Belongings and Belonging: Indonesian Histories in Inventories from the Cape of Good Hope', in Ronit Ricci (ed.), *Exile in Colonial Asia: Kings, Convicts, Commemoration* (Honolulu: University of Hawai'i Press, 2016), pp. 164–92.

Taylor, K. W., *A History of the Vietnamese* (Cambridge: Cambridge University Press, 2013).

Taylor, Miles, 'Queen Victoria and India, 1837–61', *Victorian Studies*, 46:2 (2004), 264–74.

Taylor, Stephen, *Shaka's Children: A History of the Zulu People* (London: HarperCollins, 1994).

Terretta, Meredith, 'Chiefs, Traitors, and Representatives: The Construction of a Political Repertoire in Independence-Era Cameroun', *International Journal of African Historical Studies*, 43:2 (2010), 227–53.

Thanegi, Ma, 'The Thrones of Myanmar Kings', *Enchanting Myanmar*, 2:2 (January–March 2003), www.myanmar-image.com/enchantingmyanmar/enchantingmyanmar2-2/thrones.htm.

Thant Myint-U, *The Making of Modern Burma* (Cambridge: Cambridge University Press, 2001).

Thant Myint-U, *The River of Lost Footsteps: A Personal History of Burma* (London: Faber & Faber, 2007).

Thébault, E.-P., 'Le Tragique Destin d'un empereur d'Annam', *France-Asie*, 200 (1970), 3–40.

Thein, Hla, *Myanmar and the Europeans (1878–1885)* (Yangon: Daw Thinn Thinn Mar Tun Foundation Bank Literary Committee, 2010).

Theron, Bridget, 'King Cetshwayo in Victorian England: A Cameo of Imperial Interaction', *South African Historical Journal*, 56 (2006), 60–87.

Thierry, François, *Le Trésor de Hué: Une face cachée de la colonisation de l'Indochine* (Paris: Nouveau Monde Éditions, 2014).

BIBLIOGRAPHY

Thomas, Athol, *Forgotten Eden: A View of the Seychelles Islands in the Indian Ocean* (London: Longmans, 1968).

Thomas, Martin, *The French Empire at War, 1940–1945* (Manchester: Manchester University Press, 1998).

Thompson, P. S., 'Dinuzulu and Bhambatha, 1906: An Invasion of Natal and an Uprising in Zululand That Almost Took Place', *Historia*, 58:2 (2013), 40–69.

The Times, 26 November 1894.

Tønnessen, Stein, *Vietnam 1946: How the War Began* (Berkeley: University of California Press, 2010).

Tordoff, W., *Ashanti under the Prempehs, 1888–1935* (Oxford: Oxford University Press, 1965).

Tordoff, W., 'The Exile and Repatriation of Nana Prempeh I of Ashanti (1896–1924)', *Transactions of the Historical Society of Ghana*, 4:2 (1960), 33–58.

Tran My-Van, *A Vietnamese Royal Exile in Japan: Prince Cuong De (1882–1951)* (New York: Routledge, 2005).

The Trial of Dinuzulu on Charges of High Treason (Pietermaritzburg: Times Printing, 1910).

Tronchon, Jacques, *L'insurrection malgache de 1947: essai d'interprétation historique* (Paris: Karthala, 1986).

Trong Thuoc Hoang, *Ho So Vua Duy Tan* (Laguna Hills: Thanh Huong, 1984).

Turpin, Frédéric, *De Gaulle, les Gaullistes et l'Indochine, 1940–1956* (Paris: Les Indes savantes, 2005).

Uganda Protectorate, *Withdrawal of Recognition from Kabaka Mutesa II of Buganda (Report Presented by the Secretary of State for the Colonies to Parliament)* (London: Colonial Office, 1953).

Ugwu, Ifeanyi, 'Deconstructionist Interpretations of Rotimi's *Ovonranwen Nogbaisi* in Yerima's *The Trials of Oba Ovonramwen*', *Research on Humanities and Social Sciences*, 3:13 (2013), 86–94.

Van Schaik, Sam, *Tibet: A History* (New Haven: Yale University Press, 2011).

Varga, Daniel, 'Les Vietnamiens à La Réunion, de la déportation à l'émigration volontaire (1859–1910)', *Outre-Mers*, 374–5 (2012), 233–74.

Queen Victoria, 'Proclamation by the Queen in Council to the Princes, Chiefs and People of India', London: Governor-General at Allahabad, 1 November 1858.

Vigné d'Octon, Paul, *La Gloire du sabre* (Paris: Flammarion, 1900).

Vilhena, Maria de Conceiçao, *Gungunhana no seu reino* (Lisbon: Colibri, 1996).

Vilhena, Maria de Conceiçao, *Gungunhana: Grandeza e decadência de um império africano* (Lisbon: Colibri, 1999).

Vimalananda, Tannakoon, *Sri Wickrema, Brownrigg and Ehelepola* (Colombo: Gunasena, 1984).

Vinh Sanh, Claude and Christian Vittori, *Hommage au Prince Vinh San et à l'Empereur Duy Tan* (Saint-Denis: Azalées Éditions, 2000).

Visram, Rozina, *Ayahs, Lascars and Princes: Indians in Britain, 1700–1947* (London: Pluto Press, 1986).

Vozelle, Jean, 'Béhanzin à la Martinique,' *Revue de Paris* (1 May 1898), 220–4.

Vu-Hill, Kimloan, *Coolies into Rebels: Impact of World War I on French Indochina* (Paris: Les Indes savantes, 2011).

BIBLIOGRAPHY

Vu Hong Lien, *Royal Hué: Heritage of the Nguyen Dynasty of Vietnam* (Bangkok: River Books, 2015).
Ward, Kerry, *Networks of Empire: Forced Migration in the Dutch East India Company* (Cambridge: Cambridge University Press, 2009).
Ward, Kevin, 'The Church of Uganda and the Exile of Kabaka Muteesa II, 1953–55', *Journal of Religion in Africa*, 28:4 (1998), 411–49.
Ward, Sheila, *Prisoners in Paradise* (Rose Hill, Mauritius: Éditions de l'Océan Indien, 1986).
Webb, James L. A., *Tropical Pioneers: Human Agency and Ecological Change in the Highlands of Sri Lanka, 1800–1900* (Athens, Ohio: Ohio University Press, 2002).
Welch, Frances, *The Russian Court at Sea: The Voyage of HMS* Marlborough, *April 1919* (London: Short Books, 2011).
Wickramasinghe, Nira, *Metallic Modern: Everyday Machines in Colonial Sri Lanka* (New York: Berghahn, 2014).
Wickramasinghe, Nira, 'The Return of Keppetipola's Cranium: Authenticity in a New Nation', *Economic and Political Weekly*, 26 July 1997, pp. 85–92.
Wickramasinghe, Nira, *Sri Lanka in the Modern Age: A History of Contested Identities* (London: Hurst, 2006).
Wickremeratne, Upali C., *Hearsay and Versions in British Relations with the Kingdom of Kandy, 1796–1818* (Colombo: Vijitha Yapa, 2012).
Wickremesekera, Channa, *Kandy at War: Indigenous Military Resistance to the European Expansion in Sri Lanka, 1594–1818* (New Delhi: Manohar, 2004).
Wijesinha, Rajiva, *Breaking Bounds: Essays on Sri Lankan Writing in English* (Colombo: Sabaragamuwa University Press, 1998).
Wilks, I., *Asante in the Nineteenth Century: The Structure and Evolution of a Political Order* (Cambridge: Cambridge University Press, 1989).
Williams, Donovan, 'An Echo of the Indian Mutiny: The Proposed Banishment of Bahadur Shah II to the Cape Colony, 1857', *Historia*, 17:4 (1972), 265–8.
Willis, Justin, 'A Portrait of the Mukama: Monarchy and Empire in Colonial Bunyoro, Uganda', *Journal of Imperial and Commonwealth History*, 34:1 (2006), 105–22.
Winstedt, R. O. and R. J. Wilkinson, 'A History of Perak', *Journal of the Malayan Branch of the Royal Asiatic Society*, 12:1 (1934), entire issue.
Woolman, David S., *Rebels in the Rif: Abd El Krim and the Rif Rebellion* (Stanford: Stanford University Press, 1968).
Wright, Gwendolyn, *The Politics of Design in French Colonial Urbanism* (Chicago: University of Chicago Press, 1991).
Y, Dr., 'Le Discours d'adieu du roi Behanzin', *African Heritage*, 28 January 2013.
Yafugborhi, Egufe, '100 Years of Nanna of Itsekir's "Living History"', *Vanguard*, 10 July 2016, www.vanguardngr.com/2016/07/100-years-nanna-itsekiris-living-history/.
Younger, Coralie, *Wicked Women of the Raj: European Women Who Broke Society's Rules and Married Indian Princes* (New Delhi: HarperCollins, 2003).
Zinoman, Peter, *The Colonial Bastille: A History of Imprisonment in Vietnam, 1862–1940* (Berkeley: University of California Press, 2001).

INDEX

Page numbers followed by 'fig' indicate illustrations.

Abd el-Kader, Emir 259
Abd el-Krim 3, 259, 264
Abdelaziz (sultan of Morocco) 257–8, 258fig, 259
Abdelhafid (sultan of Morocco) 257–9, 258fig
Abdullah (sultan of Perak) 105–10
African depositions
   Algeria 256
   Grande Comore 190–1, 206
   Madagascar 215, 221–7, 229
   Morocco 266–7
   Somalia 196
   southern Africa 183, 184, 193–5
   sub-Saharan Africa 178–81, 185–90, 192–3, 196–7
   Tunisia 260–4
   Uganda 197–9
   Zanzibar 195–6
Ago-Li-Agbo (king of Dahomey) 1, 192
Ahmad Urabi 6
Alamayu (prince of Ethiopia) 183–4
Alfa Yaya (ruler of Labé) 180, 186–7, 202
Alfred, Prince, Duke of Edinburgh 64
Algeria
   French conquest 255–7
   as place of exile 18, 19fig, 22, 126, 129–30, 178, 215, 220, 232, 263
Ali Shireh (Warsangali sultan) 196
Aliyu (ruler of Zazau) 196–7, 202
Alwar state 94
Amangkurat III (sultan of Kartasura) 25
Amin, Idi 199
Amin (*bey* of Tunis) 263–5
Anglo-Manipur War 94
Anglo-Sikh War 80
Annam

as French protectorate 119, 128
   see also Duy Tan; Ham Nghi; Thanh Thai
Ansari, Hamid 87
anti-colonialism *see* nationalism and anti-colonialism
Appa Sahib *see* Mudhoji II Bhonsle
Arnett, John 196–7
Ashanti state *see* Prempeh
Awadh state *see* Wajid Ali Shah

Baden-Powell, Robert 182
Bagehot, Walter 75
Bahadur Shah Zafar *see* Zafar, Bahadur Shah
Ballantyne, Tony 25, 84
Bamoun *see* Njoya Ibrahim
Bao Dai (emperor of Vietnam) 117–18, 157, 161, 166–7, 172
Bardo, Treaty of 257, 263
Baroda deposition 89–90
Bawla case 91
Béhazin (king of Dahomey) 19fig, 179fig
   descendants 1, 205, 207
   emblematic status 178–9
   life in exile 182–3, 204–5
   repatriation of remains 207
Belgian depositions 29n25
Benin monarchy 188–9
Bhutan 20
Birch, James Wheeler Woodford 106
Bonny *see* William Dappa Pepple I
Boulé, Étienne 167–8
Bourguiba, Habib 6, 259–60, 262, 263, 264
Bradlaugh, Charles 108
British Empire
   1858 Indian proclamation 87–8
   law relating to exiles 12–13

[307]

INDEX

British Empire (cont)
  nineteenth-century expansion in Asia 75–6, 105
  orders of chivalry 88
  paramountcy of 24
  rivalry with France 39, 42–3, 98–9, 190, 219–20, 232
  royal tours 64–5
  as spectacle 22, 24
  use of monarchism 14–15, 20, 22–4, 60–5, 104–5
  see also East India Company; Victoria, Queen
Brooke, Charles 105
Brownrigg, Robert 32, 34, 41–3, 45–6, 52–3, 56, 58–61, 63
Buddhism
  British protection of 47, 62, 63
  Sacred Tooth relic 38, 47, 56, 61, 63
Buganda 197–9
burials see funerals and burials; reburial of remains
Burma
  abolition of monarchy 97–100
  British as successors to Burmese monarchy 104–5
  monarchism and royalist resistance 100–1
  royal citadel and palace 98fig, 100, 104
  royal regalia 99, 103
  Shan princes (sawbwas) 104–5
Burma's Lost Royals (film) 103
Burton, Antoinette 7
Buu Lan see Thanh Thai

Cambodia 20, 119
Cameroon see Njoya Ibrahim
Can Vuong Movement 124–8
Cankili II (Jaffna king) 25
Cannadine, David 24
Catroux, Georges 128, 132
Cayla, Léon 242–3
Central African Republic 281n6
Cetshwayo (Zulu king) 25, 184, 201, 202

Ceylon
  British as successors to Kandyan monarchy 60–5
  British takeover 39–40
  contests for succession to throne 40–1, 46, 58–60
  deposition of Cankili II 25
  impact of end of Kandyan monarchy 65–9
  independence 65
  post-rebellion proclamation (1818) 62–3
  rebellions 42–7, 57–60
  role of monarchy 37–8, 60–5, 67–8
  royal tours 64–5
  see also Kandyan monarchy; Sri Vikrama Rajasinha
Chess Players, The (film) 80, 96
Chikka Virarajendra (raja of Coorg) 78–9, 82, 96
Chwa II Kabalega (ruler of Bunyoro) 197
Cohen, Andrew 198–9
Colenso, Harriette 200, 203
Colenso, John 200
colonies as places of banishment 2
commissions of inquiry 77, 79, 89, 90, 93, 192
Comoros Islands see Djoumé Fatima; Said Ali; Salima Machamba
Confucian theory of state 119
Coomarasamy see Kumaraswami
Coomaraswamy, Ananda 65
Coorg state 78–9
Cornwallis, HMS 32
Courcy, Philippe de 122, 123, 128
Cuong De, Prince 141, 148–9

Dahomey see Ago-Li-Agbo; Béhazin
Dalais, Raoul 242
Dalrymple, William 25
Damantang, Camara 180
Datia state 93
de Gaulle, Charles
  and Duy Tan 161, 169–70
  on independence for Vietnam 166
  and Mohammed V 265
  visit to Tananarive 248

INDEX

Decoux, Jean 117
degeneration theory 189
deposition and exile of rulers
  in ancient world 2
  Belgian, Dutch, German and
    Portuguese cases 25–7, 28–9n25
  early British experience 26–7
  in early modern Europe 2
  European and non-European cases
    contrasted 2–7
  European reservations and
    condemnation 198–202
  grounds, circumstances and
    procedures 10–17, 42, 69, 77–8,
    89–97, 99, 146, 183, 185–90,
    198, 209
  as kidnapping 192, 199, 227, 270
  lack of due process 32, 36, 80–1,
    107–9, 126, 136, 192, 227,
    263, 270
  legal aspects 12–13
  non-royal political exiles 2, 6
  overview 15–21, 274–81
  post-colonial cases 274
  see also trials and appeals
Dewas Senior state 93
Dias Bandaranayaka, William 43–4
Dinah Salifou (ruler of Nalou people,
    Guinea) 1, 192, 199, 202–3, 208
Dinuzulu (Zulu king) 25, 193–5,
    194fig, 207
Diponegoro (sultan of Yogyakarta) 25
Dirks, Nicholas 24
Djoumé Fatima (sultan/queen of
    Mohéli) 208–9
doctrine of lapse 76, 81
Dong Khanh (emperor of Vietnam)
    125–6, 127–8, 133, 172
D'Oyly, John 41, 42–7, 60–2
Dufferin and Ava, First
    Marquess of 100
Duleep Singh (maharajah of Punjab)
    24–5, 80, 82–4
Durand, Alfred 229–31
Dutch depositions 25–7, 28n25
Duy Tan 147fig
  accession to throne 141–2, 147–8
  capture, deposition and
    banishment 150–1
  conflict with exiled father 156–7
  death and burial 169, 171
  descendants 169
  involvement in 1916 insurrection
    149–52, 162
  life in exile 152–9
  mooted restoration as
    monarch 166–8
  during Second World War 160–8
  as short-wave radio
    enthusiast 158–9
  status as patriot 152
  successor to 151
  surveillance in exile of 153–5,
    158–9, 160–1
  vision for a unified Vietnam 164–6

East India Company
  annexations under 'doctrine of
    lapse' 76
  depositions under 26, 76–84
East Indies 25, 26–7
Egypt 28–9n25
Ehelepola 35, 41, 42, 46, 50, 56–7, 59
Elphinstone, Montstuart 79
Estéva, Jean-Pierre 260, 262
Eweka II (oba of Benin) 188
exile see deposition and exile
    of rulers

female rulers see Djoumé Fatima;
    Lili'uokalani; Ranavalona III;
    Salima Machamba; Victoria,
    Queen
feudatories 88, 96, 104
First World War 149–52, 247
Forster, E. M. 93
France
  celebrity status of Ranavalona
    in 233–8
  residual royalism 15
  surveillance of exiled rulers
    152–9, 269
  see also de Gaulle, Charles; French
    overseas empire; Vichy regime

INDEX

French overseas empire
  anti-colonial unrest 259, 264, 265–6
  gallery of deposed rulers 1
  protectorates 119–21, 128–9, 178, 192, 219–20, 228, 257, 266
  rivalry with Britain 39, 42–3, 98–9, 190, 219–20
  as Union Française 264–5, 272
  utlilisation of monarchical principle 117–19, 226–7, 228
  Vichy regime and 260, 265
funerals and burials
  Bahadur Shah Zafar 87
  Duy Tan 169, 171
  Ham Nghi 132
  Ouanilo 208
  Ranavalona III 238, 243–4
  Thanh Thai 170–1
  Vikrama Rajasinha 53–4
  see also reburial of remains

Gallieni, Joseph 215, 221–8, 233, 241, 247
Gauthier, Judith 130
gender issues 21–2
  see also homosexuality; Ranavalona III: gendered treatment of; sexual scandals
German empire 181, 257–8
Ghana (Gold Coast) *see* Prempeh
Ghosh, Amitav 25, 101, 103
Glaoui, the (pasha of Marrakesh) 266–70
Glass Palace, The (Ghosh) 25, 101
Gongalegoda Banda 60
Gooneratne, Brandon and Yasmine 60
Goscha, Christopher 117
Gosselin, Charles 123, 124–6, 127–8, 130
Govindh Singh (maharaja of Datia) 93
Gowramma (daughter of Virarajendra) 82–3
Grande Comore 190–2, 206
Great Indian Uprising 84–5
Groenhout, Fiona Elizabeth 89, 91

Guillaume, Auguste 267–8
Guinea *see* Alfa Yaya; Dinah Salifou; Samory Touré
Gulab Singh (maharaja of Rewa) 90
Guy, Jeff 25

Haile Selassie (emperor of Ethiopia) 3, 274
Ham Nghi (emperor of Annam) 1, 19fig, 131fig
  accession and installation 121
  burial and reinterment 132
  capture and deportation 125–7
  children 131–2
  as fugitive from the French 121–5, 127–8
  life in exile 129–32
  mooted restoration 132, 139
  symbolic significance 128, 132
Hamengkubuwono II (sultan of Yogyakarta) 26–7
Hancock, Keith 198
Heaton, John Henniker 108–9
Herbert, Miss (missionary) 240
Ho Chi Minh 118, 166–7
homosexuality 83, 90, 92–3, 240
Howey, Mrs 233, 239–40
Hué, battle for 121–3
Humblot, Léon 190–2, 207
Hussein Dey (*dey* of Algiers) 255

imperial governance *see* British Empire; French overseas empire
India
  deposition of Mughal emperor 84–7
  depositions under British Raj 87–97
  depositions under East India Company 26, 76–84
  Queen Victoria and deposed princes 26, 75–6, 82, 83, 94–5
  Uprising (1857) 84–5
Indore state 91
interments *see* funerals and burials
Istiqlal Party 266, 267, 269

INDEX

Jaja (ruler of Opobo) 187, 199, 201, 202, 204
Jawan Bakht 86
Jay Singh (maharaja of Alwar) 94
Juin, Alphonse 263, 266–7

Kandy, King of *see* Sri Vikrama Rajasinha
Kandyan Convention 46–7, 56, 58, 60, 62
Kandyan monarchy
  British monarchy as successor 60–5
  deposition 43–50
  Nayakkar dynasty 40, 48, 56
  post-deposition legacy and commemoration 48, 68–9
  pretenders to the throne 38
  regalia 61, 69
  role and duties 38
  see also Sri Vikrama Rajasinha
Keen, Caroline 25
Keppetipola 58–9, 68
Khai Dinh (emperor of Vietnam) 151, 172
Khalid bin Barghash (sultan of Zanzibar) 195–6, 202, 208
kidnapping 192, 199, 227, 270
Kien Phuc (emperor of Vietnam) 121
Kodagu *see* Coorg kingdom
Koh-i-noor diamond 82
Korea 28–9n25
Kothari, Uma 25
Krishna, S. M. 87
Kumaraswami 59

Laloë, Marcelle 130, 131fig
Langalibalele (Hlubi ruler) 183
Laos 20
Lawrie, A. C. 57
Lesotho 20
Lévecque, Fernand 137, 140
Lili'uokalani (queen of Hawaii) 251
Llewelyn-Jones, Rosie 25
Low, D. A. 24
Lyautey, Hubert 258–9

Madagascar
  destruction of the *Rova* 246
  French conquest and annexation 217–21
  French divide-and-rule strategy 221
  menalamba revolt 220–1
  Mohammed V's exile on 268–9
  mythification of pre-colonial monarchy 247–8
  as place of exile 18, 22, 268–9
  steps to efface monarchy 226–8
  see also Ranavalona III
Madho Singh (maharaja of Panna) 91
Madugalle 58–9
Makarios, Archbishop 6
Malaysia
  national anthem 110
  Perak sultanate 105–10
  retention of sultanates 20
Mandel, Georges 243–4
Manipur state 94–5
Maratha empire 79
Marie-Louise (Ranavalona's grand-niece) 230, 234, 235–6, 239, 241, 243
Marshal, Henry 49–50
Martinique 178, 204
Mauritius, as place of exile 59
mausoleums *see* tombs and mausoleums
Maxwell, Peter Benson 108, 152
Maxwell, William Edward 108
menalamba revolt 220–1
Mendis, Vernon L. B. 48
miscarriage of justice *see* deposition and exile of rulers: lack of due process
Mitterrand, François 267
Mohammed Ben Arafa (sultan of Morocco) 268, 269, 271
Mohammed V (sultan, later king, of Morocco)
  de Gaulle and 265
  deposition and exile 266–7
  descendants 270–1
  life in exile 268–9

INDEX

Mohammed V (sultan, later king, of Morocco) (*cont*)
   links with Istiqlal Party 266, 267, 269
   restoration 269–70
Mohammed VI (king of Morocco) 270–1
Mohéli 208–9
monarchism
   Ceylon 37–8, 60–5, 67–8
   endurance and resilience 7, 20, 277, 279
   India 88
   as platform of anti-colonialism 15–16, 57, 101
   utilisation by colonisers 14–15, 20, 23–4, 60–5, 104–5, 117–19, 226–7, 228
Moncef Bey (*bey* of Tunis) 260–5
monuments *see* statues and monuments
Morocco
   deposition and restoration of sultan 266–70
   nationalist unrest 265–7, 269
   as protectorate 257, 266
   Rif rebellion 259
Morris, Jan 22
Mudhoji II Bhonsle ('Appa Sahib') 77–8
Mughal emperor *see* Zafar, Bahadur Shah
Muhammad Abdullah Hassan 196
Mulhar Rao Gaekwar (maharaja of Baroda) 89–90
Muteba II (*kabaka* of Buganda) 199
Mutesa II (*kabaka* of Buganda) 197–9
Muttusamy, Prince 41, 50
Mwanga II (*kabaka* of Buganda) 197
Myinzaing 101

Nabha state 95
Nagpur affair 77–8
Napoleon Bonaparte 4, 209–10
Napoleon III 256
Natal 183

nationalism and anti-colonialism
   Ceylon 57–8, 66–8
   India 84–5, 95
   Madagascar 220–1, 247–8
   monarchism as platform for 15–16, 57, 101
   Morocco 259, 265–7, 269
   Tunisia 259–60, 263–4
   Vietnam 117–18, 121–3, 124–7, 148–52, 167, 172
Nayakkar dynasty 40, 48, 56
Nehru, Jawaharlal 95
'new imperial history' 21–2
Newbury, Colin 24
Nga Mauk ruby 99
Ngo Dinh Diem 118
Nguyên Thê Anh 119, 141, 172
Nguyen Van Tuong 120–4
Nigeria *see* Aliyu of Zazau; Benin monarchy; Jaja (ruler of Opobo); William Dappa Pepple I
Njimoluh Sédou 207
Njoya Ibrahim (ruler of Bamoun, western Cameroon) 180–1, 202, 207
North, Frederick 40–1

Oba Ovonranwem (king of Benin) 188–9
Obote, Milton 199
Opigez, Captain 192, 197
Ouanilo (Béhanzin's son) 204, 206, 207–8
Oudh state *see* Wajid Ali Shah
overrule concept 22–3, 24, 95, 110–11

Panna state 91
Perak sultanate 105–10
Pétain, Philippe 160, 259, 260, 262
Phan Boi Chau 148
Phan Chau Trinh 148
Phayre, Arthur 86–7, 90
Phillips, James 188, 190
Pieris, P. E. 49
Pilima Talauve (father) 40–1, 49–50, 59
Pilima Talauve (son) 41, 58

INDEX

Portuguese depositions 25, 29n25
Pouvanaa a Oopa 6
Pratap Singh (raja of Satara) 79, 80–1
Prempeh (Ashanti king)
  Baden-Powell on 182
  deposition and banishment 186
  descendants 208
  life in exile 202–4
  looted regalia 182
  repatriation 203, 205–6
  sympathy for 201–2
Prendergast, Harry 99
pretenders and claimants
  Burma 101, 104
  Ceylon 40–1, 46, 58–60, 62
  Morocco 258
  Perak 105–6
protectorates
  Annam 117, 119, 128
  Cambodia 119
  Dahomey 178, 192–3
  French, in Vietnam 119–21, 128–9
  German, over Bamoun 181
  legal aspects 9–10, 23
  Madagascar 219–20, 228
  Morocco 257, 266
  Nigeria 185, 188
  Perak 106
  Punjab 80
  Tonkin 117, 119
  Tunisia 257
  Uganda 198
  Zanzibar 195
Punjab 80
Puyi (emperor of China) 3

race and racism 21–2, 182–3, 189, 221, 242
Rainilaiarivony 216–17, 241
Raja Chulan 109
Raja Hadya Abdullah 109–10
Raja Mansur 109–10
Ramazindrazana 226, 230, 239–40, 243
Ramusack, Barbara 95

Ranavalona III (queen of Madagascar) 1, 19fig, 218fig
  as celebrity in France 233–8
  death, funeral, and repatriation of remains 238, 241–6
  deposition of 215, 221–7, 229
  and French takeover 217–20
  gendered treatment of 21, 220, 228–9, 237–8, 248–50
  life in exile 229–38
  welfare of family members 238–41
Ray, Satyajit 80, 96
reburial of remains
  Alfa Yaya 180
  Bahadur Shah Zafar 87
  Béhanzin 207
  Duy Tan 171
  Ham Nghi 132
  Mohammed Ben Arafa 271
  Mutesa II 199
  Ranavalona III 241–6
  Samory Touré 180
regalia
  Ashanti 182
  Benin 189
  British expropriation of 61, 69, 82, 99, 103, 189
  Burmese 99, 103
  Kandyan 61, 69
  Malagasy 246
  Sikh 82
reinterment *see* reburial of remains
repatriation from exile
  approvals given 82, 107–9, 170–1, 194, 202
  petitions for 107–8, 205–6
  of remains 132, 171, 199, 207, 241–6, 264
restoration of dethroned rulers
  Eweka II 188
  Mohammed V 269–70
  mooted cases 132, 139, 141, 166–8, 264
  Mutesa 199
  William Dappa Pepple 187
restoration of monarchies 188, 193, 199

[313]

INDEX

Réunion
    as place of exile 18, 22, 151–5, 191, 215, 259
    surveillance of exiled rulers 152–5, 158–9, 160–1
Rewa state 90–1
Rif rebellion 259
Ripudaman Singh (maharaja of Nabha) 95
Roberts, Michael 48
royal tours 64–5
royalty, scholarly study of 23–5
Rwanda 29n25, 282n9

Sacred Tooth relic 38, 47, 56, 61, 63
Said Ali (sultan of Grande Comore) 190–1, 191fig, 200, 202, 206–7, 208
Salima Machamba (sultan of Mohéli) 208–9
Salisbury, Lord 199
Samoa 20
Samory Touré (Wassoulou ruler) 180, 186, 202, 209
SarDesai, D. R. 109
Satara territory 79, 81
sawbwas 104–5
Saya San 101
Second World War
    Duy Tan and 160–8
    French resistance 160–3, 265
    Tunisia and 265
    see also Vichy regime
sexual scandals
    India 90–4
    Madagascar 226, 240
    Uganda 197–8
    Vietnam 135–8, 142–3, 145, 154, 156
Seychelles 18, 22, 25, 107, 108, 196, 197, 203
Shah, Sudha 25
Shan princes 104–5, 274
Shepstone, Theophilus 184
Shivaji Rao (maharaja of Indore) 91–3
Sidya Ndaté Yalla Diop (ruler of Waalo kingdom) 186, 202

Sikkim 274
Sivasundaram, Sujit 40, 60, 63–4
Sladen, Edward 99
Somalia *see* Ali Shireh
Speedy, Charles 183
Sri Lanka *see* Ceylon; Kandyan monarchy
Sri Vikrama Rajasinha 33fig, 44fig
    accession as monarch 40
    capture and deposition 43–50
    death and burial 53–4, 69
    exiled relatives, descendants and followers 54–6
    journey into exile 32–7
    Kandyan opposition to 40–2, 49–50
    life in exile 50–3
    personality 48–9
    posthumous reputation 48, 68–9
    relations with Pilima Talauve 49–50
St Helena, as place of exile 18, 22, 193, 195, 196, 202–3, 210
St Vincent 187, 204
Stanley, Lyulph (later Baron Stanley) 108
statues and monuments
    Duleep Singh 84
    Gallieni 247
    Keppetipola 68
    Nana Olomu 212n30
    Njoya Ibrahim 180
    Samory Touré 180
Stevenson, Francis Seymour 108
Supayalat (queen of Burma) 97–8, 99, 101–2, 104
Surchandra (maharaja of Manipur) 94–5
surveillance of exiled rulers 152–9, 160–1, 269
Swaziland 20

Tangier, as place of exile 258, 259, 271
Taw Phaya, Prince 102–3
Temple of the Tooth *see* Sacred Tooth relic

INDEX

Thami el-Glaoui (pasha of Marrakesh) 266–70
Thanh Thai (emperor of Annam) 134fig
  accession to throne 133
  death and burial 170–1
  descendants 169–70
  dethroning and abdication 138–41
  Duy Tan's conflict with 156–7
  exile in Réunion 156–7, 170
  exile in Vietnam 145–6
  grievous private behaviour 135–8, 142–5, 154, 157, 163
  reasons for his downfall 146
  repatriation 170–1
  sanity 136, 142, 144, 154
  status as patriotic martyr 143–4
Thein Sein 103
Thibaw (king of Burma)
  commemoration of 102–3
  deposition 97–100
  descendants' lives 102–3
  life in exile 101–2
Thompson, George 81
Thuyet see Ton That Thuyet
Tibet 274
Tipu Sultan ('tiger of Mysore') 26
tombs and mausoleums
  Ashanti 204
  Bahadur Shah Zafar 87
  Duleep Singh 84
  Duy Thanh 171
  Ham Nghi 132
  Madagascar 227, 244, 246
  Mohammed Ben Arafa 271
  Moncef Bey 264
  Ranavalona III 241, 244, 246
  Supayalat 103
  Thanh Thai 171
  Thibaw 103
  Tunisia 264
Ton That Thuyet 120–3, 125, 127–8
Tonga 20
Toussaint-Louverture, François-Dominique 6
trials and appeals 59, 86, 187, 193, 195, 196, 198, 206–7

Tukoji Rao III (maharaja of Indore) 91, 92fig, 96
Tukoji Rao III Puar (maharaja of Dewas Senior) 93
Tunisia
  abolition of monarchy 264
  deposition of sultans 257, 262–4
  as French protectorate 257
  nationalist movements 259–60, 263–4
  during Second World War 260–3
Tuong see Nguyen Van Tuong

Uganda 24, 197–9

Vellore 51, 55, 69
Vibave 58–9, 62
Vichy regime 117–18, 160–1, 260–2, 265
Victoria, Queen
  1858 Indian proclamation 87–8
  as Empress of India 83, 88
  receives Abd el-Kader 256
  sympathy for deposed princes 5, 26, 75–6, 82, 83, 94–5, 183–4, 202
Viet Minh 118, 167
Vietnam
  1916 insurrection 149–52
  abolition of monarchy 118, 172
  anti-colonial movements 118, 121–3, 124–7, 148–52, 167, 172
  battle for Hué 121–3
  Cam Vuong Movement 124–7
  French protectorates 117, 119, 128
  French use of local monarchy 117–19
  see also Bao Dai; Duy Tan; Ham Nghi; Thanh Thai
Vikrama Rajasinha see Sri Vikrama Rajasinha
Vinh San 142, 152, 160–8
  see also Duy Tan
Vinh San, Claude 169, 171
Virarajendra (raja of Coorg) 78–9, 82, 96
Vozelle, Jean 182–3

INDEX

Wajid Ali Shah (king of Oudh) 80, 81–2
war memorials 247
Wickramasinghe, Nira 66
William Dappa Pepple I (king of Bonny) 187, 202, 209
women
  female rulers *see* Djoumé Fatima; Ranavalona III; Salima Machamba; Victoria, Queen
  sexual abuse of 135–8, 146

Yusef ben Hassan (sultan of Morocco) 259

Zafar, Bahadur Shah (Mughal emperor) 85–7, 85fig, 96
Zanzibar 219
  see also Khalid bin Barghash
Zazau 196–7
Zulu kings *see* Cetshwayo; Dinuzulu

EU authorised representative for GPSR:
Easy Access System Europe, Mustamäe tee 50,
10621 Tallinn, Estonia
gpsr.requests@easproject.com

www.ingramcontent.com/pod-product-compliance
Lightning Source LLC
Chambersburg PA
CBHW071401300426
44114CB00016B/2138